Medieval History

FOR

DUMMIES®

by Stephen Batchelor

WILEY

A John Wiley and Sons, Ltd, Publication

Medieval History For Dummies®

Published by
John Wiley & Sons, Ltd
The Atrium
Southern Gate
Chichester
West Sussex
PO19 8SQ
England

E-mail (for orders and customer service enquires): cs-books@wiley.co.uk

Visit our Home Page on www.wiley.com

For general information on our other products and services, please contact our Customer Care Department within the U.S. at 877-762-2974, outside the U.S. at 317-572-3993, or fax 317-572-4002.

For technical support, please visit www.wiley.com/techsupport.

Wiley also publishes its books in a variety of electronic formats. Some content that appears in print may not be available in electronic books.

British Library Cataloguing in Publication Data: A catalogue record for this book is available from the British Library

ISBN: 978-0-470-74783-4

Printed and bound in Great Britain by TJ International, Padstow, Cornwall

10 9 8 7 6 5 4 3 2

WILEY

About the Author

Stephen Batchelor has taught Ancient and Medieval History for a number of years to a wide variety of student groups, and is currently Head of Faculty for Creative & Visual Arts at MidKent College.

Stephen has travelled extensively around the Mediterranean and worked there as an archaeological tour guide. He has written book reviews for *Current Archaeology* and *History Today* and is the author of *The Ancient Greeks For Dummies*.

Author's Acknowledgements

I would like to thank several people for their involvement in this book: firstly, thanks to Steve Edwards and all the team at Wiley who worked on the project, and to Samantha Spickernell for her enthusiastic support of the original idea. I would also like to thank my mother for her support and the loan of her spare room to use as a library, and my partner Samantha for putting up with me once again spending hours in the solitary activity of writing. Special thanks too are due to the very talented Sarah Shade for the tremendous illustration of a Viking ship that appears in Chapter 8.

Finally, I would like to thank the students at Richmond Adult Community College whom it was my pleasure to teach between 1998 and 2007. As a group they reignited by my interest in the Medieval World and their enthusiasm, ideas and desire to make the connections between so many disparate places and peoples played a big part in my thinking for this book.

Publisher's Acknowledgements

We're proud of this book; please send us your comments through our Dummies online registration form located at www.dummies.com/register/.

Some of the people who helped bring this book to market include the following:

Commissioning, Editorial, and Media Development

Project Editor: Steve Edwards

Content Editor: Jo Theedom

Commissioning Editor: Samantha Spickernell

Assistant Editor: Ben Kemble

Development Editor: Brian Kramer

Copy Editor: Andy Finch

Technical Editor: Amanda Richardson

Proofreader: Dawn Bates

Production Manager: Daniel Mersey

Cover Photos: © Photononstop/Photolibrary.com

Cartoons: Rich Tennant
(www.the5thwave.com)

Composition Services

Project Coordinator: Lynsey Stanford

Layout and Graphics: Tim Detrick, Joyce Haughey, Melissa K. Smith

Proofreader: Laura Albert

Indexer: Cheryl Duksta

Brand Reviewer: Jennifer Bingham

Contents at a Glance

Table of Contents

Introduction

I haven't always been interested in the Middle Ages. My main interest used to be the Ancient World of Greece and Rome, and the Middle Ages always seemed to me a bit like the clearing up after a particularly good party. The period can be difficult to get your head around, what with being in the middle rather than at the start or at the end. Studying medieval history often means that you have to know what came *before* and can leave you with an awful lot of questions about what happened *next*. The times were certainly confusing too, with bits of territory changing hands all the time, and just as you get used to a king or a succession of kings, they all die and somebody else takes over.

But when I found out more about the Middle Ages, my opinions changed. I began to see that a great deal of the world that you and I know today came into being during the medieval period. I realised that some of today's most pressing issues and biggest conflicts have their roots in events that happened more than 1,000 years ago. I also got to know more about the people (many of them flat-out characters) who populate the period, the fantastic castles that dot the landscape and the curious, bizarre and sometimes extremely unpleasant things that people did. In the process, I began to knit together and understand how the world got from the Roman Empire to the Renaissance – and beyond.

The more I read and discovered about the Middle Ages, the more I realised that in many ways the period has a greater relevance to my life than what happened in the time of the Ancient Greeks and the Roman emperors. Also, medieval history turns out to be just as much fun to read about as those earlier periods. If I had the chance to travel back in time to the medieval period, I'd jump at the opportunity. Well, as long as I managed to avoid the danger of violent death, the bad food, the horrid diseases and the smell (I'm confident that it would smell really, really bad).

About This Book

This book is an introduction to the Middle Ages – an attempt to give everybody the chance to get excited about the period: and what a period it was. Traditionally, people consider the Middle Ages to have lasted between 1100 and 1500, but in this book I look at what happened before then and where the Middle Ages came from. I start with the collapse of the Western Roman Empire in AD 476 and carry on to 1500 – a period of over 1,000 years! The events that I look at spanned territory from the west coast of Spain to the edges of Arabia, from Greenland to the north of the African continent. The period features countless numbers of different peoples, all moving from place to place, invading new areas and then being driven out by new sets of invaders.

The Middle Ages also featured the creation and development of many modern-day countries. Although they already existed as landmasses, France, England and Germany came into being as countries during the Middle Ages and began to develop the individual identities and cultures you now recognise.

The period also saw the first big clashes between western Europe and the near East and between the faiths of Christianity and Islam. Following the amazing Islamic conquests during the seventh century, Christianity responded with the Crusades of the eleventh to fourteenth centuries. The events and arguments of this tumultuous period are still at the centre of modern discussions and increase in relevance every day.

In addition, the medieval period is one that, save for some exceptions, historians still don't know a great deal about. New archaeological discoveries and surviving written sources, however, mean that despite the passage of time understanding of the period is growing. New pieces of information keep emerging. I'm writing these words in January 2010, and by the time you read them, hundreds of new medieval objects buried in the Earth are sure to have been discovered, enabling yet more pieces of the jigsaw to fall into place.

Conventions Used in This Book

As you may have worked out by now, one of the big issues when reading about the Middle Ages is geography. The events in this book take place over a huge canvas, and very often boundaries shift and change every few years. Maps appear throughout the book to reflect some of these changes – the most detailed is Figure 1-1 in Chapter 1 (which you can also find online at www.dummies.com/cheatsheet/medievalhistoryuk). Wherever possible I'm specific about where an event happened, but the places may not always appear on the maps.

Why is this the case? Well, some important events in medieval history occurred nowhere in particular. For example, many battles in which thousands were bashing the living daylights out of each other took place in open fields that are impossible to identify nowadays. Historians guess that these battles took place near to major towns, but this isn't always accurate. For example, the Battle of Hastings in 1066 (which I describe in Chapter 10) didn't happen in Hastings.

The other big issue when exploring medieval history is simply the huge amount that happened during the period. In all, I cover about 1,000 years of history. This book is intended as an introduction to the subject, and so obviously I can't include everything. I skim over whole groups of people and skip some series of events. Think of this book as your starting point. I hope that when you finish, you'll feel like going further, exploring other areas and seeking the answers to new questions.

An initially confusing thing about studying history is the way that we refer to centuries. Specifically, the confusing part is that the number of a century (such as the '20' in '2010') doesn't directly refer to the relevant year. For example, I'm writing this book in 2010, which falls within the twenty-first century – not the twentieth. Because we date time from AD 1 – the year that Jesus Christ was born – the first century was made up of the years between AD 1 and AD 99. When AD100 began, it actually started the second century AD. So when I mention, for example, the thirteenth century, what I'm referring to are the years between AD 1200 and 1299. Simple!

Oh yes, and just a note about language. Wherever possible I describe things in English and use English names and words. Sometimes I use terms in the original language, but I always give the English alternative. I do this for good reason. People during the Middle Ages spoke hundreds of different languages that were further broken down into numerous regional dialects. Often words are translated slightly differently or spelt in different and unusual ways. Wherever possible, I use the most common spelling of a name, place or term. But don't be surprised if you read another book or do some online research and encounter different spellings. That's the nature of historical writing. Take as an example the famous Viking, king Canute (who features in Chapter 3). He can be known as Canute, Kanute, Knut, Cnut or Canute the Great. Each is correct in its own way!

How This Book Is Organised

This book is split into six parts. Five of them are a chronological guide to medieval history and the sixth, the Part of Tens, is a series of lists of things to look into next.

Part 1: Starting Up the Middle Ages (450–800)

This part explains how the Middle Ages arose and what came before them. I look at the end of the Roman Empire, how it completely collapsed in Western Europe and how it became the Byzantine Empire in Eastern Europe. I shed some light on the 'Dark Ages' that followed and show that they aren't quite as dark as people think. I also take a look at how the areas of modern-day France and Germany came to fall under the control of one people – the Franks. Their domination became so complete that one man, Charlemagne, managed to create himself a whole new empire to play with. I also examine what was happening in Britain, where the departure of the Roman legions left a nice big hole for the Anglo-Saxons to fill.

Part II: Forming the Basis of Europe (850–1100)

The Middle Ages really get going here! In this part I look at how Europe went through massive alterations and frequent changes of rulers and even ruling peoples. I examine the Holy Roman Empire and how disputes between its rulers eventually ended in the creation of the territories that became France and Germany. I spend two chapters looking at two different peoples who had an astonishing impact during the period: the Islamic armies that swept north and westwards and the Vikings who came south and journeyed as far as North America. I also consider how the medieval Christian Church developed, how it became more complex and how divisions and tensions ultimately arose that caused it to split. I introduce you to the tough, adventurous warriors who descended from Viking stock – the Normans – and detail their conquests in England.

Part III: Waging Holy War: Crusading at Home and Abroad (1050–1300)

Part III is all about Crusading, an activity that became very popular during the twelfth century. When the Byzantine Empire suffered a series of defeats by Arab forces, the pope appealed to Western Europe to take military action and reclaim the Holy Land in the name of Christianity. His appeal was amazingly successful. Over the next 200 years, a whole series of military expeditions occurred. Most ended in abject failure, and some never even made it out of Europe. At the same time some leaders took to Crusading within Europe against those they perceived to be unchristian and enemies of the Church. This period is fascinating, full of tremendous stories that veer from the appallingly brutal to the absolutely bizarre.

Part IV: Dealing with Domestic Dramas: Parliament, Priories and Plagues (1200–1300)

In this part I show how Medieval Europe changed during the thirteenth century. This period was a time when kings were increasingly coming under pressure to give power to the nobles who served them. Some, like the weak King John of England, gave in, and parliament was created. The period also saw a massive explosion in trade as the wealthy city states of Italy began to expand their interests across the Mediterranean, taking advantage of the inroads made by Crusaders. This period also saw big changes in the Church with monasteries and religious movements becoming increasing influential. In fact, the papacy argued so much that it split with itself and several people claimed to be pope at the same time. I also tackle the grim story of the Black Death, the plague that devastated Europe for a decade and killed more than 75 million people.

Part V: Ending the Middle and Beginning the Age of Discovery (1300–1492)

When did the Middle Ages come to an end? It's a great question and in Part V I take a look at the final events, when the medieval period began to merge into the Renaissance. I recount the Hundred Years' War between England and France and the amazing battles that took place at Crecy and Agincourt. I also spend some time with the Peasants' Revolt in England, when the downtrodden had finally had enough and the Lollard movement saw them storming London and demanding change. The part ends with a chapter on the fifteenth century when the Middle Ages ceased to be: the Renaissance in Italy, the end of the Byzantine Empire and the voyages of Christopher Columbus resulted in a whole new world.

Part VI: The Part of Tens

The final part contains five brief chapters in which I give you some ideas of people and places to explore next. You can find a chapter on some of the worst kings of the medieval period (for which a lot of competition exists) as well as a chapter dedicated to ten people who really changed the world. Check out my list of the best medieval castles that you can still visit today, along with some of the more curious and unpleasant practices in which medieval people engaged. Something for everybody!

Icons Used in This Book

The book is loaded with information and occasionally I use the following icons to bring your attention to particular issues, noteworthy events or specific information:

Many documents and literary sources survive from the Middle Ages. As often as possible, I give examples. Original writing from the period has always helped history come alive to me: I hope this technique works for you, too.

I use this icon to highlight information that's really important or helps set the scene for something I discuss later in the chapter or the rest of the book.

An increasing number of films are being made about historical events from the Middle Ages. Some of them are great, and some of them are rubbish! Whenever the opportunity exists, I mention films and highlight aspects that are worth checking out.

If you're just looking for a general overview, by all means skip over sections with this icon. The information is interesting but not absolutely vital.

The book covers 1,000 years or so and a vast geographical area. Occasionally I use this icon to point out an event that was taking place elsewhere, which gives a further context to the topic at hand.

A lot of 'facts' which people think they know about the Middle Ages aren't actually true at all, as with any period of history. I use this icon to debunk myths and set the record straight. Vikings wearing horned helmets, King Alfred burning the cakes and Cnut ordering the sea to stop in front of him; they and other tales all get the MythBuster treatment!

Where to Go from Here

So what next? My advice is to start from the beginning and read on. The book is chronological and tells the story of the Middle Ages from beginning to end. Each part focuses on a different portion of the overall story, and so you can start with the period in which you're most interested.

However, each of the chapters is also like an individual essay on a specific topic, and so if you already know a bit about medieval history you can just jump straight in with a topic that interests you. For example, if you're keen on the Crusades, go straight to Part III, or if you want to find out about Joan of Arc, have a look at Chapter 23.

Alternatively, you can start with the Part of Tens, see what grabs your interest and then refer back to the relevant chapter or part. Whatever you decide, I hope you have fun!

Part I

Starting Up the Middle Ages (450–800)

The 5th Wave   By Rich Tennant

Carolingian Dynasty

"Something for the kids to play with."

In this part . . .

So when did the Middle Ages happen? The answer is more complicated than you may think. In this part I look at what happened when the Roman Empire came to an end and numerous new states and countries began to emerge. I also look at how the Anglo-Saxons made England their own and how a whole new Holy Roman Empire came into being through a man who modestly called himself Charles the Great. But this part isn't all empire building – you can also find thrilling epic poetry, a bold appearance by Attila the Hun and a homicidal German queen named Brunhilda!

Chapter 1

Journeying Back to the Middle Ages: When, Where, What, Who?

The Middle Ages – a period of roughly 1,000 years of human life in Europe and beyond – have long been the recipient of bad press. For example:

✔ Simply referring to this era as the *Middle* Ages implies that the really important bits are what happened before and after, and that the Middle Ages are just filler.

✔ Using the adjective 'medieval' carries the negative connotation that things were underdeveloped or backward.

✔ Thinking of this entire era as the Dark Ages (as a few people do) implies nothing more than century after century of wars, diseases and savagery.

In fact, the Middle Ages are an incredibly rich swathe of history. Many modern-day European countries formed during the period, and enduring aspects of present-day governments and international relations link back to this time. Advances in science and technology were enormous and far-reaching, and much of the beautiful art and buildings created during this period continue to inspire today. In addition, some truly fascinating figures made their mark on history.

Of course, like all periods of history, the Middle Ages did include bloodthirsty wars, cruel invasions, religious repression and the first great plague – the Black Death. None of these events were very much fun for the people involved at the time, but they do combine to make one hell of a story!

In this chapter I put the Middle Ages in context, zeroing in on the specific times, places and people that make up this incredible era. I also briefly look at some of the reasons why the Middle Ages remain such a fascinating period.

Pinpointing the Middle Ages: The Middle of What Exactly?

Although now quite negative, the terms 'medieval' and 'Middle Ages' were initially purely practical ways to describe a specific period of time.

The term 'Middle Ages' first came into use during the Renaissance (roughly 1400–1600). Historians and scholars in this period were great fans of *antiquity* – Ancient Greece and Rome – and were hugely influenced by the writers, philosophers and artists of the period. Antiquity came to an end with the fall of the Western Roman Empire in AD 476 (flip to Chapter 2 for more on this monumental event). Renaissance historians used the term Middle Ages to cover the period between this event and their own time.

 Of course, people living in the period didn't consider themselves to be living during the Middle Ages. The term didn't exist for them – just as Renaissance writers didn't realise that they were living in the Renaissance and people currently don't know how future scholars are going to refer to events happening today.

Having the time of their lives

The Middle Ages encompass a very long period of history. Traditionally, historians have considered the Middle Ages to have taken place between 1100 and 1500, but scholars have long argued about when the period officially starts and finishes. I've been forced to make a decision about that, too. *Medieval History For Dummies* covers the period between two key events:

- ✔ The fall of the Western Roman Empire in AD 476.
- ✔ The discovery of America by Christopher Columbus in 1492.

Of course, including Columbus takes this book into the fifteenth century (which some people may say isn't part of the Middle Ages), but the discovery of another continent really is the event that ushers in the next period of history. It also makes for a slice of history just over 1,000 years in length, which is just neat!

To put 1,000 years – a huge period of time – into context, bear in mind that fewer than 1,000 years have passed since William of Normandy won the Battle of Hastings in 1066 (which I describe more in Chapter 10). Think how much has changed since then. The aim of this book is to give you a framework of medieval history: the big issues, important developments, essential events and most significant characters.

Establishing a timeline

Clearly a period of 1,000 years requires some sort of chronology! Although you can always jump to any chapter of this book that interests you, each part focuses on a specific period, usually a chunk that's several centuries long. Here's a quick guide:

- **450–800: The Roman Empire falls and the Dark Ages begin.** As Europe experiences a series of huge people migrations, some leaders take their chances to gain territory and status. Most successful is Charles Magnus 'Charlemagne' who becomes the first Holy Roman Emperor. This period is the focus of Part I.

- **800–1100: The Middle Ages get going, and Europe begins to form.** This tumultuous time includes Islamic conquests in Spain, Viking raids everywhere and William the Conqueror waging the Battle of Hastings. Exciting times! Turn to Part II.

- **1100–1200: The Crusades sweep through Europe, the Middle East and beyond.** After the Byzantine emperor begs for help, Pope Urban II calls the rulers of Europe to retake Jerusalem. Thousands respond in the form of numerous Crusades, which result in establishing the kingdom of Outremer and a great deal else. Soldier on to Part III.

- **1200–1400: The 'High Middle Ages', during which England and France are in conflict.** A crisis in the papacy (several people claim to be the pope) occurs at the same time as the Black Death, which many people think of as a punishment from God. Pop to Part IV for more.

- **1400–1492: The Middle Ages draw to a close.** With the end of the Hundred Years' War between England and France and the destruction of the Byzantine Empire by the Ottoman Turks, the Renaissance is born and Christopher Columbus discovers the New World. I wrap up things in Part V.

Locating the Medieval World

When historians talk about the Middle Ages, they are generally talking about events that took place in and around modern-day Europe and a few adjacent areas, as Figure 1-1 shows.

As you can see, the Medieval World is based around Europe and extends to the areas around the Mediterranean Sea. The northern coast of Africa (modern-day Morocco and Tunisia), the Levantine (modern-day Syria and Palestine) and what used to be called Asia Minor (modern-day Turkey) are the virtual boundaries.

The areas included in Figure 1-1 were pretty much the limits of the known world to Western Europeans during the Middle Ages. People were aware that lands existed farther to the east and the south, but they had no real information about them. Even the basic geography of these areas on maps was unfamiliar to many people, which made the journeys of various Crusaders very difficult (Part III contains more about the Crusades). Of course, a great deal was going on in the rest of the world at this time, even though Medieval Europe wasn't aware of it!

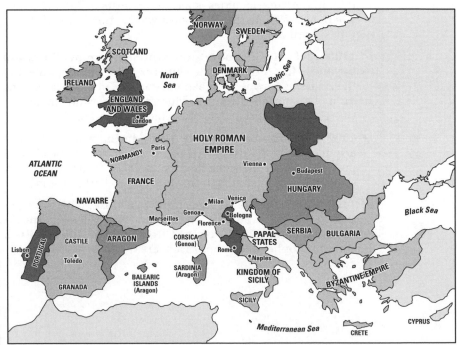

Figure 1-1:
The
Medieval
World.

Flat-packed planet?

One of the popular modern beliefs about the Middle Ages is that everybody believed that the Earth was flat; if you sailed far enough, you fell off the edge of the world. The story goes that only after Columbus reached the Americas in 1492 and returned to Europe did people believe that the planet was round.

Knowing the truth here is difficult. For instance, a huge number of writers and mathematicians suggested that the Earth was spherical for many centuries before the Middle Ages and this assertion continued throughout the Middle Ages. Then again, current historians have no idea about wider popular opinion, and so huge numbers of people may well have thought that the Earth was flat.

Getting to Know the People of the Middle Ages

The countries on the map in Figure 1-1 may look pretty familiar, but they aren't the same as their modern equivalents. Countries such as France, Germany, Spain and many others only really formed during the medieval period.

Consequently the people who lived in these areas didn't really think of themselves as French, German or Spanish. Instead they considered their identity in a much more localised way, most likely claiming their town, city or possibly principality. For example, a man from Florence may introduce himself as a Florentine not Italian, just as a woman from Burgundy in northern France would consider herself a Burgundian.

Moving around – a lot

Another complicating factor in the idea of nationality is that huge population movements took place several times during the Middle Ages. Whole societies would move geographical location because of war, disease or famine. These massive shifts mean that tracing people's lineage is extremely complicated.

A great example of the complexities of identity is William the Conqueror. Nowadays most people think of William as French, but he was actually the son of the Duke of Normandy, and thus a Norman from northern France. He was descended from a people who moved to the Loire Valley in France in around

AD 911 from Scandinavia, however, and so his ancestors were essentially Vikings. As you can see, nationality gets very complicated!

Individuals moved around a lot, too. Although many people might spend their whole lives in the same small village, they had lots of reasons for leaving to go on a journey. For example, pilgrimage was very popular and led people to undertake journeys of thousands of miles. Merchants and seamen began to make longer and more substantial journeys as trade increased in volume and reach (see Chapter 18), and some of the biggest journeys were made by clerics and Church officials travelling to religious councils and meetings.

Minding your language

With so many people moving around the continent of Europe, the languages of the medieval period were equally diverse and in constant flux.

Literacy is one of the most fascinating things about the medieval period. The vast majority of people in Europe were illiterate and so most languages were only spoken. Most literate people were within the higher ranks of society, but even then their literacy was only partial. The major written language of the day was Latin – the language of the Roman Empire, the papacy and the medieval Church – but although many people in the Church could read and write, this wasn't so everywhere. A lot of important people were only able to read. This wasn't because these people weren't intelligent enough; it was simply because they didn't need to bother. Kings, queens, lords and ladies had servants and these included scribes who would make notes and write letters for them – just as secretaries did for modern-day business people until the arrival of dictaphones and speech-recognition software!

As you can see from the map in Figure 1-2, languages varied widely throughout Medieval Europe. Many people spoke localised dialects, which were based around the contemporary indo-European languages, like the Germanic, Celtic and Hellenic languages. Eventually during the later medieval period, some of the main modern languages you know today developed alongside the modern nations themselves. English, French, German and Spanish all first came into common usage during the Middle Ages.

On a local level, however, language wasn't as simple as Figure 1-2 suggests. Large-scale population movements brought in new dialects and as a result linguistic adaptations developed frequently. This fact was particularly true in Eastern Europe, where the influx of new people from farther east constantly influenced the huge variety of Slav languages.

Figure 1-2:
Who spoke
what in the
Medieval
World.

Appreciating an Era

Although the Middle Ages are complicated, exploring this period is very much worth the effort; presumably you agree because you're reading this book!

Calling the Middle Ages 'the Dark Ages' (the period between 450–800) just isn't fair or accurate. This period – and indeed this book – is filled with deeply fascinating stories, ideas and characters.

Bucking the trend: Medieval inventions

The word 'medieval' has become a term of abuse to describe things that are backward and that ignore progress, but this usage is far from the truth. The Middle Ages saw the invention of numerous fascinating devices and new, innovative ways of doing things, some of which continue to impact your life today. Here are just three:

- **Castles:** Probably the most obvious invention of the Middle Ages, castles were first introduced in Europe in the tenth century in France. Initially built of wood, the Normans later built them from stone. In addition to influencing building and architecture for centuries to come, castles were vital tools for enforcing authority and maintaining the possession of lands – two things that medieval rulers were particularly keen on (read more about this aspect in Chapter 10). Castles worked as administrative centres too. Local rulers used castles as their bases for a sort of medieval civil service and revenue collection service. The medieval writing implement was just as mighty as the sword!

- **The clavicembalum or harpsichord:** A manuscript dating from 1397 claims that Hermann Poll invented the first stringed instrument to be played by a keyboard. In doing so he created the first harpsichord, the precursor to the piano.

- **The printing press:** Presses were used throughout the Ancient World to produce wine and olive oil, but during the medieval period the technology was used to reproduce the printed word – and truly revolutionise the world. In 1439, Johannes Gutenberg invented the first printing press in Strasbourg. You're reading this book right now as a direct result of that event! Turn to Chapters 28 and 29 for more.

Logically illogical history

One of the most interesting, but equally infuriating, aspects about studying history is the way that things suddenly change. People may spend years establishing a tradition or setting up a system of government, only for one individual or a group to do something crazy and change everything. With the benefit of hindsight, you're likely to be shocked by some of the short-term decisions that historical figures made and the chaos that ensued. The Middle Ages were particularly prone to this tendency. Near-constant regime change means that things shifted all the time and that the stability that people spent years working towards was upset by one (seemingly) stupid decision.

However, what seems illogical to you probably seemed very logical to them. Medieval people regarded life as brief and essentially training for the afterlife. They weren't necessarily making decisions with an eye on how they would play out over the next half-century or even the next ten years; it was all about making decisions for the here and now. A great example is Reynald of Chatillon, a French knight to whom I give a hard time in Chapter 15. He was a bit of an idiot, but he probably thought he was doing the right thing! In a way the decision-making process of medieval leaders isn't that different from that of many contemporary politicians. An alternative point of view would be that medieval people were focused on the very long term, in that they felt their mortal lives were preparation for the afterlife. Perversely, this meant that they made very short-term decisions for what I suppose is the ultimate long-term benefit!

Encountering fascinating people

Along with development of a host of technologies and major societal changes, the Middle Ages also witnessed a host of amazing individuals whose exploits continue to excite, inspire and amuse. Here are just a few examples of the characters that crop up in the period:

- **Henry II 'The Wrangler', Duke of Bavaria (951–995):** The German aristocracy were a fascinating and unusual bunch, and Henry is a particularly good example. Twice the Duke of Bavaria, he earned his nickname due to his difficult and quarrelsome nature, persistently starting conflicts and attempting to usurp the throne. Many of the kings themselves weren't much better; see also Charles the Fat, Henry the Fowler and Charles the Simple.

- **Fulk III 'The Black' (972–1040):** A notorious villain, robber and plunderer, Fulk was also the Count of Anjou in France. His nickname was due to his dark and savage temper that often erupted in extreme violence. He is mainly famous for two things: being one of the first great castle builders and burning his wife at the stake after discovering that she had committed adultery with a goatherd (to be fair, she was never unfaithful again). Fulk also spent a great deal of his time on pilgrimage and doing penance for his wicked acts, which makes him a great example of how the savagery of some medieval figures is balanced with extreme religious devotion. See Chapter 10.

- **Stephen of Blois (c. 1045–1102):** Stephen was the Count of Blois and one of the leaders of the first Crusade. He wrote a number of letters to his wife Adela of Normandy describing how the Crusade was going. Unfortunately he became ill when the Crusade got stuck at Antioch and returned home without having reached Jerusalem as he vowed. Unimpressed, Adele forced him to go back. He didn't make it this time either and was killed in battle on the way. See Chapter 11.

- **Peter the Hermit (c. 1050–1115):** A penniless, nomadic ex-monk who travelled around relying on the charity of others, Peter the Hermit doesn't appear to be much at first sight. He was, however, responsible for recruiting thousands and thousands of people to travel to Jerusalem as part of the People's Crusade (1096). The event was a total disaster and the vast majority were killed, but Peter is a great example of the influence of religion in the Medieval World and the power of oratory. See Chapter 12.

- **Hildegard of Bingen (c. 1098–1179):** Despite being a male-dominated age, the medieval period produced many fascinating women. Hildegard was a German writer, scholar, mystic and artist who eventually became a saint, so was a woman of many talents! During her remarkable life she founded two monasteries, composed music, wrote plays and stories, and drew beautiful illuminations for manuscripts. Hildegard is a great example of how many medieval thinkers and creative people turned their hands to all forms of art in a way that foreshadowed the intellectuals of the Renaissance. Living until she was 81 years old was something of an achievement too!

✔ **Genghis Khan (c. 1155–1227):** The great conqueror and Mongol leader was mostly active in Asia, but his activities had a profound effect on the Western Medieval World. Several of the big population movements I mention in the earlier section 'Moving around – a lot' were due to Genghis Khan's military adventures.

Many more wonderful characters appear in the story of the Middle Ages – monks, knights, kings, queens, writers and others. So turn the page and start meeting them!

Chapter 2

Finishing Off the Roman Empire and Entering the (Not So) Dark Ages

In This Chapter

▶ Watching the Roman Empire crumble

▶ Touring the Byzantine Empire

▶ Shining a light on the Dark Ages

▶ Converting the masses to Christianity

Historians use the term *Middle Ages* to represent the period of medieval history that lasted from around 1100–1500. This phrase is all very well, but the Middle Ages didn't just start suddenly in 1100; an awful lot happened before then to create the world that the Middle Ages sprung from. In this book I look at history from the fall of the Roman Empire in AD 476 through to around 1500 and to keep things simple I refer to all of it as medieval history.

In this chapter, I finish off the Roman Empire (with some help from Rome's crumbling government and attacks by the Visigoths and Attila the Hun, of course). The period that followed it has been popularly known as the *Dark Ages,* which laid the foundation for the beginning of the Middle Ages. I also look at the importance of Christianity to the early Medieval World.

Saying Goodbye to Antiquity

In this book, I define *medieval history* as the period between Antiquity (also called Ancient History) and the Renaissance. As I discuss in Chapter 1, historians are still arguing about exactly when each period finished and the next started, but whatever dates and events you pick, medieval history still covers a massive period of time – about 1,000 years, or what historians refer to as a *millennium*, from approximately 476–1500.

This book's starting point for medieval history is the end of *Antiquity*, which describes the period including the Ancient Greek civilisation and the Roman Empire and dates from around 1700 BC to AD 500. This period is fascinating, and if you want to know more about it, take a look at *The Ancient Greeks For Dummies* (Wiley, 2008) by yours truly and *The Romans For Dummies* (Wiley, 2006) by Guy De la Bédoyère.

The end of Antiquity is particularly important to understanding medieval history – most specifically the fall of the Roman Empire.

Dismantling Rome: The Empire that Died

The Roman Empire was the largest that the world had ever seen until its time. For nearly 1,000 years, the vast majority of Europe and the Mediterranean was ruled in the name of a single city and its emperor. At its height (around AD 120), the Empire stretched from the western coast of modern-day Portugal to the Tigris and Euphrates Rivers, which flow today through Iraq. Figure 2-1 shows the Empire's huge expanse.

Figure 2-1:
The Roman Empire in c. AD 120.

Standing for greatness

The Roman Empire was able to flourish spectacularly for nearly 1,000 years because it possessed a tremendous army that protected its borders. For nearly 500 years Rome flourished as a republic before expanding even further and more successfully under the emperors like Augustus (reigned 27 BC–AD 14), Tiberius (AD 14–37) and Trajan (AD 98–117). Unlike most other civilisations in Antiquity, Rome had a *standing army*, a group of professional soldiers who joined for the employment. With thousands of men devoted to policing and protecting it, the Empire was safe from invasions and able to add aggressively to its territory. This situation in turn meant more land and more tax and produce from its provinces, which enabled the Empire to further increase the size and strength of the army.

Splitting the Roman Empire

For many years from 27 BC the Roman Empire was successfully run by one man – the emperor – and by the political and administrative system of which he was the head. By the fourth century, however, the Empire was starting to break apart. It was effectively divided in two when Emperor Constantine (306–337) moved the capital and seat of the Empire from Rome to his new city of Constantinople on the Bosphorus (modern-day Istanbul).

In the years that followed, the Roman Empire split into two distinct sections. This arrangement was formalised in 395 with the death of Emperor Theodosius, the last emperor to rule the combined Roman Empire. He named two of his sons as joint heirs: Arcadius was given the Eastern Empire and Honorius the Western Empire.

Another big change made during the reign of Theodosius was the conversion of the Roman Empire to Christianity, which became its official religion. Christianity had been growing in influence for the past 150 years, and Constantine had publicly converted during the civil war that gave him control, and privately converted on his deathbed. In the eastern areas, the shift to Christianity didn't make for a massive change, but the effect in the West was far more profound, because the Christian Church was at that time less well established in Western Europe. See the section 'Spreading Christianity' later for more details.

As well as the geographical split, the Roman Empire also had linguistic differences. The Western Empire was uniformly thought of as 'The Latin Empire', because it still used Latin as its official language of communication, whereas (Ancient) Greek was the dominant language in the Eastern Empire.

Although the Western Empire was the oldest part, it was also very much the lesser part. Despite its huge geographical span, the area was considerably less well developed. Historians calculate that by around the year 400, the Eastern Empire had about 900 cities, all of which were thriving economies. By contrast the Western Empire sported only just over 100 cities.

Beginning the breakdown: The Visigoths

The Western Roman Empire suffered a series of massive setbacks in the fifth century, which involved attacks from tribes and groups beyond its borders.

Since the late fourth century, barbarian peoples to the east had continually attacked and invaded one another. One such group was the Huns, fearsome warriors from the central part of Russia known as the *steppes*. As nomads who never stayed in one place for long, settled or built towns, the Huns had to keep moving to find new lands to live off. The Huns's movements unsettled other groups, pushing everyone farther westwards towards the Western Empire. The later section 'Trying to manage a new threat: Attila the Hun' has more about the Huns.

In 376, a massive horde of German peoples (displaced by the Huns and known as the Visigoths) crossed the river Danube (see Figure 2-1) and invaded the Western Roman Empire. A massive battle at Adrianople in the year 378 saw the Western Roman army destroyed and Emperor Valens killed.

The Visigoth leader Alaric then led his people into Greece and spent the next decade rampaging around the Western Empire. Emperor Honorius didn't have the money to bribe the Visigoths to stop or an army strong enough to fight them. In 410 the Visigoths attacked and sacked Rome. It was the first time that the city had been successfully attacked since 390 BC, 800 years earlier.

Adding more destruction

The Visigoths were just the first of many groups to attack the Western Roman Empire. Throughout the fifth century, more and more peoples from Eastern Europe successfully made their way across the borders:

- ✔ The Visigoths eventually settled in southern Gaul (modern-day southern France).
- ✔ The Burgundians also settled in Gaul.
- ✔ The Vandals invaded Spain, destroyed Roman rule in the region and then moved on to North Africa.

Increasingly, the old Roman institutions of power began to ebb away. An emperor was still on the throne, but his court was now based in the city of Ravenna, Italy, rather than Rome. The Eastern Empire was suffering attacks too, so there was no chance of unifying the two empires under one single emperor. Meanwhile, people in the provinces of Western Europe were increasingly under the control of the leaders of the Visigoth tribes who had successfully invaded. The once powerful civil service and administration of the Roman Empire lost its influence; loyalties to local tribal leaders and representatives of the Christian Church replaced long-standing affiliations with the Empire as people looked to the faith for leadership rather than to a distant emperor. Many people in the farther reaches of the Western Empire must have believed that one of these groups was more protective of their interests than the officials of the emperor.

Whole regions of the Western Roman Empire eventually broke away and were declared independent kingdoms by the Goth leaders that ruled them. The age of Roman rule was coming to an end.

Trying to manage a new threat: Attila the Hun

The nomadic lifestyle of the Huns drove the Visigoths westwards into Roman territory, and in 450 the Huns themselves also made the move into Western Europe, attacking the wealthy Visigoth kingdom of Toulouse, in modern-day France.

The Huns were led by a man named Attila, who lived c. 410–453. He was feared throughout Europe for the savagery with which he fought battles. Initially the Roman Emperor Valentinian III approved of and agreed to Attila's movement into the Western Empire; he thought he would use the Huns to win back the regions that Rome had lost. How wrong he was.

Huns on the run

At first the Huns's invasion of Visigoth-occupied areas in 450 went to plan, with Attila proving very successful.

The Huns uniformly fought as cavalry and used a special type of bow known as the composite bow. Made from horn and sinew, this weapon was much lighter than the wooden bows that Roman archers used. Consequently the Huns were fast, deadly and very difficult to fight against.

Later in the year 450, however, Attila received a very surprising letter from Honoria, the sister of Emperor Valentinian III. The letter suggested that she would marry Attila if he would have her and that this arrangement would make him heir to the Western Empire. This was an amazing thing for a member of the Roman nobility to do. Most historians cite her reason as being that she was trying to escape from her betrothal to a senator that Valentinian III had forced her into. Her solution was fairly imaginative, but it had massive consequences!

Valentinian III was appalled when he discovered the letter and wrote to Attila cancelling the offer. Fearing that the Huns would turn against him, the emperor flipped sides and made a pact with the Visigoth King Theodoric to try and expel the Huns from the Western Empire.

The two armies clashed near the French town of Chalons, and the Roman allies won a surprising victory over the Huns. It would be the last big victory that a Roman army would ever win.

Attila in Italy

By 452 Attila was back, this time invading Italy and hoping to claim the Western Roman Empire for himself.

During this campaign, Attila successfully sacked many towns and villages in northern Italy. Much of the population fled, looking for new places to live that were safe from further attacks by the Huns. A few hundred people ended up making their way to the Venetian Lagoon and the small islands within it. They were joined by others fleeing invasions in the sixth century and the new communities they formed eventually became the city of Venice that played a vital role in the later Middle Ages (I talk more about the merchant city of Venice in Chapter 18).

Attila moved south in Italy but was eventually halted at the River Po. His army had been travelling for a very long time, and disease had broken out. He was forced to turn back and make for his stronghold across the Danube.

By early 453, Attila was dead. Accounts of his death vary, but the most commonly cited cause is that he suffered some kind of internal bleeding and choked to death on his own blood. Another account suggests that he died of a haemorrhage on his wedding night with a new bride, or even that he was murdered by her. Attila was 47 years old.

Crowning the last Emperor: Romulus Augustulus

Attila's death gave no real respite to the dying Western Roman Empire. One side effect of Attila's invasion was that some of his people stayed behind. One such man, Orestes, had been a secretary to the Hun leader.

Orestes joined the Western Roman Army and rose through the ranks to a high position. In 475, Orestes was appointed as *Magister Militum* (supreme commander) by the then emperor Julius Nepos. The political situation within the Western Empire was clearly desperate if such a relative newcomer as Orestes was able to rise to this position so quickly.

So why did the Roman Empire collapse?

The reasons behind the fall of such a mighty institution as the Roman Empire have always intrigued historians, and they have tried to explain the event ever since:

✔ The first historian to try was Vegetius (dates uncertain) who probably wrote soon after the collapse of the Western Empire. He blamed its demise on the increasing 'Germanisation' of the Roman Army brought on by incorporating barbarian mercenaries.

✔ The English historian Sir Edward Gibbon (1737–1794) wrote the most famous analysis of the collapse, *The History of the Decline and Fall of the Roman Empire*. His contention was that the Roman Empire collapsed because of a loss of 'civic virtue' among its citizens, the fact that they didn't take active roles in defence and administration.

Without the involvement of Roman citizens, the army and civil service more easily fell under the control of 'barbarian' non-Romans. Gibbon also blamed the impact of the conversion of the Roman Empire to Christianity. Gibbon was a protestant, so was happy to blame the Church of the Roman Empire, which was Catholic.

✔ Most modern scholarship focuses on the movement of peoples that took place beyond Rome's borders. These large population shifts created impacts that no empire could have dealt with at any time. Additionally, rather than an inevitable decline, most modern historians explain the collapse as the result of a number of related movements and events, all outside the control of the Empire.

Orestes soon used his new position to lead a revolt, seizing the capital of Ravenna in the process. For reasons that are unclear, Orestes didn't declare himself as emperor, preferring instead to hand the title to his 13-year-old son. The boy was given the names of Rome's founder (the mythical Romulus) and the man many considered its greatest emperor (Augustus). The 'ulus' was added to the end of the name as a diminutive, meaning literally 'Little Augustus'. He was crowned on 31 October 475. Despite the grand references, however, young Romulus Augustulus's reign was short, and he was never truly in power either, acting more as a figurehead for his father.

Within only a few weeks, the new emperor's power base had almost completely disappeared. The army revolted under the leadership of a man known as Odoacer. Like many of the men who supported him, Odoacer was a barbarian mercenary. He demanded that Orestes hand over a third of the land in Italy for Odoacer to establish his own kingdom. Orestes refused and was executed.

Odoacer went immediately to Ravenna and captured the young emperor. Augustulus was forced to abdicate in August 476 after only nine months as emperor. Odoacer sent a letter to Zeno, the Eastern Roman Emperor, declaring that he would rule the Western lands in his name. Zeno wasn't really of a mind to do anything about it and agreed. Check out the later section 'Enduring in the East: Byzantium' for what happened in the Eastern Empire.

Therefore, in August 476, the Western Roman Empire came to an end. No longer ruled by an emperor and rapidly dividing itself into smaller kingdoms, the domination of the city of Rome that had lasted 1,000 years came to an end with barely a whimper.

Enduring in the East: Byzantium

While the Western Roman Empire was breaking apart (flip to the earlier section, 'Dismantling Rome: The Empire that Died', the Eastern Empire thrived and continued to do so for many years to come. Since the official division of the Roman Empire in 395, the Eastern Empire had forged its own separate identity, and modern scholars now refer to it as the Byzantine Empire. Figure 2-2 shows the extent of this kingdom.

The Byzantine Empire was known as such because in 330 Emperor Constantine established the new capital city of Constantinople on the spot of a much older city – the ancient port of Byzantium.

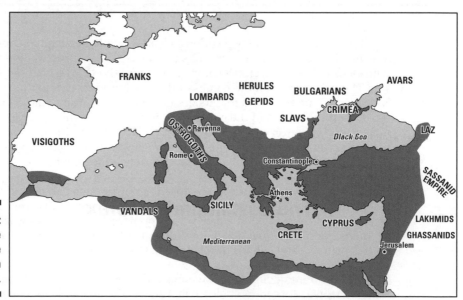

Figure 2-2:
The Byzantine Empire in the year 550.

Although technically part of the Roman Empire, the Byzantine Empire was very different from the Western Empire. In addition to having many more cities than in the West, other pronounced differences included the following:

✔ **The Greek background:** The Byzantine Empire had its origins in Greek culture rather than Latin. The official language was Ancient Greek, and the art and culture were highly influenced by the Classical Greeks.

✔ **The Patriarch:** The dominant figure in the Western Christian Church was the pope (see Chapter 1), but he never held complete sway over the Eastern Church. The main man in the Byzantine Empire was the *Patriarch of Constantinople*, who was effectively the pope in the East. He was, however, subservient to the Byzantine Emperor – a fact that the Church in the West found increasingly difficult to stomach (see Chapter 9).

✔ **The history of religious differences:** Although Christianity was more widespread in the East, it was also much more debated and discussed. In the West, the pope proscribed what people should believe, whereas the East had a much greater history of academic debates. Numerous heretical movements grew up in the Byzantine Empire including Arians (check out the later sidebar, 'The Arian difference', for more), Nestorians and others. Although the beliefs of these various groups were unorthodox and condemned by the Western Catholic Church, they were often supported by Byzantine Emperors and Patriarchs.

✔ **The Emperor and his court:** The Eastern Empire continued to have an Emperor, and his influence and celebrity were far greater than those of any recent Western Emperor. The Byzantine Emperor was considered to be the closest person to God and therefore a higher being than all others. Byzantine Emperors lived a life of total luxury and ceremony. Visiting dignitaries had to get through hordes of flunkeys and advisors to get even a glimpse of the Emperor (turn to the later sidebar 'The Byzantium complex'). This situation in the East was a totally different world to that of the leaders who emerged in the West (see Chapter 4 for more about the early Western rulers).

TECHNICAL STUFF

The Byzantium complex

The word *Byzantine* is used these days to describe something that is incredibly complex and difficult to work out. For example, someone may say, 'This train timetable is far too Byzantine to understand!' This modern use of the word has its origin in the old Byzantine Empire. The Emperor's court was incredibly complex, filled with different levels of advisors, servants, eunuchs and secretaries who made up his civil service. Trying to get a clear, simple answer was a challenge – hence what came to be known as Byzantine complexity.

The Byzantine Empire far outlasted its western neighbour. Throughout periods of expansion and reduction, it lasted all the way through until 1453 when the Ottoman Turks finally sacked Constantinople.

Due to its geographical location, the Byzantine Empire is mostly on the periphery of the story of Medieval History and the focus of this book. East and West do continue to collide and collaborate, particularly over various religious matters and during the Crusades (see Part III of this book), but the Byzantine Empire has its own rich and fascinating history. If you want to find out more, you'll just have to wait for *Byzantine History For Dummies*!

Delving into the Dark Ages

The period immediately after the fall of the Western Roman Empire in August 476 is traditionally known as the *Dark Ages*, during which huge migrations of people took place and new states and countries came into being in Northern Europe. (In Chapters 3 and 4, I examine exactly what happened and how the new societies were developed.)

The Dark Ages roughly cover the years 450–800 – which comprises the early part of the Middle Ages – and received its name for two reasons:

- Early historians regarded the period after the Roman Empire as regressive and backward, a time during which a lot of learning and knowledge were lost and people moved back to living simpler lives in smaller communities.

- Fewer written sources are available, and so historians knew far less about what actually happened during this time than, say, during the Roman Empire at its height.

More recently, many historians have revised these views. As researchers have discovered more about what went on during the Dark Ages, the period has become considerably lighter! Instead of a backwards step, this era was the beginning of the formation of Western Europe as you now know today. Many of the reasons for this change in opinion are due to advances made in medieval archaeology, in particular since the 1950s. For a good example of this, look at the section on archaeology in Chapter 3.

Migrating during the fifth century

Part of the reason that the Western Empire came to an end was down to the huge movements of people westwards (as I mention in Chapter 1 and the earlier sidebar 'So why did the Roman Empire collapse?'). These migrations saw large numbers of people who spoke Germanic languages moving into vast areas of territory that the retreating Roman army had vacated.

King Arthur: Man or myth?

A classic example of myth and history from the Dark Ages is the figure of King Arthur. Most historians now agree that the man recognised as King Arthur was a British tribal leader who led the defence of Britain against invasions by the Saxons in the sixth century (turn to Chapter 3 for more details). As a famous figure during his own time, stories abounded about him and became folklore tales. The deeds of other people were probably attributed to him too, as a famous figure can become a magnet for such stories. The stories would then have been passed verbally between families and generations.

In the twelfth century, Geoffrey of Monmouth wrote a book of these stories called *The History of the Kings of Britain*. As a consequence of this book, the version of the legend of King Arthur that has become popular in fact came into being around 500 years *after* he was (probably) alive!

The legends and stories of King Arthur in Monmouth's work and subsequent writers, including Chrétien de Troyes, Thomas Malory, Alfred Lord Tennyson and T.H. White, are fabulously entertaining – but they bear no relation to the life that the man actually lived.

The vast majority of these people were illiterate, which has made tracking their movements extremely difficult because they never wrote their own histories. Most of the evidence available for this period is based on archaeology or the writings of later historians. Because much of the available history has been handed down verbally between generations, the history can take on qualities of *mythtory* – a mix of actual historical fact and mythical stories or folk tales. Often the only reliable information that exists is the names and sequence of leaders.

Moving on up with the Merovingians

Medieval Europe was essentially a blank canvas after the fall of the Roman Empire, and strong leaders were able to exploit the resulting power vacuum. One of the most successful was Childeric, who became the first of the 'Merovingian' kings – descendants of a quasi-mythical figure called Merovech whom you can read all about in Chapter 4.

Meeting the first medieval diplomat: Childeric

In common with many other Dark Age leaders, Childeric's life is largely a mystery. Born in the first half of the fifth century (historians don't know the actual date), Childeric succeeded his father as king of the Salian Franks in 457. Childeric's people were a relatively small group of Franks who lived in what is now The Netherlands, just above the river Rhine. This area is known as Salland today.

By the fifth century, the Salian Franks had moved into northern Gaul, establishing their home city in Tournai (modern-day Belgium). They were a pagan people who worshipped their own gods.

Although a relatively small group, they became more influential through Childeric's political manoeuvring. He collaborated with various groups of Romans and also with the Church to protect his territory. When the Western Roman Empire came to an end, he was a well-known and influential leader.

Achieving great things: Clovis

When Childeric died in 481, he was very much top dog in the region of northern Gaul. His power was transferred to his son Clovis, who grabbed his chance.

During his reign, Clovis was able to unite all the Franks in Gaul by assassinating several kings and fighting successful wars. Although Clovis's tactics involved nothing particularly unusual, he was able to gather support from the Romans still living in northern Gaul by recognising that, regardless of tribal allegiances and geography, the one factor that brought all Romans together was the Christian Church. He gave up his own pagan beliefs and converted to Christianity, using the power of the Church to further increase his support.

Historians know a fair amount about Clovis because of the work of historian Gregory of Tours (539–594). Gregory was a bishop who wrote an account of his own life and career in the Church. Fortunately, he also devotes three chapters to events before his own lifetime, and he describes Clovis's conversion to Christianity. Despite the attempts of his wife to convert him, Clovis had remained resistant to Christianity until he was struggling in a battle against the tribe called the Alamanni:

> *'Jesus Christ,' he said, 'you who Clotild maintains to be the son of the living God, you who deign to give help to those in travail and victory over those who trust in you, in faith I beg the glory of your help' . . . Even as he said it, the Alamanni turned their backs and began to run away.*

Following these events, Clovis immediately converted to Christianity. To understand why his plan was so smart, you need to consider how influential the Church had become, which is just what I do in the next section.

Spreading Christianity

Although the Roman Empire had officially become Christian in the fourth century, Christianity was far from dominant in Western Europe when the Western Roman Empire came to an end. Historians estimate that in the year 400, the majority of people in Western Europe followed *polytheistic religions*, meaning that they worshipped one or more pagan, that is, non-Christian, gods.

The Arian difference

Many of the people who moved into Western Europe during the collapse of the Roman Empire were nominally Christian but wouldn't have been considered so by the Catholic Church. Their form of belief was known as *Arianism*, a distinct form of Christianity considered heretical by the papacy and named after a man called Bishop Arius (c. AD 250–336) from Alexandria in Egypt.

Specifically, Arians believed that Christ was lesser than God and not formed of part of him. They regarded the Holy Spirit as being lesser still and subservient to Christ. This belief contrasted with traditional Catholic belief, which held that the Holy Trinity were all born of God and eternal like Him, and balanced in status and importance.

These differences might not seem like much on paper, but Arian beliefs were massively controversial and influential. Arianism, in various forms, thrived throughout Western Europe until it was finally suppressed in the seventh century, and carried on for even longer in the east.

Arianism is just one of the hundreds of heresies that abounded during the Middle Ages; you can read about some others in Chapter 14.

Just about 500 years later, the situation was incredibly different. By 900 virtually the whole of Europe was Christian, and the Church was the dominant force in politics and economics. Understanding how this amazing change took place is key to understanding the Medieval World.

Living on the edge

The Frankish king Clovis (check out the earlier section 'Achieving great things: Clovis') took power in large parts of Northern Europe and made a deal with the Catholic Church, which gave Catholic priests and missionaries the opportunity to seek to convert Clovis's people to the Catholic faith. The Church tended to try and convert only those within the boundaries of the old Roman Empire, believing that people who lived outside it did so for a reason – basically, the will of God was that they remain outside the Empire and continue with their pagan beliefs.

Of course, many Catholics lived outside the borders of the old Roman Empire as well. They had settled in parts of the world that were beyond Roman control even when the Roman Empire had been at its height. The Church didn't forget these people and bishops were frequently sent out to minister to them and their spiritual needs. Although they weren't specifically sent out for the purpose, these men ended up becoming the first Christian missionaries.

Encouraging the Irish: Palladius

One of the best and earliest examples of the early missionary phenomenon is Bishop Palladius. Palladius had experienced an exciting early life, having been kidnapped and sold into slavery as a young boy. Fleeing to the Church, he became a noted Christian scholar and in 431 the pope sent him to Ireland in a bid to convert its pagan people. Details of what Palladius did are scarce, but by the time he died (around 460) a significant Christian community and Church had been established in Ireland and Palladius was later made into a saint. His successor in Ireland did pretty well too! The man who replaced Palladius was known as Patricius in Latin and later became the St Patrick that is still celebrated by Irish communities around the world on 17 March.

Scared to death – of death

The increase in Christianity across early Medieval Europe significantly influenced people's attitudes towards life throughout the age and beyond. During the later medieval period (after 1150), Christianity was particularly focused on the afterlife and ensuring progress to Heaven. In a way, your earthly life was just an opportunity to make sure that you didn't condemn yourself to Hell through sinful acts.

These are some of the key things that later medieval Christians believed:

✔ **Judgement:** Whenever people died, their souls underwent judgement during which God's emissaries decided whether they would go to Heaven or Hell depending on how free of sin their souls were. Judgement didn't happen immediately upon dying though, and the dead would have to wait in their graves for the judgement to be made. The person doing the judging was St Michael who would weigh the souls of the dead to find out how much sin they contained.

✔ **Purgatory:** If people's souls weren't completely free of sin, they entered Purgatory. This place was a state of purification where the soul underwent cleansing before it progressed to Heaven. People would say prayers for deceased individuals to try and ease their passages through Purgatory towards Heaven. In the thirteenth century the idea developed of purgatory being an actual 'place', a kind of waiting room where those who had yet to be judged awaited their fate. Purgatory is still a major part of Catholic religious practice today.

✔ **Indulgences:** Medieval Christians were desperate for assurance during their lifetimes that their souls would eventually make it to Heaven and grasped at opportunities to guarantee their futures. Later in the Middle Ages, from the thirteenth century onwards, people undertook *indulgences* – good works or deeds that offset sin and assured you a place in Heaven. The greatest indulgence ever offered was to go on Crusade (see Chapter 11) – the pope claimed that doing so would cleanse away all previous sin. Eventually indulgences took on a financial form too, and the dead could leave money to pay clerics to pray for their souls.

✔ **Fear:** Absolute dread of Hell and Purgatory is one of the main reasons why the Church held such a powerful grip on the medieval imagination and became so influential over the following centuries.

Chapter 3

Settling in England with the Anglo-Saxons

> *Wondrous is this stone-wall, wrecked by fate; the city buildings crumble, the works of giants decay.*
>
> –'The Ruin', an Anglo-Saxon poem describing England after the Romans left.

*J*ust like the rest of Europe, England entered a period of change and migration following the fall of the Roman Empire. Although the pace of change wasn't as great as that of the Carolingians in France (as I describe in Chapter 4), a new kingdom began to emerge in England by the middle of the ninth century. Much of the early history of England from this period is vague and difficult to pin down, but this chapter serves as a guide to what happened during the 300 or so years after the end of the Roman Empire.

Keeping On Moving On: Early Migrations and Anglo-Saxon Action

In AD 410 the Roman emperor Honorius pulled the Roman army out of Britain – effectively abandoning the province – and left the indigenous population to defend themselves. What happened immediately following this withdrawal is unclear.

The island probably didn't have an overall controlling force, and seems to have broken down into a number of smaller kingdoms. The immediate problem faced by the indigenous population of England was the threat of invasion from the Picts to the north, and whilst attacks did come the threat from the north was soon replaced with a far bigger threat from across the sea.

Stepping in to help (and hinder): The Saxons

A host of stories exist as to how the Saxons came to be in England. Some accounts describe Saxon invasions that occurred in Kent and Sussex during the period. Another account cites a decision attributed to one king called Vortigern, whereupon in the middle of the fifth century the kings in the east of England invited some Saxon mercenaries from the Low Countries (modern-day Belgium and The Netherlands) to come and help defend their territory. Most likely, the sudden arrival of hordes of Saxons in England was a mixture of invasion and invitation. (See Chapter 25 for more about Vortigern.)

The Saxons were joined in England around the same time by a people from north-east Germany known as the Angles. The indigenous people of England probably didn't make much distinction between them and, as a result, we refer to those people who crossed the sea and settled as *Anglo-Saxons*.

Unfortunately, the bold idea of inviting the Saxons over didn't work; the kings ran out of supplies and were unable to pay their new army. Some historians argue that, in turn, the Saxons then revolted, creating a much bigger war closer to home for the kings to deal with. Things seem to have come to a head in the late fifth century. The crucial point in the struggle is a battle at a place known as *Mons Badonicus*. This conflict is a bit of a problem for historians because nobody is entirely sure *when* it happened or even *where* it took place! The battle is likely to have occurred between the years 490 and 517, but no definite date is known. Equally a whole variety of sites in western England and south Wales have been suggested as the battlefield.

Historians do know that this battle was a massive confrontation between a mix of indigenous Britons and an Anglo-Saxon army – and that the British won. The Anglo-Saxon advance was halted for many years as a result of this defeat. However, *Mons Badonicus* turned out to be the last stand for the indigenous British against the Anglo-Saxons. During the sixth century the invaders strengthened their hold over what we would now think of as the British Isles, and gradually reduced opposition.

The real King Arthur?

One of the stories about the battle of *Mons Badonicus* is that King Arthur was the leader of the British forces. (Check out Chapter 2 for more on Arthur.) The only account of the battle is a very brief mention by a British monk called Gildas who lived in the sixth century. He doesn't mention anybody called Arthur, but more recent speculation suggests that the leader of the British was a man called Ambrosius Aurelianus,

a former Roman military commander. Many people think that this leader was the basis for the legend of King Arthur.

A version of this story is shown in the film *King Arthur* (2004), featuring Clive Owen in the title role. The film is based on a heavily adapted version of a story that's historically dodgy to begin with, but the movie is good fun and the battle scenes are great.

Due to the lack of written historical sources, most knowledge of this period is derived from archaeological finds in England. Some of these discoveries have been quite large (see the later sidebar 'Finds of the century'), particularly in eastern England and along the river Thames. These locations make sense because large numbers of Saxons first arrived in Eastern England, and they would have colonised here and used the river to travel farther west.

Setting up the Super Seven: The heptarchy

By the late sixth century, most of England was under Anglo-Saxon control. However, this situation didn't mean that a single ruler controlled the territory. Anglo-Saxons arrived in tribes, and these various groups secured large chunks of territory that each became separate smaller kingdoms (see Figure 3-1):

- ✔ The four major kingdoms were East Anglia, Mercia, Wessex and Northumbria.
- ✔ After these were founded, the Saxons also gained control of Kent, Essex and Sussex.

Each kingdom had its own king, and so the period is sometimes known as the *heptarchy*, an Ancient Greek word meaning 'seven realms'. Recently historians have criticised the term as misleading because the seven distinct and separate kingdoms existed independently of each other, but it is still the best way to describe how the original seven kingdoms came into being.

Figure 3-1:
The Anglo-Saxon kingdoms around the year 600.

The wars also created separate sub-kingdoms within the kingdoms. For example, in Northumbria two smaller sub-kingdoms called Bernicia and Deira developed and stayed independent for some period of time. Also, places such as the Isle of Wight and, for a time, Cornwall, existed independently from the heptarchy. New kingdoms emerged too; Lindsey and Hwicca (both of which appear in Figure 3-1) were small kingdoms based in Lincolnshire and Worcestershire respectively that were subsumed into other, more powerful kingdoms within a century or so.

A certain amount of disunity is always likely when a tribal people establishes itself in a large new landmass, and something similar happened in Germany at the same time (turn to Chapter 4 to find out more).

Deciding who is king of kings

The rulers of these kingdoms were effectively like tribal chieftains and the tribal system still operated. In this system, all people within the tribe were united in their total loyalty to a leader who made all decisions for his people and fought as a warrior. Consequently, the tribal nature of the kingdoms meant that the kings were often at war with one another, which is what happened throughout the next 200 years, as conflicts flared between rival kingdoms. Occasionally, one king became the most powerful and dominated the others. The top king would be known as the *Bretwalda* or 'ruler of Britain', but this title wasn't permanent or formal, and was just something that kings claimed from time to time.

Offa of Mercia (died 796) is a good example. Mercia was one of the more powerful kingdoms and over a period of about 20 years, Offa managed also to get his hands on East Anglia and absorb Kent and Essex into his realm. Offa was a successful king because of his drive and personality: it was a dog eat dog world. When he died, his son Ecgfrith succeeded him, but he lasted barely six months before being ousted by a rival. Offa's story just goes to prove that this tribal method of ruling wasn't a system.

Becoming unified

The tribal king drama finally came to an end in the ninth century when nearly all Anglo-Saxon England was unified under one king, Alfred the Great (flip to Chapter 6 for all about Alfred). However, full unification didn't occur until Edgar I, who reigned between 959–975. Edgar was known as 'The Peaceful', because his reign finally brought an end to civil war between the kingdoms. Within 100 years of his death, in 1066, the problem was solved for good with William the Conqueror bringing a complete end to Anglo-Saxon rule in England (as I describe in Chapter 10).

Cnut: Not a Cnutter!

One of the most famous kings of the Anglo-Saxon period is Cnut, also known as Canute. Cnut was the Viking king of Denmark and Norway, but also became king of England in 1017 when he married Emma of Normandy, the wife of the previous king, and ruled through a regent. He's a very interesting character in that he ruled internationally and was also responsible for making lots of laws, many in a letter he wrote to the English people that still survives.

However, Cnut is most famous for an old story that is often wrongly told, in which he tried to use his powers as king to stop the sea. This summary is unfair on Cnut, and the full story is rather different. Twelfth-century writer Henry of Huntingdon first reported on Cnut and described him as having done this futile act precisely because he wanted to show his smarmy courtiers that the power of a king has limits.

According to Henry, as the tide flowed around his robes, Cnut said 'Let all men know how empty and worthless is the power of kings, for there is none worthy of the name, but He whom Heaven, Earth, and sea obey by eternal laws.' According to Henry from this point onwards Cnut never wore his crown again, as a symbol that he was just a man.

Cnut was a genuinely Christian king who journeyed to Rome to witness the coronation of the Holy Roman Emperor in 1027. On his return he wrote his famous letter to the English people. It contains 20 points, in one of which Cnut claims, 'And I inform you that I will be a gracious lord and a faithful observer of God's rights and just secular law.' The irony is that this most thoughtful and pious of Anglo-Saxon kings has been associated with a story that people think shows him to be a power-mad megalomaniac!

Christianising England, again

The new kings of England weren't the only change that came with Anglo-Saxon rule. Many social and cultural changes took place, and I talk about them in the later section 'Assessing the Anglo-Saxon Impact'. One important change, however, was reaffirming England's Christian orientation again.

Under Roman rule, the province of Britain had been Christian since the fourth century, but the Germanic tribes that came to England after the fall of the Roman Empire were pagan. Historians aren't sure, but after the Roman Legions left many of the indigenous British people most likely returned to their former religions. Therefore, when Anglo-Saxon power was established, the Catholic Church in Europe looked to convert the new leaders of England.

Going on the Gregorian mission

The first conversion attempt came in 597 and was known as the Gregorian mission, because it was sent by Pope Gregory, or Gregory the Great. Augustine, the prior of a Benedictine monastery (Chapter 18 has lots more on Benedictine monks and other monastic orders), led the mission and landed in Kent with 40 missionaries. King Aethelbert, the leader of Kent at that time, allowed the mission to travel through his lands, and Augustine and his crew arrived at Aethelbert's court at Canterbury and began preaching to the local community. Key to this was Aethelbert's wife Bertha. She was already a Christian and persuaded her husband to take a more tolerant attitude than he had previously – a key intervention as it turned out. Augustine and his followers were amazingly successful, and within four years the king himself had converted to Christianity.

Aethelbert's conversion gave Augustine great power. The pope had already decreed that all British Christians treat Augustine as their leader. As a result of his success in Kent, Augustine became the leader of the English Church and the first Archbishop of Canterbury, a role that remains central to the Church of England today because Canterbury was the first bishopric to be established during the conversion.

Within a few years another bishopric had been established at Rochester and soon London and the kingdom of Essex had them as well. For his part, Aethelbert became a passionate campaigner for Christianity, and the religion spread quickly throughout the south of England.

Forming new, Christian England

Throughout the seventh century, the re-conversion of England continued. One of the biggest events came in 655 when King Penda of Mercia was killed in battle. Up to that point, Mercia had remained pagan, but Penda's successor, Cenwalh of Wessex, brought both kingdoms together under his Christian rule.

The Venerable – and Productive – Bede

By far the best source for Anglo-Saxon history is a chronicler known as Bede, or 'The Venerable Bede'. Scholars consider him to be the first real English historian and so he's also known as 'The Father of English History'. That title is quite a lot to live up to, but Bede was definitely an extraordinary figure – and his own life was fairly interesting too.

All that historians know about Bede comes from his own writings in which he says he was born around 672 and sent to a monastery when he was seven years old. He stayed in monastic institutions for the rest of his life and was involved in a number of religious debates and controversies. He is most famous for his writing, most notably the *Historica Ecclesiastica*, a history of the Church in England, which is written in Latin and spread over five books, weighing in at around 400 pages. The books took Bede around 30 years to write and they detail the history of England between the arrival of Julius Caesar (55 BC) all the way up to AD 731. His was an incredible undertaking, but a life in religious institutions meant that Bede had access to all the existing documentation.

Bede died four years after the books's completion in 735, probably in his late 60s. The *Historica Ecclesiastica* is by far the most consistent and detailed narrative of the Anglo-Saxon period up to Bede's death. He was very clear on his reasons for writing history as the following quote shows:

> *For if history relates good things of good men, the attentive hearer is excited to imitate that which is good; or if it mentions evil things of wicked persons, nevertheless the religious and pious hearer or reader, shunning that which is hurtful and perverse, is the more earnestly excited to perform those things which he knows to be good, and worthy of God.*

By the end of the seventh century all the Anglo-Saxon leaders claimed to be Christian. They probably weren't Christian as you would understand the term today, but they claimed Christianity as their religion and allowed people to worship, which meant the religion was able to flourish and the Church go on to become a powerful institution.

Not everybody was a practising Christian. Forms of pagan worship survived, particularly in the countryside, and people were allowed to worship as they desired. The tradition of English folklore is based in this rural paganism, and it continued to flourish throughout the Middle Ages and beyond.

Assessing the Anglo-Saxon Impact

The Anglo-Saxons made a bigger impact on England than just redrawing the map, bringing with them a new organisational and cultural approach. In this section I look at the many ways that Anglo-Saxon rulers changed England.

Governing England: Resistance is feudal

The biggest impact the Anglo-Saxons had on England was the establishment of the method of government and administration that we refer to as the *feudal system*. A huge debate exists about when the feudal system first came into being in the world, but the Dark Ages (c. 450–800) saw it spread across mainland Europe and become the most common method of government of the day. The system wasn't political and had no voting; instead, it was a system of economic organisation, and it stayed in place for centuries.

The key element of the feudal system was that it made a firm connection between land and service. A lord or noble owned land and would make grants of it, known as *fiefs*. However, a lord could only grant land to somebody that was his *vassal,* meaning someone who had sworn an oath of loyalty to him and promised to pay him *homage.* Paying homage involved making a public demonstration of loyalty to the lord, kneeling before him and making the oath. The oath had two parts. Not only did the vassal promise loyalty to the lord, but also promised to give him military service, to fight for him in wars. In return for this, the vassal would receive his fief or grant of land which he could work, or get others to work for him, and live from the profits of the land. That wasn't the end of it, though – the vassal had to pay a portion of the profit to his lord.

This feudal organisation ran right the way through society. Nobles paid homage themselves, to kings, and even kings paid homage. The fact that the king of England had to pay homage to his French counterpart for the lands that he held in France was a key part of the continuing warfare between the two countries in the later Middle Ages (see Chapters 17 and 21).

For most people, the feudal system meant that they were tied to the land they worked on because they didn't own the means of their own livelihood, and had to stay loyal to their feudal lord or face a life without land or income. This restriction of liberty eventually resulted in several peasant uprisings in the fifteenth century (see Chapter 22).

Medieval people wouldn't have considered themselves to be living in a feudal system because the term itself was first used during the sixteenth century and came into popular use during the Enlightenment, in the eighteenth century.

Laying down the law

The Anglo-Saxons had their own laws, which they brought to England. You may be surprised to find out that pagan settlers had a very well-defined code of law, but this was definitely the case! Also, England had lost most of its organisational processes when the Roman Empire collapsed and its administrators left the former province. The resulting gap was large, and history's most surprising legal eagles were happy to fill it! The laws that they introduced stayed in place until the Norman Conquest in 1066.

Getting the word out

The law these days is complex: to get something done, you consult an expert, such as a solicitor. In the Medieval World things were rather different. In Anglo-Saxon England, law was made by the king: existing laws were in place and he chose to add to them if he so desired. As with conversion to Christianity, King Aethelbert of Kent (see the section 'Going on the Gregorian mission') was one of the first to augment the laws of his kingdom.

The new laws were distributed throughout his lands and posted up so that all literate people were able to read them. The laws were also written in the Germanic languages or dialects spoken by the Anglo-Saxons (mostly 'West Saxon') rather than Latin – the first set of European laws to be written in any other language.

Law-making quickly became complicated, because each king was different and the changes introduced by say, the king of Mercia, differed from those in Northumbria, Kent or Essex. If you were going to do something wrong or make a claim, you were best off doing it on your own turf!

Going to court (sort of)

Anglo-Saxon legal cases were heard in front of an assembly of freemen. These assemblies had various names depending on the location, such as 'borough courts' and 'shire courts'. Individuals brought prosecutions by making accusations about other people.

The proceedings weren't trials in the modern sense. Instead, the accused people had to take an oath that they were innocent and also provide others to make similar oaths testifying to this fact. Sometimes these supporting oaths were not enough to defeat an accusation, perhaps because the accused was unable to provide enough people to make oaths in support or because others with more status said that the person was guilty. If individuals were found guilty, the normal punishments were fines. If you were unable or didn't want to pay, you had to go through a horrible ordeal.

Surviving trial by ordeal

Trial by ordeal is one of the most famous – and nastiest – aspects of the Anglo-Saxon world. Common men (in other words, men that weren't members of the nobility) unable or unwilling to pay their fines had a choice between facing one of three ordeals:

- ✔ Being tied up and thrown into a pool of water. If you were guilty, you sank; if you were innocent, you floated!

- ✔ Carrying a red-hot piece of iron for a specific distance. If you succeeded, you were deemed innocent.

- ✔ Putting your hand in a pot of boiling water and lifting out a heavy stone.

As if these options weren't bad enough, different levels to the trial also existed, as this example suggests:

> *And if the accusation be 'single'* [that is, a lesser crime] *the hand is to be plunged in up to the wrist to reach the stone, and if it be 'three-fold'* [more serious], *up to the elbow.*

Unfortunately, simply lifting out the stone wasn't enough. The proof or guilt of innocence rested on how the wound developed:

> *And he is to undergo it, and they are to seal up the hand; and after the third day they are to look and see whether it be corrupt or clean within the seal.*

Basically if your wound became infected, you were guilty as well! The ordeal wasn't just reserved for common men. One version of it was for priests, which involved forcing them to eat huge amounts of consecrated bread (as used in mass). If they were unable to eat and choked or vomited, they were guilty! Punishments were fixed rather than decided upon after a verdict had been reached, so everybody would have known what was likely to happen to the accused if he was found guilty.

Enjoying Anglo-Saxon culture

When the Anglo-Saxons arrived in England, they brought their culture – which resembled that of the Germanic peoples of Central Europe – with them.

Surveying the laws of Whitred

A great example of Anglo-Saxon law is the law code of King Whitred of Kent, who ruled between 690–725. Interestingly, his laws show the clear links between the king and the Church, including how powerful bishops had already become.

The laws were a very mixed bag, focusing on things such as regulating holy days in the calendar and banning unlawful marriages, indicating the extent of Christianity's influence at the time. Some of the listed punishments were very curious: for example, if servants worked on their own business on holy days, they had to pay a fine or be flogged, whereas freemen were fined and the person who reported the offence received half the fine as payment!

Positing poetry

For a warlike people given to savage activities such as 'trial by ordeal' (which I describe in the earlier section, 'Surviving trial by ordeal'), the Anglo-Saxons were surprisingly fond of poetry and pretty good at producing it. Like many cultures they used poetry as a way of recording history and it was often passed down orally between generations. Some of these poems went back a long way in time and were probably first composed by German tribes that fought against the early Roman Emperors during the first two centuries AD.

Most of the poems deal with the deeds of heroes and warriors fighting at battles that probably had some basis in history but had changed and altered across the generations. Only fragments of some of these poems survive, but you can still get an idea of how evocative they were.

Early Viking raids on Britain (flip to Chapter 8 to discover the deeds of the Vikings) are recorded in the most famous of these epic poems, known as _The Battle of Maldon_. The poem celebrated the battle that took place at Maldon, on the coast of Essex, in 991. The following section describes how the over-confident leader Byhrtnoth allowed the Vikings to invade his territory and was killed trying to defend it. In this English translated extract, one of his followers laments his death:

> _Here lies our leader, hewn down, an heroic man in the dust. He who now longs to escape will lament for ever. I am old, I will not go from here, but I mean to lie by the side of my lord, lie in the dust with the man I loved so dearly._

Getting epic: Beowulf

The most famous Anglo-Saxon poem is the epic _Beowulf_, which was composed by an anonymous eighth-century poet. The poem is an adventure story about a young warrior called Beowulf from the Geat tribe in Sweden. Although probably composed in England, the poem is written in the original Germanic language of the poet and concerns mythical events in Scandinavia.

The famous opening lines call you to gather round and listen to a great story:

> _Listen! The fame of Danish kings, in days gone by, the daring feats worked by those heroes are well known to us._

The poem comes in two parts. In the first, the young Beowulf helps a king to defeat the mythical monster Grendel and then his mother who comes to avenge him. The second part is set 50 years later after Beowulf has become king of the Geats and is called to defend his people against a dragon. The poem has a lot more going on, but to tell you would spoil the adventure!

Try looking out for a modern translation of Beowulf. The poem has a bad reputation because of the dusty old translations that people studied at school 40 of 50 years ago. Seamus Heaney's translation from 2001 is a version that really brings the language and characters to life.

Despite being more than 1,200 years old, *Beowulf* is still big news at the box-office. Several film versions have been made over the last ten years, but the one most worth a look is the animated version from 2007, featuring the voices of Anthony Hopkins, Angelina Jolie and many others. The computer-generated imagery gives the movie a slightly otherworldly feel that makes sense for a myth: and the monster Grendel is really quite scary!

Affecting language for centuries

Anglo-Saxon rule continued in England until the defeat to William of Normandy at the Battle of Hastings in 1066 (check out Chapter 10 for more), but their impact on government and culture lasted far longer. For example, this book is written in English, the earliest form of which was Anglo-Saxon.

After the Norman invasion of 1066, Anglo-Saxon developed into the language generally referred to as Old English. In turn, this language developed into the Middle English Chaucer and Shakespeare used. Middle English is much more recognisable by English speakers of today. So, the fact that British historians traditionally felt that culture left England with the Romans is rather ironic – the Germanic people that arrived soon after the Romans left actually kick-started the development of the language that those historians wrote in!

Finds of the century

Much of what historians know about the Anglo-Saxon period comes from archaeological finds in England. Probably the most famous discovery is Sutton Hoo near Woodbridge in Suffolk. This site includes two burial grounds from the sixth and seventh centuries where a huge amount was found including a full ship burial, which provides great insight into Anglo-Saxon burial practices and the design of their ships. Nobody is sure who was buried in the ship, although it must have been somebody of great importance and status. One claim is that it was a king called Raedwald who ruled at the beginning of the seventh century, but this theory has never been proven.

Since Sutton Hoo was first excavated during the Second World War, several other major sites have been uncovered elsewhere in England and more continue to be discovered. As recently as September 2009, the biggest ever find of Anglo-Saxon gold was found in Staffordshire. A man with a metal detector came across a massive horde of Anglo-Saxon artefacts numbering more than 1,500 pieces and dating from sometime around the year 700. The complexity and skill of design in some of the artwork is greater than anything previously seen, and as a result historians have revised their theories on the nature of Anglo-Saxon England.

History is changing all the time – especially as researchers keep on digging up more of it!

Chapter 4

Organising Early France & Germany: The Merovingians and Carolingians

During the first few centuries following the fall of the Roman Empire in the year 476, nearly all the European territories experienced new rulers and big population movements. In Central Europe – the old Roman province of Gaul and home to modern-day France and Germany – large sections of territory gradually came under the control of the Franks (turn to Chapter 2 for more details), who had recently converted to Christianity.

Over the next few centuries, Frankish domination increased under two dynasties – the Merovingians and Carolingians. In this chapter I explore the people who made up these dynasties and how they rose to power.

The period that I cover in this chapter is a difficult one for modern historians to write about because of the large gaps in knowledge, one of the reasons that it has often been referred to as 'The Dark Ages', but researchers have put together a framework that explains how one family came to rule half of Europe. So here goes!

Making Major Moves: The Merovingians

The Merovingians were descended from a people called the Salian Franks, who had lived in the area that now forms the modern-day, south Netherlands, to the north of the river Rhine. During the fifth century, they moved westwards and began to establish themselves in what is modern-day France, as Figure 4-1 shows. Merovingian history is quite difficult to trace because they were always falling out with and fighting each other in civil wars – a reflection of their origins as a tribal people. Nevertheless they still managed to hold on to power in this area until the middle of the eighth century.

Figure 4-1:
The
Frankish
Kingdoms
511–751.

Merovingian is a wonderful word, and it seems to have come from a man called Merovech who first led these people on their journey west in the early fifth century. He was the grandfather of Clovis, who was the first to establish rule and also adopt Christianity (flip to Chapter 2 for more details on Clovis). Historians don't really know anything about Merovech himself; he's one of those almost mythical figures who were quite common during the Dark Ages, but a real historical figure would have existed.

The term Merovingian is strictly appropriate only to describe the ruling class of this people. Historians typically refer to the people in general as *Franks*. At the time, they were also known as the 'long-haired' Franks because of their fashion for wearing hair over the collar, which was notably different from their Roman predecessors.

Amassing land

The Merovingians made fast work of adding to their territory. When Clovis I died in 511, they had gained control of the whole of the old Roman province of Gaul except Burgundy, and by the middle of the sixth century, they had added the Provence region to their territory.

During this time the Frankish lands were divided into two distinct territories:

- **To the east** was Austrasia (East Land), which incorporated eastern France, Germany, Belgium and southern The Netherlands.
- **To the west** was Neustria (West Land), which incorporated the majority of the west of France.

At various points territories broke away or tried to separate, but these attempts never succeeded. Austrasia and Neustria lasted throughout the Merovingian period.

Squabbling constantly

The Merovingians managed to conquer a great deal of territory, but ruling it successfully became more of a problem because they were unable to stop fighting each other.

Descendants of Clovis and their sons ruled all the territory, but wars between the relatives were pretty much constant. Brief periods of unity were immediately followed by civil war when a ruler died, due to the fact that his territory would be split between his sons. The normal tradition seems to have been to fight your brothers on an annual basis and because all the rulers came from the same family, grievances and the desire for vengeance lasted through generations. Family dinners must have been fun!

Bad, bad Brunhilda

One of the biggest causes of discontent in the Merovingian world was a woman called Brunhilda, who lived from around 543 to 613. Her life is too eventful even for a feature film – it would require a mini-series! She's a fascinating character and a great example of how treacherous the Merovingian kingdoms were.

Brunhilda was a Visigoth princess who grew up in the Visigoth kingdom in Spain. She married King Sigebert I of Austrasia and was the first foreign noble to marry a Merovingian. Sigebert's brother Chilperic obviously liked the idea because he married Brunhilda's sister Galswintha, who was murdered within a year, probably by Chilperic and his mistress.

Brunhilda was devastated at her sister's death and persuaded Sigebert to go to war with Chilperic over it. Sigebert won the war but was soon assassinated by his brother's agents, and Brunhilda was captured and imprisoned in Rouen. Despite her imprisonment, she had clearly maintained her ability to bewitch Merovingian men because shortly afterwards she married Merovech (not the semi-legendary figure who gave his name to the Merovingians), the son of her bitter enemy Chilperic! The two immediately set about planning to make Merovech king. As a result Chilperic declared the marriage invalid and forced his son to go into a monastery. Merovech went on the run and ended up committing suicide.

Meanwhile, Brunhilda seized the throne of Austrasia for herself, claiming that she was acting as regent for her eldest son from her first marriage! Over the next 30 years, the regencies and murders continued furiously as Brunhilda continued to manipulate all sorts of Merovingian men into doing what she wanted and even led troops into battle herself.

Brunhilda was eventually captured in the year 613 by a king called Clotaire II, who became sole ruler of the Merovingian kingdoms. She was put on trial and accused of the murder of ten Merovingian kings. This number was pushing it a bit, but probably not too far off the mark! She was convicted and punished by being torn apart between two charging horses as a symbol of how her acts had ripped the kingdoms apart.

Constant war between the kings came at a tremendous cost. The competing Merovingians were always campaigning for the support of the nobility, which made the nobility extremely powerful and weakened the royal line. Most historians agree that the last truly independent Merovingian king was Dagobert I, who died in 639.

In the period that followed, the kings became more like ceremonial figures, with the real power residing with their barons, nobles and generals. New positions of power developed, most importantly the role of 'Mayor of the Palace' – a chief administrator to the Merovingian king who effectively controlled the kingdom (see the later section 'Making the most of the mayor'). Under these circumstances, a whole new line of rulers developed – the Carolingians. I talk about how this transition happened in the later section 'Rising to Power: The Carolingians'.

Pondering Merovingian power

The Merovingian period didn't last very long, only a couple of centuries, but it was still rich and interesting. After all, they were the first people to come to power in mainland Europe after the fall of the Roman Empire, which meant that they were effectively starting with a blank canvas.

Absolute power?

The Merovingians were originally a tribal people, a fact that shows in the way they organised their society. The king, like a tribal chief, was an absolute ruler with total authority. All territory and wealth that was gained was also his, which is one of the reasons why people were so keen to try and set themselves up as king!

Kings were able to nominate their successors and transfer all territory and property to their children. Of course, these decisions were rarely respected and civil war was usually the result. But the Merovingians placed the bloodline and relationship to the throne above any other quality.

The Merovingian kings also kept themselves apart from the administration of their kingdom, as I discuss in the following section. In this way they resembled the Byzantine emperors (check out Chapter 2 for more details on these rulers), detached from ordinary people and seen as being closer to God (also see the later sidebar 'Kings after death').

Replacing the Romans: The rise of comites

The fact that Merovingian kings kept themselves separate from the administration of their kingdoms meant that they needed an aristocratic class to run them. The Merovingian Empire was massive, covering a huge landmass. Under the Romans, it had been run and organised by a combination of the civil service, the army and the Church – and so the leadership and management gap was enormous.

The Merovingian solution was to create a whole new class of people to carry out the administration of the kingdoms. These people were given the title of *comites* (counts), an old Roman military term. Their roles were incredibly wide-ranging and included collecting taxes, organising the courts and justice, and even recruiting and administering the army.

Over time the comites grew into incredibly powerful and influential people. The Merovingian kings could make as many decisions as they liked, but they were unable to implement any of them without the comites.

Kings after death

The Merovingians converted to Christianity during the sixth century, and their faith added a great deal to their mystique. Merovingian money and patronage was responsible for the Christian faith spreading throughout Austrasia, Neustria and beyond. Many Merovingian kings founded churches and monasteries, and a number of them were subsequently made into saints. These new saints were immensely popular in their local areas, and as a result cults arose that were devoted to them. These cults also meant that many of the ensuing civil wars also took on regional and religious elements.

Hagiography (the writing of saints' lives) was the most popular form of Merovingian literature, and it usually emphasised the healing powers that the tombs of the saints possessed. Accordingly the tombs of the Merovingian kings became the first real pilgrimage sites of the Medieval World. The Merovingians may not have been interested in administering their kingdoms, but they did manage to generate a tourism industry!

Rising to Power: The Carolingians

During the eighth century something significant changed in the Frankish world. Gradually, year on year, the practical power of the Merovingian king became less and less, while that of his advisors grew (as I relate in the earlier section 'Pondering Merovingian power'). Within 100 years the Merovingian royal line had ceased to exist, and a new and more powerful family were running the Frankish Empire – the Carolingians.

The Carolingians didn't just come out of nowhere. They had always been an important aristocratic family in the Frankish world. Their name in medieval Latin was *kairolingi*, meaning 'the descendants of Charles'. The Charles in question was Charles Martell (c. 688–741) (turn to the later section 'Hammering the Merovingians: Charles Martell' for more on Charles).

Making the most of the mayor

For generations the Carolingians had been a part of the Merovingian administration, holding powerful posts as comites and dealing with financial and military matters (the earlier section 'Replacing the Romans: The rise of comites' talks more about comites). During the eighth century, they got their hands on the most powerful job of all.

The key position that enabled the Carolingians to ascend to power was that of *Mayor of the Palace*, known in Latin as *major domus* from which the term 'major-domo' derives. Although this title may not sound like much, almost like some kind of butler, Mayor of the Palace was the lynchpin position in the old Merovingian kingdoms:

- ✔ The Mayor controlled access to the king and anyone wanting to speak with the king had to go through the Mayor of the Palace.
- ✔ The Mayor was the key decision maker on policy. All the comites in charge of finance, justice and the army reported to him.

Simply put, the Mayor was the power behind the throne and the man who kept the kingdom running. The wide-ranging power of the Mayor was one of the main reasons why the king was seen as a rather ethereal, mystical figure.

Running in the family

During the late seventh and early eighth centuries, one family came to dominate the position of Mayor in Austrasia. At the time this family was known as the 'Pippinids', because most men in the family took the name Pippin. For the best part of a century, fathers and sons of the Pippinid clan took the role of Mayor and handed it on, massively building up their power base as they did so, and eventually granting themselves the title of *Duke*. This title came from *dux*, an old Roman title that had been used to confer widespread military powers. In adopting this title, the mayors were claiming total command of the military in the Merovingian kingdom.

Everything changed in 714 when the serving Mayor, Duke Pippin II, died without a legitimate heir. Instead, power was passed to an illegitimate son born to him by a concubine. The child's name was Charles Martell.

Hammering the Merovingians: Charles Martell

Charles Martell was an amazing success as Mayor of Austrasia. Like those before him, he assumed the title Duke of the Franks and proved to be an incredibly successful general – so successful that he earned the nickname of 'The Hammer'. He's reputed to have lost only one battle and is probably most famous for defeating a large Muslim army at the Battle of Tours in 732, a victory you can read about in Chapter 7.

Tearing up at Tertry

One of the first events that showed how powerful the Mayors had become was the battle of Tertry in the year 687. The battle in the Somme region of the north of France was the climax of a brief civil war between Neustria and Austrasia and their respective Mayors. The conflict took place despite the fact that a Merovingian king, Theuderic III, was still in power.

The Austrasian Mayor was called Pippin of Herstal (see the following section 'Running in the family'), who defeated his Neustrian counterpart Berthar and replaced him as Mayor with one of his own supporters. This appointment increased the power of the Austrasian Mayor and also diminished the influence of the king.

Charles didn't have things easy to begin with. Within a year of assuming his father's title, he was challenged as Mayor of Austrasia by a pretender from Neustria called Ragenfrid: a three-year civil war followed. Charles won it comfortably, but showed mercy to his enemies. He also unified both Austrasia and Neustria under his control.

By this point Charles was effectively the absolute ruler of the Frankish world. A Merovingian king was still in place, but the position had become purely ceremonial. The armies were at the command of Charles, which meant that he was in charge. He used his power to expand Frankish interests and territory by fighting a series of successful foreign wars to the east and west, as well as into Saxon territory in the north. Charles carried out this expansion while still claiming only the title of Duke of the Franks.

After the Battle of Tours, fought against the Muslims in 732, Charles continued with his campaigning up until 737 when the Merovingian king, Theuderic IV, died without an obvious successor. Charles didn't grab the throne, however, and instead it lay vacant. Although the fact that Charles didn't grasp such an obvious opportunity to make himself king seems strange, he already had all the power he needed.

Playing with power after Charles: Pippin

When Charles died in 741, he was able to divide up the Frankish lands as if he were a king and give them to his sons. He split the kingdom in two, giving Austrasia to his elder son Carloman and Neustria to his other son Pippin. Each son also took the title of Mayor of the Palace in their respective kingdoms.

Usually such a split between brothers meant a civil war in the making, but this time things didn't work out like that. Not to say that everything was hunky-dory; the brothers did have another half-brother called Grifo, who was immediately imprisoned when they took power. That's the way to do it!

Working as a puppet master

When the brothers took power, the position of Merovingian king was vacant. One of Carloman's first acts was to nominate a Merovingian noble called Childeric to take the throne. Shortly afterwards, in 747, Carloman decided to abdicate and spend the rest of his days in a monastery.

All this manoeuvring was doubtless down to Pippin III. He's often known as Pippin 'The Short'. We don't know if he was unusually small but if so he certainly made up for his lack of stature with his impact on history.

Pippin was now the sole Mayor and also kept the title Duke of the Franks. To make him look even more legitimate, Pippin retained Childeric on the throne, but the people considered that a king who owed his very existence to Pippin and Carloman was a bit of a joke. Pippin was now in total control of the Franks and he made the most of it.

Making the case for king

Understanding the mind of Pippin and his motivations is almost impossible, but most historians believe that even before he took power he was determined to become the first Carolingian king. His actions certainly bear this idea out.

After he was in supreme power in Austrasia and Neustria, Pippin began his campaign to become king. His first act was to write to Pope Zachary, asking him who he felt truly held royal power in the Frankish lands. This question was a tricky one for the pope; he was aware that he may well need the help of the Frankish king in the near future. The Lombards in northern Italy were making claims for some of the papal estates there, and the pope would need some military support to stop them. With this situation in mind, Zachary replied that the man with real power not also having royal power seemed unusual – he was basically giving Pippin approval to make himself king.

Pippin didn't hang around and announced that at present the throne was vacant. Instead of declaring himself king, he summoned a council of Frankish nobles and comites in the year 751 and asked them to elect a king. Whether any other candidates were involved is unclear, but historians do know that Pippin's army was present to encourage people to make the correct choice!

The Archbishop of Mainz crowned Pippin at the town of Soissons in 751. His coronation set an important precedent – a group of nobles who were technically in competition with him elected him king of the Franks. This important principle stayed in place for generations, all the way through the medieval period, and showed that the king of the Franks represented real military and political power. This selection process was a world away from the old Merovingian system of quasi-mystical rulers.

Pippin's coronation was recorded in a contemporary chronicle as follows:

> *751 – In this year Pipin was named king of the Franks with the sanction of the pope, and in the city of Soissons he was anointed with the holy oil by the hands of Boniface, archbishop and martyr of blessed memory, and was raised to the throne after the custom of the Franks. But Childerich, who had the name of king, was shorn of his locks and sent into a monastery.*

Expanding the realm

Pippin made great use of his new power and set about securing the borders and expanding the territory of what had now officially become *his* kingdom. His first efforts were directed at northern Italy and the Lombards. He owed the papacy a favour for their support of him, and he didn't forget it. Attacking the Lombards paid further dividends for him when Pope Stephen II awarded him another title – Patrician of the Romans, which effectively made him the official military protector of the papacy and Christian interests in Europe. This title was really the first step on the way to becoming Holy Roman Emperor, which Pippin's son Charles achieved in the year 800 (check out Chapter 5 for more on the man who would become Charlemagne).

Pippin took his responsibilities seriously and carried on the work of Charles Martell with campaigns against the Islamic armies in Spain and southwest France. He drove them out of the Narbonne region in 759 and as a result was able to add Aquitaine to the growing Carolingian Empire. By the time of his death, nearly all modern-day France was under his control.

Popping off and positioning Charlemagne

Pippin died in 768, aged 54, having fallen ill on campaign. As the first Frankish king, the arrangements for his succession set a precedent. He'd stated that the old Salic Law (the law of the Salian Franks) would apply, so his territories were divided between his two sons, Charles and Carloman. Whilst the Merovingians had always divided inheritance like this, Pippin as the first Carolingian king was setting a new precedent that would have far-reaching consequences for the development of Europe (see Chapter 6).

Within 50 years his eldest son, Charles, had taken things even further, being crowned Holy Roman Emperor and extending the borders of Frankish territory far beyond what Clovis and the early Merovingian kings would have believed possible (you can follow the rise of Charles in Chapter 5).

None of that would have been achieved without Pippin. The Carolingian line went on to rule as kings and emperors until 1122. Not bad for a little guy!

TECHNICAL STUFF

One dodgy document

The period of negotiation between Pippin and Pope Stephen II saw the emergence of one of the most infamous documents in history. The 'Donation of Constantine' was alleged to have been an imperial decree written by the Roman Emperor Constantine I (272–337). In the document, Constantine (who resided in Constantinople) gave control of a large portion of territory in the Roman west to the pope – in particular, lands in Italy and the city of Rome itself. Pope Stephen would have used this decree to help convince Pippin to give the lands he won from the Lombards back to the papacy, which Pippin did, as he was effectively just restoring them to their previous owner. These lands then brought huge revenues to the papacy for the next 1,000 years.

The only problem? The Donation of Constantine was a fake! Even then, people were suspicious of the sudden emergence of such a useful 400-year-old document. By the Renaissance, various people had been recorded as saying that the document was both a fake and the main reason why the papacy had become so corrupt (Chapter 19 has more on this period in papal history).

Modern historians pretty much universally agree that the document was faked, but as to when and by whom they are at a loss. Wherever it came from, the document did its job; Pippin gave the lands back to the papacy, and an important precedent was established.

Chapter 5

Becoming Great: Charlemagne and the New Roman Empire

In This Chapter

▶ Defending the papacy and reaping rewards

▶ Creating and ruling the Holy Roman Empire

▶ Instigating the Middle Ages

A leading Frankish family, the Carolingians, emerged during the seventh century and gained the upper hand in parts of what is modern-day Germany (see Chapter 4). But their power trip didn't stop there, by the middle of the eighth century, the Carolingians went from dominating a single area to taking control of the whole Frankish kingdom and then developing an empire that reunited Europe for the first time since the fall of Rome.

Much of this tremendous achievement comes down to one man – Charles the Great (who lived from 742 to 814), literally 'Charles Magnus' or Charlemagne as he would become known. In this chapter, I examine Charlemagne's early successes, dissect his relationship with the papacy and explore his lingering impact on Europe for generations to come.

Growing into Greatness: Charles's Early Years

Charles was born in 742 in Liege (a town in modern-day Belgium) and was the eldest son of the Frankish king Pippin III (see Chapter 4). When his father died in 768, Charles succeeded him and jointly ruled the kingdom with his younger brother Carloman. As is typical of these dual-ruling situations, Charles and his brother didn't get along, and sharing power proved to be problematic. War seemed inevitable between the brothers until Carloman suddenly died in 771.

Tall stories?

Although little is known about what Charles looked like, a physical description by contemporary writer Einhard (c.774–840) emphasises the king's height and bulk. Now, medieval chroniclers typically describe great leaders as being tall and often most likely over-egg things, because in general people were slightly shorter in the Middle Ages.

In this case, however, the larger than life qualities turn out to be true. In 1861, scientists opened Charles's tomb and using the bones within, reconstructed his skeleton. They found that he would have measured about 190 centimetres (6 feet, 3 inches) – tall for the period and exactly the height that Einhard quoted.

Even at the time, many considered Carloman's death suspicious, but all sources point to natural causes, with an unstoppable nosebleed (probably as the result of an internal haemorrhage) most commonly cited as the reason. Whatever the cause of his brother's death, Charles became the sole ruler of the Franks at the age of 29.

Laying into the Lombards

Like his father Pippin III, Charles was responsible, as Frankish king, for defending the papacy and its interests. Soon after he became the sole ruler, the new pope, Hadrian I, put this duty to the test. Hadrian needed help reclaiming lands that had been taken by Desiderius, king of the Lombards (see Chapter 4). After Charles held an unsuccessful conference with Desiderius late in 772 (during which Desiderius denied all charges and refused to give back the lands), Charles decided to side with Hadrian and go to war.

In 773, Charles crossed the Alps and laid siege to the Italian city of Pavia, which was controlled by the Lombards. Desiderius fled to Constantinople to seek the help of the Byzantine emperor, and the Lombard resistance petered out. By 774, Pavia had surrendered, and the pope granted Charles a large amount of new land, including Tuscany, Venice and the island of Corsica. Hadrian also gave Charles the title of *patrician*, an old Latin term from the Roman Empire that indicated military governorship of an area.

Suffering a small setback in Spain

After his campaign in Italy, Charles's next rescue act involved campaigning in what is now Spain. About two thirds of the country was under the control of various Muslim leaders whose predecessors had conquered the territory during the seventh century (see Chapter 7 for the full story). These leaders were now coming under threat from a man called Abd ar-Raham I, the emir (governor) of Cordoba.

The various Muslim leaders appealed to Charles for help. He enthusiastically agreed, seeing a good opportunity to develop his profile as a Christian monarch and potentially take back lands from heathens. Charles's agreement to help the Muslim leaders was motivated mostly by the idea of promoting his own image. If he could potentially take back European lands from those Muslim leaders, he could do so in the name of the Catholic Church. It was an astute political move that bore similarities to the motivation of many knights of the First Crusade in 1097 (see Chapter 12). It also has a resonance to some more recent conflicts and invasions, such as the removal of Saddam Hussein from power in Iraq in 2003.

So, in 778, Charles led an army across the Pyrenees into Spain. For the first time in Charles's career, the campaign didn't go well. Charles's army went as far as Zaragoza where he was forced into retreat. As he travelled through the Roncevaux pass in the Pyrenees on his return, a Basque army attacked his rearguard, destroying and stealing his baggage train. This setback was the only real failure of Charles's entire reign.

Interestingly, this relatively chastening defeat inspired the earliest known work of French literature. *The Song of Roland* takes the form of an epic poem of some 4,000 lines and provides a fictionalised account of the campaign and the defeat and slaughter at Roncevaux.

In the poem, the character Roland is represented as Charles's right-hand man who leads a heroic last stand against the Basques. The poem was first written down in the eleventh century but is likely to have been composed much earlier. It became hugely popular towards the end of the ninth century and remained so throughout the Middle Ages, kick-starting a whole literary genre of epic poems telling of heroic deeds, known as *chanson de geste*. This genre remained popular all the way through to the Renaissance.

Wrestling with the Saxons

During the years that Charles spent abroad, he also worked to solve problems within and just beyond his original kingdom. Throughout the late eighth century, he fought a number of campaigns against the Saxons who bordered his territory. All the campaigns were fought in the name of the Catholic Church, and many conquered Saxons were baptised and converted to Christianity. All told, Charles was at war against the Saxons for almost 35 years.

Charles's leadership secrets

Throughout his life, Charles was almost constantly at war – winning territory, expanding his kingdom and then defending it from internal and external attack. He was successful at war for several reasons:

🖙 **All in the family:** As soon as they were of age, Charles appointed his sons to positions of authority within his territory. His two sons Pippin and Louis were named, respectively, king of Italy and king of Aquitaine (a territory now in southern France). They were well placed to deal with any threats to the territory and were trusted by Charles to follow his orders without question.

🖙 **Powerful protectors – on horseback:** Charles's elite bodyguard, known as the Scara, travelled with him at all times. They took the form of a cavalry unit, which was especially useful during difficult missions that required greater mobility. Using

cavalry in this way was unusual at the time and often gave Charles a significant advantage over most of his adversaries on the borders of the Frankish kingdom who predominantly used slower-moving infantry.

🖙 **A diplomat and a warrior:** Although Charles fought many wars, they always served a wider purpose and were, generally, last resorts. He was happy to use diplomacy when appropriate, but if that failed, he would resort to warfare. This combination of negotiation and military prowess made him both respected and feared, and also tied the fortunes of the papacy to him, which eventually resulted in his coronation as emperor by the Pope, leading to the formation of the Holy Roman Empire (see the later section 'Becoming Emperor: Charles to Charlemagne').

The chronicler Einhard gives some (typically biased) reasons for the lengthy war:

> *As to the Saxon war, no war ever undertaken by the Franks was waged with such persistence and bitterness, or cost so much labour, because the Saxons, like almost all Germans, were a ferocious folk, given over to devil-worship, hostile to our Faith, and they did not consider it dishonourable to transgress and violate all law – be it human or divine.*

Extending his reach

During the 780s, Charles went even farther, campaigning against the Avars, an Asian people who had invaded Hungary, and crossing the Elbe river to take on the Slavs, the people that bordered his kingdom. Although these territories never fully came under Charles's control, he made significant territorial gains and saw huge numbers of people convert to Christianity.

As Figure 5-1 shows, around this time Charles's empire spanned a large amount of Western Europe, by far the biggest single holding since the fall of the Roman Empire.

Figure 5-1: The extent of Charles's empire.

SAXONY
THURINGIA
BAVARIA
ALAMANNIA
AQUITANIA BURGUNDY LOMBARDY
GASCONY PROVENCE
CORSICA

Frankish Empire – at accession of Charles

Conquests of Charles to 814

Becoming Emperor: Charles to Charlemagne

By the end of the eighth century, Charles was already ruling over and fighting to protect a land empire, when a series of circumstances finally led to Pope Leo III officially crowning him emperor in 800.

In 799, Pope Leo was in a bit of trouble. He'd become increasingly unpopular in the city of Rome due to his preference for Charles as a protector instead of various Roman nobles. Eventually a group tried to seize the pope with the intention of mutilating him by putting out his eyes and cutting out his tongue!

Understandably, Leo fled to Charles at Paderborn (in modern-day central Germany) for protection. In November 800, Charles marched into Italy and held a council on 1 December where he forced the Romans to accept Leo as their pope.

Gaining a crown

When Charles attended mass on Christmas day 800, Leo approached him while he was praying and placed a crown on his head, calling him *Imperator Romanorum* – emperor of the Romans, the first such emperor since Romulus Augustulus in the year 475, more than 300 years earlier. At the time this act appeared to be a surprise to Charles (or Charlemagne as he was known following his coronation), but most historians now believe that he and Leo had been planning it for some time.

Charlemagne's coronation was a momentous event, not so much for what it led to but what it signified. Leo offered no information as to whether Charlemagne was just emperor over the city of Rome – or over all the territory that used to be a part of the Roman Empire. For his part, Charlemagne definitely interpreted his crown as being given the power by God's representative on earth to rule all the territory that he had spent the last 30 years adding to his kingdom.

Historians have spent years arguing over whether Charlemagne was a Roman Emperor in the same vein as the emperors of the original Roman Empire, like Augustus, Tiberius and Marcus Aurelius (see *The Romans For Dummies*) – he wasn't really. These original emperors had been absolute rulers with godlike status who lived in fabulous, billionaire-style luxury. This wasn't really the case with Charlemagne. Although his empire had a big geographical span, he had created it out of a political alliance with the Church and he himself was a very different kind of figure to his ancient Roman forebears.

The world had changed significantly from the days of the original Roman emperors. But whatever the differences, Charlemagne can undoubtedly be called the first Holy Roman Emperor.

Defining the Holy Roman Empire

The *Holy Roman Empire* came into being with Charlemagne and carried on in various forms for more than a thousand years, until the last emperor Francis II (who abdicated in 1806). By Francis II's time, the term 'emperor' had effectively become a ceremonial title that signified very little in terms of actual territory.

Throughout the period of the Holy Roman Empire, the territory within fluctuated hugely, although its core was always rooted in Central Europe and modern-day Germany. Under Charlemagne the empire was at its largest and most powerful, spanning territory that included modern-day France, Belgium and Germany with parts of Italy and the island of Corsica.

Although the Holy Roman Empire seems to be a title conjured out of nowhere, you can break the phrase down to understand its meaning:

- ✔ **Holy:** The pope gave Charlemagne his title; therefore it came directly from God. Charlemagne was also the military protector of the papacy and, if you like, God's general.

- ✔ **Roman:** Rome wasn't a territory technically under Charlemagne's control, and few subsequent Holy Roman Emperors controlled it, but Charlemagne was crowned in the city. Also, all the territory under his control had been part of the Roman Empire at its original height.

- ✔ **Empire:** Charlemagne's territory was international, giving him control over a large number of kingdoms – thus, an empire.

Many people have argued that the Holy Roman Empire was really none of those things! However, from the thirteenth century onwards the title came into common use and historians have always referred to it as such. If you think about it in the terms I set out above, the name does kind of make sense!

By making Charlemagne an emperor, Pope Leo III set a huge precedent, suggesting that the person holding the title King of the Franks or the Papal protector also deserved the title of emperor.

However, Leo also set another rather more long-standing precedent – that the title of emperor was in the power of the papacy to give. Emperors didn't make themselves; they were made by the Church. This precedent was one that caused huge ructions throughout the Middle Ages, igniting continual squabbles between popes and would-be emperors (see Chapter 13 for more details). I wonder if Leo realised the trouble he would cause?

Bickering with the Byzantines

Charlemagne's wasn't the only empire, however; to the east, the Byzantines ruled from Constantinople (modern-day Istanbul). Unsurprisingly the Byzantines refused to accept Charlemagne as an emperor, regarding him as a usurper. Although Charlemagne was very unlikely to try and unify the whole Roman Empire by attacking the Byzantines, he did control territories in Italy and the Adriatic, areas that the Byzantines also desired to control. The relationship between the Holy Roman Empire and the Byzantine Empire continued to be one of mutual distrust.

We are family

Charlemagne was very keen on using his sons as a way of stabilising his control over territory. In addition, he had a very interesting way of dealing with the female members of his family. He had at least ten wives and concubines during his lifetime and through them he produced around 20 children, the vast majority illegitimate.

He treated his daughters in what was (even for the time) a rather unusual way. He forced them to stay at his court and forbade them to marry. His reasoning was that any marriage outside the family would create new branches of aristocrats that threatened revolt or challenge to his sons. As a consequence, he allowed his daughters to take lovers and took care of any children produced from them. The arrangement was both liberated and highly restrictive.

Official contact between the two courts continued because the Byzantines still held some territory in northern Italy. But then in 804 the people of Venice chose to break away from Byzantine control and submit to Pippin (Charlemagne's son, who he had made king of Italy). A series of military engagements followed with Byzantine fleets raiding the Italian coast. Finally, by 810, the Venetians had had enough and asked to return to Byzantine control.

Pippin agreed to this change and the Byzantines transferred control of the Istrian peninsula (the western coast of modern-day Croatia) to him as compensation. The Byzantine emperor, Michael I, recognised Charlemagne as an emperor as part of the deal.

Living and Ruling as Emperor

Being emperor didn't make a huge difference to Charlemagne, but the situation did a lot to reinforce the position of Leo III (see the earlier section 'Becoming Emperor: Charles to Charlemagne'). For the remaining 14 years of his life after gaining his crown, Charlemagne continued to rule as he always had. Interestingly, since becoming sole king of the Franks, Charlemagne had run his territory much in the style of an old Roman Emperor; ruling from afar and almost constantly engaged in campaigns to strengthen and defend its borders. This was very different to any other ruler at the time.

Although Charlemagne continued to spend a great deal of time away on campaigns, he also continued to spend every winter in the town of Aachen (in the northwest of modern-day Germany, close to the Belgian border). This town quickly became the centre of his empire and the base of his court.

Unlike Roman Emperors, Charlemagne was not a prodigious builder, but he did construct a building known as the Palatine Chapel in Aachen. Originally this building was the private chapel attached to his own palace, but it later became Aachen Cathedral and was the site at which all future German kings were crowned. Charlemagne was buried there after he died in 814, and you can still visit Aachen Cathedral today.

Making reforms

Throughout his reign, Charlemagne attempted to closely manage his empire by installing practices that were common throughout, rather than leaving local dukes and barons that swore allegiance to him to administer it. He was far more successful in doing so than any of his successors.

Thinking economically

Amongst Charlemagne's greatest achievements during his reign were the economic changes that he made, creating an entirely new economic system for Europe in the process.

Until the time of Charlemagne, the whole of Europe used the 'sou', the nickname for the *solidus*, the gold coin introduced by the Roman Emperor Diocletian around 500 years earlier. The problem with the sou was that following the collapse of the original empire, the availability of gold had declined rapidly. Thus, a sou in the year 800 was made with less gold than it had been in the centuries before and was worth much less.

As a consequence, ordinary people traded with localised coinage produced in their town or area. This practice, however, made any commerce outside a person's own town very difficult, because prices and coinage values differed hugely depending on where you were in Europe.

Charlemagne's solution was to introduce a brand new currency: the *livre carolinienne*, or Carolingian Pound. This new unit of currency was minted from silver, which was much more widely available, and a Carolingian Pound was worth around 20 old sous. Charlemagne immediately began to issue smaller denominations of this currency, known as *deniers*, that had his image and titles branded on them.

Charlemagne developed this new coinage in partnership with King Offa of Mercia (the Anglo-Saxon King in England; see Chapter 3) and accordingly the new coinage became international across Europe; if you like, a first real attempt at the Euro!

Charlemagne also introduced a new accounting system in his empire and forced everyone to adopt it. He also banned money-lending, which had a very negative impact on Jewish communities around Europe. The majority of moneylenders in Medieval Europe were Jewish because their faith allowed them to carry out the practice, unlike Christianity which classed money lending or *usury* as a sin. As a result, Jewish communities throughout the Holy Roman Empire were harshly affected by the reforms.

Education, education, education!

Having established his court at Aachen, Charlemagne encouraged the study of the liberal arts and took tuition himself from men such as Einhard in subjects such as astronomy, mathematics, rhetoric and theology. He also encouraged his family to be educated and take part in artistic pursuits. Aachen also became a beacon for huge numbers of artists, writers and intellectuals who travelled to the town in hope of securing Charlemagne's patronage and approval.

Charlemagne's conquests also extended a great deal of educational reform across Europe. As territory was added to his empire, he ensured that monastic centres were set up. As I note in Chapter 2, monasteries had many functions beyond the religious, in particular providing education to the poor and working as *scriptoria*, centres where classical texts were copied and reproduced. Indeed, many of the surviving works of classical Latin by writers such as Cicero, Tacitus and Pliny exist because of the work of Carolingian scholars in *scriptorias*.

Not getting it 'write'

Despite devoting a great deal of time to educational reform and his own studies, Einhard notes that Charlemagne took up the idea of writing only late in his life and never really mastered it.

Because Einhard doesn't really mention the Emperor's reading ability, some people have suggested that Charlemagne may have died completely illiterate. True or not, the fact that such a rich, powerful and well-born young Frank as Charlemagne had not been brought up to be literate suggests how low levels of literacy were at the time in Northern Europe. To be illiterate wasn't a stigma at the time though, and very many well-born people would've been illiterate or at least unable to write. A clear distinction existed at the time as reading could be a necessary skill for the wealthy, but any writing or note taking could be done by servants.

Finding things grim up north

Although Charlemagne continued to campaign during the last years of his life, his most significant military engagements were with the Danes who lived in Jutland (part of modern-day Denmark). The Danes were a non-Christian race about whom Charlemagne would have known little.

During Charlemagne's rule, the Danes were led by a man called Godfred. In 808, Godfred built a huge earthwork rampart across the isthmus of Schleswig. Known as the *Danevirke*, this structure prevented any land army from crossing into the Jutland peninsular and allowed Godfred and his fearsome warriors to raid with impunity.

Godfred led a series of piratical raids into Charlemagne's territory, ravaging many of the towns of Frisia, in modern-day northern Germany. For a time Godfred appeared to be threatening to take things further, but in 811 he was murdered, probably by an assassin working on Charlemagne's orders. Power passed to Godfred's nephew, Hemming, who signed a peace treaty with Charlemagne.

Although the impact on Charlemagne's territory wasn't massive, Godfred's attacks were one of the first examples of Danes and other Scandinavians raiding far from home. These raiders eventually became known as the Vikings. Read more about them in Chapter 8.

Passing On: Charlemagne's Legacy

Charlemagne never intended to nominate a single successor. Soon after becoming emperor in 806, he made plans to divide his empire into three kingdoms, ruled by his sons Charles the Younger, Pippin and Louis, none of whom would be senior to another or receive the title of emperor.

Unfortunately for Charlemagne, this shared family dynasty was never to be. By 811, both Charles and Pippin had died. So in 813, knowing his time was short, Charlemagne granted Louis (then the King of Aquitaine) a half-share in the current empire and made him co-emperor.

Louis returned to Aquitaine from Aachen, but not for long. After spending the autumn hunting, Charlemagne came to Aachen for the New Year but in January fell ill with pleurisy. On 28 January, 814, he died aged 61, a ripe old age for the time. He was buried in state in Aachen Cathedral and succeeded as emperor by Louis.

Charlemagne's life was an interesting and dynamic period of history, but his achievements far outweigh what even he can have imagined. Although his empire soon broke up, aspects of his reign survived for much longer:

- **The beginnings of France and Germany:** By expanding the Frankish kingdoms into an empire, he gave separate identities to the lands now thought of as France and Germany. Ruled by two of his sons, these areas effectively became separate monarchies, which was the first step on the road to medieval France and medieval Germany (see Chapter 6).

- **The idea of Europe:** By creating an empire and ruling it as a homogenised state, Charlemagne gave a common identity to people living in Northwestern Europe that they hadn't previously possessed. Linguistic barriers were broken down as a result.

- **The practice of medieval trade:** Charlemagne's economic reforms outlived him by hundreds of years. The coinage and trade regulations he established helped break down barriers in the new Europe and contributed to a more geographically unified identity.

- **The spread of Christianity:** Charlemagne's conquests and (sometimes forced) conversions led to the Catholic Church growing in power and influence, extending the reach of the papacy ever further.

In short, Charlemagne effectively created the Middle Ages!

Part II

Forming the Basis of Europe (800–1100)

The 5th Wave   By Rich Tennant

376AD – THE VISIGOTH MIGRATION

ROME

"Okay, this is us."

In this part . . .

As Medieval Europe came together, many of the countries you now recognise emerged. This part covers the amazing journeys that Arabs and Vikings undertook, the exploits of William the Conqueror and an almighty dust-up between the Eastern and Western Churches. If you have a slightly gory side, you're sure to enjoy some fantastically nasty Viking activities and the downright foul Fulk of Anjou. But don't worry, you also encounter fascinating theological points of view and the accurately named Louis the Pious.

Chapter 6

Laying the Foundations of Europe

· ·

· ·

At the end of Charlemagne's reign in 814, Europe had been changed forever. Although his Empire crumbled in the hands of his successors, the territorial divisions that he created helped to form modern-day Europe. In this chapter, I look at the development of Europe in the early Middle Ages by Charlemagne's various Frankish successors and the unification of England by one man – Alfred the Great.

Following Charlemagne: Louis the Pious

Charlemagne's younger son Louis was named King of Aquitaine (southern France) in 781 and reigned as joint emperor with his father before Charlemagne's death in 814 (flip to Chapter 5 for all about Charlemagne). During this period Louis closely followed his father's example as ruler.

To try to put right the losses suffered by Charlemagne in his 778 Spanish campaign, Louis led his own campaign into Spain in 801. He managed to recover the city of Barcelona from the Emirate of Cordoba and reinforced Frankish control over the Basque population and the area of Pamplona south of the Pyrenees.

After Charlemagne died in 814, sole rule of his empire transferred to Louis. Upon hearing the news of his father's death, Louis hurried to Aachen and arranged a coronation ceremony (he wasn't crowned by the pope until 816). He then set about creating a new council of advisors.

Louis was very different from his father. His reign was characterised by piety and a determination to rule as a Christian monarch, earning him the name 'Louis the Pious'. In addition to calling on religious figures for advice, he made huge changes to the Frankish Church. Although his reign was no great success, many of the changes he made to religious practices far outlived him.

Dividing up authority

With the borders of his kingdom secure, Louis set about ensuring its government by appointing members of his immediate family to positions of authority, much as Charlemagne had done. Louis's three sons from his first marriage – Lothair, Pippin and Louis – were all involved in the government of Aquitaine and now in governing his empire.

However, Louis's boldest move was to incorporate a number of figures from the Church into his government. Chief among his advisors were two men, Ebbo and Benedict:

- ✓ **Ebbo** (c. 775–851) was born a peasant in the territory of Charlemagne. He was educated at court and became chief-librarian and then chancellor to Louis. On his succession, Louis appointed him as the bishop of the city of Rhiems. As a result, Ebbo became hugely influential, preaching to the people of the empire in the north and seeking to convert the Danes to Christianity.

- ✓ **Benedict** (c. 747–821) was a Benedictine monk who exerted great influence over Louis's thinking. On his advice, Louis ensured that all monasteries in the empire followed Benedictine practice. This meant that the Benedictine order very quickly became the most influential, with its practices being implemented across the whole Holy Roman Empire. Other religious orders did prosper, but the patronage of Louis gave the Benedictines a big advantage.

Pondering mortality: The ordinatio imperii

In 817 Louis was involved in a nasty accident in Aachen. A wooden gallery that he was crossing collapsed, killing many and nearly killing the emperor. This brush with death inspired Louis to make arrangements for his successors. The plan that he made (known as the *ordinatio imperii*) was to massively influence how succession was treated throughout the medieval period.

Louis divided power as follows:

- ✓ **Lothair** was nominated as successor and immediately made Louis's co-emperor. After Louis's death, Lothair was to be the senior ruler above everyone else.

> ✔ **Pippin** was proclaimed as King of Aquitaine.
>
> ✔ **Louis** was proclaimed as King of Bavaria.
>
> ✔ **Bernard of Italy** (the son of Louis's dead brother Pippin and so cousin to Louis's sons) was allowed to keep the title of King of Italy (which he'd inherited from his father years earlier).

Louis further stated that when any of the lesser kings died, they were to be succeeded by their sons. If any of these lesser kings died childless, their lands reverted to Lothair or whoever was in his position.

Louis's arrangement placed his first born son in a position of absolute authority. This act set a tremendous precedent – that power should transfer to the first born son. Although Louis didn't write a document or publish an edict stating this, his action was taken as an example for centuries to follow and became common practice throughout much of Medieval Europe. In some countries it remains common practice today (for example, Prince Charles – as the first born son – is the first in line to succeed Queen Elizabeth II of the United Kingdom). Louis wasn't the first to name his first born son as successor, but his power and influence made doing so a hugely important statement.

Behaving less than piously

Clearly Louis pretty much divided his territory between his three sons. The real loser was Bernard of Italy, who was Louis's cousin but now lost out to his younger second cousins despite being a closer relative to Charlemagne and having been appointed by him. When Bernard made public proclamations that he would revolt, Louis took his army to Italy, captured Bernard and took him back to France.

The fate of Bernard was unpleasant to say the least. Put on trial for treason, he was convicted and sentenced to death, although on appeal the sentence was 'reduced' to blinding. Blinding wasn't an uncommon punishment in the Medieval World and was particularly used in the Byzantine Empire. Unfortunately, the job was botched, and Bernard died of his injuries two days later. (Other people associated with Bernard suffered unpleasant fates too; Theodulf of Orleans was put into a monastic prison and died soon after. Many claimed that he was poisoned on the orders of Louis.)

Bernard's death plagued Louis's conscience and, in 822, he carried out a penance to atone for it. In front of Pope Paschal II and a whole host of dukes and men of the Church, Louis confessed not only to Bernard's death but also to many other minor sins.

Although he may have saved his immortal soul, Louis's confession did nothing for his earthly reputation. His standing was diminished in the eyes of the other nobles because it was completely unprecedented for a king or emperor to admit to his failings in front of his subordinates. Although well intentioned, Louis's behaviour had the effect of lowering his status at a time when civil war was about to erupt.

Marrying again – and fuelling civil war

The key motivator for civil war was Louis's marriage to his second wife, Judith, in 820, and the fact that three years later she produced a son, called Charles. Louis's subsequent attempts to involve Charles in his succession plans alienated his sons from his first marriage and plunged the empire into civil war.

Between 829 and 840 three separate uprisings took place that pitted Louis against his sons and their supporters. Twice, agreements were reached, and twice they were broken shortly afterwards. Eventually, when the third struggle came to an end in 840, Louis agreed to divide the empire into three. Louis divided the territory into East, West and Middle Francia. Lothair and Louis II were awarded territory along with Louis's son Charles (known as Charles the Bald – see the later sidebar 'The bald truth') from his second marriage. Louis's other son, Pippin, had died in 838, creating the vacancy that Charles was now able to fill. It was a complicated situation (have a look at the family tree in Figure 6-1)!

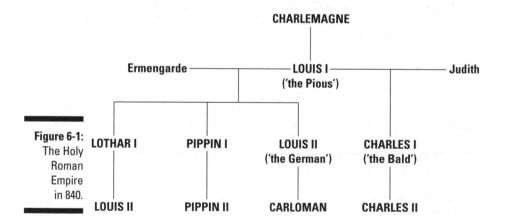

Figure 6-1: The Holy Roman Empire in 840.

Louis didn't have too long to watch over his new arrangement; he died soon afterwards at the age of 62. The majority of his reign had been spent dealing with the internal divisions in his empire caused by his relations – but the religious changes he made, particularly elevating the Benedictines over other monastic orders, carried on for hundreds of years.

Slicing Up the Pie Again: Lothair 1 and Afterwards

Although Louis's arrangement made Lothair overlord of his brothers's territory (see the earlier section 'Pondering mortality: The ordinatio imperii'), they didn't respect the agreement. In 841, his brothers revolted against him and Lothair's army was defeated by their combined force at Fontenay (near Auxerre in modern-day France). Lothair was forced to negotiate.

The three brothers met at Verdun in Lorraine, southern France, in the summer of 843. They needed to come up with a lasting settlement that gave each satisfactory territory and confirm Lothair I in his position as emperor.

What actually happened was that the Empire was chopped into three parts:

- ✔ **Lothair I** took the central portion of the Empire, which became known as the Middle Frankish Empire, consisting of everything between northern Italy and the Low Countries in the north, including the imperial cities of Aachen and Rome. Whilst Lothair didn't directly control Rome (it was under the official control of the pope) he acted as its military protector, and so Rome and all the papal estates came under his remit.

- ✔ **Louis II** took the most easterly part of the Empire – everything beyond the River Rhine. As a result of this Louis has also been referred to as Louis 'the German'. His territory forms part of what is referred to as Germany in the modern world; at the time it would have been considered as the eastern Frankish kingdom.

- ✔ **Charles the Bald** received the western portion of the Empire (modern-day France). Within this area Pippin II was made King of Aquitaine (in the south) but only under the authority of Charles.

Figure 6-2 shows the Empire and its territories after the Treaty of Verdun.

The land divisions in the Treaty of Verdun had a major impact on Europe for more than 1,000 years, for example:

- ✔ The empire was sectioned up entirely to please the individuals concerned, not taking into account the people who lived within the territories, the languages they spoke or their own culture. By creating these divisions the treaty effectively created the modern European states of France and Germany and made the land between them open to questions of ownership – questions that were fought over until the Second World War (1939–45).

- ✔ The way the treaty defined individual territories made governance by a single ruler very difficult. Future Emperors would struggle to maintain authority over the whole empire, but none would have the control that Charlemagne, Louis the Pious and, briefly, Lothair I enjoyed.

Lothair died in 855 and was succeeded by his eldest son Louis. He took the title of Louis II as emperor (not to be confused with the other Louis II – his uncle – who was also known as Louis 'the German'). His reign was chaotic and full of revolts and challenges to his power. When he died in 875, he had no son and named one of his cousins, Carloman (the son of Louis the German), as his successor. This arrangement didn't work because both Louis the German and Charles the Bald were still alive and contested the title of Emperor between them. Charles eventually won the title but died in 877, leaving the throne vacant. Just over 60 years after the death of Charlemagne, the Holy Roman Empire descended into anarchy.

The bald truth

Historians have long argued over why Charles was known as 'The Bald'. Records indicate that Charles was not bald at all – he was actually pretty hirsute – and so his nickname was clearly some kind of joke. (These kinds of descriptive epithets appear frequently throughout the Middle Ages: the ninth century also produced 'Charles the Fat' and 'Louis the Stammerer' but in most other cases they were actually true and weren't just jokes!)

Charles the Bald may just have been an ironic comment because of the man's general hairiness, but some historians suggest the name may also have come from the fact that he spent so many years without a crown while his half-brothers had already been made into kings – thus, without a crown, he was bald. Granted, either joke is pretty weak, and the nickname was probably not popular with Charles.

Whatever the actual inspiration for the name, a man called Hucbald wrote a poem during the ninth century called 'In Praise of Bald Men'. In the poem he suggests that bald men had a natural ability to become leaders, warriors and intellectuals! Of course, Hucbald lived and worked at the Imperial school that Charles founded, and so he may have had an ulterior motive for writing it. Perhaps he was trying to make Charles feel better about his nickname?

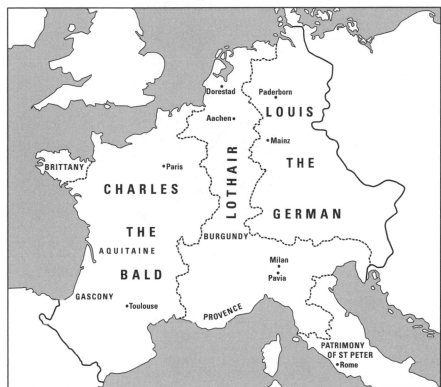

Figure 6-2:
Europe after
the Treaty of
Verdun
in 843.

Forging a New England: Alfred the Great

While the Treaty of Verdun was roughly establishing the modern states of France and Germany (see the preceding section), things were heating up across the English Channel.

Like much of the rest of Europe, England was coming under threat from the Vikings (I write about these Danish warriors in more detail in Chapter 8). Indeed, much of northern and eastern England came to be under the control of the Danes, who had been regularly invading and then settling since the beginning of the century. (Historians now call this area *Danelaw* – a term that originally meant 'the rule of the Danes' – see Figure 6-3.) During the latter half of the century, young Alfred – the first and only English king to be called 'The Great' – led a furious and successful defence against them.

Figure 6-3:
King
Alfred's
'England'.

That he was given the name so soon after Charlemagne (who was known as Charles 'The Great' – see Chapter 5) is interesting, but no obvious connection seems to exist between the two. Calling a ruler 'great' had been going on for years; Alexander the Great (353–323 BC) and Pompey the Great (106–48 BC) were famous 'greats' from the Ancient World. Alfred was probably just called great because of what he did, rather than because of people who had gone before.

Preparing for great things abroad

Alfred was born in 849 as the youngest son of Aethelwulf the King of Wessex in the southwest of England. A surprising amount of information about Alfred's life is available today because a man called Bishop Asser wrote a biography of the king's life in 893.

For example, Asser relates that at the age of five Alfred was sent to Rome to be educated, a trip that instilled a passion for learning that stayed with him throughout his life. The visit to Rome would have had a profound effect on Alfred. He stayed there for two years and the city and his experiences there would have been incredibly different to anything that he had seen in Anglo-Saxon England. It may be that in going to Rome Alfred was being groomed for a role in the Church, because with three older brothers he was unlikely to have become king. Events, however, didn't turn out that way.

While Alfred was in Rome, his eldest brother Aethelbad led a revolt against their father the king. Shortly afterwards, brother Aethelbert staged another revolt. By 866, both brothers were dead and the third, Aethelred, took power. In what proved to be a wise move, Aethelred took the precaution of naming Alfred as his successor in case he fell in battle.

By the end of 870, the Vikings were attacking the kingdom of Wessex and over the course of a few months, nine battles were fought to keep them out. In March 871, Aethelred was killed fighting the Vikings at a place called Merton. Alfred became king at the age of 22.

Turning things around

As the newly crowned king, Alfred took on a losing battle with the Vikings, fierce raiding warriors from Denmark (read more about them in Chapter 8). For the next five years he struggled to prevent them from taking control of large parts of southern England. Through a mixture of diplomacy and paying large bribes, Alfred was able to buy enough time to organise a counter-attack. Eventually he retreated to his fortress of Athelney in the Somerset marshes (see Figure 6-3). Times were desperate for Anglo-Saxon England, with Wessex the only kingdom able to resist the powerful invaders.

Burning the cakes – or cooking the books?

The enduring story about Alfred burning the cakes allegedly took place during his flight to Somerset and his subsequent attempts to organise a militia. According to an often repeated incident, a peasant woman gave Alfred shelter and asked him to watch her cakes as they cooked. Alfred, lost in thought about his military problems, forgot to watch them and they burned. The woman returned and scolded him before realising who he was and begging him for

forgiveness, but Alfred claimed that he was the one who needed to apologise to her.

In 2007, a historian claimed that the story was stolen from a legend about a fantastically named Viking leader, Ragnar Hairybreeks, who attacked Anglo-Saxon England around 100 years before Alfred's day. The historian claimed that Alfred's biographers lifted the story to build up his reputation as a leader with the common touch: a case of medieval spin-doctoring perhaps?

Alfred finally emerged in May 878, meeting the invaders at Ethundun in Wiltshire, southwest England (see Figure 6-3). His new army (see the next section 'Reorganising the military') won a famous victory, and he pursued the fleeing enemy to their stronghold at Chippenham. After a short siege, the Vikings were forced to surrender. Alfred demanded that the Viking leaders convert to Christianity.

The *Anglo-Saxon Chronicle* records the events as follows:

> *Three weeks later King Guthrum with 30 of his men who were the most important in the army came to him at Aller* [near Athelney] *and the King stood sponsor to him at his baptism there. And he was twelve days with the King, and he honoured him and his companions greatly with gifts.*

Alfred's success didn't stop in 878. The following year he quelled an uprising by some Vikings who had settled in Kent, before travelling on to London. The city had been in decline for hundreds of years, but Alfred set about refortifying it, making use of the old Roman walls and extensively rebuilding the centre of the city.

Alfred rewarded himself for his success by beginning to refer to himself as 'The King of the Anglo-Saxons'. This shift in titles was an important change – he was now claiming dominion over all the lands of southern England, rather than just Wessex. England had its first real king. Alfred couldn't lay claim to the whole of England though; the north of England was still firmly under the control of the raiders from Denmark who had settled there.

Reorganising the military

A large reason for Alfred's success came down to a huge military reorganisation that began with his exile at Athelney and carried on for the rest of his reign. The changes he made created systems that were used all the way through to the Norman invasion of England in 1066 (the Normans are the subject of Chapter 10).

Elevating the army

Initially, Alfred struggled with the lack of an established army. In modern times, most countries have a *standing army*, a body of paid, professional people whose jobs are to serve in the army. In the Medieval World, such an arrangement was very unusual. Instead, armies were usually composed of men who had been recruited or forced into fighting, usually because their interests were directly threatened. In the case of England in the ninth century such an arrangement was known as the *fyrd*: a militia raised from local farmers.

Alfred significantly altered the fyrd way of fighting, turning this peasant militia into a standing army. During his period in isolation, Alfred organised training for large groups of local farm workers and garrisoned the soldiers in towns around Wessex. Around 30 of these garrisoned towns were established between 878 and 892, securing the kingdom against further invasion. Alfred also organised his own nobles and supporters into groups of mounted warriors, one of which was always in the field. Having a sort of mobile strike force enabled him to react quickly and nip any invasion in the bud.

None of these changes were particularly new or advanced, but they brought the kind of military organisation to England that hadn't been seen since the Romans left more than 400 years earlier.

Improving the navy

Another of Alfred's innovations was the construction of a fleet of ships when, in 897, he began experimenting with naval warfare. As with the cavalry force, his thinking must have been to intercept raiders before they made too much headway. (History notes only one engagement; an encounter with a small group of Viking ships in a river somewhere in the south of England.)

Alfred was the sort of character to whom stories attached themselves (see the earlier sidebar 'Burning the cakes – or cooking the books?'). Among these too-good-to-be-true tales is the notion that the fleet built in 897 was the first of its kind and that Alfred was the founder of the British Navy. Not true! The *Anglo-Saxon Chronicle* notes that a small Viking fleet had been defeated all the way back in 851 by another brother of Alfred's – Athelstan. Alfred as founder of the British Navy is just another example of successful figures having all the accomplishments of the period attributed to them.

Influencing others after his death

Throughout his life Alfred struggled with an unnamed illness that modern scholars suggest may have been Crohn's disease, making his achievements all the more remarkable. The exact date of his death is uncertain, although most writers suggest the year 901, in which case he would have been 52. Like many medieval leaders, Alfred was made into a saint by the Catholic Church. His saint's day is the 26 October (the reputed day of his death).

Alfred's rule left southern England incredibly changed: secure from attack and capable of striking first. Anglo-Saxon England grew from this template and prospered over the next 150 years before the Norman invasion (turn to Chapter 10 for more).

Chapter 7

Linking East and West: Islam in Europe

For around 200 years, from 650 to 850, the kingdoms of Western Europe lived in fear of massively successful Muslim armies that had overthrown the Byzantine and Persian empires in the east. These dramatic events in the east were rapidly followed by huge conquests in Western Europe.

The most notable aspect about the early Muslim conquests was the speed with which they took place and the vast distances that the armies covered in relatively short periods of time. Invading Muslim armies spread across the Mediterranean and into North Africa, Italy, Spain and even France. By the ninth century, well-established Muslim kingdoms existed in Southwest Europe. Their culture mixed with the established cultures, creating something new and very different that lasts to this day.

This chapter explores the Muslim conquests of the seventh and eighth centuries and the kingdoms that these military campaigns established.

Storming In from the Desert

To the Byzantines and Persians, the people to their south – whom they called 'Arabs' – were something of an unknown quantity. For years the Arabs had just paid annual tribute to whichever of the empires was in pole position and were seen as a disparate and unthreatening people: all that was to change very, very quickly.

Going back to the beginning

The story of the Muslim conquests begins with the death of the prophet Mohammed in the year 632. Mohammed had been active in two cities south of the Persian Empire – Mecca and Medina (both in modern-day Saudi Arabia). Ten years before his death, Mohammed became a prophet for a new religion – *Islam* – which literally means 'submission'. Mohammed claimed that only one god existed, *Allah*, and that only total submission to Allah's will would allow people salvation and entrance to the afterlife. Those who devoted themselves to these beliefs were known as *Muslims* ('those who submit').

REMEMBER

What's in a name?

Dealing with the early history of the Muslim peoples and their involvement in the Middle Ages can sometimes be very difficult. Historical documents use a number of different terms to refer to them.

✔ *Moors* or *Saracens* were commonly used terms to describe people who had come from the east to the west. Note that 'Moor' and 'Saracen' are in no way polite or appropriate terms to use nowadays.

✔ *Moors* or *Moorish* can have a more specific meaning – individuals who lived in Muslim Spain between the eighth and sixteenth centuries and their art and culture. For instance, when applied to a building the term refers to the style of architecture then in vogue.

✔ *Muslim* is quite simply a term used to describe a believer in or an adherent of Islam. Throughout this chapter I use 'Muslim' to describe the people that came from the east to the west. Defining these people geographically is often difficult, due to the vast numbers of people involved and the fact that people from other nations or areas joined with them. The one big connection between all the various groups is their faith, so 'Muslim' is the most useful collective term.

✔ *Arab* is a word used to describe a whole variety of people from different places and ancestral backgrounds for whom the connection is the language of Arabic. The term doesn't describe a particular place or people and, in the modern world, Arabic people are more likely to describe themselves by a regional term that sounds closer to home, such as Egyptian, Palestinian or Saudi.

Another feature of Islam as interpreted by Mohammed's followers was the ultimate goal of converting the whole known world to the Islam faith. Consequently, when a newly formed Muslim army marched north from the Persian Empire in 634 it was something completely new. Like many other armies that had gone before, this army was bent on conquest but it also had a broader overarching aim – to encourage territory and people to convert to Islam. Whereas other invading forces may have been happy to sue for peace or diplomatic terms, this army wanted more.

The religious commitment and drive of this new Muslim army made it different to anything that had been seen before. The army generated an incredible momentum as people and places voluntarily converted to Islam, and the army grew with new recruits whose commitment was down to wanting results in more than just pay and booty. Muslim rulers did prove to be tolerant of some other religions (see the section 'Living Under Muslim Rule' later in this chapter) but the zeal of the army was so great that many thousands of people still converted.

Within three years, the Byzantines and Persians had been routed at every turn. This new army of Islam comprehensively defeated the Persians and forced the Byzantine army back north into Anatolia (modern-day Turkey), clearing the way for an invasion and occupation of both Syria and Egypt. Using Syria as a new base, Muslim forces then pushed farther south into modern-day Iran and Iraq, capturing the city of Persepolis in 650 and the territory around the Oxus River in 651. In only 20 years, they managed to secure territory that was equal in size to that of the old Roman Empire at its height in the second century AD.

Powering up the caliph

The ruler of this new state was known as a *caliph*, literally meaning successor to the prophet Mohammed. The title also meant 'representative', because the caliph was also Mohammed's representative on Earth.

Initially at least, a caliph was chosen via an election among the remaining companions of Mohammed, but in time that system became unworkable and a new hereditary system was put in place by the third caliph, Uthman (644–656). Uthman was from an aristocratic family called the Umayyads and from that point on the Muslim empire in the south was known as the Umayyad caliphate.

The position of the caliph was extraordinarily powerful due to his combined role as both religious and military leader. The situation was equivalent to combining the role of pope and Holy Roman Emperor to create one all-powerful figure whose word was absolute. Not only did this individual claim to be the mouthpiece of the prophet Mohammed (and thus, in turn, Allah himself), but also he had the command of the army to back his authority: powerful indeed.

Sunni and Shi'a

Despite the power of the Umayyads in the southern areas of the Muslim empire, some opposed the Uthman family seizing control of the caliphate. A large body in opposition felt that Ali, the son-in-law of Mohammed, should be the person to create a dynasty. This difference became the principal point of debate between *Sunni Muslims* (who supported Ali) and *Shi'a Muslims* who sided with the Umayyads. The divisions between Sunni and Shi'a continue to this day.

Heading west

Throughout the seventh century, the Muslim conquests continued. Having seized Egypt (639), the next target was North Africa. By 709, virtually the entire peninsular was under Muslim control and considered part of the Umayyad caliphate.

The Byzantines made several attempts to intervene but were ultimately unsuccessful. Further attempts were prevented when a Muslim army laid siege to Constantinople between 674–678 and then again around 35 years later. With North Africa under Muslim control, the armies of Islam were able to cross the Mediterranean and invade mainland Europe.

Seizing Hispania

At the beginning of the eighth century, the modern-day country of Spain was still known by its old Roman provincial name, Hispania. The Visigoths, who invaded from the east and settled during the collapse of the Roman Empire, ruled the country.

The Visigoths were Christian, not wholly dissimilar to the Franks (see Chapter 4), and the Visigoth king ruled from a capital in Toledo. Similar to and predating Charlemagne (whom I write about in detail in Chapter 5), the Visigoths were also consistent builders and filled Hispania with churches.

Vanquishing the Visigoths: Tarik

Historical accounts of the Muslim invasion of Hispania are almost non-existent, and so historians must rely upon later Muslim commentators. According to these records, in 711 a man called Tarik-Ibn-Ziyad crossed from North Africa with an army of around 15,000 men.

A by-product of Tarik's crossing of the Mediterranean was that the island of Gibraltar got its name. Tarik's fleet used the mountainous island as a staging post for its invasion and the site was forever after known as 'Tarik's Mountain' or *Jabal Tariq* in Arabic, which eventually became *Gibraltar*.

Tarik's army was made up largely of Berbers. These people from the deserts of North Africa had recently converted to Islam after being incorporated into the Umayyad caliphate in the early years of the eighth century. The zeal with which conquered peoples converted to their new faith was vital, because it gave the Umayyad caliphate a steady supply of recruits to its armies. The continual cycle of conquests, garrisoning troops and further conquests was possible only because the Muslim armies grew to match demand. The fact that people were converting to a religion that made holy war an act of faith virtually guaranteed that the caliphate was able to produce zealous and determined soldiers wherever it went.

Some commentators suggest that the Visigoths were unprepared for the Muslim invasion and mistakenly considered Tarik's fleet to be a large group of merchant vessels. Whatever the case, the Visigoth king, Roderic, took the field against the invading force. What followed was an absolute disaster for the Visigoths. Although they possessed a force that was possibly twice as large as the invading army, the Visigoths were savaged by repeated hit and run attacks and suffered a comprehensive defeat. Roderic and nearly all the Visigoth ruling class were killed, and their civilisation came to an end, virtually at a stroke.

The majority of Spain was now under Muslim control – a situation that remained unchanged for several hundred years. The Muslims named their new state *Al Andalus* from which derives the modern name for a section of southern Spain, Andalucía. For several decades the new territory was ruled in the name of Tarik until in 756 a rival called Abd ar-Rahman emerged.

Taking over: Abd ar-Rahman

In 750, the Umayyad caliphate was overthrown as the result of an uprising known as the Abbasid Revolution. A new caliphate was founded, the Abbasid caliphate, whose ruling families claimed descent from a man called Abbas ibn Abd al-Muttalib who had been one of the uncles of the Prophet Mohammed.

Many leading Umayyad families fled from Damascus, and among them was a young man called Abd ar-Rahman. The grandson of the recently deposed Umayyad caliphate, Abd ar-Rahman was an extremely charismatic and powerful figure. Arriving in North Africa in 755, he very quickly garnered popular support and crossed to the new territories of Al Andalus. Proclaiming himself as the true representative of the Umayyad caliphate, Abd ar-Rahman effectively started a civil war in Al Andalus, in which he was victorious.

In 756, he made the politically astute move of calling himself an *emir* or governor-general, rather than a caliph. This title suggested that he was still ruling in the name of his deposed grandfather, rather than his own. (An *emirate* was a term used much like *province* in the old Roman Empire. It meant somewhere that was governed by an individual who was ruling in the name of somebody else.)

The new emirate became a safe-haven for anybody who had been displaced by the revolution in the east. Abd ar-Rahman placed his family in positions of authority throughout the emirate, turning it into a caliphate in all but name. In 763, he managed to repel an invasion by Abbasid forces and hold on to the territory. When he died in around 788, his favourite son, Hisham, was named as his successor. Hisham took the title of caliph, and the Umayyad emirate continued all the way through until the eleventh century.

Venturing Farther Afield

The advance of Islam didn't stop with Spain. Military expeditions extended the reach of Muslim power into France, Italy and locations even farther away from the Umayyad caliphate. Figure 7-1 shows just how big the Muslim world had become by the middle of the ninth century. In just over 200 years the scale of conquest was astonishing.

Hammering into France

Following the successful invasion of Spain in 711, successive Umayyad leaders ordered expeditions farther east, across the Pyrenees and into modern-day France. These efforts were extremely successful with Muslim armies reaching north to Aquitaine and Burgundy and as far as Bordeaux.

In 732, a fresh invasion proceeded along the Loire Valley. On 10 October, somewhere between the towns of Poitiers and Tours, the Muslim army met with a Frankish force led by Charles Martell, a general who served the Merovingian kings (flip to Chapter 4 for more).

Several accounts exist of the ensuing battle. A Muslim chronicler writing in 754 describes it thus:

> *After each side had tormented the other with raids for almost seven days, they finally prepared their battle lines and fought fiercely. The northern peoples remained as immobile as a wall, holding together like a glacier in the cold regions. In the blink of an eye, they annihilated the Arabs with the sword. The people of Austrasia* [modern-day eastern France and western Germany], *greater in number of soldiers and formidably armed, killed the emir, Abd ar-Rahman, when they found him, striking him on the chest.*

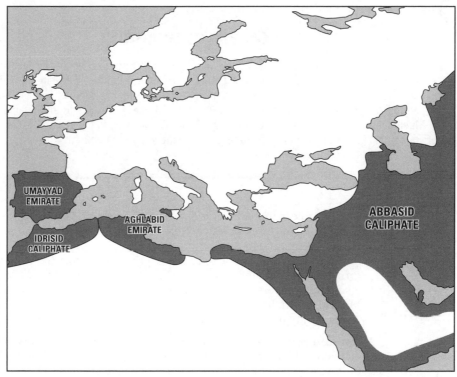

Figure 7-1:
Muslim ter-
ritories in
the western
Medite-
rranean
c. 850.

Although several small Muslim expeditions were launched up until 735, Martell's victory effectively ended the Muslim advance in mainland Europe (and earned him the nickname 'The Hammer'!). Many scholars argue that if Martell hadn't proved victorious, France would have fallen to Muslim rule. Still, just over 100 years after the death of Mohammed, the forces that marched in his name had conquered almost as far as Paris: an astonishing achievement.

Reaching into Italy

From the seventh century onwards, Muslim forces also made moves on the Italian peninsula and its islands. The greatest Muslim success around the peninsula was the conquest of the island of Sicily. The island was first seized in 827 when the Byzantine governor surrendered to the Abbasid emir of North Africa, Ziyadatt Allah. Over the following two centuries, a variety of different Muslim powers held Sicily, and the island was lost to the Normans only in 1061 (see Chapter 10 for details). Accordingly, Sicily became a small-scale Muslim state right in the heart of the Mediterranean.

Eastern extension

Muslim conquests didn't take place only in Western Europe. At the same time as their expansion in the west, the armies of Islam expanded the caliphate farther east. In 738, a Muslim army was defeated at the battle of Rajasthan in Northern India. Despite this setback The Abbasid caliphate eventually stretched from the western coast of Spain to the Ganges in India, an empire more than twice as large as that of Rome or Alexander the Great. Look at Figure 7-1 again and imagine that the area is twice as big; then you'll have some idea of the size of the empire.

The Muslim rulers introduced great changes to Sicilian society, the majority of which were uniformly positive. Here are just a couple of examples:

- **Irrigation.** They introduced new irrigation systems that increased productivity for small farmers. This change put the brakes on the large-scale landowners whose big, collective farms had dominated agriculture on the island. Irrigation also led to the growing of new crops, such as citrus fruits like lemons and oranges and also pistachio and sugarcane.

- **Buildings.** They were prodigious builders, like the Romans before them. The city of Palermo in particular saw a rash of new public buildings, many of which you can still see today in the suburb of Kasr.

IN THEIR OWN WORDS

The changes to Palermo were recorded by a traveller called Ibn Jubair who visited the town during the eleventh century:

> *The capital is endowed with two gifts, splendor and wealth. It contains all the real and imagined beauty that anyone could wish. Splendor and grace adorn the piazzas and the countryside; the streets and highways are wide, and the eye is dazzled by the beauty of its situation. It is a city full of marvels, with buildings similar to those of Cordoba* [The Emirate in Spain], *built of limestone. A permanent stream of water from four springs runs through the city. There are so many mosques that they are impossible to count. Most of them also serve as schools. The eye is dazzled by all this splendor.*

For a brief period, Muslim success in Italy extended even beyond the Sicilian conquest. In 847, an invading army captured the coastal city of Bari, established an emirate on the eastern Italian mainland (probably as a satellite from Sicily) and built a mosque. Ultimately the emirate was held only until 871, but the three emirs who ruled from Bari managed to turn the city into an enclave of Muslim power and culture on mainland Italy.

Living Under Muslim Rule

Muslim rule directly impacted the lives of ordinary people in the conquered lands. The new rulers regarded the indigenous population as *dhimmi*, literally 'those under protection'. In practice, they were protected from external threats and allowed religious freedom, and thus Christianity and Judaism lived alongside Islam in conquered territories. People were able to convert from dhimmi status to Islam, and evidence indicates that many people did. These conversions were entirely voluntary and never forced. (Mohammed had classified both Jews and Christians as 'People of the Book', and they were very much considered and accepted minorities.)

Muslim rulers, however, required that the dhimmi remain loyal to the state and also pay a tax known as *jizya* and a land tax called *kharaj*. The dhimmi's inferior status was reinforced by being banned from building anything higher than the buildings of their Muslim rulers and wearing anything that was more luxurious. Furthermore, the dhimmi had to follow certain rules of Islam, including no public drinking of alcohol and not having any kind of contact with Muslim women.

These rules were obviously not that hard to live by. When the Normans conquered Sicily in the eleventh century, they encountered many Greek-speaking, Christian communities living quite successfully with dhimmi status.

Waxing lyrical: Moorish poets

The cultural impact of the Muslims on the conquered territories was considerable. Although many of their new discoveries in science and technology were gradually superseded by developments in Western Europe, one popular fascination did endure – so-called Moorish poetry.

Moorish poetry was particularly beloved in Al Andalus and elsewhere in Muslim Spain. European readers enjoyed the poems's genuine and everyday voices and descriptions of ordinary experiences, all of which contrasted sharply with the epic and somewhat distant nature of poetry at the time.

Here's a good example by a poet whose name has long been lost:

> When I sent you my melons, you cried out with scorn,
> They ought to be heavy and wrinkled and yellow;
> When I offered myself, whom those graces adorn,
> You flouted, and called me an ugly old fellow.

Encountering Slaves and Pirates

In addition to extremely successful conquests, the Muslim impact on Europe also led to increases in slave trading and piracy. Neither activity was anything new – or solely a Muslim endeavour – but during the fractious times between 700 and 1100, the business of piracy was booming.

Selling people

Prior to the Muslim conquests, slavery existed and even thrived in various regions and at various times. Ancient cultures, in particular the Roman Empire, were built on the labour of slaves, and a life of slavery was the likely future for captured prisoners of war. Furthermore, the trade in slaves had been going on for centuries, but this activity grew hugely in the Mediterranean between the years 700 and 1100, becoming the biggest market anywhere in the Medieval World.

Incidentally, the word 'slave' comes from the term 'Slav', which Muslim traders used to describe Eastern European people who were taken prisoner and then transported to Africa, the East and elsewhere.

Balancing supply and demand

By the tenth century, in some parts of Northern Europe the number of slaves was substantially falling. However, many commentators argue that elements of the feudal system and the conditions of the lowest class of peasantry in Medieval Europe weren't actually that far from slavery. Check out Chapter 22 for how this 'slavery by another name' eventually resulted in peasant revolts.

By the millennium, only England in Northern Europe still had a high slave population. In the years that followed the Norman conquest of England in 1066, slavery was all but abolished, leaving the Muslim Mediterranean as the slavery hotspot of the Medieval World.

One reason for the continuation of the slave trade even beyond the millennium was the regular supply of 'product' on to the market. Almost continuous warfare between Christians and Muslims resulted in a steady supply of tradable prisoners of war. The economic impact of war was important, too. Families that had been impoverished by war or the general harshness of medieval life would sell their children into slavery as they struggled to feed many mouths: a horrifically pragmatic solution to a shortfall of money and food.

A respectable trade

One reason why the slave trade endured was that selling people was generally considered to be an entirely respectable way to make money. The attitude of the Catholic Church to the slave trade was very equivocal, depending on whether the individuals concerned were pagan or Catholic Christian.

Of course, the Church frowned upon the enslavement of Catholic Christians and considered releasing them to be a good deed.

However, the Church didn't force slave owners to release their slaves and had no problem with Christians who wanted to keep pagans as slaves, or indeed pagans trading slaves with each other.

In short, the Church didn't consider the slave trade illegal or sinful. Indeed several popes were rumoured to have made up shortfalls in Vatican funds by dabbling in the market!

Travelling the route

Between the seventh and tenth centuries, the slave trade predominantly consisted of people from the Slavonic countries in Eastern Europe being captured by agents of the slave traders and transported through Central Europe to Al Andalus (modern-day Spain), and then on to Africa and the East. The final destination for many of these unfortunate people was the Byzantine Empire (where slaves were still used to a very great extent) or Syria and Arabia, the heartlands of the Muslim world.

Key factors in these trade routes were the *mercaderes*, Jewish merchants who supervised the transport of slaves between Eastern Europe and the Pyrenees, skirting round the territories where the slave trade was illegal.

Working in a harem

European slaves who were exported east frequently ended up in the *harem*, the private quarters for the many wives of the caliph. Large harems existed in Cordoba, Seville and Granada in Spain, but many slaves travelled east to work at courts in the heart of the Muslim east. European women were particularly popular as *odalisques* – women who worked as servants to the caliph's wives or as entertainers or guards.

A common misconception is that women who made this journey were effectively prostitutes; it wasn't quite like this. A harem would contain a large number of women, sometimes hundreds, each with a specific role within the incredibly luxurious and opulent setting. Their role wouldn't always be sexual and the standard of living would be almost unimaginably better than where many of them had come from. Equally, however, the women completely lost their liberty and would never be able to return home. A high price to pay.

East to West: The trade route back

The trade in people went from east to west as well. Some Europeans bought young Muslim slaves. The following bill of sale from 1248 describes the purchase of a young Muslim girl by people in Marseilles:

May the nineteenth, in year of the Lord 1248. We, William Alegnan and Bernard Mute, of Cannet, have sold jointly in good faith and without guile to you, John Aleman, son of

Peter Aleman, a certain Saracen maid of ours, commonly called Aissa, for a price of nine pounds and fifteen solidi in the mixed money now current in Marseilles.

Aissa's stay with John Aleman didn't last long. A second bill of sale exists showing that she was sold on quickly to a man called Peter Bertoumieu for a profit of five pounds.

Ending the trade?

As the Middle Ages progressed, slavery was made illegal in Northern Europe. William the Conqueror banned the practice in England during the eleventh century, and the Church in Germany, England and Ireland outlawed it. The decree of the Council of London put the matter this way in 1102:

> *Let no one presume for the future to enter into that nefarious business by which they were accustomed hitherto to sell men like brute animals in England.*

Despite this condemnation and others, however, the slave trade continued unabated in the Mediterranean and Africa throughout the Middle Ages and into the modern world with another Muslim civilisation, the Ottoman Turks, who captured Constantinople in 1453. Amazingly – and upsettingly – the last slave in Constantinople (sold to traders in Ethiopia) was finally released only in 1918.

Hunting the seas: Pirates of the Mediterranean

Like the slave trade, piracy had been an occupation in the Mediterranean for hundreds of years prior to the Muslim military expeditions, but growth in trade following the Muslim conquests greatly increased the volume of vulnerable shipping. The pirates who preyed on these vessels became feared throughout the Mediterranean and beyond.

Muslim pirates

Muslim pirate attacks mainly occurred along the coasts of southern France and northern Italy with the pirates basing themselves in relatively small concealed coves and tiny islands. The island of Crete – captured by pirates in 824 – was the centre of the pirating industry and used as a base for raiding over the next 150 years.

As the pirates's attacks became bolder and bolder, they eventually went so far as to sail up the Tiber and attack Rome in 846. That attack devastated the city and caused a great deal of damage to the buildings of the Vatican.

Fuelled by successful raids farther inland, the pirates also targeted overland trade routes, in particular passes that were the only route across mountain ranges. For instance, after visiting Rome in 911, the Bishop of Narbonne was unable to return to France because a group of Muslim pirates controlled all the Alpine passes.

The Narentines

Muslim pirates weren't the only threat to shipping in the Mediterranean. The Narentines, based on the Dalmatian coast (the coast of modern-day Croatia), successfully raided around the Adriatic Sea for hundreds of years.

The Narentines were pagan, Slavic people who had originally migrated to the area in the sixth century. The area of the Dalmatian coast had been a hotbed of piracy since Greco-Roman times, and the Narentines quickly revived the tradition, raiding eastern and southern Italy with alarming frequency. By the ninth century they were successfully raiding up and down the Italian peninsular, including the mercantile centre of Venice. In 887, the Narentines defeated the Venetian fleet in a full-scale naval battle – a victory that's still celebrated in Croatia on 18 September each year in a festival called 'The Marathon of Galleys'.

The Narentines raided according to a strict pirate code. Ships (known as *Sagena*, meaning arrow) were rented out to pirates who organised the raids. The proceeds were split exactly 50:50 between the pirate and ship owner, just as they were between boat owners and fishermen. When you think about the risks that the pirates were taking, the boat owners had a pretty good deal!

Losing Power

Muslim rulers held territory in Western Europe for hundreds of years, but experienced a gradual and inexorable weakening of their position given the continual attacks from Christian powers. This weakening – known as the *Reconquista* – took place over several hundred years. Muslim influence came to an end in 1492 when the last surviving Muslim territory, the kingdom of Granada, fell to the Catholic leaders of Spain.

Although the power was gone, the Muslim influence lives on. Visiting the Iberian coast or Sicily, you can't fail to see the architectural and cultural influences of a society that sprang out of the desert nearly 1,500 years ago.

Chapter 8

Invading from the North: The Vikings

. . . .

In This Chapter

▶ Figuring out the origins of a civilisation

▶ Raiding and plundering with the Vikings

▶ Living like a Viking

▶ Tracking a global legacy

. . . .

Between approximately 800 and 1050, Western Europe experienced a new and dangerous threat. Fierce warriors from the extreme north of Europe raided and plundered their way around the coastline before moving inland to tackle towns and cities. These invaders travelled far and wide across the globe – west into the snows of Greenland, east as far as Kiev (in modern-day Ukraine) and south into the western Mediterranean.

The Vikings had a massive, lasting impact on Western Europe, and their expansion and colonisation was ultimately responsible for a great deal more, such as the creation of the state of Normandy and William the Conqueror (see Chapter 10 for more details). These Vikings are what this chapter is all about.

Transitioning from Norsemen to Vikings

The Vikings truly were 'men from the north' or 'north men', which is the origin of the word *Norsemen*. They were nomadic warriors from Scandinavia (Denmark, Norway and Sweden) whose incredible success in piracy and trading led to them dominating more than 150 years of medieval history.

The word *viking* first appears in Old Norse (the language that the Vikings spoke) and is spelled *vikingr*. In Old Norse stories, known as *sagas*, the word *vikingr* was used to mean one who travelled overseas. At some point during the ninth century the term *wicing* appears in the Anglo-Saxon language and refers to a pirate – although *wicing* may originally have meant going to a *wic*, or a trading place. Whatever the exact source of the word *viking*, people with two different languages used the term to refer to the activities of overseas raiders, and *viking* was originally used as a verb, not a noun. By the way if you want to try out 'Old Norse' today the closest modern equivalent is Icelandic!

The Vikings didn't refer to themselves as such. They thought of themselves as Norsemen. But some of them certainly engaged in 'viking' activities!

Career change?

One of the big unsolved mysteries of medieval history is why so many Scandinavian people suddenly turned from their traditional occupations of trading and fishing to piracy. One theory is that the population had outgrown the agricultural potential of their mostly wooded homeland. Even today Scandinavia (Denmark, Norway and Sweden) is a heavily wooded place, thick with forests.

A more interesting theory, however, is that Scandinavian traders suffered hugely from troubles that hit the silver trade during the 820s. Many Scandinavians had profited hugely from purchasing the silver of the Muslim Abbasid Empire (which I discuss in Chapter 7) from towns in Russia and bringing it to the territories of the Holy Roman Empire (see Chapter 5). When the silver trade dried up, the people of the north used the geographical knowledge they'd gained from trading to become successful pirates.

Even if problems in Arabia didn't motivate the shift to piracy, the Scandinavian people's worldly experience aided their transition from Norsemen to Vikings. And their extensive travels show just how international the medieval period actually was.

Attacking the British Isles

Historians consider the Viking Age to date from 800 (the time of Charlemagne's coronation as Holy Roman Emperor; flip to Chapter 5 for more) to 1066 (the Norman conquest of England; turn to Chapter 10 for all about the Normans). The fact that such an important period in medieval history is known as 'The Viking Age' reflects the huge impact of the Vikings.

The first recorded Viking attacks were on the northeastern coast of Anglo-Saxon England. Early Viking raiders targeted monasteries because of the wealth they held. Between 793–795, the monasteries of Lindisfarne, Jarrow and Iona were attacked and badly damaged. In the next few years, many more monasteries were attacked and for a time they ceased to exist in northeastern England. Viking raiders also attacked Irish monasteries with similarly disastrous effects.

The Viking attacks were devastating, particularly because they were made on holy sites. The *Anglo-Saxon Chronicle* regarded 793 as being full of portents of doom:

> *This year came dreadful fore-warnings over the land of the Northumbrians* [northeastern England], *terrifying the people most woefully: these were immense sheets of light rushing through the air, and whirlwinds, and fiery, dragons flying across the firmament. These tremendous tokens were soon followed by a great famine: and not long after, on the sixth day before the ides of January in the same year, the harrowing inroads of heathen men made lamentable havoc in the church of God in Holy-island, by rapine and slaughter.*

All the early Viking raids followed a pattern: small numbers of ships raiding targets close to the coast that were easily accessible. The raiders almost completely destroyed their targets because they didn't intend to return and wanted to take as much booty as one trip would allow and do as much damage as possible.

Raiding farther afield

By the first half of the ninth century, the Vikings were raiding farther afield and more ambitiously. Mainland Europe was their next target and during the 830s, the empire of Louis the Pious (described in Chapter 6) came under serious attack. The important trading centre of Dorestad in northern Germany was a popular early target, as well as towns and ports along the northern coast of France.

Springtime in Paris

Many of the popular stories and ideas concerning the Vikings are untrue. (I bust some of the biggest myths in the later section 'Dispelling misconceptions about the Vikings'). However, one episode that historians have verified is the Viking attack on Paris.

In 841, a Viking fleet sailed up the river Seine, threatening towns hundreds of miles from the coast. After four years of rampaging, they threatened Paris in 845. The Carolingian mayor of Paris eventually bought them off with a payment of 7,000 pounds of silver. A second attack took place in 885, but the invaders were driven back, this time for good.

Due to the extended distances that the raiders were travelling, they began to push farther inland. Raids in Ireland went towards the centre of the island, and the raiders spent the winter there in 841–842, consolidating their position. In fact, the encampment that the Vikings established carried on after they left and eventually became the settlement that is now known as Dublin. The Vikings also wintered elsewhere in France and England.

Although Viking raids were widespread, they weren't random attacks by barbarian hordes. The Viking people were traders for centuries before becoming raiders and they knew markets and areas that were popular with merchants. As their piracy affected trading patterns, they kept up with economic changes and political changes throughout Europe.

The Holy Roman Empire was racked with civil war under Louis the Pious (as I describe in Chapter 6), and the Vikings took advantage of this instability. Eventually, in the 860s, the Empire recovered, but over the next 150 years the Vikings periodically took advantage of political crises in Western Europe to increase their raiding activity.

Sailing Far and Wide

The Viking attacks on England, Ireland and mainland Europe were only the beginning of their adventures: few places in the Medieval World escaped the Viking influence. As Figure 8-1 shows, they went an awfully long way in search of plunder and riches.

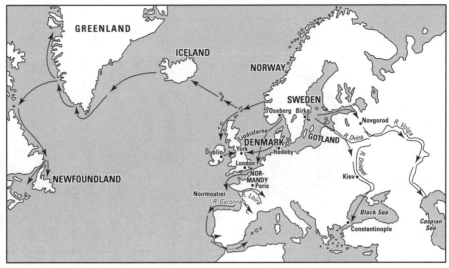

Taking long journeys on longships

The ships they travelled in, known as _longships_, were integral to the success of the Vikings. The Scandinavians had originally developed these vessels for long-distance trading, but the Vikings managed to adapt them easily for their new purposes.

Two different kinds of Viking ships eventually emerged:

✔ The _drakkar_ was the traditional Viking longship. The name comes from the Norse word for dragon and was given to the boats because of the large pointed construction that jutted out from the prow. These boats had very long, narrow hulls that enabled them to sail in shallow water and easily land on shore for attacks. The ships were large and carried up to 100 men (see Figure 8-2).

Drakkars were equipped with both oars and sails, allowing greater freedom of travel because the crew didn't have to rely on the wind. In fact, with the use of a specially adapted spar, called a _beitass_, which was mounted on to the sail, they were able to sail against the wind.

✔ The _knarr_ was a more traditional type of merchant vessel with a much broader hull and deeper draft than the _drakkar_. Not as manoeuvrable, knarrs were mostly used for transporting supplies on journeys and bringing booty home. Very often knarrs towed smaller boats behind them in order to land people and supplies closer to shore.

Figure 8-2:
A Viking
drakkar.

Despite carrying the crew hundreds of miles across rough seas, Viking vessels were hardly first-class ocean liners. With no real cover on the longships, passengers were exposed to the elements and got what sleep they could by huddling around the benches. Storage space was limited, and supplies were very basic. Often the sailors existed on little more than dried fish.

Colonising: Creating a new home away from home

Viking raiders weren't the only Scandinavians who made incredibly long journeys by boat. Increasingly in the ninth century, Vikings settled in other parts of Europe. Entire families travelled together and shared the hardships and exposure to the weather.

One of the first of the new settlements was made by a group of Scandinavians who sailed up the Rhine and its tributaries in the 850s. Led by a man from Denmark called Harald and his nephew Roric, this group negotiated with the Holy Roman Emperor, Lothair I (turn to Chapter 6 for more on Lothair). He allowed them to settle around Dorestad in northern Germany on condition that they defend his kingdom from further attack – probably by raiding Vikings!

In 866, a Viking force seized the English city of York and settled there, but further attacks south were driven back and eventually defeated by Alfred the Great (Chapter 6 contains all the details of Alfred's campaign). The settlement at York (known as 'Jorvik') was a success though, remaining under Scandinavian control for the next 200 years until England was conquered by William of Normandy in 1066 (see Chapter 10).

The last successful colonisation came in 911 when a group of Vikings were granted territory by the Frankish king Charles 'The Simple'. Led by a man called Rollo, the descendants of this Viking group became the fearsome Normans. See Chapter 10 for the full story!

Shifting from raiders to traders

The Vikings led relatively simple lives, and the booty they took was often used for legitimate trade. Their longstanding interest in travel and commerce meant that the new Viking settlements quickly became busy medieval trading centres.

One of the Vikings' most profitable lines of business was the slave trade, which was practised throughout Europe and linked with Muslim traders in the Mediterranean (see Chapter 7 for more on this practice). Prisoners taken by the Vikings in northern England, for example, potentially ended up as slaves in Arabia.

In addition to taking booty, the Vikings also ran a kind of protection racket where the payment of a tribute protected an area from further attack. The fact that they then ploughed their ill-gotten gains into legitimate business activity is somewhat reminiscent of organised crime!

Reaching into Russia

Some of the longest Viking voyages were to the east. As traders, the people of Scandinavia had made connections with towns in Russia during the eighth century. In 860, a Norseman called Rurik followed trade routes and settled in Russia, near the town of Novgorod.

As with other Viking colonies in Europe, the population in Russia prospered, and the descendants of Rurik journeyed farther south, gaining control of the city of Kiev under the leadership of two men called Askold and Dir. The descendants of these people became know as Varangians and held power in various parts of Russia all the way through until the seventeenth century.

Did the Vikings discover America?

An enduring question is whether the Vikings ever reached mainland North America. Consensus among historians is that they did indeed sail that far from their Scandinavian homeland.

In the tenth century, Vikings led by Erik the Red had colonised Greenland, forming small communities that acted as staging posts for journeys farther west. The most successful of these journeys were led by a man called Leif Eriksson, who at the beginning of the eleventh century journeyed as far as Newfoundland, the island to the east of Canada. The area Eriksson reached became known as *Vinland*, a Norse term that meant 'pasture land' or 'meadow land'.

Evidence suggests that the settlers in this colony travelled even farther, perhaps to the North American mainland. If they did, they reached there nearly 500 years before Christopher Columbus. When you consider what conditions must have been like crossing the Atlantic in longboats, this feat is absolutely incredible!

Connecting with Constantinople

Vikings even made their presence felt in the Mediterranean. During the ninth century longships had sailed around the Atlantic coast of Spain to attack ports in the western Mediterranean, but the Vikings in the Byzantine capital of Constantinople were far more unusual. These Vikings had made their way to the eastern Mediterranean via Russia and the Black Sea. Even more intriguing – they quickly found work in Constantinople.

The huge, tall and blond-haired Scandinavian warriors must have seemed fairly remarkable to the eastern Greeks. Various Byzantine emperors recruited them into their armies during the tenth century. Eventually, in 998, the emperor Basil II brought in some 6,000 Viking mercenaries to form the core of what eventually became known as the Varangian Guard. This elite unit served as personal bodyguards to the emperor. The Varangian guard continued until late into the fourteenth century and took part in all the major conflicts of the Byzantine period, as well as the crusades (which I write about in Part III).

Living the Viking Life

Viking society was organised much like that elsewhere in the Medieval World. A king ruled over all the other people, who were divided into three distinct social groups:

- ✔ **Jarls** were members of the aristocracy. Like earls in other medieval societies, jarls owned a great deal of land and were the only people other than the king permitted to have an armed force or *hird*.

- ✔ **Karls** were land-owning farmers and the majority of people in Viking communities. Socially this group was extremely broad and diverse, with wealth and relationship to the aristocracy determining a person's level of influence.

- ✔ **Thralls**, or slaves, were the lowest social class, working as unpaid labourers for the farming class. Trade in slaves was one of the Vikings' biggest businesses. As the Vikings were non-Christian, they were initially unaffected by the Church's ban on slavery and continued a healthy trade. (See the later section 'Stopping the slave trade' for information on the gradual decline of trading.) Thralls had absolutely no rights and were kept by the owners in the same fashion as their livestock. Many thralls were prisoners taken from other countries, but native Scandinavians lived as thralls if they were homeless and starving. The life of a *thrall* was incredibly hard and *manumission* (release from the bonds of slavery) was extremely rare.

Examining Viking religion and beliefs

The Vikings were a pagan people whose beliefs formed what modern scholars call a *folk-religion* – one that isn't centrally organised. Individual Viking tribes and peoples had slightly (or sometimes wildly) different beliefs and worshipped in their own ways instead of through a prescribed code from formal religious leaders.

Norse mythology served as the basis for their beliefs. This collection of stories is chock full of gods, heroes, legends and sagas – rather like ancient Greek mythology. Norse mythology is a massive subject and too big to go into here, but the most important point is that it valued the role of the warrior and placed huge emphasis on bravery and success in war – an important factor in ensuring a successful afterlife.

The power of life and death

Masters had the power of life and death over their thralls and it seems to have been put to use through the process of human sacrifice. Viking funerals were spectacular affairs, and according to legend, thralls were often sacrificed so that they were able to continue serving their masters in the next life. Female slaves suffered terribly, being repeatedly raped and then strangled and stabbed. The multiple rapes were supposed to ensure that the slaves' bodies transported 'life force' to their dead masters.

Norse saga poems regularly mention human sacrifice. In one poem, when the hero Sigurd dies he is followed to death by the sacrifice of others:

> Bond-women five shall follow him,
> And eight of my thralls, well-born are they,
> Children with me, and mine they were.
> As gifts that Buthli his daughter gave.

Scholars long thought that human sacrifice was present only in myths and sagas, but archaeological discoveries in Jutland (in modern Denmark) have revealed bodies of people who were strangled as part of some kind of ritual, leading some scholars to suggest that human sacrifice was all too real.

According to Norse belief a deceased person could progress to three possible destinations:

- ✔ **Valhalla:** Valhalla was the destination for great heroes who died in battle or in a heroic way. The word translates as the 'hall of the chosen ones' where heroes would feast in eternity.

- ✔ **Hel:** Hel, which translates as the 'covered hall', was the middle ground for people who had neither excelled or disappointed. Norse belief was that people would be reunited with their loved ones and relatives there, but it wasn't seen as a nice or magical place.

- ✔ **Nifhel:** The place where you really didn't want to go, nifhel was the 'dark hall' occupied by people who had broken oaths or not lived up to the ideals set up by Norse mythology.

Like most pagan religions, Norse religion didn't offer specific ethical or moral rules to live by, as other religions do; it just offered possible venues for the afterlife. Instead, Vikings looked to the words of their poets and writers for examples to aspire to.

Poetic sagas were popular works that featured the escapades of heroes, as well as some moral instruction. For example, *The Sayings of Odin* (the king of the Norse gods) contains the following advice:

> *Be a friend to your friend; match gift with gift. Meet smiles with smiles, and lies with dissimulation. . . . Generous and brave men get the best out of life; they seldom bring harassments on themselves. But a coward fears everything, and a miser groans at a gift.*

The poem contains 164 stanzas – all containing similar advice. Viking lives were a curious mix of this simple ethical code and incredibly savage warfare and piracy.

Grinding their axes: Viking warfare

Norse sagas contain many accounts of the exploits of heroes and warriors, and the majority of them are broadly similar.

From their first appearance to their eventual decline, Viking warriors fought in roughly the same way and with the same weapons. Any 'free' Norseman was required to own weapons, and their quality was an important marker of social status. The main weapons included the following:

- **Axes** are the weapons for which Vikings are most famous. Originally the same implement that was used to chop wood, battle axes developed into true weapons with longer shafts and heads measuring up to 50 centimetres, or 20 inches. Axes were less effective in battle than swords because they were cumbersome and difficult to manoeuvre among tightly pressed bodies on the fighting fields.

- **Swords** were the most expensive weapon that Vikings used, so your sword was seen as a real symbol of prestige. Made of refined carbon steel, the sword was the work of a genuine craftsman. The majority were manufactured outside of Scandinavia and imported or stolen during raids. Typically only around 80 centimetres, or 31 inches, long, Viking swords were quite short weapons, rather like the *spatha* that the Roman army used. A sword was highly manoeuvrable – particularly when compared with an axe.

- **Spears** were used for thrusting as well as throwing. They were considered cheap weapons, commonly available and easy to replace.

- **Knives,** particularly the *seax*, were quite large weapons, almost the size of small swords. They were usually employed as secondary weapons or side-arms, particularly during close quarters in battle.

All Viking warriors protected themselves with oval shields made of wood and wore some kind of armour, typically made of thick leather. Although examples of Viking chain mail have been found, they were very unusual and would have been extremely expensive. As with all medieval warriors (see Chapter 11 for more on 'knights'), the owner's wealth and status determined the type and quality of armour.

Visiting the Vikings: Ibn Fadlan

One of the reasons why historians know so much about the Viking world is a travel memoir written by a man called Ibn Fadlan. The Abbasid caliph (flip to Chapter 7 for more on the Islamic caliphs) sent Ibn Fadlan on a diplomatic mission in 921, during which he visited a Viking colony on the Volga River in modern-day Russia.

His resulting document is a fascinating account of two very different civilisations coming together. The Volga Vikings were traders rather than raiders, but their lifestyle was likely to be similar to other Viking communities. As a Muslim, Ibn Fadlan was fastidious about cleanliness and was appalled by what he saw as the dirtiness of Viking society (although, in fact, the Vikings were comparatively clean-living for medieval times).

He is also the main source for information on Viking funerals, including very detailed descriptions of an elaborate ceremony involving the burning of a ship that held the body of a deceased Viking chieftain.

Dispelling misconceptions about the Vikings

The Vikings were a brutal people who practised human sacrifice and whose economy was based on rape, pillage and the slave trade; so, unsurprisingly, lots of myths and misconceptions have grown about them over the centuries.

Here are a few of the best-known Viking tales – along with the facts:

- **Horned helmets:** Many modern illustrations and representations of the Vikings show them wearing horned helmets, but the vast majority of them probably didn't do so, possibly aside from at occasional religious ceremonies. This type of headgear would have been incredibly cumbersome in battle and probably quite dangerous to their own side! As for a horde of rampaging Vikings charging up a beach wearing horned helmets – it never happened!

- **Lack of hygiene:** Blame anti-Viking propaganda for the idea that the Vikings were smelly savages who lived filthy lives. In fact, the Scandinavian peoples were more fastidious about washing than most of their contemporaries, insisting on bathing one day a week and regularly washing their hair. For one thing, completing the incredibly long sea journeys that Vikings embarked on would have been impossible without massive disease problems – if the Vikings hadn't been concerned with cleanliness.

- ✔ **Skull cups:** Another enduring Viking myth is the notion that they turned human skulls into drinking vessels. Yes, ritual drinking was a big part of Viking life, but no evidence survives to suggest that they drank from the skulls of their enemies.

- ✔ **The Blood Eagle:** The *Blood Eagle* was a particularly savage form of execution that appears in Norse saga poetry. The process involved cutting into a victim's ribs by the spine and then breaking the ribs so they looked like blood stained wings. The lungs were then pulled out and salt was poured into the open wounds. Most modern scholars believe that technique was hardly ever used and is probably quoted by Christian sources in anti-Viking propaganda.

Although the Vikings were a savage and violent people, they quickly adapted to their surroundings and integrated with indigenous peoples. A lot of recent scholarship has focused on this flexibility, and suggests that by the eleventh and twelfth centuries Viking people were almost indistinguishable from their neighbours, leading the quiet and peaceable lives of farmers with only their Scandinavian names to distinguish them.

Viking women?

Although the history of the Viking world is dominated by men, it's important to emphasise the role that women played in the civilisation. Technically, no such thing as a Viking woman existed as the word *vikingar* is only used to describe men, but none of what I describe in this chapter could have been achieved without women.

Typically in the Norse world, women were in control of the hearth and home, with a particular focus on the food supply (including responsibility for animals and the dairy) and the provision of clothing. These two responsibilities were absolutely vital in the processes of immigration and colonisation that many Norse communities went through. Norse society changed with these processes and also with the coming of Christianity, and women's roles changed as a result. Suddenly women began to have a political influence as Norse women married foreign nobles to cement alliances, and also started to be more publicly involved in religion.

One rune stone from Sweden shows a Norse woman called Ingirun who travelled to Jerusalem on pilgrimage – an amazing journey, and one that was much longer than those undertaken by many of her male *vikingar* forebears!

Declining and Leaving a Legacy

Historians generally consider that the Viking Age lasted for around 150 years, up to the middle of the eleventh century. At no single point did the Viking civilisation die out, but about this time they cease to appear as frequently in chronicles and narratives.

Changing with the times: Testaments and trade bans

Part of the reason for this gradual disappearance may be because many Viking peoples had emigrated and effectively integrated, living relatively peaceful lives in places such as France and Russia. Other factors, however, may also have contributed to the change, as the following sections reveal.

Getting religion

The coming of Christianity to Scandinavia was one of the major factors in the decline of the Vikings. Christian missionaries first began to make successful inroads into the northern reaches of Europe in the eleventh century, and the new religion quickly took hold of people's imagination.

As a result, the old pagan ways fell out of favour. Viking civilisation was tribal, and the decision of the king or chieftain was final. Those chiefs who converted to Christianity violently enforced their new faith on everyone. Non-believers were driven out or killed and with them went many tribal traditions, in particular the demands of the warrior culture for conquest, booty and glory.

Chief among the leaders bringing change was Olaf Haralddson, the king of Norway from 1015–1028. Although some conversion had already taken place in Scandinavia, historians consider Olaf the main reason that Norway converted to Christianity.

Olaf's methods of conversion were notably bloodthirsty and similar to those he used to punish military enemies. Conversion worked, however, and the Norwegian Church was founded in his lifetime. After his death Olaf was made into a saint by the Catholic Church. (For information on the spread of Christianity elsewhere, see Chapter 9.)

Stopping the slave trade

The spread of Christianity also affected the slave trade. During the late eleventh and early twelfth centuries, the Catholic Church made a number of pronouncements on slavery, in particular banning the trade of Christian people as slaves (see Chapter 7 for more details). These pronouncements presented serious problems for slave traders, not so much because of a lack of supply but due to a fall in demand. In the twelfth century, the Catholic Church completely banned slavery in all Christian countries.

Evading raiding

Raiding became more difficult, too. The gradual settling of the medieval kingdoms such as France and England into large states with strong and consistent rule meant that these territories became significantly better organised and able to defend themselves.

As raiding became more difficult and the profits dried up, the practice eventually died out. By the thirteenth century, the Vikings were taking part in crusades sponsored by the Catholic Church (see Chapter 14), and Denmark and Sweden were involved in the creation of the biggest medieval trading guild – the Hanseatic League (see Chapter 18). The Viking Age was truly at an end.

Reaching far and wide

The Vikings are dominant figures in medieval history. Their impact was varied and widespread, and their regular appearance in medieval chronicles show how much of an influence they had on their contemporaries.

One major impact arose from the Vikings who eventually settled in Northern France. Led by a man called Rollo, these Norsemen were the founders of Norman civilisation. The huge warriors who helped William of Normandy invade England in 1066 were pretty much Vikings through and through. Read all about them in Chapter 10.

Another noticeable impact of the Viking world is the huge population movements that the civilisation inspired. Viking communities settled all over the world, as far apart as Newfoundland and Kiev and in places as diverse as Iceland and modern-day Turkey. These people didn't just keep to themselves: they slowly integrated and became part of their wider communities.

Researchers using genetic techniques to trace population movements have closely followed a genetic class known as 'Haplogroup 11', a group whose Y-chromosome indicates that they link back to the original Vikings. Unsurprisingly, of course, about 40 per cent of adult males in Scandinavia belong to the group, but significant populations also appear all around the world, in America as well as Europe. One study in Liverpool suggests that males born in families who had lived in the city for more than 200 years were 50 per cent more likely to have come from Haplogroup 11. Whatever else the Viking Age produced, it may be that one of the Beatles was a Viking descendant!

Chapter 9

Splitting the Church: Schisms between East and West

By the ninth century, Christianity had spread throughout Western Europe and beyond. The Church had an incredibly powerful hold on the minds and lives of the vast majority of people in the Medieval World.

Some areas, however – particularly in the eastern Mediterranean – were still independent, and the ninth century saw the first big division, or *schism*, between the Western Roman Church and the Greek Eastern Church of the Byzantine Empire (see Chapter 2). This break, which historians call the *Photian Schism*, served as a prelude to the *Great East-West Schism* of 1054.

In this chapter, I explore the big arguments – often about seemingly small things – that broke out between the Eastern and Western Churches.

Walking the Walk: Early Medieval Missionaries

Following the death of Jesus Christ in AD 30, Christianity spread throughout Europe. Within 300 years it was the official religion of the Roman Empire and when, less than 200 years after that the Empire fell, Christianity and the Church survived and prospered.

TECHNICAL STUFF

Pinpointing paganism

The word *pagan* is often confusing as it tends to conjure up ideas of worshipping bizarre ancient gods. What it really means is 'non-Christian' and with regard to the Roman Church in the Middle Ages it meant not conforming to their beliefs. Hence, people who were Christian but had slightly different views to the Papacy could be considered pagan. You can read about some of the Crusades that were targeted against these people in Chapter 16.

In the following centuries, mass conversions took place across Western Europe with previously pagan peoples turning their backs on their beliefs and way of life and embracing Christianity. This transformation is all the more remarkable when you consider the absence of television, radio or any form of mass media and the fact that the vast majority of people were illiterate. Thus, spreading the word of God involved travelling and speaking to people – lots of travelling and speaking! The people who devoted their lives to this enterprise were known as *missionaries*.

Being a missionary was a tough role with a lot of dangers and expectations to live up to. The ultimate example of a missionary was one of the first, St Paul, in the first century AD. After his conversion on the road to Damascus, he devoted his life to travelling and spreading the word of God, as recorded in detail in books throughout the New Testament.

During the eighth and ninth centuries, the Roman Church appointed and funded Christian missionaries who journeyed to various locations throughout Europe. They turned out to be amazingly successful. Figure 9-1 shows how much of the Medieval World became Christian by AD 850.

Although missionaries frequently travelled in small groups of 20 or fewer, their work was still incredibly dangerous. For many pagans, their religious practices defined their way of life – something these tribes were unlikely to give up easily.

Following the leader of the pack: Boniface

Probably the greatest of the early medieval missionaries was Boniface, who lived c. 680–754. Boniface was an Englishman whose father was probably an Anglo-Saxon. Known initially as Winfrid, he was educated in a Benedictine monastery before becoming a priest. In 716 he embarked on his first missionary journey to Frisia on the northern coast of Germany, a territory that was pagan at the time.

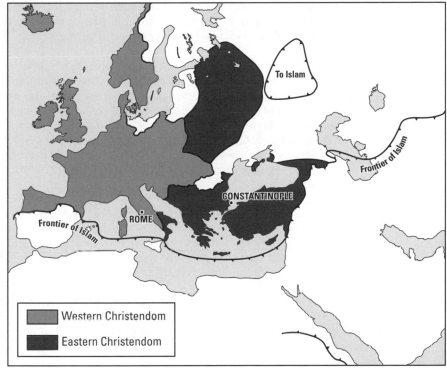

Figure 9-1:
Areas of
Europe
converted to
Christianity
by AD 850.

To Islam

Frontier of Islam

Frontier of Islam

CONSTANTINOPLE

ROME

Western Christendom

Eastern Christendom

Initially, Winfrid didn't fare well but he returned in 718 to much greater success, and soon gained the support of the Carolingian rulers of the area that we now think of as Germany (see Chapter 4 for more on the Carolingians).

One of Winfrid's most famous acts was to chop down a tree known as 'Thor's Tree' – an oak tree that local people had dedicated to the pagan god Thor, in a small town called Fritzlar (in the centre of modern-day Germany). Winfrid personally chopped it down and invited the pagan god to strike him down: Thor didn't. The story spread rapidly and showed Winfrid as somebody who had defied the gods and survived and it gave his message a lot of credence with his audience.

Over the next 30 years, Winfrid led near continuous missions to convert the German people. He was armed with the support of Pope Gregory II, whom he visited in 730 and who made him the Church's official *legate* (representative) in Germany. After receiving his title, Winfrid took the name Boniface, meaning 'good deeds', and used his new authority to establish churches and appoint his followers as bishops to run them.

Boniface's correspondence with the Church survives and highlights the missionary zeal of this period. Take a look at the following extract from Pope Gregory II's letter of introduction to the leaders of Thuringia (central Germany):

> *We pray also that as far as the work of our holy religion requires, you will seek consolation from this Holy Apostolic See* [the jurisdiction of the pope], *who is the spiritual mother of all believers, for as you are her sons and joint heirs of a kingdom that has a royal Father it is fitting that you do so. We bid you to show obedience in all things to our dearest brother Boniface, now consecrated bishop, who is well grounded in all the traditions of this Apostolic See. We send him to you to preach and instruct you in the faith and we urge you to cooperate with him in working out your salvation in the Lord.*

Over the next 30 years Boniface continued to work throughout the Carolingian kingdom, seeking to convert its inhabitants. In 754, Boniface went on a final mission to Frisia. On this occasion, he was attacked and beheaded by a group of armed men who believed that he was carrying large amounts of gold in chests. (The containers actually held his books.)

Boniface was made a saint by the Church and is still the patron saint of Germany. In the years that followed Boniface's death, Charlemagne (to whom I devote Chapter 5) forced the conversion of thousands of people to Christianity.

East is East

Missionaries ranged far and wide during the medieval period, but surely the most amazing journey undertaken was a mission to China led by a man called John of Monte Corvino towards the end of the thirteenth century. Pope Nicholas IV sent John and a group eastwards, where they were well received by the Mongol leader Kublai Khan.

The mission was a great success with John and his fellow missionaries translating the Psalms and the Gospels into the Mongol language and establishing a training school: around 6,000 people converted to Christianity. Missions continued throughout the first half of the fourteenth century, and a sizeable Christian community was established in the town of Quanzhou (now in southeast China) which had strong connections to the West through the trade in silk.

However by the middle of the fourteenth century Europe was feeling the effects of the great plague known as the Black Death (check out Chapter 20). The population of Europe was devastated by the Black Death, which also made long-distance travel even more difficult and dangerous than normal. Because they would move from place to place, missionaries came to be seen as likely carriers of the disease. Also, in China, the indigenous Chinese people revolted against Mongol control in 1368 and established a new rule – the Ming Dynasty – under which the Christians were driven out.

In an amazing story that would make a great film, the final mission sent in 1370 disappeared without trace!

Taking God on tour: Cyril and Methodius

The Roman Church in Europe wasn't the only religious institution seeking to convert pagan peoples. The Eastern Byzantine Church was also very active in sending missionaries abroad during the eighth and ninth centuries.

In addition to religious fervour, very real practical concerns motivated the leaders in Byzantium. The territories to the north of Constantinople, or Istanbul as it is known today, (modern-day Bulgaria and beyond) were filled with nomadic warriors who had moved westwards. An obvious benefit of converting these people to Christianity was that the Byzantine emperor automatically became their overlord. As would happen many more times, Christianity and politics became usefully linked.

The two most famous and successful Byzantine missionaries were Cyril and Methodius. These brothers were born in the Greek city of Thessalonica in the first quarter of the ninth century. After the death of their father, they came under the protection of a powerful Byzantine official called Theokistos. His wealth and status afforded the brothers an excellent education in both theology and languages.

Cyril's first experience of missionary work was some successful journeys to the Abbasid Caliph during the 850s, but in 862 he and his brother embarked on the mission for which they became famous. They were sent to the kingdom of Moravia (in the area of present-day Slovakia) following a request from Ratislav, the Prince of Moravia, for Christian missionaries.

The request was certainly odd. The Moravians were a pagan, Slavonic people, and Ratislav had previously rejected Christianity. Four years before, missionaries from the Roman Church had been violently expelled, because Ratislav was concerned that they were the beginnings of an attempt to add Moravia to the Holy Roman Empire. Ratislav's call to the Byzantine emperor wasn't because he suddenly wanted to embrace Christianity, but because he wanted Byzantine support against any future attempt by the Roman Empire to seize his territory!

Cyril and Methodius's mission proved to be the first of many 'conversions' based purely on political necessity and serves as an example of the tensions that eventually caused the schism between the Eastern and Western Churches (see the later section 'Splitting the Church: The Great Schism').

The script for Scripture

Despite the fact that the origin of their mission was political, Cyril and Methodius worked hard to convert the Slavonic people of Moravia. The brothers stuck at their task for the rest of their lives and were both *canonised,* or made into saints, after their deaths.

One of the by-products of their efforts was that they had to find some way of transcribing the Bible from Latin into the language of the Slavs.

In the process, they developed the *Glagolitic alphabet,* a method of transcribing the Slavonic language. Eventually this method of transcription became known as *Cyrillic,* and the *Cyrillic Alphabet* is still used by many languages today such as Russian, Bulgarian, Macedonian and Ukrainian. This translation of the Bible into another language was one of the first, and it was very unusual. The first full Bible in English wasn't produced until 1535, hundreds of years later.

Experiencing conversion issues

The mass conversions that took place during the eighth and ninth centuries didn't have an instant impact on the way that people lived their lives and in some cases the conversions were used for distinctly non-Christian ends. Although some people fully embraced Christianity, conversion gave others the opportunity to use the already harsh punishments available to them to enforce a new set of rules.

For instance, Mieszko I of Poland officially declared his kingdom Christian in 966 and began appointing bishops from among his own supporters. Some of the measures imposed by these new bishops were ghastly. Sources from the period report that people who broke official fasts were punished by having their teeth punched out. More severely, people accused of immorality had their genitals mutilated or sliced off altogether – a far cry from the Christian message that missionaries such as Boniface and Cyril had tried to bring to the world.

Creating Cracks in the Church: The Photian Schism

The mission of Cyril and Methodius to Moravia (see the preceding section) illustrates the increasing tension and sense of competition between the Western (Roman) and Eastern (Byzantine) Churches, as well as how religious arguments and conflicts in the Medieval World were very often based on political issues. In addition, as a result of the Muslim conquests of Europe in the seventh and eighth centuries (which I describe in detail in Chapter 7), most of the old Christian centres in what had been part of the old Byzantine

Empire (modern-day Turkey, Syria and Palestine) had declined and were ruled by Islam, racking up the potential for conflict even more.

Pitting the pope against the patriarch

By 800, the Christian world was dominated by two cities – Rome and Constantinople. The differences between these Western and Eastern cultures were wide and grew increasingly contentious.

Unsurprisingly, the biggest problem between the Church in Rome and the Church in Constantinople was the question of who was in charge:

- ✔ **In Rome,** the head of the Christian Church was the pope. The first pope had been St Peter the apostle, and the office of pope was considered to be that of God's emissary on earth. The pope was considered to have a hotline to God and his job was to spread the word of God to the Christian peoples. The Roman Church maintained that anybody who disagreed with the pope or papal decisions was in effect arguing against the decisions of God – not a wise move in the Medieval World.

- ✔ **In the Byzantine Empire,** the situation was different. The leader of the Church here was the patriarch (effectively an archbishop) of Constantinople (see Chapter 2 for more details). The patriarch was appointed by the Byzantine emperor, whose authority was absolute. The emperor was believed to be chosen by God and to interpret His will. Therefore, the emperor, not the patriarch, was the true rival of the pope.

Debating doctrine and dogma

In addition to the large-scale power struggles, theological arguments were always raging between and within the two Churches. Clerics and theologians were fractious people; most of them were able to start an argument in an empty room.

For example, the two Churches differed greatly in how they treated and interpreted the Gospels. The Western Church relied on the pope's interpretation for instruction, whereas the Eastern Church took a much more academic and philosophical view. To the latter, interpretations of the Gospels were something to be discussed and debated by clerics and academics in an abstract way, rather than necessarily automatically obeyed. This approach also meant that the nature of Christian belief amongst ordinary people was much more varied and less dogmatic.

These two very different outlooks were never really going to meld together. Even now, nearly 1200 years later, massive divisions and differences still exist between the two churches. As recently as 2001, the Greek Orthodox Church refused to allow Pope John Paul II to visit Athens until he formally apologised for the years of conflict between the two Churches.

Slash and burn – Iconoclasm

The Eastern Byzantine Church experienced its own divisions over the practice of *iconoclasm*, literally 'image breaking' in Greek. Iconoclasm was the practice of destroying *icons*, images of religious figures.

During the eighth century an outbreak of iconoclasm occurred throughout the Byzantine Empire. Iconoclasts believed that creating images of Jesus or the Holy Family was unholy, because these individuals were perfect and divine and no image ever would be.

Unlike many theological arguments, iconoclasm was widespread among the common people as well as academics and theologians. Outbreaks began in the far east of the Byzantine Empire, possibly inspired by the rise of Islam nearby. Incredibly violent confrontations took place in cities with many people losing their lives. Large fights broke out between iconoclasts and *iconodules*, people who defended the right to make icons. The movement was finally ended by the Council of Nicaea in 787, when the Emperor Constantine VI declared:

> *We declare that we defend free from any innovations all the written and unwritten ecclesiastical traditions that have been entrusted to us. One of these is the production of representational art; this is quite in harmony with the history of the spread of the gospel, as it provides confirmation that the becoming man of the Word of God was real and not just imaginary.*

Iconoclasm never really took hold in the Western Church, where the making and perfecting of religious images continued, and continues to this day. The sudden and violent explosion of iconoclasm on the Eastern Church, however, is more evidence of how different religious life was in the two parts of the Medieval World and the inevitability of some kind of split.

Talking different: All Greek to them

Another big difference between the two Churches was the different languages. The common language, or *lingua franca*, of the Western (Roman) Church was Latin. All correspondence, official business and conversation of the Eastern (Byzantine) Church, however, was carried out in Greek. The mass – the central element of Christian services – was the only aspect of Eastern Church life that wasn't in Greek. Linguistic issues of understanding the Latin mass in Greek were at the root of many of the arguments and disputes.

Coming to a head in 863

Given the tense situation between the Western and Eastern Churches, the political forces in Rome and Constantinople looked set to explode at any moment. The explosion came in 863, quite spectacularly, in the dispute known as the *Photian Schism*, the first big falling out between the two Churches. The Photian Schism was eventually followed by the much more far-reaching *Great East-West Schism* in the eleventh century (see the later section 'Splitting the Church: The Great Schism').

Elevating Photios

Essential to the Photian Schism was the decision by the Byzantine emperor Michael III in 858 to appoint a man called Photios to the office of patriarch of Constantinople. Numerous problems accompanied this appointment:

- Michael III had to depose the current patriarch, a man called Ignatios.

- Photios was an extremely wise and learned academic and theologian, but he wasn't a priest. The appointment is not unlike making the English writer and intellectual Stephen Fry Archbishop of Canterbury!

- Ignatios was treated very poorly. He was accused of treason, didn't have a formal trial and was thrown in prison.

- Michael III didn't ask the pope for permission.

Unsurprisingly when Pope Nicholas I heard about Michael III's activities, he was outraged. The pope sent some of his envoys to investigate in Constantinople, but they were pressured into approving the appointment by the Byzantine emperor at a *synod* (a church or ecclesiastical council) in 861.

Retaliating against the pope

The tension didn't end with the visit. When the envoys eventually returned to Rome, Nicholas I was outraged at their actions. In 863 he excommunicated Photios and demanded that Ignatios be reinstated. For his part, Photios wasn't keen to follow orders and excommunicated the pope in return! (See the sidebar 'Communicating excommunication' for more on this practice.)

Photios claimed that he had excommunicated the pope for a relatively obscure theological difference known as the *fillioque clause*, a debate that questioned whether Jesus the Son was of equal divinity to God the Father. Typical of the relatively obscure issues that made up arguments between Eastern and Western clerics, the issue remained unsettled for the best part of 20 years.

Of course, politics and empire were also big factors in Photios's actions. His direct challenge to the pope's authority was symptomatic of another issue: the kingdom of Bulgaria, immediately north of Byzantium, had recently converted to Christianity. From Photios's point of view, why should the Bulgars be loyal to the pope in Rome when the emperor (Michael III) was their next door neighbour? More importantly, to the Byzantines at least, the emperor wanted to become the Bulgars's overlord so that Bulgaria would be an ally rather than a threat.

Resolving the dispute

The Photian Schism rumbled on for a number of years. In 879, after both Ignatios and Nicholas I had died, Photios was officially recognised by the Western Church as patriarch. In exchange, the Byzantines nominally handed religious control of Bulgaria to Rome. (But in reality, the Bulgar king, Boris I, continued to treat the Byzantine emperor as his ruler.)

The dispute was never really resolved, and theological disagreements rumbled on over the next two centuries (check out the following section 'Splitting the Church: The Great Schism'). Although the Photian Schism wasn't the final break between the Eastern and Western Churches, relations between pope, patriarch and emperor were never the same again.

Splitting the Church: The Great Schism

For 200 years after the Photian Schism, relations between the Western Church in Rome and the Eastern Church in Constantinople continued to be difficult and the problems unresolved. The biggest problem was that the Eastern Church continued to practise the policy of *Ceasaropapism*, by which the Byzantine emperor (rather than the patriarch or pope) was the dominant force in the empire and the master of the Church.

Ceasaropapism put the Church under the influence of whoever was emperor at the time (with the emperor settling all big religious questions and theological debates). The pope wasn't happy with this policy because the Western Church believed that only the pope was able to communicate the word of God.

Of course, loads and loads of other smaller but still significant issues divided the two Churches. In addition to the *fillioque* issue (see the earlier section 'Retaliating against the pope'), the Western Church used unleavened bread during communion services (the Eucharist) whereas the Eastern Church used leavened bread. Whilst Eastern priests were allowed to marry, the Roman Church discouraged priests from doing so, eventually going so far as to ban them from doing so in 1139. These differences were the cause of the biggest ever breach between the Eastern and Western Churches – the Great Schism. And everything came down to a letter.

Writing a letter with enormous impact: Michael I

In 1054 Michael I, the patriarch of Constantinople, did an extraordinary thing. He sent a letter to Pope Leo IX that kick-started the Great Schism. In the letter he addressed the pope as 'brother' rather than 'father', indicating that he saw the pope as his equal rather than his superior. Michael then openly criticised the Western Church for various things, in particular using unleavened bread in the communion service. Michael described these practices as 'Judaistic' and therefore not Christian.

Why all the fuss over unleavened bread? The Eastern Church insisted that unleavened bread shouldn't be used in religious services because the Old Testament featured its use, whereas Jesus Christ in the New Testament used leavened bread. For the Eastern Church, any action of Jesus cancelled out practices featured in the Old Testament. Therefore, any practices similar to those celebrated in the Old Testament were like that of the Jewish faith, which explains the 'Judaistic' comment in Michael I's letter to the pope.

Unsurprisingly Michael's letter went down rather badly with the pope. Leo IX died soon afterwards (although probably not from shock) but only after he had made plans to denounce Michael.

Just before Leo's death, an embassy was sent to Constantinople with the intention of settling the debate. One of Leo's senior clerics, Cardinal Humbert, led the delegation, which arrived in Constantinople in April 1054. Michael pretty much gave the group the diplomatic cold shoulder and refused to accept their authority over him. Subsequent news of Pope Leo's death didn't improve the strength of Humbert's case.

Humbert and his fellows, however, continued their efforts. After Michael refused once more to discuss the issue with them, Humbert took extraordinary action. During Mass one morning in Hagia Sophia (Byzantium's most holy church, and now converted to a mosque that you can still visit in modern-day Istanbul), Humbert burst through the doors and marched up to the altar. Pausing a moment for dramatic effect, he planted the *Papal Bull* (the seal of the pope) on the altar and marched out again. The message was clear: the Eastern Church had been excommunicated.

Constantinople was in uproar, and Michael I took the popular step of a return volley, by excommunicating the Western Church (see the sidebar 'Communicating excommunication'). From that point on, the two Churches were formally divided never to join together again. A Great Schism indeed.

Trying to heal the breach

The excommunication wasn't like a declaration of war, and priests didn't physically fight each other. The schism was largely a political and academic exercise; the impact on ordinary people was slight (see the earlier sidebar 'Communicating excommunication'). The problems between the two Churches had been bubbling away for years and, regardless of Michael I's actions, the division would have happened sooner or later.

Subsequent attempts to try and heal the breach and relations between the two Churches resulted in decidedly mixed results:

- ✔ Divisions between the two Churches were dealt a serious blow when a Frankish army attacked Constantinople in 1204 as part of the Fourth Crusade (flip to Chapter 16 for more on this episode).

- ✔ Around the time of the First Crusade, the pope and the Holy Roman Emperor came into conflict. The resulting 'investiture dispute' centred around who had the right to appoint bishops (more details in Chapter 13).

- ✔ The fractious Western Church actually split with itself in the fourteenth century! Excommunications flew all over the place and at one time three people claimed to be pope! Read all about this great story in Chapter 19.

Communicating excommunication

Excommunication literally means that somebody or something is denied membership of a religious community. When you're denied 'communion', you can't take part in the religious service of the same name and therefore can't share the rite of Christ that it entails.

Excommunication of a single person was a serious matter. Being denied the right to participate in religious service essentially prevented that person from entering Heaven – the most serious punishment in the Medieval World (see Chapter 2). Despite its seriousness, excommunication was not uncommon; men like Philip II of France and John I of England were excommunicated, and the Holy Roman Emperor Henry IV was excommunicated twice (see Chapter 13).

A whole Church excommunicating another means that one Church refuses to recognise the legitimacy of any part of the other Church. Therefore, any mass held by the excommunicated Eastern Church, and all its priests, became illegitimate in the eyes of the Western Church, and anybody attending those services or ministered to by those priests was similarly not legitimate.

As serious as excommunication sounds, the vast majority of medieval people in western Europe were probably unaware or unconcerned by the implications of one Church excommunicating another Church. After all, they still thought their priest was a priest!

Chapter 10

Revving Up the 'Real' Middle Ages with the Normans

In This Chapter

▶ Getting settled with the Normans

▶ Waging the Battle of Hastings

▶ Securing lands with castles

▶ Heading into southern Italy with the de Hauteville clan

*A*sk anybody for an important date from the Middle Ages, and the likely answer is 1066 – the year of the Battle of Hastings. According to this famous and often-told story, William of Normandy (popularly known as William the Conqueror and William the Bastard) invaded England, King Harold received an arrow in the eye during the battle and, following his victory, William seized the crown of England for himself.

But 1066 is notable for more than King Harold looking up at an inopportune moment! For a start, William was in essence a Viking (turn to Chapter 8 for all about the Vikings), and other Norman invasions were also taking place elsewhere in Europe. Furthermore, the results of the Battle of Hastings went far deeper than just the appearance of a new king. The Normans made massive changes to England; the structure of society changed, economic policies changed and the landscape was altered with a huge number of new buildings.

In this chapter I look at how the Normans came into being and the massive impact they had across the Medieval World. Many people consider that the Middle Ages truly began towards the end of the eleventh century – the time that William was remodelling England in his own design – so get ready, the 'real' Middle Ages start now!

Stormin' Normandy

Most people associate the Normans with France and the area still known today as Normandy. Less well-known is the fact that when William the Conqueror invaded England in 1066, the Normans had existed for only about 150 years. The following section explores the Norman's meteoric rise to power.

Settling in Northmannia

In the early years of the tenth century, a group of Vikings from Scandinavia settled and made a community alongside the Seine river in northwestern France. This activity was fairly typical of the Vikings, because they travelled and settled all around Europe (Chapter 8 contains much more on the Vikings).

Of course, the new Scandinavian visitors weren't exactly popular with the local Frankish population, who referred to them as *northmanni* (literally 'men from the north'). Traditionally the northmanni were feared for their savage attacks in which villages were burned and Christians sold into slavery. The Viking presence was most certainly viewed as threatening.

However, the Viking settlements in this region proved to be different. Their leader, a man called King Rollo, met with the Frankish king Charles 'The Simple' in 911. Charles was understandably keen to strike a deal with the Vikings because of their very threatening presence. He offered Rollo his daughter as a wife along with large chunks of territory in northern France (these would go on to become the area known as Normandy). In exchange Charles wanted Rollo to cease attacks on local villages and convert to Christianity. Rollo readily agreed.

According to a man called Dudo who wrote a history of the Normans, the meeting with Rollo was successful until Charles asked him to make the traditional gesture of homage and kiss his foot. Rollo refused but asked one of his men to do so:

> *And the man immediately grasped the king's foot and raised it to the mouth and planted a kiss on it while he remained standing, and laid the king flat on his back.*

Despite this unfortunate misunderstanding Rollo still got his land, and what ultimately became the Duchy of Normandy was born.

Building up the Duchy of Normandy: Gold and Frankish sense

The original Viking settlers in the newly founded Normandy were a relatively small group of aristocrats. In order for their territory to grow, they needed to attract other people. During the tenth century, they absorbed many of the native Frankish population as well as other Vikings who travelled to join the soon thriving community.

Despite Rollo agreeing to be baptised as a Christian, he and the Vikings clung to their old traditions, such as speaking the Norse language and remaining remote from the politics of the Frankish world.

After Rollo's death in 932, the duchy passed to his son William Longsword. Although William continued to speak Norse, he began to follow some Frankish traditions. For example, he minted his own money in the town of Rouen, something that was common amongst medieval rulers in Central Europe but not in Scandinavia. It was similar in style and value to that of Carolingian coins (check out Chapter 5 for more on Charlemagne and the Carolingian dynasty).

William also involved himself more in Frankish politics. Despite being the ruler over his own kingdom, he was still a vassal of the Frankish king and required to play a part in the administration of the kingdom. The period of William's reign was very fractious in the territories of the Holy Roman Empire and involved a civil war between three pretenders to the Frankish throne. William took advantage of the situation, by attempting to expand his territory.

His first target was modern-day Flanders, to the northeast of Normandy. He also led raids westwards against the Bretons in Brittany These activities made him unpopular and he was assassinated in 942 during an ambush planned by the Count of Flanders.

William's death brought to an end the more aggressive Viking-like policy of expansion through raiding. Over the next century, Normandy quietly consolidated under the long-term leadership of Duke Richard I and his successor Duke Richard II. During this period links with Scandinavia gradually faded and Northmannia truly became Normandy.

Normandy was a fully functioning part of the Frankish Empire with a Christian Church, a leader who ruled like other Frankish counts and acceptance as part of the Frankish world. As Figure 10-1 shows, by the middle of the eleventh century, Normandy was a sizeable and significant territory – but the eyes of its new ruler, Duke William I, were trained overseas on Britain.

Figure 10-1:
France
around the
year 1050.

Mounting the Norman Invasion – 1066 and All That!

Normandy's period of quiet expansion came juddering to a halt in 1026 when Duke Richard II died. His eldest son took the throne as Richard III but was unseated by his brother Robert only ten months after his coronation. The two brothers and their supporters fought each other, and Richard finally gained Robert's subjugation but died within a year; sources suggest that he was poisoned.

Technically the title should have passed to Richard's young son but he was shepherded off to spend his life in a monastery by the treacherous Robert, who assumed the title of Duke of Normandy.

Claiming William 'The Bastard'

Having won his throne through treachery, Robert found allies difficult to come by and was very swiftly attacked internally and from beyond the borders of the duchy. He was forced to make deals to hold on to power and was quite ineffective as a ruler. Eventually he decided to embark on a pilgrimage to Jerusalem in an attempt to gain divine assistance. Unfortunately, this surprising move didn't work.

He died in July 1035 in the city of Nicaea on the way back from Jerusalem; most historical sources claim that he was poisoned. He was 35 years old and didn't name a legitimate heir.

Magnificent devil

Robert's life was eventful and relatively brief. The changing names that he was given over the years indicate how opinions and reputations were swift to change in the Medieval World:

✔ During his lifetime and after the suspected poisoning of his brother, Richard III, he was referred to as Robert 'The Devil'.

✔ Following his death on pilgrimage and the successes of his son William, he was called Robert 'The Magnificent'.

In the absence of a legitimate son, Robert was forced to select his illegitimate seven-year-old son William as heir. Nothing is certain about who William's mother was. Some sources say that she was the daughter of an aristocrat, others that her father was a common tradesman. A debate exists even about her name, although most people refer to her as Herleva. Whoever she was, she hadn't been married to Robert but such relationships out of wedlock between nobles and women possibly from the lower orders weren't uncommon. However, the fact that William wasn't legitimate and his young age made his selection as heir doubly risky.

Making friends and foes

William (who would go on to be known as William the Conqueror) had an incredibly precarious upbringing. Fortunately, he was able to rely on the support of Robert's barons who were loyal to him. He needed them, because the first two decades of his reign saw full-scale revolts against him led by competing lords such as Guy of Burgundy.

Although he was initially supported by the king, Henry I of France eventually betrayed William. At the beginning of the 1050s, he fought an exhausting war with the king. During this period he was ably supported by Baldwin, the Count of Flanders, whose daughter, Matilda, he had married in 1050. This relationship proved extremely handy in 1060 when King Henry I died, because his son and the heir to the French throne was under the guardianship of Flanders. William stopped fearing any threat from the south and turned his eyes north, across the channel.

Looking towards England

By the 1060s William was in an excellent position. He was young, successful and politically secure with allies to the northeast of him in Flanders and all his foes to the south too weak to make a challenge. He was at the head of an extremely tough and well-trained army, whose recent battle experiences had only made them tougher. Although Normandy was an independent state, its soldiers were still as fearsome as their Viking ancestors – physically large and ferocious in battle. Norman troops were feared throughout France.

The mindset of a medieval lord may seem strange to modern eyes. People today would perhaps be satisfied with such a strong position, but William was always unlikely to settle for what he had. He could have remained content with his lot, but his rivals would have perceived this behaviour as weakness.

Simply put, standing still was fatal for a medieval ruler. From William's point of view, he had to seize on his rivals's temporary problems to make further ground for himself, so that when they were ready to challenge him again he would be that much stronger. This mindset was common among medieval nobles, but even so William's move to invade England was a surprise.

So why did a Norman count, only five generations removed from his Viking ancestors, think that he had a claim to the throne of England? Surprisingly, the answer comes down to his aunt! William's great-aunt Emma had been the wife of the English king Ethelred (known as the 'Unready'). Their son Edward, who had grown up in Normandy, inherited the throne in 1042.

Despite being the king of England, Edward didn't have much love for his country. He had grown up in Normandy and liked the lifestyle that he'd enjoyed when living there with his cousin William. Norman sources state that when Edward fell ill in 1064 and had to choose an heir, he named William. William may well have known about this for some time as some sources suggest that Edward made the promise to him as far back as when he visited England in 1051.

Unfortunately things weren't quite that simple. Edward appears to have been a little over generous with his bequests, because two other people also claimed that he'd named them as his heir (to be fair, one was called Harold and the other Harald, and so some confusion was understandable):

✔ The first claimant was Harold Godwinson, the earl of Wessex, the largest of the English earldoms.

✔ The other claimant was Harald III of Norway, a Viking king not far removed from William's ancestors.

Although both claimed that Edward had verbally offered them the throne, when Edward died in January 1066, Harold Godwinson was crowned as the new king of England – and a whole heap of trouble started brewing.

Invading England: The Norman Conquest

The news of Harold's coronation was not well received in Normandy. William wrote to Pope Alexander II demanding support for his claim to the throne and received a consecrated papal banner, with which he later rode into battle.

More importantly, William immediately began to plan an invasion. He managed to put together an impressive force at the Norman port of Dives-sur-Mer. His army numbered around 7,000 men from his own forces, mercenaries, allies and a number of foreign knights. He also put together a fleet of 600 ships to carry them across the channel.

William was ready to go by July 1066, but terrible weather delayed his departure. In the end, the delay proved extremely fortunate for several reasons:

- With the imminent danger passed, Harold moved his ships from the south coast back to London, to keep them safe during the bad weather. This move left the way clear for William's invasion. On 8 September 1066, Harold also disbanded his army.

- Another heap of trouble was brewing in the north. Edward's other 'successor' – Harald III of Norway – was about to begin his own invasion of England. Only a couple of weeks after Harold Godwinson disbanded his army, Harald III landed near York with a large Viking force.

King Harold was forced hastily to reassemble his army and make the long march north. While he was absent from the south, on 12 September, William attempted to cross the channel, but was forced to turn back by strong winds. On 25 September, King Harold defeated Harald III in a tough battle in the north.

On 27 September, as Harold made his way back from York, William and his Norman fleet finally sailed. They landed at Pevensey Bay and then made their way to a site near the modern town of Hastings.

Waging the Battle of Hastings

William's first act was to establish a wooden castle as a base of operations. (Building castles was something that William continued to do throughout England during his conquests; see the later section 'Constructing Castles: The New Big Things' for more details.)

The armies of Harold and William met on 14 October at a place called Senlac Hill, around six miles or ten kilometres north of Hastings and the site of the modern-day town of Battle. Both sides were fairly evenly matched in terms of numbers: figures suggest that the Norman army was around 8,500 as opposed to around 7,500 English troops. Aside from the numbers, the Normans had two big advantages:

- **William's army was faster and more mobile.** The vast majority of Harold's troops fought on foot, whereas William had something like 2,200 cavalry available.

- **William's army was in better condition.** Harold's army had fought an exhausting battle in York only three weeks before and then marched swiftly back to the south. They were in far from peak condition.

Harold's army was made up of two different types of troops:

- ✔ The *housecarls,* who were his own personal troops (and those of his other noble supporters), professional warriors who had professed personal allegiance to their lord.

- ✔ The men of the *fyrd,* men from the earldoms of England who were less well armed and experienced.

The Battle of Hastings was fought in a way not dissimilar to many other medieval battles and so its details are worth examining. Figure 10-2 illustrates the main moves that took place during the battle, including the following (the numbers relate to the arrows on the plan):

1. The Normans began with a barrage by their archers against the English infantry, hoping to make breaks in the line before trying to charge it.

2. The Norman infantry charged up the hill at the English, while the English in turn bombarded them with rocks, javelins and anything else to hand.

3. The two infantry lines came together in vicious hand-to-hand fighting. The battle must have been much tougher than the Normans were expecting because their archery barrage hadn't been as effective as they had hoped against the English stout shields.

4. William sent in his cavalry much more quickly than he intended to support the infantry. The two sides fought hard for about an hour before some of the Norman cavalry began to fall back under pressure.

5. The English were tempted into chasing the fleeing Normans – a move that fatally broke apart their infantry wall. The Norman cavalry then reformed and charged back up the hill, cutting a swathe through the stranded English.

6. The English at the top of the hill began to fall back, and William ordered his archers to fire over the infantry line and into the mass of men who were confused about where to move.

The impact of this final step was devastating. According to many sources, Harold was fatally wounded by an arrow in the eye. In the confusion that followed, the Norman cavalry charged again and the battle turned into a rout. Modern scholars believe that around 5,000 English and 3,000 Normans were killed – around 55 per cent of those who took the field. Harold was dead, and England had a new king – William I of Normandy.

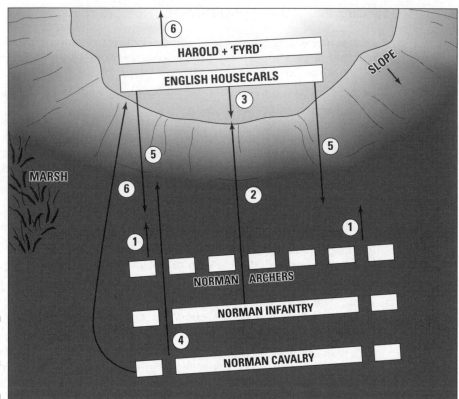

Figure 10-2:
Plan of the
Battle of
Hastings.

A well-spun tale

One of the reasons historians know so much about the Battle of Hastings is the existence of the *Bayeux tapestry*, which was originally displayed in Bayeux Cathedral in France. Despite the name, it isn't strictly speaking a tapestry but a massive piece of embroidered cloth (69 metres or 226 feet long), which depicts the events from the beginning of 1066 to William assuming the throne after the Battle of Hastings.

Along the way many of the most famous scenes are depicted, including Harold's death, possibly caused by an arrow. (Indeed, the tapestry is the main source for this detail.) One section shows a warrior with an arrow in his eye and has 'Harold' written above it. Next to him is another warrior being killed who has the Latin *infectus est* ('has been killed') written above him. The story of Harold's death by an arrow comes from this part of the tapestry, although whether the two pieces of writing both refer to the man with the arrow in his eye isn't clear.

The tapestry also depicts a few startling things. Halley's Comet appears, something that would have been interpreted as a bad omen at the time, and various other strange figures and situations crop up, events that nobody has yet managed to explain satisfactorily.

The biggest mystery, however, is who ordered the tapestry to be made. Many people have cited Matilda, William's wife, as having ordered it, but most scholars suggest that it was probably Bishop Odo, William's half brother. Nearly 1,000 years after it was made, the tapestry is still on display in the town of Bayeux and a full copy is displayed in the English town of Reading.

Transforming England: Normanisation

The story of how William brought England under his control is almost as fascinating as how he came to invade it. In the 21 years of his reign, William transformed England from how he had found it on arrival into a fully functioning Norman state, along the lines of the duchy he had left behind but on a much, much bigger scale. The following sections detail this transformation.

Building towers of power

One of the most obvious changes following William's coronation was the sight of castles springing up all over the English landscape. You can read all about them when I look at castle building in the later section 'Constructing Castles: The New Big Things'.

The most impressive of all William's buildings is the Tower of London. William constructed the White Tower (as it was known) in 1078, and it still stands impressively today. With walls 4.5 metres (or 14.5 feet) thick and reaching a height of 27 metres (or 88.5 feet), the tower dominated the landscape for miles around and served as a very visible sign of the new force in town.

Ringing the changes

William didn't stop at just changing the landscape, he also fundamentally changed the nature of society. French immediately became the language of choice among the new aristocracy and stayed that way for about the next 300 years.

The old Anglo-Saxon aristocracy was virtually eliminated, with lands seized and given over to Norman (or Norman-friendly replacements). Anglo-Saxons were eliminated from positions of influence. Many fled and some were sold into slavery. Within 20 years of the Battle of Hastings, 90 per cent of the land in control of the old aristocracy had been transferred to that of the new Norman overlords – an amazing pace of change in any time period.

These changes in power were backed by a complete rewrite of the English legal system: Norman law was brought in to replace it. The power of earls who were so much part of the feudal system in Anglo-Saxon England (see Chapter 3) was massively reduced. William allowed them to control only one shire apiece.

Instead, control of local areas was transferred to local towns and brought under organised central control. This administrational task was a massive one and to help with the process William ordered the making of an amazing new survey – the Domesday Book.

Published in 1086, the Domesday Book was a staggering achievement and a vital aid in bringing England under Norman rule. Initially designed as a way of assessing the levels of tax that were liable under the reign of Edward the Confessor, the book turned into an assessment of the wealth of the entire nation. The survey took a year to complete and gave William a total reckoning of what he was due, both in general taxes and in revenues derived from *Crown lands,* or areas owned by the king.

The Domesday Book's name comes from the old English word *dom*, which translates as 'doom' and means reckoning or accounting for. The book certainly meant doom for some people, because its judgement was final and appeals were forbidden.

A total of 13,418 places are listed in the Domesday Book, which was originally written in Latin, still at this time the language of administration across the whole of Medieval Europe. All the lands, livestock and possessions in the country were gathered together under the *fiefs* (see Chapter 3) of which they were a part, rather than geographically by town or city.

The following entry from the Domesday Book is taken from a section concerning the land of a man called Robert Malet who lived in Norfolk:

> *Fredrebruge Hundred and half Glorestorp. Godwin, a freeman, held it. Two carucates of land in the time of king Edward. Then and afterwards 8 villains; now 3. Then and afterwards 3 bordars; now 5. At all times 3 serfs, and 30 acres of meadow. At all times 2 carucates in demesne* [the whole of the land in question associated with Robert Malet's manor]. *Then half a carucate of the men, and now. Woods for 8 swine, and 2 mills. Here are located 13 socmen, of 40 acres of land…At all times 8 swine, then 20 sheep, and it is worth 60 shillings.*

A *carucate* was the unit of land area used throughout the book for taxation purposes. It was a measure of land considered to be big enough for a tiller of eight oxen to plough during a season. *Socmen* were tenants who worked on the land in question, so here there were 13 tenants working on the land.

The Domesday Book was a huge success that allowed William and his successors the financial freedom to implement other control measures, including the use of castles and knights.

Constructing Castles: The New Big Things

Another important method used by William the Conqueror to enforce his authority over England was the building of castles. Castles are one of the two main things that people associate with the Middle Ages along with knights, but both took a while to become mainstays of the Medieval World. Indeed, only in the eleventh century did both of these institutions become commonplace.

The next sections focus on medieval castles (I examine the development of the knights in Chapter 11).

Defending your land and hosting guests

In a way, castles were no great invention. From the earliest days after the break-up of the Roman Empire, the more important men in European society had lived in large houses along with their retinues. Over time, new aristocracies emerged, and men took titles such as duke, earl or baron. None of these titles really signified anything different from each other, but by the eleventh century these men were becoming extremely powerful and in control of huge areas of land – which needed protecting and defending.

The word castle comes from the Latin word *castellum*, meaning a fortified place. Many towns and cities in the Ancient World were fortified, but the difference with a castle is that it was a deliberately fortified dwelling, rather than a palace in a fortified town (such as the palaces in which a Roman Emperor may have lived).

Castles were both defensive and offensive structures. You were able to hide in one from attackers but also use one to attack, by building it in your enemy's territory. When William the Conqueror won at Hastings in 1066, he used castles for both of these purposes – to secure what he had and to push farther inland to grab more territory.

Castles also had a social function. Kings and lords lived and conducted all their business and administration in castles, and visitors were received and feasts and revels also held there. A castle was the dominant building in the local area, both physically and in terms of its relevance to people's lives.

Touring early buildings: Motte and bailey castles

In the early centuries after the fall of Rome (roughly from 450 to 750), fortifications tended to be made by adapting existing buildings that had fallen into disrepair. By the tenth century a new and clear pattern for building fortifications emerged, and in the eleventh century it was introduced to England by the Normans.

The earliest examples of these buildings were known as *motte and bailey castles*, which involved creating a large hill (known as the *motte*) and surrounding it with a water moat or some kind of ditch. The structure built on top of the hill was known as a *bailey* or *keep*. Everything was placed in the bailey, including residential areas, stables and a water well, so the bailey was a simple and effective place of security.

Fulk of Anjou: A model builder

The Count of Anjou in France, Fulk 'The Black' – who is, as I relate in Chapter 1, infamous for burning his wife when he suspected her of adultery – is also known for his castle building. Indeed, he was one of the first major builders.

Fulk built castles for a variety of reasons but mostly as a very visible symbol of his power and a method of intimidating the population of Anjou. Very often these structures were not great works of architecture but just simple buildings, set up on a motte or a naturally raised piece of ground. The keep or *donjon* that he built at Montbazon (in the Loire region of central France) is still standing and is a great

example of the many such buildings that Fulk constructed.

Fulk's last building, however, was a church. As he grew older he became terrified of the prospect of not reaching Heaven because of his wicked behaviour. At a place called Conquereuil, in northwest France, where he had once won a great victory, he founded a large church. Unfortunately for Fulk on the day of its consecration, the building was partly blown down by the wind. To his enemies this event was evidence of divine judgement!

Visiting medieval castles

By the eleventh century, castles had developed considerably from their motte-and-bailey predecessors. Variations appeared all around Europe, but in essence functioning medieval castles were built of stone and always contained the following key elements (as Figure 10-3 shows):

- The **keep**, or *donjon*, was the largest tower and central feature of a castle. This structure housed the residing ruler and his retinue and provided storage. The keep was the most secure spot in the castle; people flocked to it during crisis or attack.

- The **outer walls**, or *curtain walls*, surrounded the keep and central area. They were a second layer of defence, separate from the keep or (if the castle had one) the bailey. Gradually, *turrets* were developed on the walls to give an extra level of observation of the surrounding area.

- The **gatehouse** provided access through the wall into the central area. A gate was a castle's potential defensive weakness, and so it was fortified more than elsewhere on the walls. A later development was the *portcullis*, a latticed gate made of wood or metal that was raised and lowered to admit people.

- The **moat** was a deep ditch dug around the castle and filled with water. The moat served as a first line of defence, and a drawbridge that lowered from the gatehouse was used to cross it.

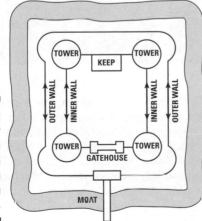

Figure 10-3:
Plan of
a typical
Norman
castle with
common
elements.

As the medieval period continued, castle building became more sophisticated with other elements becoming standard. For example, the use of *crenellations* or *merlons* – the battlements put on top of towers that look like teeth sticking up – and the slots built into walls that gave cover to archers as they fired down on attackers were key innovations. Other types of openings, known as *murder holes*, were left in the walls so that defenders were able to drop objects such as rocks or pour boiling water on to the heads of attackers. Sneaky!

All these developments meant that attacking a castle became increasingly difficult and costly. *Siege warfare* techniques were developed to cope with the new defences (check out Chapter 12 and the section on the siege of Antioch).

Figure 10-4 shows Tonbridge Castle, the first castle that I ever saw because it stands in the Kent town where I grew up. Originally a motte-and-bailey castle, the stone structure was built in the late eleventh century by William Rufus, the son of William the Conqueror, after having burnt down the original structure to punish the owner who'd rebelled against him. The picture below shows a twin-towered gatehouse that was constructed on the site around 1260 and is still open to visitors today.

Figure 10-4: Two medieval castles: Tonbridge gatehouse (left) and Bodiam (right).

Figure 10-4 also shows Bodiam Castle in Sussex. This brilliantly preserved castle is an ideal site to visit to get a real idea of what Medieval castles were like. The structure was built much later than Tonbridge Castle in the late fourteenth century by Edward Dalyngrigge to defend against a possible French invasion during the Hundred Years' War (which I cover in Chapter 21). Bodiam is in superb condition and a typical example of the period. For more great castles, cross over to Chapter 27.

Property prices

Building castles wasn't cheap. Early castles were made of wood, but stone soon became the standard building material with the outer walls and keep almost certainly being made of stone like sandstone, limestone, flint or hard chalk.

Unless the builder was able to quarry stone nearby, it had to be moved to the site, which was time-consuming and expensive. Workers's wages may have been low on a daily basis, but building a castle took about five years and hundreds of labourers. The keep alone of Dover castle on the south coast of England took five years to build between 1182–1187, at a cost of about £4,000 (equivalent to nearly £480,000 today).

Castles also cost a fortune to maintain and improve. Documents show that the English king Henry II (1154–1189) spent around £1,400 over eight years on the upkeep of Orford castle (in Suffolk, eastern England). This equates to about £168,000 these days; and Orford was a small castle with just the one tower. Big money, especially when you consider that England had hundreds of castles at this time, and they all required repair and maintenance.

Journeying South: The Normans in the Mediterranean

William the Conqueror's achievements were amazing, but he wasn't the only Norman to venture farther afield than northern France. Before William's conquests, other Normans had also made their presence felt much farther south in Italy and particularly on the Mediterranean island of Sicily.

Fortune hunting in southern Italy: the de Hauteville clan

The story of the Normans in the Mediterranean really begins with a man about whom historians know virtually nothing. Tancred de Hauteville (980–1041) was a minor Norman noble in charge of a number of small villages on the Contentin peninsula in Normandy. He seems to have led a fairly uneventful life with the exception of the fact that he sired 12 sons.

Three of these sons – William, Drogo and Humphrey – turned up in Italy in the 1030s as mercenaries in a Byzantine army that was trying to retake the island of Sicily from its Muslim rulers (flip to Chapter 7 for all about the

Islamic invasions). Although the expedition was a failure, the de Hautevilles obviously liked what they saw during their foray in Italy. The rest of the family soon travelled there in an attempt to find their fortune. Chief among them was Tancred's sixth son Robert, known as Robert Guiscard the Cunning.

Men like Guiscard were euphemistically known as 'adventurers'. Essentially they were *brigands* or robbers who made their money from a mixture of criminal activities and hiring themselves out as mercenaries to local lords. Robert's brothers had done well for themselves by seizing territory from local rulers and then claiming the titles for themselves. Robert's brother William (known as 'Iron Arm') proclaimed himself Duke of Apulia (Apulia is the 'heel on the boot' of southeast Italy), and his brother Drogo succeeded him on his death.

The political situation was so chaotic that various members of the de Hauteville clan were able to hold on to this territory. Lands in southern Italy were in dispute between the papacy, the Byzantine emperor and the Holy Roman emperor, none of whom were able to take back the land.

The criminal life of these Norman adventurers did, however, come under fire in 1053, when Pope Leo IX attempted to take back southern Italy. But his German army was soundly thrashed by the Normans in a battle at Civitate. This defeat brought an end to papal resistance of the de Hauteville clan. In 1059 Pope Nicholas II presented Robert with a banner proclaiming him as the rightful Duke of Apulia and Calabria. Crime does pay after all!

Setting their sights on Sicily

With Norman rule in Southern Italy official, the de Hauteville clan wasted no time in trying to take things further. Their next target was the island of Sicily, which had been under Muslim rule for several hundred years.

In 1061 a Norman force under Robert Guiscard and his younger brother Roger began their attacks on Sicily. They met with continued success until 1064 when they were defeated by a Muslim fleet off the coast of Palermo. Roger wasn't held off for long though. Palermo finally fell in January 1072 and over the next 15 years Roger, now calling himself Roger I, completed his total conquest of the island. Still not satisfied he added Malta to his growing empire in 1090.

Taking on the Empire

As Roger's successes continued, his brother Robert was hardly slacking. In 1081 Robert launched an incredibly ambitious attempt to attack the Byzantine Empire! His first target was the port of Durazzo (on the western coast of modern-day Albania), from where he intended to march overland along a road known as the via Egnatia to Constantinople itself. His initial attempts to attack Durazzo were scuppered, but he returned and laid siege to the port, finally taking it, only to lose it again a year later.

Still not satisfied, he launched a naval attack in 1084 on the Byzantine island of Corfu. He successfully defeated a mixed army of Byzantines and Venetians but caught typhoid and died in the summer of 1085 at the age of 70.

In a little over a generation, the Normans in Italy went from being a band of 'adventurers' to the most feared military force in the Mediterranean. Norman rule in Sicily continued until the thirteenth century, and their influence can still be seen all over the island in the castles that remain, like the amazing black stone castle of Aci Castello built in 1076. Their success mirrored that of their Norman contemporary, William the Conqueror, in England.

European warriors smashing their way around the Mediterranean was something of a dry run for the next stage of medieval history. Farther to the east, a new conflict in which the Normans played a major role was about to begin. Read all about the Crusades in Part III!

Part III
Waging Holy War: Crusading at Home and Abroad
(1050–1300)

The 5th Wave   By Rich Tennant

Oh for gosh sake, Richard! It's a couple of mice in the basement stealing grain. Quit making a crusade out of everything!

In this part . . .

Part III is about Crusading, which was all the rage between the eleventh and fourteenth centuries. An incredible sequence of events led the armies of Western Europe to invade the Holy Land and establish a whole new kingdom – Outremer. These action-packed years feature an amazing cast of characters: swashbuckling heroes such as Richard the Lionheart, inspirational leaders such as Saladin and absolute idiots (Reynald of Chatillon, anyone?). And don't forget the Crusaders who ran out of steam halfway through their mission and decided to sack Constantinople instead.

Chapter 11

Uncovering the Origins of the Crusades

During the period between the Norman Conquest of England (in 1066) to around 1250, the focus of the powerful military and religious leaders of Europe switched from their own immediate concerns to events taking place thousands of miles away – the now infamous Crusades.

In a series of extraordinary events, rulers and leaders from all across Europe made their way to the Holy Land to recapture the city of Jerusalem from the Muslim peoples. Along the way, new kingdoms were established, atrocities committed and a whole new chapter of history written.

This chapter is all about why the Crusade came about, what motivated the First Crusade of 1097 and, in particular, why people felt that they were serving God by killing foreigners. This period in history was extraordinary and is one over which controversies continue to this day – where the word *crusade* is used to describe a totally different type of conflict taking place in our own time.

Read on and find out more!

Seeking the Causes of the Crusades

The main reason that the European countries gave for undertaking the Crusades – and a series of European campaigns over the next 200 years directed at the Muslim World in the East – was to retake Jerusalem, which the Fatamid caliphate had captured. The Muslims, however, had seized Jerusalem in 688 (journey to Chapter 7 for more details), more than 400 years before the First Crusade.

The actual motivations behind the Crusades are more complicated and include the following:

- The Byzantine Empire had got itself into a bit of a bother with the battle of Manzikert in 1071 (this situation was probably the most significant cause).
- The European nobles wanted new territory.
- The pope was determined to call men of war into Christian service.
- The excess of skilled fighting men – *knights* – meant that many didn't have lands to defend, were desperate for a cause and wanted to make their name and win riches and glory.

The following sections explore all these reasons and more.

Going berserk at Manzikert

By the eleventh century, the Christian Byzantine Empire was in serious trouble. During the early years of the century a new and powerful enemy had emerged – the Seljuk Turks, who delivered a crushing blow to the Byzantines in a battle at Manzikert (near Erzurum in modern Turkey). The Seljuks were a nomadic people who came from central Asia and began to strike at the heart of modern-day Iran. Having seized power from the previous Muslim regime, they converted to Islam and started to move farther west.

The Battle of Manzikert

The Seljuks advanced into the eastern borders of the Byzantine Empire. In 1067, they captured the province of Armenia and clearly didn't intend to stop there.

Byzantium had other problems, too. The emperor at the time was a young boy, Michael VII, whose mother was ruling in his stead. As the Seljuk threat advanced, she married the commander of the Byzantine army, Romanus Diogenes, and made him emperor.

In August 1071, Romanus advanced against the Seljuks with an army of around 100,000, but the battle proved a disaster. Treachery and misinterpreted instructions resulted in a Byzantine defeat. Although the losses weren't huge, the Byzantines lost central Anatolia (modern-day Turkey) to the Seljuks and must have feared greater losses to come.

A cry for help

Although the Seljuks didn't press on to Constantinople, the Byzantine Empire continued to be under threat. Over the next 20 years, the Seljuks carried on their campaigns elsewhere. They began by sweeping up the ports on the Levantine coast and, in 1085, captured the ancient Syrian city of Antioch from the Byzantines.

Byzantium was also trying to deal with the activities of the Norman adventurer Robert Guiscard who tried to invade Greece in the same year. (Guiscard was the sixth son of Tancred de Hauteville who you can read all about in Chapter 10.) After Guiscard's death, however, the relationship between the Eastern and Western Churches thawed a bit. Pope Urban II lifted the excommunication on the Byzantine emperor Alexius (turn to Chapter 9 for more details), who wasted no time in pushing his advantage. In 1095, at an embassy in Piacenza, his envoys made a formal request for protection from the Western Catholic Church.

A monk called Bernodl of Constance relates what happened:

> *An embassy of the emperor of Constantinople came to the synod and humbly begged the lord pope and all the faithful of Christ to send some help to him for the defence of the Holy Land against these pagans.*

The pope in question was Urban II. He agreed to Alexius's request and began the call for a Crusade.

Hungering for land

The Crusades appealed to noblemen for several reasons, but the acquisition of new land was paramount. Medieval Europe was a very dangerous place with near continual warfare between various aristocracies on the continent. The sons of ambitious nobles employed armed knights in these battles (see the later section 'Bringing on the knights' for more details).

A desire for more land drove this state of continuous warfare. Europe had only a finite amount of land, and the sons of the aristocracy who weren't in line to inherit wanted to find some for themselves. Suddenly Urban II was offering them the opportunity to invade a whole new region with lots of land for the taking. Many of the nobles who joined the first Crusade had just this objective in mind.

Calling for Crusade

Between the summer of 1095 and July 1096, Pope Urban II went on tour in an effort to recruit people to the relief effort for Constantinople. He travelled through northern Italy, all around France and sent letters to the people of Flanders, Italian cities and elsewhere. The Byzantine envoys probably only expected a few mercenaries. Instead, the pope went on a massive recruitment campaign and called on Christian warriors to arm themselves for a war in the East.

Going on the Crusade was a considerable commitment. Uprooting your life, leaving your wife and children, travelling thousands of miles and then fighting a horrifically dangerous war against relatively unknown enemies was a huge sacrifice.

Urban was a pretty good salesman, however, and had some very tempting deals on offer. Specifically, the pope offered an *indulgence* (see Chapter 2) to anyone going on Crusade. By doing this Christian service, people were able to have all their sins up to that point forgiven. He put the offer this way:

> Whoever for devotion alone, not to gain honour or money, goes to Jerusalem to liberate the Church of God can substitute this journey for all penance.

All a crusader's sins would be wiped away, as would any that were committed on the Crusade itself (which was clearly going to involve a lot of murder and pillage).

The idea of an indulgence was electric to the medieval mind. As I discuss in Chapter 9, medieval people were obsessed by the idea of the afterlife and getting into Heaven. Urban II was offering a guaranteed ticket.

Urban II had hoped for a response from the military classes, but he received more than he bargained for. His message appealed to all members of society and spread like wildfire across continental Europe. People with no money, status or military experience were fired up by the idea (see Chapter 12 for more on *The People's Crusade*). The old, the poor, women and children all went on this adventure because of the opportunity of pilgrimage. What had begun as a call for military assistance became something more like a population movement. Some modern historians estimate that almost 60,000 people would've been involved.

Bringing on the knights

The class of society that Pope Urban II had in mind when he called people throughout Europe to go on Crusade were the new warriors of Europe, the knights.

Knights played a hugely important part of the success of the Normans in northern France and elsewhere, and by the time of the First Crusade, they were the dominant military class in Europe. The following sections examine who and what the knights were. By 1000, having a castle was the mark of a serious ruler in Europe (Chapter 10 contains loads more info on castles). As a way of protecting land and imposing your will on the local population, castles were unrivalled – but they needed staff.

During the same period, nobles and aristocrats began to keep large retinues of heavily armed men. These *cnichts* were used to brutally suppress local people. (Indeed, *cnicht* is an old English word that describes the basest type of servant and in a way, that's what these men were.) Like mafia enforcers, cnichts ensured that taxes were paid, laws obeyed and men volunteered for military service. Without land themselves, a cnicht was tied to a master, who also paid for his expensive weapons and armour. A crucial distinction was that *knights* were mounted warriors and could afford to equip a horse.

The duties and experiences of a cnicht contrast sharply with what being a knight eventually came to signify as the Middle Ages continued – that is, a wealthy warrior who was able to afford his own warhorse. Knighthood in this later era was also associated with chivalry and honourable conduct (see Chapter 16 for more), but at the time of the Crusades, knights were effectively mercenaries for hire. Just the type that Urban II was looking for.

Things that go bump on a knight

The main things that made the knights so different from other fighting men was their incredibly expensive arms and armour. The different types of armour varied between places and periods but the basic elements remained the same:

✔ **Mailcoat:** By far the most expensive element of a knight's armour was the chainmail undercoat that was worn with sleeves and reached down to the knees. Known as a *hauberk*, it was made up of hundreds of individual iron links that were joined together by hand. Hauberks took a great deal of time to make and cost a fortune.

✔ **Helmet:** All knights wore some kind of helmet. Originally this helmet was just a bowl type hat that sat on top of a chainmail hood. During the Middle Ages, however, helmets developed, initially in terms of new shapes that better deflected blows and then into full head helmets with visors.

✔ **Body armour:** Individual pieces of body armour were worn on the arms and legs and varied hugely in size and style throughout the period and in different geographic regions. The most common elements were *greaves* that protected the lower leg beneath the knee and *gauntlets* that covered the hand and forearm.

The costs of these items varied depending on quality and design. Knights without much cash could have worn some leather armour pieces but for most iron would've been essential. Estimating the expense is difficult, but fully arming a man and supplying him with a horse and weapons was probably equivalent to the price of a house today. Obviously knights needed to be the sons of successful men or have their armour bought for them.

Charge of the rather heavy brigade

The armour that knights wore (see the earlier sidebar 'Things that go bump on a knight') made them far safer from attack than normal cavalry soldiers. In addition, two other innovations made knights more mobile and useful in battle:

✔ **Stirrups.** Stirrups were first introduced to Europe sometime during the ninth or tenth centuries. Previously riders rode without them. With the addition of stirrups, men were able to ride with greater control using only their feet.

✔ **Lances.** The greater control that stirrups brought to riding also allowed knights to carry long poles (up to four metres or 13 feet in length) in the crook of their right arms, while holding a shield in the left. Knights then charged forward, directly at enemy infantry lines – to devastating effect.

Heavily armoured, mobile and effective from distance, knights were a terrifying weapon of war and social control.

Murder practice: Tournaments

Around the same time that mounted knights became common in Medieval Europe, tournaments also developed. During these competitive events, knights practised combat skills for the entertainment of an audience. Inevitably, they sometimes killed each other, although this wasn't the intention!

The main event was the *estor* or charge, where two lines of knights charged at each other with lances. These events turned into proper battles with people severely injured and killed as a result. Individual knights were captured during the melee and allowed to return to where they came from only if an extremely expensive ransom was paid to their captors. It was a high-risk activity, but the rewards were great; knights could make fortunes from ransoms and it was a good way of gaining international honour and prestige.

By far the most glamorous event of tournaments was the *joust*, where two knights on horseback and armed with lances and shields charged at each other in one-on-one combat. Eventually, during the thirteenth century, the joust took over as the main event from the *estor*, and huge sums were gambled on the results by the watching masses. Jousting was incredibly dangerous and people did die, although killing your opponent wasn't the objective. The tournament was also associated with fighting for the hand of a lady and an element of chivalry that you can read about in Chapter 26.

Venturing into the Kingdom of France

Following the treaty of Verdun in the ninth century (which I discuss in Chapter 6), the western territory of the Roman Empire known as *Western Francia* – modern-day France – had become distinct and separate from other parts of continental Europe.

Finding your way round France

By the time of the First Crusade, medieval France was a very different place compared to the years of the Carolingian rulers (see Chapters 5 and 6). It had many and varied independent rulers, all protecting their own interests with the skilful use of knights.

As a large slab of land, France had traditionally been thought of as being divided into two distinct sections. As far back as the Roman Empire, France had been divided into two provinces and since then the north and south had been treated independently (see Figure 11-1).

✔ **The southern area,** known as Aquitaine, didn't have a king as such. Instead, one of the leading counts assumed overall rule and took the title of Duke of Aquitaine. Historically the Count of Poitou, one of the leading towns in the region, took the lead.

✔ **The north and upland areas** were much more complex:

- To the west, the count of Brittany pretty much ruled it as a separate state.

- To the northeast of Brittany was Normandy, whose interests had expanded across the channel to England (see Chapter 10 on William the Conqueror).

- To the northeast even farther was Flanders, which the Vikings had previously occupied before Count Baldwin II forced them out at the beginning of the tenth century.

- To the east, the territory was known as Burgundy. This area was a loose collection of old dukedoms that had been ruled by the Carolingians (the family of Charlemagne) since the eighth century (see Chapter 6). However, by the eleventh century these territories were in the hands of people who had no allegiance to the Holy Roman emperor.

France was a patchwork of different territories and dukedoms. But in the middle of it all was the king of France. Where had he come from?

Meeting the king of France

Since the Treaty of Verdun in 843, somebody had traditionally been called the king of France, but the position was nothing like as grand as it sounds. The actual territory that the king ruled was only that part of France known as Isle de France, the area immediately around the city of Paris, hemmed in by the lands of various other dukes and lords such as Anjou, Flanders and Normandy.

Figure 11-1:
Medieval
France in
around 1100.

In the second half of the tenth century, the Carolingian rulers were struggling in France. Links with the emperor in Germany were not as strong as they had been, and the Carolingians were forced to give away land to the indigenous Franks to gain their support.

During this period a man called Hugh Capet succeeded to the throne in 987. He took advantage of the weakness of the Carolingian ruler, held on to his title and was able to pass it on to his successors. Throughout the tenth and eleventh centuries, France essentially had its own independent king. Technically he was the overlord of all the other dukes and counts who ruled in Francia – but things didn't quite work out like that. The king's power in the north was weak, and the aristocrats of Aquitaine virtually ignored him, but that situation would change over the next 100 years as the king's power grew. By the late eleventh century the king of France had become a truly serious player on the international stage.

Extending the call to France

Unsurprisingly, all the competing aristocrats in France were almost con-stantly engaged in warfare or diplomatic skulduggery. The huge growth in the numbers of knights in France and their ever more violent and aggressive actions were of concern to the papacy.

As I mention in the earlier section 'Calling for Crusade', going on a Crusade answered the warrior noble's desire for land and provided an outlet for their knights's aggression. For these reasons, Pope Urban II spent much of his time travelling around France, preaching Crusade.

The effect of Urban's call on the people must have been electric. Here was God's representative appearing in front of them and calling them to come to war.

Preparing for the First Crusade

So who actually went on Crusade? Pope Urban II probably didn't expect the more powerful figures in Europe to go. The king of England, the Holy Roman Emperor or the king of France were unlikely to take the pledge.

As rulers of large territories – and constantly threatened with invasion by their neighbours – they were unable to leave their kingdoms, because they weren't sure that they'd have a kingdom to come back to. (In addition, the pope and Roman emperor weren't on speaking terms due to the 'Investiture Controversy', which I cover in detail in Chapter 13.)

Instead, Urban II was targeting the second-tier of European nobility with his call for Crusade. These men were the younger brothers of rulers, discontented nobles or professional 'adventurers' such as the Normans. These men had something to gain from Crusade. With their ambitions frustrated at home, the Crusades offered chances to forge new kingdoms, along with guaranteed places in Heaven.

Meeting some notable Crusaders

The response from nobles across Europe to Urban's call was almost over-whelming. Following is a list of the leading warriors of the First Crusade (con-fusingly, several of them seem to have been called Baldwin):

- **Hugh of Vermandois:** The younger brother of the king of France, Hugh was by far the most high-profile nobleman on the list.

- **Raymond of Toulouse:** The most senior and experienced warrior to go on the First Crusade, Raymond previously fought the Muslim armies in Spain. He wanted to be the official leader of the First Crusade, but Urban II said no.

- **Adhemar of Le Puy:** The official and spiritual leader of the Crusade, bishop Adhemar of Le Puy was tasked by Urban II to choose a Christian monarch for Jerusalem after it was re-conquered. Everybody thus wanted to be Adhemar's new best friend.

- **Godfrey of Bouillon, Eustace of Boulogne and Baldwin:** Best described as the 'Lorraine Gang', Godfrey was the Duke of Lower Lorraine and his younger brother Eustace was the Count of Boulogne. The third brother Baldwin had no actual title and worked as an officer for Godfrey.

- **Bohemond of Taranto:** The first of the Norman contingent to embark, Bohemond was part of the de Hauteville family and a descendant of Robert Guiscard (for more on this adventurer, check out Chapter 10). He abandoned his territorial plans in southern Italy to join the Crusade.

- **Tancred de Hauteville:** Tancred was Bohemond's nephew, another de Hauteville. Without a dukedom or principality of his own, the Crusade presented a great opportunity for him.

- **Robert of Normandy:** A northern Norman, Robert was the eldest son of William the Conqueror and the current Duke of Normandy (and was known as Robert 'Curthose' meaning 'short stockings', as a patronising nickname). To raise the capital needed for the expedition, he pawned his lands to his brother William II, the king of England, and was one of the first to sign up.

- **Stephen of Blois:** A Norman nobleman, Stephen was married to Adela, the sister of Robert of Normandy. He didn't want to go on Crusade, but his wife wanted him to. She won and he went.

- **Baldwin of Flanders and Baldwin of Alost:** Two relatively minor noblemen from areas of Northern France, both Baldwins had held and lost titles in their homeland. The Crusade represented a real opportunity to make good elsewhere.

The knights of the First Crusade were a fearsome bunch of warriors, each bringing a private army of men and a mighty ego. Pope Urban II considered the Crusade to be a religious enterprise and chose a cleric, Adhemar of Le Puy, to lead it. Unfortunately, Urban underestimated other factors, specifically rivalry between the knights, the desire for land and antipathy towards the Byzantine Empire. Indeed, these factors almost undermined the Crusade before it got going.

Planning the journey

Ego clashes and arguments over leadership weren't the only problems facing the First Crusade. Those who went on the expedition faced an imposing physical trek of around 3,000 miles (or 4,800 kilometres) to reach Constantinople. The first leg of the planned route involved moving south through Italy, crossing the Adriatic to Greece and then moving overland to Constantinople.

Medieval travellers had limited knowledge of distances and travel times. Upon reaching Constantinople, the vast majority of the Crusaders would literally have reached the end of their knowledge of the world. Even those few who had seen a map would have mistakenly believed that the holy city of Jerusalem was at the centre of the world (see Chapter 1). In fact, upon leaving Constantinople in April 1097 one crusader wrote to his wife that he expected to take Jerusalem and return home by Christmas! As it turned out his army didn't even reach Jerusalem until June 1099, more than two years later.

Covering travel expenses

The journey during the Crusade proved arduous, lengthy and also extremely costly. Any nobleman embarking on the expedition had to provide for all the men in his army. This obligation meant paying for weapons and armour as well as the potentially ruinous expense of feeding them on the long, long march.

Robert of Normandy pawned his lands to his brother William II to raise enough money to go on Crusade. In turn, William had to get the money from somewhere in order to pay Robert. William of Malmesbury, a twelfth-century English historian and monk, describes the fundraising as follows:

> *Rufus* [William II] *therefore imposed an insupportable tax throughout the whole of England. Many bishops and abbots came to Rufus's court complaining about its severity, saying that they could not pay without driving away the peasants. The courtiers, with their usual sarcasm, replied: 'Do you not have reliquaries made of gold and silver, full of dead men's bones?'* . . . *almost everything that the holy frugality of our ancestors had saved up, the greed of those robbers spent.*

The disrespect shown to holy relics in the desperation to raise money really did foreshadow the atrocities that would occur during the Crusades.

Chapter 12

Waging the First Crusade: 1096–1099

. . . .

In This Chapter

▶ Joining up with the People's Crusade

▶ Upsetting the Byzantines with the First Crusade

▶ Getting stuck in siege warfare at Antioch

▶ Founding Outremer, the kingdom beyond the sea

. . . .

*I*n 1096, the First Crusade was (finally) ready to begin (check out Chapter 11 for the gen on what led to the Crusade). A lengthy, arduous journey lay ahead into a land about which the vast majority of the papal army had only the sketchiest of ideas.

No grand plan existed – other than to march to Jerusalem and take it back. The leadership of the whole enterprise was constantly challenged, and the Byzantine emperor, Alexius Comnenus I, was justifiably nervous about a Western army arriving in his capital, and he put up a diplomatic (rather than militaristic) fight.

Strap yourself in. This chapter is one bumpy ride through two unofficial Crusades and the papal army's official First Crusade.

Participating in the People's Crusade

The preaching of Pope Urban II made a massive impact in Medieval Europe (as I describe in Chapter 11). While the great and the good jockeyed for position in the official papal army that assembled in Italy, another far more radical group of Crusaders also began to make its way to the Holy Land in an effort known as the People's Crusade, also known as the Peasants' and Paupers' Crusade.

Palling around with Peter the Hermit

Urban II wasn't the only person to preach Crusade. Many of his bishops and priests took the message to their people, and other unofficial recruiters and preachers took to the streets themselves. The most famous and successful of these latter preachers was a man known as Peter the Hermit (whom I mention in Chapter 1).

Peter the Hermit was born around 1050 and came from Amiens in France. He was a nomadic ex-monk who relied on the charity of others to live. In fact, he spent most of his time travelling around talking to people, and so he wasn't really much of a hermit. Peter the Nomad would have probably been a more accurate description.

He apparently tried to make a pilgrimage to the Holy Land, only to be stopped by the wars in the Byzantine Empire. Taking Urban's call to Crusade as his cue, Peter now travelled around northern France recruiting a huge mob of common people to join him on pilgrimage, and help him to go back and clear the way to Jerusalem.

Peter was astonishingly successful in recruiting people to join his journey. Crowds were awed by his inspiring preaching and enthusiastically joined up because going on pilgrimage was effectively an *indulgence* (Chapter 2 has the lowdown on the granting of indulgences by the Church), something that granted you likely access to Heaven. What Peter and other prophets like him were offering was an organised pilgrimage to the Holy Land – the ultimate spiritual destination on Earth. People jumped at the chance.

Marching with the great unwashed

The People's Crusade was completely unofficial and left months before the official papal army. Gathering in the German town of Cologne, approximately 40,000 people left in April 1096. To put this number in perspective, it would have been around 10,000 more than the population of a city like Paris at the time – an immense body of people.

This number was made up of a huge variety of different people: young men and women, children, the old, the poor and even the sick. Some modern historians have suggested that there were possibly some armed nobles involved who were so keen to get going that they couldn't wait for the 'official' First Crusade.

Unfortunately, going on pilgrimage, especially to somewhere as far away as Jerusalem, was really hard work; it was even more difficult if you were poor. With no money to buy supplies, the Crusaders had to steal and rob their way to Constantinople.

The Byzantines must have been pretty surprised and rather confused to see the pilgrims arrive in August 1096. The emperor had requested a Christian army from the east. Instead over 30,000 largely unarmed peasants appeared before the city walls!

It must have been a bizarre sight. The chronicler Anna Comnena (see the later sidebar 'Lady of letters') describes the scene as follows:

> *There was such universal eagerness and enthusiasm that every highway had some of them; along with the soldiers went an unarmed crowd, more numerous than the sand or the stars, carrying palms and crosses on their shoulders, including even women and children who had left their own countries.*

Lady of letters

One of the best sources for the events surrounding the First Crusade (including the People's Crusade) is Anna Comnena, daughter of the Byzantine emperor Alexius Comnenus. Born in 1083, she was brought up in the cultured and academic court of the emperor and educated far beyond the level of many Western kings.

Anna wrote a life of her father, known as the *Alexiad*, which provides an unrivalled account of the attitudes of the Byzantines towards the First Crusade. As the emperor's daughter she had complete access to people and documents. Although she was writing 40 years after the events took place, she gives a sharp impression of the Byzantine concerns, particularly that the Crusaders were going to just come and attack Constantinople. She also makes very clear her distaste both for Islam and for the type of Christianity practised in the Western Roman Church. The *Alexiad* is now available in modern translations and is well worth checking out for a beautiful glimpse into a moment in time nearly 1,000 years ago.

Her own life wasn't without incident. In 1118 when her father died, she made an attempt to convince him to nominate her husband (Nicephorus) and not her brother John as his heir. Alexius refused, and Anna spent some time in a convent, away from court, while her loyalty to the new regime was tested.

Falling apart

After reaching Constantinople, the People's Crusade fell into a bit of a shambles. No real leadership was in place, and the soldiers from France, Germany and Italy ran amok whenever they encountered a chance for profit.

Members of the People's Crusade crossed the Bosphorus in September 1096 and slowly made their way towards the town of Nicaea. Although the territory was notionally in the hands of the Seljuk Turks, relations with the Byzantines were good and no army came to attack them.

Instead, the Crusaders filled their time by brutally mistreating the local population – raping, pillaging and torturing their way through local communities.

Eventually the majority of them made their way to the fortress of Xerigordon and settled there, which was a big mistake. The Seljuk Sultan immediately sent an army to lay siege to the fortress. The Crusaders hadn't realised that the only accessible water was outside the fortress; within a week they were drinking their own urine and the blood of their animals.

The Turks then tricked the remaining Crusaders by telling them that those at Xerigordon had also captured Nicaea and were taking all the booty for themselves. When the Crusaders left their camp, they were almost immediately ambushed by Turks. Nearly 20,000 people were slaughtered.

Peter the Hermit wasn't with these unfortunate Crusaders. He had travelled back to Constantinople to ask Alexius for reinforcements. Before he reached the city, his People's Crusade was annihilated.

Persecuting Jews

The People's Crusade (see the preceding section) wasn't the only unofficial Crusade that set off before the official papal army left Italy. Furthermore, the first victims of a Crusade army weren't Turks or Greek Christians – they were the Jews of Europe. (See the later sidebar 'Blameless murder? The logic of extermination' for more on these soldiers's motives.) One of the main motivations was a radical preacher known as Folkmar who corrupted the preaching of Urban II and encouraged people in Central Europe to target non-Christians closer to home. The Jewish population were by far the most obvious target.

A bunch of fairly thuggish knights led by Emich, Count of Leisingen, began their own Crusade shortly after the People's Crusade. Emich was allegedly a fanatical Christian who claimed to have a cross branded on to his chest. During April and May, he and a small army of one or two thousand made their way across Germany, attacking Jewish communities as they went.

The Jewish populations of Spier, Worms, Mainz and Cologne were brutally attacked by Emich and his men. When local bishops tried to prevent the slaughter, they were attacked as well. Emich went as far as to attack the palace of the Bishop of Worms where 500 Jews were sheltering.

The chronicler Solomon bar Simson describes the slaughter.

> *This man showed no mercy to the aged, youths or maidens, or babes, or sucklings, not even the sick . . . putting all to the sword and disembowelling pregnant women.*

Similar atrocities took place elsewhere in Germany, but all these groups of thugs came a cropper when Emich and his followers arrived in Hungary. By this point, they had run out of supplies or money to buy them and began to pillage around the countryside. The king of Hungary acted quickly, and his men attacked and scattered Emich's army. Many were slaughtered, and others wandered off to join other Crusade armies. Emich himself returned home where he was mocked for his failure to reach Jerusalem. Hardly an adequate punishment for his crimes.

Blameless murder? The logic of extermination

The horrific pogrom against the Jews was only the first example of the appalling atrocities that took place during the Crusades. Emich and his relatively small band targeted the Jews of Germany because they were alien and foreign. They also viewed the Jews as the people who had killed Christ. Of course, none of this makes any sense because Jesus was Jewish too, but the Crusaders had been fired up by papal rhetoric and the promise that any sins that they committed would be forgiven.

Emich's terrible acts were entirely down to him and didn't spread but the same attitude was behind the Crusaders's willingness to murder Greek Christians, Muslims, Arabs and Turks. All these non-European Christian people were alien, and eliminating them was not considered a sin.

Although the action of various Crusaders may seem inhumane and insane, similar brutal, horrific thinking was responsible for the Holocaust during the Second World War less than 70 years ago, as well as the more recent ethnic cleansing in former Yugoslavia and ongoing atrocities in Africa.

Heading East

Unsurprisingly after the events of the People's Crusade (which I describe in the earlier section 'Participating in the People's Crusade'), the Byzantine emperor, Alexius Comnenus, was very suspicious of the official papal army when it approached Constantinople in 1097. This army arrived in its various regional groups, and all but its leaders were kept in camps outside the city walls.

Taking Alexius's oath

Alexius asked that all the Crusade leaders swear an oath of loyalty to him. In particular, this oath set out that any territory the Crusaders took from the Turks would be handed back to Byzantium. Alexius set up a system where each leader was invited to the palace to swear the oath, and then the leader and his army were ferried across the Bosphorus before the next one arrived.

If any leader refused to take the oath, Alexius cut off his supplies. The system worked well. Godfrey of Bouillon kicked up a bit of a protest, but Alexius swiftly sent his troops out to knock his followers around, and Godfrey and the other lords soon fell into line. Alexius was just as capable of using the carrot as well as the stick; some leaders were offered riches; Geoffrey of Bouillon himself received a 'mound of gold and silver'!

The only nobleman to refuse absolutely was one of the last to arrive – Bohemond, the Norman lord of Taranto. Only after he'd asked Alexius to make him commander of all the Byzantine armies in the East and was told in response that it wasn't appropriate to do so did he take the oath. Anna Comnena (see the earlier sidebar 'Lady of letters') seems to have had a bit of a love-hate relationship with Bohemond, deploring his conduct but writing almost admiringly of the powerful impression that he made. I think that she quite fancied him really, but you be the judge:

> There was a certain charm about him, but it was somewhat dimmed by the alarm that his person as a whole inspired; there was a hard savage quality to his whole aspect, due I suppose, to his great stature and his eyes; even his laugh sounded like a threat to others.

Making moves on Nicaea

Finally across the Bosphorus, the papal army began its march into Anatolia (in modern-day Turkey). Western Anatolia was under the control of a Seljuk Sultan called Kilij Arslan, but most of the population of the territory were

Christian. The Sultan himself was away, fighting a rebellious emir (provincial governor). He was forced to abandon his plans and march back west as quickly as possible.

The Crusaders first target was the city of Nicaea, where the People's Crusade had been routed. The army quickly laid siege. Brief skirmishes took place when Turks attacked Raymond of Toulouse's forces, but they were quickly driven off.

Overall, however, the siege didn't go well, because the Crusaders didn't have the necessary heavy siege equipment and the people inside the city were well supplied. In addition, the city was on a lake and the Crusaders didn't have boats to stop the Turks from rowing across it to get supplies. Six weeks later, and the Crusaders were still stuck outside Nicaea. (See the later sidebar 'A, B, Siege! A guide to siege warfare' for more on this subject.)

While the Crusaders were held up outside Nicaea, the Byzantine emperor Alexius took the initiative. A Byzantine force carried out secret negotiations with the Turkish commanders and then rowed across the lake to take the fortress.

The Crusaders were not amused and Alexius had to buy them off with gifts of gold to the leaders, but his efforts showed how serious he was about keeping hold of his territory. The papal army was forced to pack up and trudge off down the road to its first proper battle.

Tactical clashes

The knights of the Crusading army were fearsome fighters (for more on this, see Chapter 11). Heavily armoured, they were also fast and able to mount devastating charges against enemy infantry. These characteristics made them particularly successful against Western European armies who tended to fight in tight formations.

Unfortunately for the knights, the Seljuk Turks didn't often fight in this manner. Simply put, the Turks's tactics were the precise opposite of the Crusaders. The Turks tended to be lightly armed with bows and rode small quick horses, ideal for quick attacks and counter-attacks followed by swift retreats. They wore down an enemy by continually making small-scale but devastating attacks and retreating to distance. The papal army was quite capable of charging the Turks, but the latter were unlikely to stay still long enough for the charge to take full effect.

To defeat this new adversary, the Crusaders had to change the tactics that had previously served them so well.

Achieving the first victory at Dorylaeum

The Crusaders left Nicaea in June 1097 and made their way farther down the Anatolian coast. The massive army of around 35,000 was really too big to travel together because finding supplies was difficult. At this point, they split into two sections: the Franks and men from Lorraine under the leadership of Raymond of Toulouse and the Normans and the rest with Bohemond as leader.

As both sections approached the town of Dorylaeum, Bohemond's advance party first came under attack from the Turks, and he made a huge tactical change (see the earlier sidebar 'Tactical clashes'). Instead of charging at the enemy, Bohemond drew up his forces in a defensive formation with the knights protected in its centre. Over several hours, the Turks threw everything at this defensive wall with continual assaults that gradually wore down the defenders.

Eventually, just as the line was about to break, Raymond of Toulouse and the second army approached. At this point Bohemond ordered his knights to go on the charge, and they flew at the now exhausted Turk troops, who scattered. The papal army won the day. More significantly, it was the last time that the papal army were truly challenged on its way through Anatolia.

An interesting note was made by the anonymous writer of a source called the *Gesta Francorum* (the 'Deeds of the Franks') who was an eyewitness to the battle. The writer notes that the real architects of the victory were the women of the Crusader party who continually supplied the fighters with both water and encouragement, both of which activities would have been incredibly dangerous in the heat of battle.

Establishing a new state in Edessa

Dorylaeum was a great victory, but the tensions between the Crusade leaders continued. Also, conditions deteriorated as they travelled farther east. The heat was appalling and even worse for men wearing chainmail and heavy armour. The atmosphere further declined as arguments erupted over how to make the journey down to the Levantine coast.

As Figure 12-1 shows, several Crusaders were tempted into going out of their way into Armenia. Local guides had told them that the Christian city of Edessa would welcome support against the Seljuk Turks. Edessa was the biggest and wealthiest city in the region and a very important trading centre on the Euphrates river.

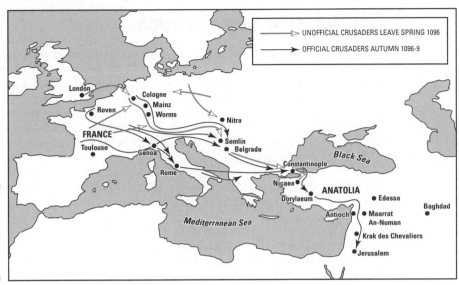

Figure 12-1:
The route
of the First
Crusade
1096–1099.

Baldwin of Boulogne was the leader who made the move, arriving in Edessa in October 1097. A man called Thoros ruled Edessa, and Baldwin asked that, in exchange for his help against the Turks, Thoros formally adopt him as heir. Baldwin went through a formal ceremony that involved both men getting inside one big shirt and rubbing their chests together; Baldwin then did the same with Thoros's wife. After this ceremony, he officially became their son and heir.

In a shocking move shortly afterwards, traitors killed Thoros. The chronicler Fulcher of Chartres writes of Baldwin's reaction to the news:

> *Baldwin and his people were greatly saddened at this, since they were unable to obtain mercy for the prince* [Thoros]. *Nevertheless, Baldwin received the principality by the gift of the people.*

Fortunately for Baldwin, he was able to overcome his grief and become the new ruler of Edessa, which became the first Crusader state. Baldwin married a local princess and set about ruling his new kingdom, leaving the rest of the papal army to get on with the original intention of the First Crusade – taking Jerusalem.

Laying siege on Antioch

While Baldwin was setting himself up in Edessa, the papal army hit a major obstacle – the city of Antioch (see Figure 12-1) the modern-day Turkish town of Antakya. Antioch was the biggest city on the Levantine coast (modern-day Syria) and a hugely important place for the Eastern Christian community. The vast majority of the population were Christian from various parts of the Byzantine Empire, and it is claimed that the city was the site of the first-ever Christian community, established by the disciples Barnabus, Paul and Peter in the first century AD.

In addition, for the Byzantine emperor Alexius, Antioch was second in importance only to Constantinople for the following reasons:

✔ Antioch was rich, seriously rich. The city formed the link between the trade routes to the east and the Mediterranean. All trade heading west passed through the city, and traders had to pay taxes before proceeding to the port of St Symeon.

✔ Antioch was extremely fertile and able to produce a huge amount of food from farmland within the city walls.

To land-hungry Crusaders from Western Europe, Antioch must have seemed like an absolute paradise: one that they had to take for themselves.

The impossible job

Unfortunately for the Crusaders, the city had been under the control of the Turks since 1084 and was incredibly well-defended. The walls of Antioch were 25 miles (or 40 kilometres) long and completely surrounded the city. Along the walls were almost 400 towers from which sentries were clearly able to observe the movements of any attacking army. As if this situation wasn't tough enough, the city had excellent water supplies and was full of good farmland.

Crusader Stephen of Blois wrote to his wife Adela as follows:

> *We found Antioch to be enormous beyond belief, and very strong and well fortified. More than 5,000 Turkish soldiers had flocked within the city not to mention the countless other peoples within.*

With Antioch seeming so impregnable, the only way it was likely to fall was through treachery. Given that the city was full of Christians, these individuals must have appeared as likely threats. Therefore, the Seljuk governor immediately imprisoned the Christian Patriarch and expelled all the Christian leaders.

REMEMBER

A, B, Siege! A guide to siege warfare

Laying siege to castles, fortresses and cities was a large part of medieval warfare. The process was difficult, incredibly dangerous and very time-consuming. You had essentially two options: starve the enemy into submission, or storm or break down the walls, taking your target by force.

Siege machines were essential to both options. Some of the common weapons and tactics included the following:

✔ **Battering ram:** Usually the trunk of a massive tree, this large piece of wood was repeatedly rammed against walls or gates. The downside of rams was that they were slow to move and that the men using them were very exposed to enemy arrow fire.

✔ **Catapult:** Various slightly different types of catapults existed, known as Mangonel, Trebuchet or Onager. They were all built using a counter-weight to fling projectiles at the walls of the target. Heavy objects were hurled from a large bucket or sling at the end of the arm. Catapults were also used to hurl burning objects such as oil in an attempt to start fires within the town or castle and thus force the defenders to flee.

✔ **Mining:** Attackers tried to bring walls down by digging under them and setting fires in an attempt to decompose the cement, so that they were able to knock out individual stones. Needless to say, mining was incredibly dangerous and unreliable.

✔ **Petard:** The petard was invented towards the end of the medieval period (around the end of the fifteenth century), coinciding with the first use of gun powder. A small charge was laid at the base of a wall and exploded in an attempt to bring down the structure. Effectively, it was a small bomb, rather like a modern firecracker, but more powerful and far less stable. Early attempts were not successful, and attackers tended to blow themselves up rather than the walls.

The word 'petard' is the reason for the expression 'hoist by his own petard', meaning someone who is harmed by his own plan to harm another. Petards were so unreliable that this expression was quite accurate!

✔ **Siege tower:** Used frequently during the Crusades, these tall wheeled towers were pushed up to the walls and allowed attackers to climb on to the city walls. Giant screens surrounded the towers and protected the attacking troops from arrow fire by the defenders.

✔ **Spreading disease:** Some attackers also tried biological warfare. Using catapults they flung diseased corpses (human or animal) over walls or dumped them into the water supply. The effects could be devastating.

Frustration on the Antioch front

The siege of Antioch didn't go well. The Crusaders made sporadic raids against the walls of the city but were nearly always driven back before they made any impression. In response the Turks led frequent (and successful) sorties out to harass the Crusaders.

The Crusaders had to settle down for what promised to be a long siege. This meant spending huge amounts of money on siege towers and establishing permanent watch towers around the city. For these constructions they needed a huge amount of wood and were forced to scour the surrounding countryside for timber.

The other problem was that the Crusaders were suffering much more from hunger and disease than the people inside the city. Each knight had to pay for his own food and that of his men. Supplies were short and prices extortionate. Large numbers among the armies died from starvation or diseases that struck because they were so weak. As winter dragged on into 1098, the situation became worse and worse.

Bohemond makes a deal

By June 1098, the siege had dragged on for eight months, and many of the papal army were ready to pack up and go home. Desertions were commonplace.

Just at this point, Bohemond got hold of some important news. One of the guards on a tower in the Antioch walls known as the 'Two Sisters' had a grudge against the city governor Yaghi-Siyan and was prepared to betray him.

Bohemond didn't reveal all this information to the other Crusade leaders. He told them only that he was going to launch an assault and if he was successful he would demand full control of the city. Wearily, and not expecting him to succeed, the other leaders agreed to his demands.

Bohemond's friendly guard let his men in through a window in the tower. They spread quickly and silently through the city. Within minutes the city was theirs and an appallingly savage rampage followed. Turks were hunted down and eliminated, and thousands were raped and killed, including many Christians.

Counter-attack – and a miraculous lance!

Only days after entering the city, the papal army found itself under siege from a Turk general called Kerbogah, who came from the west with a huge relief army. After months of siege, the papal army was in a terrible state – ill, exhausted and unable to find any food in Antioch, still starving. The population inside the city had eaten their way through supplies and much more was lost in the rampage that followed its fall to the Crusader army.

Assistance came, however, in an unexpected way. Within Antioch's walls, the Crusaders found a small length of iron buried underneath the Cathedral. The Bishop of Le Puy proclaimed the artefact to be a piece of the Holy Lance, the spear that pierced the side of Jesus when he was on the cross; he announced that it would help lead the army to victory against Kerbogah.

The Crusaders certainly needed the help. The army was on its knees, but on 28 June it left the city to face the Turks. The few hundred mounted knights shambled out across the plain when suddenly a miracle occurred: the Turks broke up and fled.

According to the Bishop of Le Puy, the Turks's retreat was due to the Holy Lance. Witnesses claimed to have seen an army of white robed horsemen charging down from the hills led by St George!

The truth is a little easier to believe: Kerbogah had been betrayed by his generals, who had hatched a political plot against him. They intended to 'throw' the battle to damage his reputation and get him executed by the Seljuk Sultan. Whatever the reason, however, Antioch now belonged to the papal army, and the Crusaders now had a hugely important staging post on their way to Jerusalem.

Capturing Jerusalem

After the unlikely success at Antioch, the papal army was set to march farther south towards its ultimate goal of Jerusalem and establishing a new Kingdom of Jerusalem.

Negotiating with the Egyptians

Before the Crusaders even left Antioch, a big part of what they needed to do had already taken place. During the spring of 1098, the camp outside Antioch had been visited by ambassadors from the Fatamid vizier of Egypt. The Fatamid Caliphate had previously been the controllers of the whole of Palestine (see Figure 12-1), including Jerusalem, and had lost the area to the Seljuk Turks in 1070.

While the Crusaders had been making their slow progress from Constantinople to Antioch, the Egyptians had attacked the Turks in Palestine and were at the point of recapturing it. The vizier wanted to stop the Crusaders from coming any farther south and so was prepared to offer Christian pilgrims free passage in the Holy City but not control of it.

The Egyptian offer must have been attractive to the exhausted army outside Antioch, but three months later, after taking the city and enjoying victory over Kerbogah, the world looked very different. The 'miracle' of the Holy Lance was still fresh in the Crusaders' minds, and they now considered themselves unbeatable. Although the Egyptians weren't the Turks, they still weren't Christian. To leave the Holy City in their hands would leave the job half done. They rejected the vizier's offer and began planning their next move.

Stumbling onward

The leaders of the Crusade were unable to decide what to do next:

- ✔ Hugh of France had had enough. He considered Jerusalem saved and sailed back to France with his men.

- ✔ Bohemond and the others were still arguing about who controlled Antioch and were held up for several weeks while they resolved the dispute. Bohemond won and, to the huge annoyance of the Byzantine emperor Alexius, began to refer to himself as the prince of Antioch.

In the end, the less prestigious nobles took to the road to Jerusalem first. Poor and hungry, they lived off the land and raided the local area for food. They were particularly savage and became known as 'Tarfurs', from the Arabic word meaning 'without money'. By this time the army of 35,000 had shrunk to nearer 14,000 with fewer than 1,500 knights.

On the road south, they were forced into a shocking act – cannibalism. The chronicler Guibert of Nogent describes the unpleasant tale:

> When at Ma'arra – and wherever else scraps of flesh from the pagans' bodies were discovered; when starvation forced our soldiers into the deed of cannibalism . . . the Tarfurs, in order to impress the enemy, roasted the bruised body of a Turk over a fire, as if it were meat for eating, in full view of the Turkish forces.

The remaining papal army took six months to make its way the relatively short distance from Antioch to Jerusalem. The slowness was partly due to various unnecessary fights against the remaining Turks, an extended stay in the port of Tripoli (where the Crusaders were royally entertained by the local emir) and another long siege at a place called Arqa.

Retaking the city

On 7 June 1099, the papal army finally arrived at the outskirts of Jerusalem – more than two years after first setting out. A first attack on the city failed, and the papal army settled down for what seemed like yet another lengthy siege.

A piece of good fortune occurred, however, during preparations for the siege: Tancred de Hauteville came across a huge amount of timber in the most unlikely of circumstances. Radulph of Caen explains:

> Tancred was suffering from severe dysentery, but did not spare himself from riding even though he could barely sit on his horse. The nuisance kept

forcing him to dismount, go away from the group and find a hiding place . . . while Tancred was relieving himself he faced a cave in the rock opposite, where found hundred timbers lay open to view.

The results of Tancred's unfortunate affliction were a huge bonus because timber was scarce and the army was now able to construct vast siege machines with which to attack the city. (See the earlier sidebar 'A, B, Siege! A guide to siege warfare'.)

By the middle of July, the Crusaders were ready for a full-scale attack. The papal army that attacked on 15 July was only 20,000 strong. More than half the original number had died or deserted at some point on the two-year journey to Jerusalem. Raymond of Toulouse led the assault and it was almost immediately successful.

What followed was a horrendous slaughter. Tancred and his men desecrated the most holy place of the Muslims, the Dome of the Rock. Others forced their way into a mosque and killed everyone inside. Another party burned down a synagogue in which the Jewish population were sheltering. The atrocities were appalling and thousands and thousands of people were slaughtered, the corpses piling up outside the city gates so high that they towered over the walls.

The Crusaders had regained Jerusalem, but at a huge cost. The incredible mission that Pope Urban II had requested had arguably been a success, but the pope himself never found out; he died two days before messengers arrived in Italy with the news.

Establishing the Kingdom of Jerusalem

After the papal army regained Jerusalem, more problems started. The big issue was what to do with the city. Pope Urban II had originally stated that a new Christian state should be founded. By slaughtering all the non-Christian people of the city, this aim had been achieved by default; the big question was who was now to be in charge.

Selecting a leader

In a surprisingly democratic move, the Crusade leaders decided to vote on who should be the new king. The first vote went to Raymond of Toulouse, but he turned the job down because he felt that it was impious to rule with a crown in the city of Christ. The rest of the knights didn't share Raymond's reticence, and so they voted again.

This time the vote went to Godfrey of Lorraine. He accepted but taking his queue from Raymond, he refused to call himself king and took the title of 'Defender of the Holy Sepulchre (tomb of Christ)'. With Jerusalem in the bag, three Western European nobles now ruled three Eastern states: Baldwin in Edessa, Bohemond in Antioch and Godfrey in Jerusalem.

Of course, plenty of other Eastern cities and ports were available for capturing. Within a few months, a man called Daimbert arrived. He had been the archbishop of Pisa and was sent by the pope to be the new Patriarch of Jerusalem. One of his first acts was to make Tancred 'Prince of Galilee'. This new title gave Tancred the right to look for his own lands, and he soon attacked the port of Haifa.

With so much territory under Western control, the Holy Land and territories to the north were soon referred to as *Outremer*, or the kingdom across the sea. In many ways Outremer was just like Lorraine or Aquitaine, a collection of individual principalities that were more or less loyal to an overall lord (Godfrey in this case) with the pope as religious leader.

Over the next two centuries Outremer developed into a quite extraordinary place where Western Europeans lived side by side with, and even married, their non-Christian counterparts (flip to Chapter 14 for more details).

Taking charge: Baldwin 1

As events turned out, Godfrey of Lorraine didn't defend the Holy Sepulchre for very long. Within a year of being chosen, he was dead and a new leader was required. Godfrey's brother was Baldwin of Edessa and he naturally assumed that the job was his for the taking. Daimbert, however, wasn't keen and asked Bohemond to stop him, but unfortunately for Bohemond he got himself captured by the Turks. Therefore, nothing could stop Baldwin from marching from Edessa to Jerusalem.

On Christmas Day 1100, Baldwin was crowned King of Jerusalem, becoming one of the most powerful men in the world in the process. His reign, however, didn't last, Jerusalem fell once more and within 50 years, a call for a fresh Crusade arose (check out Chapter 14 for the full story).

Chapter 13

Struggling for Power: Popes Versus Monarchs

In This Chapter

▶ Pursuing papal reform

▶ Going toe-to-toe with Henry IV and Gregory VII

▶ Nabbing Normandy with Henry I

▶ Halting the investiture crisis with Henry V

The end of the eleventh century was a time of great upheaval throughout Western Europe, and in this chapter I take a look at the important issues and arguments that took place. In addition to the First Crusade (which I cover in detail in Chapter 12), the largest disagreements featured two rulers named Henry and tough questions about whether God had empowered popes or monarchs to make important decisions.

Of course, whenever you combine the nature of God and the use of political power, the results are potentially controversial – and this period was no exception. The intense disagreements and efforts to resolve matters resonated deeply throughout Europe for the rest of the medieval era.

Getting Busy with Pope Gregory VII

Outside of the leaders and personalities involved in the First Crusade, the eleventh century in Medieval Europe was dominated by Pope Gregory VII.

Gregory VII was born around 1020 in Tuscany, Italy, and (unfortunately for him) named Hildebrand. From humble origins (his father was a blacksmith), the young Hildebrand moved to Rome to study and rose quickly through the ranks at the Vatican to become a leading cardinal.

One of the most influential and high-profile medieval popes, Gregory was a prime mover behind the two big issues of the era: papal reform and the investiture controversy.

Taking a broader view of the Church's role: Papal reform

The young Hildebrand developed a definite (and different) view of the place of the Church in the Medieval World. To his mind the Church was absolutely central to everything in existence. God founded the Church, and so by extension it was responsible for all sections of society and had supreme authority over all human structures. The pope was God's regent and the ultimate decision maker on any matter. Whilst most popes would have agreed with this view, few lived in the ideal in the way that Hildebrand eventually did.

Hildebrand's beliefs obviously put him at odds with kings and rulers of his time and served as the main issue behind the subsequent *investiture controversy* (see the following section 'Putting people in power: The investiture question'). However, Hildebrand also recognised that the pope had to work with rulers in order to reach the people in their territories – although he never considered them to be on an equal footing with the pope.

Given his high standards, Hildebrand believed that the medieval Church of his day wasn't really up to scratch. In particular, he wanted to eliminate two significant, ongoing Church practices:

- **Clerical marriage:** Unlike the Greek Eastern Church in the East (flip to Chapter 9 for more), the Roman Catholic Church wasn't in favour of priests marrying. Despite this stance, huge numbers of priests in Western Europe were married or living with women and having illegitimate children.

- **Simony:** The practice of *simony*, selling religious offices for profit, was widespread throughout Europe as rich men effectively bought parishes and bishoprics for their younger sons who would not inherit the family estates. Simony also involved religious officials taking money or fees for hearing confession or praying for the souls of the dead.

Creating and stating new rules

In April 1073 Pope Alexander II died. Hildebrand was chosen as his successor with huge popular support, and yet his election was controversial. People later criticised the fact that he'd been elected by a small group of cardinals with a baying mob of popular supporters outside. Nonetheless, Hildebrand took the name Pope Gregory VII and quickly went about making big changes that pitted him against some of the most powerful people in Europe.

Gregory's first acts were attempts to reconcile the papacy with the Norman adventurers who had taken control of Southern Italy (turn to Chapter 10 for much more on these Normans). His efforts didn't work, and so Gregory excommunicated the Norman leader Robert Guiscard. He clearly wasn't in the mood to mess around.

In 1075 Gregory really made his mark when he published a list of 27 rules known as the *Dictatus Papae*. This hugely controversial document caused uproar throughout Europe. In it Gregory set out the beliefs that he had formed as a young man, principally that the Roman Church was founded by God and the power of the pope was the sole universal power.

The first three rules alone were enough to cause massive controversy:

- ✔ The Roman Church was founded by God alone.
- ✔ The Roman pontiff (the pope) alone can with right be called universal.
- ✔ The pope alone can appoint, depose or reinstate bishops.

In February 1075 the rules were confirmed by Gregory, crucially including the last rule above that the pope alone was able to appoint (known as investiture), depose or reinstate bishops.

Putting people in power: The investiture question

The *Dictatus Papae* challenged the principle of *investiture*, the process of putting people in positions of power in the Catholic Church. Previously in Medieval Europe, the thinking was that God appointed kings, and kings in turn were responsible for appointing their own churchmen within their kingdom. Gregory took a different view.

The power to appoint Church leaders was extremely important because the clergy, and in particular bishops, had responsibilities beyond their religious activities. Bishops were also important statesmen involved in their local economies and played key roles in educating the local people and administering justice. Consequently, rulers wanted to be able to fill these roles with their own choices. A king's ability to select bishops was also a useful way to dispense *patronage* (in other words, favours to people to make them loyal) to nobles and supporters whose sons were then rewarded with religious offices.

This practice clashed with everything that Gregory VII believed. To him the pope was the absolute authority, closer to God than any secular monarch. Clearly a clash was going to come and it ended up being with the greatest of all medieval monarchs – the Holy Roman Emperor.

Henry IV fights back

The emperor in 1075 was Henry IV. He was only 25 years old and had experienced a difficult early reign during which his mother, the empress Agnes, served as his regent until he reached the age of 15 and officially came of age. During this period he was kidnapped by treacherous German nobles, and even by 1075 he wasn't totally secure in power.

The *Dictatus Papae* was a real threat to a ruler with an unsteady grip on power. The rules cut off an important mechanism for Henry to secure territory and place men he trusted in positions of influence. Henry wasn't going to take Gregory's proclamations lying down.

Henry's first protest to the pope came in the form of one of the most fascinating surviving letters from the medieval period. In it Henry makes all sorts of claims against Gregory VII and winds up calling for the election of a new pope. Incendiary stuff to say the least and an amazing record for us to still have now!

The following two excerpts, from the beginning and end, give a fair picture of the letter's general tone:

> *Henry, king not through usurpation but through the holy ordination of God, to Hildebrand, at present not pope but false monk . . .*

> *. . . Thou, therefore, damned by this curse and by the judgement of all our bishops and by our own, descend and relinquish the apostolic chair which thou has usurped. Let another ascend the throne of St Peter, who shall not practise violence under the cloak of religion, but shall teach the sound doctrine of St Peter. I Henry, king by the grace of God, do say unto thee, together with all our bishops: descend, descend, to be damned throughout the ages.*

Henry then went one better. Specifically flying in the face of the *Dictatus Papae*, he appointed his own man as Bishop of Milan, despite the fact that Gregory had already announced his preference.

The pope's weapon of mass deposition

Unfortunately, Henry bit off more than he could chew. The normal papal response would have been to excommunicate him, but Gregory had a far more powerful weapon at his disposal.

Outrage!

The historian Anna Comnena (see Chapter 12) gives a remarkable account of quite how savage the argument between Gregory and Henry had become. Henry delivered his reply to the Pope by sending his envoys to the papal court. Anna describes in detail the way that Gregory treated them:

> *To begin with he outraged them savagely, then cut their hair and beards, the one with scissors, the other with a razor, and finally*

he did something else to them which was quite improper, going beyond the insolent behaviour one expects from barbarians, and sent them away. I would have given a name to the outrage, but as a woman and a princess modesty forbade me.

Strong stuff indeed, although Anna was fairly anti-Gregory to start with, describing him elsewhere as the *'abominable pope'*!

Rule number 12 of the *Dictatus Papae* gave the pope the right to depose emperors. As well as treating Henry's messengers poorly (see the sidebar 'Outrage!'), Gregory sent back a stinker of a letter not only excommunicating Henry, but also deposing him as Holy Roman Emperor. Normally a pope wouldn't be able to back up this sort of threat. After all, the fact that the pope didn't have an army was the whole reason behind establishing the title of Holy Roman Emperor in the first place (see Chapter 5 for more details).

On this occasion, however, Gregory was in a powerful position. He had other people to fight his wars for him. The German nobles who had been trying to overthrow Henry for years now had the perfect excuse to do so. Henry was an illegal ruler, even the pope said so! Within weeks of Gregory's order of deposition, Henry was fighting off rebellion throughout his empire.

A barefoot apology at Canossa

Henry was unable to fight the fierce Germans and was forced into a humiliating climb-down. In 1077 he travelled to Italy to meet with Gregory at Canossa and beg forgiveness. Like any other person wanting forgiveness, the pope ordered Henry to do penance, specifically standing barefoot in the snow while wearing a hair shirt. As a result of this display, Gregory lifted both the deposition and excommunication.

Henry IV was legal again, but his status didn't really help his problems back in Germany. Rudolf of Rheinfelden had declared himself the king of Germany and had the support of papal officials who were visiting Germany. Rudolf continued to do so despite events at Canossa and the civil war in Germany carried on for several more years.

Not the marrying kind

Although Gregory VII is most famous for his arguments with Henry IV, he was also responsible for a number of other reforms, including the following:

✔ Although Gregory didn't ban priests from marrying, he did issue an edict that released people from obedience to any bishop that allowed priests in his bishopric to marry. This action probably didn't stop priests from carrying on as normal, but it did put the onus on bishops to put their house in order.

✔ Gregory followed up this edict with an order that allowed bishops to deprive clerics who married of their revenues.

His real concern was that the clergy should be completely celibate, whereas previous popes had considered that marriage was preferable to unmarried relationships. Neither policy proved hugely successful, but Gregory did raise the issue of clerical marriage, an issue that never went away again.

Excommunication – again and again!

Later in 1080, Gregory excommunicated and deposed Henry for a second time!

After Canossa, Gregory had sensibly kept out of the civil war in Germany, refusing to take sides. In early 1080, however, Rudolf appeared to be getting the upper hand. Gregory made his choice and declared Rudolf the true king, again deposing and excommunicating Henry IV.

Bad move. Within six months Rudolf was dead. In any case this second deposition wasn't well received by German nobles or by some clerics and officials at the Vatican. No real grounds existed for it and Gregory's enemies saw the act as a cynical and vengeful thing to do.

In addition, the second excommunication didn't affect Henry too much. He summoned a council of clerics at the German town of Brixen and they decided that the deposition was ridiculous and unfair. They excommunicated Gregory in turn, and nominated a man called Guibert of Ravenna to be Gregory's successor as pope.

Gregory on the run

Henry IV took things even further in 1082 by marching on Italy. As Henry advanced south, Gregory fled and went into exile at Sant Angelo from where he issued more excommunications, this time targeting both Henry and his newly appointed pope, Guibert. Henry ignored Gregory's actions and marched into the city of Rome. In the face of Henry's army, most of Gregory's supporters deserted him and appointed Guibert as the new pope (Clement III) on 24 March 1084.

Clement's appointment was the end for Gregory VII. Gregory was forced to turn to Robert Guiscard – who he'd previously excommunicated – for help! Although Guiscard's army moved north and managed to force Henry IV back to Germany, Gregory was completely without support in Rome and never returned to the city.

Instead, Gregory spent his last days in a palace by the sea in the town of Salerno under the protection of his new Norman allies. He still considered himself pope, but nobody else did. He died the following year in 1085. Apparently, the day before he died he renounced all excommunications that he had made except for two: his successor Guibert and his mortal enemy Henry IV.

Although Gregory died a failure, the issue that he brought to life – investiture – rumbled on for decades without complete resolution.

Expanding the Kingdom: Henry 1 of England

The Holy Roman Emperor Henry IV wasn't the only person called Henry who caused a stir during the late eleventh century (see the earlier section 'Getting Busy with Pope Gregory VII'). Henry I, the Norman king of England, was also on the scene. Henry I's reign is notable for the amount of political skulduggery in which he was involved, and at which he proved very successful.

Going from fourth to first

Henry was the youngest son of William the Conqueror (check out Chapter 10 for all about William). Henry was born in 1068, two years after his father had won the Battle of Hastings and set about the conquest of England. As the youngest of four sons, Henry was the least likely to inherit the crown and was destined for a career in the Church and expected to become a bishop. Consequently he was the best educated of the boys and was given the name 'Beauclerc', meaning 'fine scholar'. As it turned out all that learning was lost to the Church.

Bullying baby brother

In 1081, however, Richard, the second oldest of the brothers, was killed in a hunting accident. William the Conqueror made a very clear statement of what should happen by making the following succession plans among his three surviving sons:

Making the most of marriage: Choosing a wife

Shortly after grabbing the throne, Henry made a very clever marriage move. He married Edith, the daughter of King Malcolm III of Scotland. This arrangement combined Henry's kingdom with his closest neighbour and linked him with Edith's great, great uncle, Edward the Confessor.

Edward the Confessor had originally promised England to William the Conqueror and so

Henry's new connection, along with the fact that he'd been born in England, immediately made Henry more palatable to the vast majority of the English population, who were Anglo-Saxon. The Normans weren't too keen, but Henry made Edith change her name to Matilda, his mother's name and a good Norman one.

- ✔ William Rufus was to receive England and become King William II.

- ✔ Robert was to receive the Duchy of Normandy and become Duke Robert II.

- ✔ Henry was to receive no lands at all, just the considerable sum of 5,000 pounds in silver. (Henry was very obvious in his disappointment, but to no avail.)

When William died in 1087, the succession went to plan, and Henry was out in the cold. His brothers obviously saw Henry as a threat, because they formed something called the *Accession Treaty*, which stated that should William II or Robert II die their lands went to the other and not Henry.

Seizing the throne of England

In August 1100, like his brother, William II was killed in an accident while hunting in the New Forest. (Hunting was clearly a dangerous pastime in Norman England!) Adding to the drama of the situation was the fact that Duke Robert II still hadn't returned from the First Crusade (which I describe in Chapter 12), and so nobody was around to enforce the Accession Treaty.

Henry seized his chance. On the premise of burying his brother's body at Winchester Cathedral, Henry seized the royal treasury that was located there. With nobody to stop him, he forced the leading barons to support him and was crowned as the new king of England, Henry I.

Laying down the law and nabbing Normandy

A few months later, Henry's brother Robert II of Normandy returned from the First Crusade. Robert refused to accept Henry as king and almost immediately led an invasion of England designed to unseat him. The invasion didn't go well, and again Henry used diplomacy to his advantage and forced Robert to sign the Treaty of Alton. This treaty forced Robert to recognise Henry as king and in return Robert was paid 2,000 silver marks. Robert hadn't done as well out of the Crusade as he'd hoped and needed the money, and so he was forced to accept.

The Treaty of Alton was good business but expensive. It needed to be renewed annually, which meant continually paying out another 2,000 silver marks to Robert. By 1105 Henry was tired of the drain on his revenues and decided to invade Normandy.

The two armies first encountered each other outside a small village called Tinchebray. A messy, running battle followed that dragged on for several hours spread out over a large site. Eventually Robert's army was forced to fall back and Robert himself was captured by Henry's men.

Nearly 20 years after he had been comprehensively cut out of things when his father died, Henry had reunited England and Normandy. He returned across the channel and had his brother imprisoned in the Tower of London.

Horrible Henry?

Henry is famous for being a clever politician, but many stories suggest that he could be brutally unpleasant if required. For example, after Robert had been imprisoned for a while in the Tower of London, he was moved to Cardiff and kept under house arrest. Stories suggest that when he tried to escape and was recaptured, Henry had his eyes put out so that he was unable to do it again.

Another story tells that Henry personally threw a disloyal town councillor called Conan Pilatus from the top of the tower of Rouen. Even more disturbing is a tale that suggests that Henry allowed his two granddaughters to be tortured and mutilated in a disagreement between two of his barons.

Although historians can't ascertain whether these stories are true, they do fit with the callous way in which Henry treated his own brothers. Some people even accuse Henry of being behind William II's 'hunting accident' in 1100. He was part of the hunting party that day, so you probably wouldn't bet against it!

Presenting the Charter of Liberties

Many of Henry I's acts as king impacted upon the international stage, but the one that most affected England was the *Charter of Liberties*. This amazing document, announced soon after Henry's coronation in 1100, was one of his smoothest political moves.

The nobility had criticised Henry's predecessor, William II, over how he treated them and the Church. By marrying Edith of Scotland, Henry made himself more popular with the Anglo-Saxon population of England, which squared him with the Church and the Norman nobility.

Immediately on taking power, Henry produced a document that appeared to put limits on what he was able to do as king. Instead, it was really a public relations exercise to suggest that Henry would return to the ways of his father, William the Conqueror. The document was never really enforced, but it created the right impression and featured the following points:

- Limiting the ways that the king was able to take taxes from his barons.
- Preventing the king from taking tax on top of military service.
- Promising to cancel all debts that were owed to William II.
- Discontinuing the practice of the nobility being forced to pay fines when they committed a crime.

- Granting the right to a trial to nobles accused of crimes. This promise was a relief for the nobles who had been continually ripped off by William with fines for crimes that they probably hadn't committed.

The most important aspect of the charter was that it suggested that the king was in some ways accountable to his barons, which was a first. In fact it was never really followed closely but the Charter of Liberties paved the way for the biggest charter of all, the Magna Carta, signed by King John in 1215 (see Chapter 17 for more details).

Dabbling in investiture

An interesting aspect of Henry's reign was that he was drawn into his own arguments around investiture (see the earlier section 'Putting people in power: The investiture question').

Between 1103 and 1107, Henry fell into a big argument over making appointments within the Church with Pope Paschal II and his own Archbishop of

Canterbury, Anselm. In the end a compromise was reached and written up in the Concordat of London in 1107. Henry gave up the right to appoint bishops, agreeing that it was the sole preserve of the papacy, but insisted that bishops still had to pay homage to him in secular matters. This compromise was a subtle solution to an argument that had been raging for more than 50 years and that was about to kick off again in mainland Europe (see the next section 'Dealing with Unfinished Business: Henry V').

Dealing with Unfinished Business: Henry V

The Holy Roman Emperor Henry IV died in 1104. He had never truly regained control of his empire after the civil war that followed his first excommunication (discussed in the earlier section 'Henry IV fights back'); when he died, a fresh civil war was in progress.

In the year of his death he had been fighting against a rebellion led by his son, Henry, who he had made king of Germany in 1099 and who would go on to succeed him as emperor, as Henry V. Eventually Henry IV's enemies persuaded the young Henry to act as a figurehead for a fresh attack, and this attack was the one that finished off Henry IV.

At the age of just 18, Henry V was a young king and immediately faced the same problems as his father: subduing the rebellious elements among the German aristocracy and getting himself recognised as Holy Roman Emperor. He spent the first few years of his reign 'cleaning up' and successfully defeating Robert II of Flanders, who had attacked his lands in the northwest.

Henry V had high hopes of securing the support of the pope. The current incumbent Paschal II supported Henry's rebellion, and in turn Henry V supported Paschal against his (Henry's) father. However, none of this mattered in regards to the old argument of who had the right to appoint bishops (investiture).

Henry V was in exactly the same position as his father had been: he needed to nominate his own bishops. Henry V carried on doing so in the early years of his reign, which brought him directly into conflict with Pope Paschal II.

Gaining Paschal's agreement

In 1107 Paschal II reaffirmed his policy on investiture at the council of Troyes in France. Both the king of France and Henry I of England backed down (see 'Putting people in power: The investiture question' earlier in this chapter). Only Henry V refused to do so. The situation was a stalemate: Paschal and Henry V were unlikely to change their minds. The problem was that Henry hadn't yet been crowned as Holy Roman Emperor and sooner or later he expected to be.

Henry continued to correspond with Paschal about his coronation, but the response was always negative. In 1110 Paschal went further and renewed his position on investiture. Henry decided to adopt his father's solution to problems with a pope and invaded Italy with his army in 1111.

Paschal II was in no position to resist him as he completely lacked military support. Henry didn't need to promise to give up his investiture rights in return for being crowned emperor and also for the pope to confirm that the empire in question was the whole of Christendom, meaning that Henry V was then superior to every other monarch throughout Europe, Byzantium and the new crusader states in the Middle East! It helped that Henry had kidnapped and kept him prisoner for 61 days until he eventually gave in and acceded to Henry's demands. Henry was thus crowned emperor in April 1111, keeping his right to investiture in the process.

Reaching resolution with the Concordat of Worms

Henry V received a great deal out of Paschal II in 1111, but the situation was never likely to last.

In 1116 Pope Paschal officially removed his support for investiture by secular rulers. This action was followed up by the Archbishop of Milan calling for Henry to be excommunicated. In an almost exact replay of his father's career, Henry V took his army back across the Alps and into Italy. Just like Gregory VII, Paschal was forced to flee but not before publishing Henry's excommunication. A chaotic situation followed with Henry proposing an anti-pope, Paschal dying and an official new pope (Gelasius II) being appointed before dying himself only 18 months later!

The situation was finally resolved in 1122. The newly appointed Pope Callistus II sent his envoys to meet Henry in the German town of Worms. At the meeting, Henry V renounced his rights to investiture. Instead, the clergy themselves would now elect bishops, much as they elected the pope. The emperor was to oversee the process but was unable to interfere. Finally the question of investiture seemed to be resolved in a manner that satisfied both Church and state.

Comparing the Ends of Two Henrys

The activities of Henry I in England (check out the earlier section 'Expanding the Kingdom: Henry I of England') and Henry V in Germany dominated the first quarter of the twelfth century.

The end of the reigns of Henry I and Henry V was very much the end of an era:

- **The reign of Henry V ended in 1125.** His last act was to lead a campaign against Louis VI of France. He died a short time afterwards in the town of Utrecht. His marriage to Matilda was childless and he had no male heirs to inherit the kingdom of Germany or to make a bid for the title of emperor. The Salian dynasty – Frankish kings and emperors since 1024 – officially came to an end.

- **The reign of Henry I ended in 1135 (under rather fishy circumstances).** Matilda and her husband (Geoffrey) produced the heirs that Henry I desired, but while visiting them he ate too many lampreys – a fish of which he was particularly fond – and died a few days later (aged 67, a good age for the time). The fact that Henry I died without a son as an immediate heir to the throne is something of a surprise. Although he was married twice, he was never short of female company and holds the record for the greatest number of acknowledged illegitimate children by an English king – 25!

Making the most of marriage: Dynastic match ups

By 1125, Henry I was getting very good at making political gains out of marriages. He had already persuaded the nobility of England to accept Matilda as his heir and when Henry V died that year, she became the most sought-after widow in Europe. Matilda and Henry V's marriage hadn't produced any children and therefore whoever married her now had a chance of creating the next generation of heirs to the English throne.

Her father made a political choice based on the continuing problems between Normandy and Anjou. Henry I chose to marry Matilda to Geoffrey, the count of Anjou. Again Henry I's political judgement was spot on because Geoffrey and Matilda's marriage went on to produce the *Plantagenet dynasty*. (Geoffrey referred to himself as 'Plantagenet', the name of the flower that was his emblem.) It didn't immediately work out as Henry had planned, though, as England was plunged into anarchy when Henry died in 1135. Eventually, however, the issue was resolved and members of the Plantagenet dynasty would go on to rule England all the way up until 1485.

Both England and Germany fell into anarchy after their leaders's deaths, which was particularly disappointing after Henry I's extensive dynastic planning. The nobility of England and Normandy had sworn allegiance to Matilda to honour her as the new Queen of England. Unfortunately things didn't quite work out like that. The Norman aristocracy considered Geoffrey of Anjou an enemy and refused to acknowledge his wife as their new monarch. All Henry's careful political plotting came to nothing.

Instead a man called Stephen claimed the English throne. Stephen was the nephew of Henry I, the son of sister Adela. What followed was a period known as 'The Anarchy', a lengthy struggle between Matilda and Stephen for the right to rule England, which rumbled on for over 25 years and wasn't truly settled until 1153.

Stephen's reign as king didn't go terribly well. In fact, things went so badly that you can read all about him in Chapter 25, which describes ten rubbish kings!

Chapter 14

Waging the Second Crusade and Crusading at Home

*T*he First Crusade (which I describe in Chapter 12) was a success. The papal army retook the Holy City of Jerusalem as well as a fair amount of other territory along the path to their destination. New European kingdoms and principalities were established, and a whole generation of Franks and other European people were born thousands of miles from their ancestral homes.

Of course, all this activity was happening during the volatile Middle Ages, and so it wasn't going to last long. Within 50 years of the capture of Jerusalem in 1099, the Pope called for a second Crusade, and this time Europe's big hitters were involved.

Maintaining Semi-Order in Outremer

After the First Crusade recaptured Jerusalem, Baldwin of Boulogne (previously the ruler of Edessa) was appointed king to rule over it (check out Chapter 12 for all about Baldwin). In addition to the Holy City, European armies had also taken control of other large cities and ports such as Edessa, Antioch, Tripoli and Acre (see the map in Figure 14-1). This loose federation of cities very much resembled those of Medieval Europe politically, with a king as overlord to a number of nobles who ruled under his authority. Europeans called this entire region of Crusader states *Outremer*, the land beyond the sea.

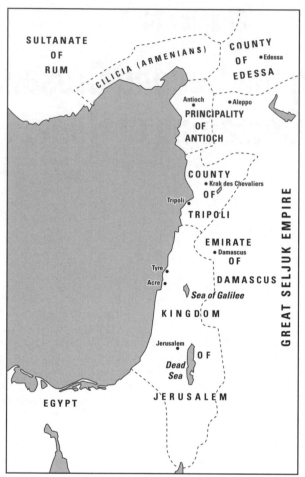

Figure 14-1:
The
Crusader
states
around the
year 1140.

The Muslim leaders of the near-east took the invasion of their territories rather lightly. They had no clear or coordinated way to respond to the occupations, and for the ultimate leader, the Seljuk Sultan based in Baghdad (in modern-day Iraq), affairs in Outremer were very much on the periphery of his empire and of little concern.

Securing Jerusalem and the other cities, however, was only half of the job for the Crusaders. Keeping hold of the region proved much more difficult. On a local level, Muslim people were prepared to take matters in to their own hands, as I discuss in the next section.

Responding to Holy War

The early years of Outremer were successful. In 1109 a Frankish army captured the important port of Tripoli after a near five-year siege and followed up with the sacking of Beruit in 1110. Homeless people fled from these areas to the remaining Arab strongholds of Aleppo and Damascus, the populations of these cities swelling by thousands as a result.

Whereas the Muslim leaders chose to placate the Franks by signing peace treaties, others who weren't leaders turned to extreme action. A man from Aleppo called Abu al Fadil ibn al Kashshab was the first. Appalled by appeasement, he complained to Ridwan, the Seljuk ruler of Aleppo. His complaints were ignored, and so al Fadil took direct action. Gathering together a group of Sufis (a mystical Muslim sect) in February 1111, he set off to Baghdad to persuade the Sultan to act, setting off a full-scale riot during which the holiest places in the Sultan's own mosque were destroyed.

The uprising worked. The Sultan's attention was finally drawn to the problems in Aleppo and Damascus. He announced 'Holy War against the infidel enemies of God' and invoked *jihad*, the Islamic term meaning 'struggle in the cause of the prophet'. Just as Pope Urban had called for a Holy War to retake Jerusalem, the Sultan now called for Jihad to take it back.

All the Frankish successes in Outremer were suddenly thrown into a new light. The Crusader states now looked very small and vulnerable in comparison to the vastness of the Seljuk Empire and the hordes that their Sultan commanded. The Crusaders did manage to resist the first attempt at jihad, however, which had been led by a man called Mawdud (who was assassinated before he was able to attack the Franks). Nevertheless, the possibility of jihad showed the true weakness of the Crusaders' position.

In 1118 King Baldwin died. His cousin, Baldwin of Edessa, replaced him as Baldwin II. Although the Franks continued to hold power, the vast majority of people living in Outremer were not European Christians. Constant appeals were made by the Frankish leaders in Outremer for more Europeans to settle in the new land but, despite the riches on offer, the response was slow. Many pilgrims visited Jerusalem, but few stayed. Those who did stay were shocked by the way Christians and Muslims had integrated and brought with them Western European values and ideas, which only increased tensions between groups.

Life in Outremer was a tinderbox. The only surprise was that things didn't begin to fall apart until 1144.

The Knights Templar

One of the major developments following the foundation of Outremer was an increase in pilgrimages to Jerusalem. With European-occupied cities now lining the route to the Christian Holy Land, huge numbers of people began making pilgrimages on an annual basis. But the journey was still hazardous. Although many cities were friendly to pilgrims, the lands between the cities were full of bandits, in particular the route between the port of Jaffa and the Holy City.

In 1119 two French knights, Hugues de Payens and Godfrey de Saint-Omer, came up with the idea of founding an order of armed monks to protect pilgrims. They gained the permission of King Baldwin II and established themselves on the Temple Mount of Jerusalem in what had been the Al Aqsa Mosque, reputedly the site of the original temple of Solomon. From this location, they took their name, the Knights of the Temple.

Within a century the order had become one of the most powerful forces in the Medieval World. Shrewd business dealings made them extraordinarily rich, and they extended their military activities into Eastern Europe. Their numbers grew larger and larger. Loyal only to the order and their Grandmaster, they were effectively a state within a state and became feared by European monarchs. In 1305 Pope Clement V ordered their dissolution and over the next few years a bloody persecution was the result (Chapter 16 contains more on the Knights Templar).

Due to their secrecy and air of mystique, the Templar order still fascinates writers and conspiracy theorists today. You can visit their old headquarters, Temple Church in London, and read all about them in *The Templar Code For Dummies* by Christopher L. Hodapp and Alice Von Kannon (Wiley, 2007).

Stepping up jihad in Edessa

All the cause of jihad really needed was an effective leader, and in 1126 Imad ed-Din Zengi stepped on to the scene. Originally the military leader who put down a revolt against the Sultan in Baghdad, Zengi was made emir (provincial governor) of Aleppo and Mosul in 1128 and began to covet Damascus to gain complete control of the region.

At the time, Damascus was friendly with the Crusader states and so Zengi set about trying to undermine their relationship, which wasn't too hard. The Frankish leaders had a habit of falling out with each other anyway, and rarely needed the help of anybody else! Zengi wanted to isolate Damascus so that the city would either need him to come to its aid or be unable to resist his military advances. He never did manage to take advantage of the situation, and in the end his first target was much further north – the city of Edessa.

In 1144 Joscelin, the European ruler of Edessa, had a major argument with his immediate overlord Raymond of Antioch. Edessa lost the military support of Antioch and became a particularly tasty target for Zengi.

Crusading queen – Melisinde of Jerusalem

One of the most influential figures in Outremer during this period was Queen Melisinde of Jerusalem, who lived around 1105 to 1161. Melisinde was the eldest daughter of Baldwin II of Jerusalem and his wife, an Armenian princess called Morphia. Throughout the first half of the twelfth century Melisinde was probably the most influential political figure in the kingdom of Outremer, actively ruling as Queen of Jerusalem for over 20 years.

Throughout this period Melisinde was consistently undermined by her extremely unpleasant husband, Fulk of Anjou, who had ascended to the throne with her as joint ruler in 1131. This joint accession hugely offended the noble class of Jerusalem, for whom Melisinde was the true royal because she had the blood of Baldwin's family. The husband and wife grew hugely estranged and things reached a boiling point in 1134 when Fulk accused his wife of adultery with Hugh II, the Count of Jaffa. Fulk had bitten off more than he could chew and the nobility of Outremer, including the Patriarch of Jerusalem, sided with Melisinde. Fulk was forced to retract his accusations and return to his wife. From that point on he was utterly sidelined and Melisinde became the greatest political influence in the land.

All this time Melisinde was technically ruling for her young son Baldwin III who had not yet come of age, but hers was no regency by committee – Melisinde was the true queen. Fulk died in a hunting accident in 1143 that for once seems to have actually been a genuine accident!

In 1148 Melisinde was heavily involved in the council at Acre that decided the actions of the Second Crusade and was one of the few people to survive with her reputation unscathed from the debacle at Damascus that followed. Unsurprisingly, Melisinde wasn't keen to give up the reigns of government when Baldwin came of age and eventually she was forced into virtual civil war with him. In 1153 they were reconciled and Melisinde went into effective retirement concentrating most of her time on being a patron of the arts. She died in 1161 and the historian William of Tyre paid tribute to her as follows:

> 'She was a very wise woman, fully experienced in almost all affairs of state business, who completely triumphed over the handicap of her sex so she could take charge of important affairs.'

Whilst this account may seem patronising to us now, from a medieval writer in a society that was hugely dominated by men it was a tremendous compliment. After all, Melisinde enjoyed the longest and least-interrupted reign of any monarch in the history of Outremer. She serves as an important reminder of how some medieval women were able to rise above the restrictions of their society to truly make a mark on history.

Zengi and his forces attacked a Seljuk prince who was loyal to Joscelin. When Joscelin and his army left Edessa to support the prince, Zengi attacked the city. Although Edessa was surrounded by huge walls and towers, no army was in place to man the defences. Without any military support from Antioch, Zengi's army took the city quickly. According to the chronicler Michael the Syrian:

The Turks [Seljuk Turks] entered Edessa with staves and swords drawn, indiscriminately slaughtering the old and the young, men and women, priests, deacons, monks, nuns, infants at the breast, and those promised to each other in marriage! The Syrian boar was victorious and devoured the sweetest fruit!

For the Crusader states, the fall of Edessa increased anxiety of attack but didn't hugely change their lives – at least initially. After all, Edessa was the most far flung of the Crusader kingdoms and somewhat remote from the others (as the map in Figure 14-1 shows). Still, the situation was unstable and ripe for fears to get whipped into a frenzy.

In the Arab world, however, the fall of Edessa was hugely important, because it raised spirits and demonstrated that the Franks were beatable and cities could be retaken. Ironically, Zengi never lived to realise these dreams. He died in 1146, killed by one of his own eunuchs whom he threatened after catching him drinking from his own personal wine goblet!

Catching Crusade Fever

The First Crusade had drawn huge support from around Europe, but most of that support came from second-tier nobility without any direct involvement from the Holy Roman Emperor or any of the leading monarchs.

After the fall of Edessa, the situation changed in Europe, and the stakes rose even higher. Although it didn't impact too much on Outremer, the fall of the first Crusader state created a big splash in Europe, which had grown used to stories of Frankish success.

Calling for another round

In 1145 Bishop Hugh of Jebail led an embassy from Outremer to Pope Eugenius III in Rome. Hugh presented the fears of the people of Outremer and requested help. Pope Eugenius went straight to the heart of the matter and decided the quickest way to help was a new Crusade. He is unlikely to have viewed it as the 'Second Crusade', which is more a modern term. Contemporary people would have just regarded it as another Crusade.

Eugenius III acted quickly and addressed a letter to the French king, Louis VII and the whole of the French nobility.

In his letter, Eugenius not only addressed religious devotion, but also clearly stated that Crusaders would receive more than spiritual benefits by participating in the new mission. He promised that individuals who went on Crusade would have their property legally protected under the authority of the Church while they were away (losing their home property had been a big problem during the First Crusade). Furthermore, Eugenius promised that participants wouldn't end up out of pocket:

> *Whoever is oppressed by debt, and undertakes this holy journey with purity of heart, shall not pay interest on the money he has not repaid; and if others on their behalf, have been imprisoned because of interest, by our apostolic authority we absolve them from their obligation and their pledge.*

In other words: crusade now – pay later! Eugenius was offering the deal of a lifetime. Not only were the nobility able to save their souls by going on Crusade, but they also had the personal guarantee of the pope to protect them and their property financially while they sought new fortunes abroad. Furthermore, although many people had died on the First Crusade and in the military operations since, according to the pope they would have all gone to Heaven. He was effectively giving potential recruits a personal guarantee. Unsurprisingly, many found the offer very attractive.

Broadening the appeal: Bernard 'The Honey Tongued'

Although Pope Eugenius's offer was brilliant, it was somewhat wasted on King Louis VII who had already decided on making a journey to Outremer several months earlier before the Pope had made his appeal. Louis agreed to go on Crusade, and he actively recruited others to the cause, incorporating his expedition with those planned by other people.

Bernard of Clairvaux made by far the greatest effort on the French recruiting front. A close friend of the French king, Bernard was the greatest orator of the age and spent 1146–47 travelling around France, the Low Countries (modern-day Belgium and The Netherlands) and Germany, preaching to the multitudes and developing a reputation of 'Bernard the honey tongued'. Despite the fact that he preached only in French and Latin, many people who didn't understand either language were still convinced to take part in the cause! (This 'miracle' led to Bernard's canonisation in 1174.)

If anything Bernard was probably *too* successful. Eugenius had intended that only monarchs and nobility take part in the Second Crusade, envisioning a purely military expedition. But Bernard spoke to all classes in society. Indeed, to him anybody that didn't go on Crusade was a sinner. Bernard's message made an impact on everybody.

Joining the party: Conrad III

Although Eugenius III had conceived of a purely military expedition drawn from France and Italy, the Second Crusade quickly took on a life of its own. During Christmas 1146 the German king, Conrad III responded to the pope's call and announced that he too was taking the cross and making the journey to Jerusalem.

Conrad was an interesting character. He had tried to make himself German king following the death of his uncle, Henry V in 1125 (see Chapter 13), but that process ended up taking 13 years and a series of wars before his title was confirmed. Leaving nothing to chance, Conrad took advantage of the pope's offer to secure all lands of Crusaders by having his son crowned as his successor before he left for the Holy Land.

At the time, no one held the title of Holy Roman Emperor, although several claimed it. Conrad frequently referred to himself as emperor, as do several sources at the time, but no pope ever crowned him with that title.

Going on Crusade – without leaving Europe

The enthusiasm for a new Crusade was reflected by more than just individuals travelling with the armies of Louis VII or Conrad III to the Holy Land. A whole other range of military expeditions took place during the middle of the twelfth century, focusing on populations within Europe.

Many people saw the preaching of Bernard of Clairvaux (see the preceding 'Broadening the appeal: Bernard 'The Honey Tongued') and others as a way to justify their own mercenary desires and often horrible actions. In some cases, their claims and justifications were very dubious indeed.

Tussling with the Jews

As during the First Crusade (turn to Chapter 12 for more details), the first victims of the new expedition were the Jewish communities of Europe. While the armies gathered in Germany to accompany Conrad III to the Holy Land, various leaders decided to attack the Jewish populations of Cologne, Mainz, Worms and elsewhere. Jews and many others who felt threatened fled their homes and found sanctuary in the city of Nuremburg.

At this point Bernard of Clairvaux intervened. Bernard seems to have shared the prevailing view of his time that the Jews were the killers of Christ and as such were enemies of God. Even so, he preached that Jews shouldn't be killed in return:

> *The Jews are not to be persecuted, nor killed, nor even forced to flee. God says 'Slay not my enemies, lest my people forget' [Psalm 59.11]. Alive, the Jews are signs to us, a continual reminder of the Lord's passion.*

Whatever the logic behind his statement, the pogroms stopped, but this wouldn't be the last time that Jewish communities were attacked in the name of Crusade (see Chapter 16).

Wounding the Wends

Another target closer to home were the Wends, Slavic people who lived in northeastern Germany and had been a continual enemy to the German kings. During the two decades prior to the Second Crusade, the bishops of eastern Germany had been trying to convert the pagan Wends, without a great deal of success. In 1147 several German princes were given papal permission to try rather more violent tactics.

A mixed force of German and Danish warriors attacked the Wendish fortress of Dobin in the northeast of Germany. The attack was successful, and the inhabitants of the local area converted to Christianity. However, by the time the armies had made their way back west, the Wends of Dobin had resumed their pagan lifestyle.

The only real result of this forceful conversion attempt was that the Wends now paid a higher annual tribute to their German neighbours. So the effort wasn't so much a Crusade as a protection racket!

Battling in the Baltic

The even odder Baltic Crusade took place in 1147. Vladislav the Duke of Bohemia, motivated by the words of Bernard of Clairvaux, decided to take the fight to a people known as the Pomeranians, who lived between Germany and Poland on the southern shore of the Baltic Sea. The Crusaders considered the Pomeranians to be pagan.

Vladislav's forces laid siege to the Pomeranian capital of Stettin. In response, the inhabitants of the city raised crosses above the city walls and declared their willingness to convert to Christianity. This tactic scuppered Vladislav's plans for conquest because the bishops of Saxony immediately intervened and decided that a peaceful conversion should take place.

Vladislav returned home having lost many men and gained no new territory. Still, with the mass conversions, Bernard of Clairvaux was probably pleased with the result!

Punishing Portugal

In a truly curious incident, Portugal was the most easterly country in Europe attacked during the Crusades and technically the farthest from Jerusalem!

As elsewhere, the call for Crusade had been effective in northern Europe. In the summer of 1147, a group made up of Crusaders from England, Normandy, northern Germany and the Low Countries (modern-day Belgium and The Netherlands) set sail around the Atlantic coast of modern-day France and Spain on their way to the Holy Land.

Their reasonably large contingent of around 150–200 ships encountered bad weather during the voyage and they were forced to dock at the city of Oporto, where they met with the Portuguese king Afonso I. Although he was technically king, he was still seeking to drive out the Moors (Muslim invaders) who had for so long dominated the country. At the time, Afonso was laying siege to the Moors in the city of Lisbon.

Afonso persuaded the Crusade army to join the siege and help him. It took four months, but finally in October the Moorish leaders surrendered. A mass slaughter followed, and many of the Crusade army stayed behind to enjoy the riches of Portugal. One of their number, Gilbert of Hastings, was elected as the new Bishop of Lisbon. The pope officially approved their victory and it became considered one of the acts of the *reconquista,* or reconquest, when lands that were formerly in Christian hands were retaken from the Muslim rulers who'd seized them.

Therefore, the first attacks against Muslims during the Second Crusade took place far, far from the Holy Land. And, in the event, the Portuguese Crusade was a whole lot more successful than the official expedition proved to be.

Venturing East Again: The Second Crusade

Personalities with large egos dominated the Second Crusade. Pope Eugenius III, Bernard of Clairvaux, King Louis VII of France and King Conrad III of Germany were all involved in the expedition, each having their own ideas about how it should proceed.

In particular, the kings of France and Germany both felt that they ought to be in charge. As a result, two separate armies were engaged on the Second Crusade and were essentially in competition to see who won the most fame and glory.

The two armies travelled separately to the Holy Land, setting off in early summer 1146, the Germans in May and the French in June. Like the First Crusade, the journey was extremely hard with the two armies virtually living off the lands around them as they went.

Determining precisely how many people were involved is difficult, but Conrad had at least 20,000 men and Louis around the same number. Including all the other people associated with armies and the baggage train, around 50,000 people made their way towards the Byzantine city of Constantinople.

Going with the Germans

Conrad III and his army left from Vienna accompanied by the German cardinal Theodwin as the Pope's representative. They faced a potentially tricky journey as King Geza II of Hungary was technically an enemy of Conrad's, and they would need to pass through Geza's territory. As it turned out he let the Crusaders pass through unhindered. A good job too otherwise the Crusade might have been fairly brief!

Meeting up with Manuel the unwelcoming

The Byzantine emperor in 1146 was Manuel Comnenus, the son of Alexius I who had experienced the First Crusade. Based on his father's experiences, Manuel took a fairly sceptical view of how much benefit Byzantium would derive from the enterprise and was very concerned about two European armies arriving at his capital. (The situation wasn't helped when German soldiers caused a riot in the Byzantine city of Phillipopolis after trying to kill a juggler who was so good they suspected him of practising witchcraft!)

Accordingly, when Conrad arrived at Byzantium, Manuel persuaded him to move on and not wait for Louis as he had previously agreed to. Conrad was itching to get with things and didn't take too much persuading. A good move for Manuel but not, as things turned out, for Conrad.

Experiencing defeat at Dorylaeum

Conrad and his army marched on, led by Greek guides supplied to them by Manuel. Somewhere on the road to the town of Dorylaeum, however, the guides deserted them. The Germans were left without the local knowledge they needed to find water and shelter, but they struggled on down the eastern road.

Just at their weakest point, Conrad's army was surprised by a huge Turkish force, led by the son of Kilij Arslan, who had been defeated by the army of the First Crusade at Dorylaeum (as described in Chapter 12). The Turks were looking for revenge, and they got it. The exhausted and thirsty Germans were taken completely by surprise and massacred. One chronicler paints a grisly picture of the attack:

Nothing could be heard except the depths of grief and the groans and crashes of the dying; on the other side nothing but the awful shout of 'Death to the pilgrims!' as the Saracens [Seljuk Turks] *urged each other on with mouths contorted like dogs.*

Of Conrad's army, only around 2,000 men remained. Conrad himself travelled back to Constantinople while what was left of his army joined up with the French as they made their own way eastwards.

Following the French

The French portion of the Second Crusade didn't go particularly well. Continual attacks from Seljuk warriors reduced Louis's army to stragglers, and the lack of available supplies made their problems even worse.

Eventually they reached the port of Attalia (in southeast modern–day Turkey) and hit another problem – the fleet provided by Manuel to take them to Antioch (see Figure 14-1) was too small. Louis made a cold-blooded decision, taking the majority of the ships for himself and his household, he set sail for Antioch leaving the rest of his army to travel overland and fend for themselves.

The marching force had a desperate time. Lacking supplies and under constant assault, barely half Louis's men made it to Antioch. Louis himself was fine, arriving at Antioch in fine style in March 1148.

Encountering Nur ed-Din: A new enemy

By the time the now combined army of the Second Crusade reached their destination, the Holy Land had changed hugely. The depleted army of the Second Crusade was going to face a new and different threat in the form of one man – Nur ed-Din.

Nur ed-Din was the second son of Zengi, the emir of the cities of Aleppo and Mosul who had captured Edessa in 1144 (see the earlier section 'Stepping up jihad in Edessa'). Chaos initially followed his father's death in 1146, which the Franks tried to exploit by taking back lost forts and territory. Their efforts didn't last long, however; Nur ed-Din seized control of his father's power base in Aleppo and in a series of bold moves set about securing Seljuk territory.

SEEN ON SCREEN

'My husbands and I': Eleanor of Aquitaine

Arriving at Antioch with King Louis in 1148 was his wife, Eleanor of Aquitaine. Accompanying your husband on Crusade was unusual – particularly for such a high-profile wife – but throughout her life, Eleanor proved to be a controversial figure.

Eleanor was the daughter of William, Duke of Aquitaine, and when she married the French king, the union brought together the two most powerful noble families in France.

Various reasons were suggested at the time to explain why she accompanied her husband, ranging from her own pious devotion to a combination of her supposed infidelity and Louis's insane jealousy.

Whatever the case, rumours of infidelity dogged her at Antioch (see the later section 'Losing focus in Antioch'). On the journey home she and Louis fell out in spectacular style, even making the journey on separate ships! On reaching France, they applied to Pope Eugenius III for an annulment to their marriage, but he initially tried to reconcile them. As the marriage had yet to produce a son (they had produced two daughters), Louis was keen to end the marriage as well. In the end Louis managed to have the marriage dissolved on the basis of *consanguinity*, which means that they were too closely related (Louis and Eleanor were cousins, four times removed). Theirs doesn't sound like a happy marriage at all. It seems that Eleanor was never very satisfied by Louis, whom she described as 'more monk than man'!

With the marriage over, Eleanor became one of the most eligible single women in Europe, more for her vast land in southern France than for her personal charm, although this was considerable. Several suitors tried to woo her, but she eventually married Henry, Duke of Anjou and Normandy. Within a few months he also became King of England, Henry II. Theirs was another tumultuous marriage, but the absolutely huge territories that they controlled kept them together for political reasons. She bore Henry II five sons and three daughters and lived through a civil war (see Chapter 15) that saw her imprisoned in England for 16 years.

Eleanor outlived her second husband and died in 1204 aged 82, which was impressive for the time. She had a remarkable life that saw her involved with just about every key figure of the age. No other woman in the medieval period made such an impact or inspired so many later writers. To this day historians still write biographies of Eleanor and novelists produce fictionalised versions of her life. With a life so rich and interesting it can't have been too difficult to do! She was memorably portrayed by Katherine Hepburn, in the film *The Lion in Winter* (1966), who provided just the right mix of beauty and fierce intelligence.

Ignoring Mosul, Nur ed-Din focused his attentions on Aleppo and, more importantly, Outremer. Like his father before him, his goal was to seize control of Damascus which, at the time, was still on good terms with Outremer.

Despite being only 29 in 1146, Nur ed-Din was an inspirational leader. He surrounded himself with Islamic scholars and academics and made full use of their teachings to inspire jihad among his followers. He took a hard line, going as far as to ban anybody who served in his retinue from drinking alcohol.

Losing focus in Antioch

As if Nu red-Din wasn't a tough enough enemy to face, Louis VII was making something of a mess of his time in Antioch. He was received with massive splendour by Raymond of Antioch, who personally was keen on forcing Nur ed-Din as far away from his city as possible and hoped at some point to take back Edessa, too.

Unfortunately for Raymond, Louis had no intention of fighting Nur ed-Din by himself. His only target was Jerusalem. Conrad III and the small number of his troops that remained had already set sail for Acre (check out Figure 14-1) with the intention of meeting Louis in Jerusalem.

As if things weren't bad enough, rumours were flying around Antioch that Louis's wife, Eleanor of Aquitaine, had begun an affair with Raymond who also happened to be her uncle! One explanation for the rumours could have been that both Eleanor and Raymond spoke the southern French language of Occitan that was unintelligible to outsiders. Modern historians still debate whether there was anything more substantial to the rumours; whatever the truth, Eleanor doesn't seem to have been terribly happy with Louis.

When Louis announced that he was intending to march to Jerusalem, Eleanor apparently demanded to stay behind. Louis's response was to send his men to kidnap her and bring her by force to his camp outside the city. Another chapter in a stormy marriage!

Louis set sail for Jerusalem with a furious wife and left behind a disappointed and angry Raymond of Antioch. Unfortunately, things were only going to get worse.

Dead-ending at Damascus

Eventually the significantly reduced army of the Second Crusade staggered south. In the end only the German contingent reached Jerusalem, where the most pressing question was what to do next. The city itself was secure, and the only territory that had been lost was Edessa, which Louis had recently decided not to attack with Raymond.

The Frankish leaders came to a shocking decision. At a council at Acre in May 1148, they elected to attack Damascus. This decision was bizarre for several reasons, including the fact that the city was their only ally in the Seljuk Empire and Unur, the governor of Damascus, had been on friendly terms with the Franks for decades.

The motivations behind the decision are cloudy at best. The only notion that makes much sense is that the Franks wanted to strike at the heart of Nur ed-Din's ambitions by capturing the famous city before him. Some historians suggest that Queen Melisinde of Jerusalem persuaded them to attack the city, but she would have only been pushing at their existing desire to win a famous victory.

Whatever the reason, it was a bad idea because Damascus had previously proved to be all but impregnable to invading armies. Neither Zengi nor Nur ed-Din had managed to take it, and little reason existed to see how a weakened Frankish army would succeed.

The chronicler William of Tyre describes the difficulties of taking the city:

> *On its western side and its northern side Damascus is surrounded far and wide by orchards like thick groves which stretch out for five miles or more towards Lebanon . . . these orchards provide a valuable defence for the city . . . it was in this place that our princes had initially decided to attack.*

These dense orchards were difficult to move through and full of towers and defensive earthworks that prevented an attacking army from moving quickly or staying undetected.

Incredibly, when the Crusader forces attacked on 28 May 1148, they managed to seize control of the orchards and force the Damascene army back into the city. But having won such a great position, they threw it away.

When Muslim reinforcements began to appear from the north, the Crusaders left the orchards to go back to the plains because they feared that their camp would be attacked. The orchard was immediately reoccupied by the Muslim army from Damascus. When they reached the plains, the Crusaders realised that they were now outside the virtually impregnable northern walls of the city and no water supply in the area existed because the governor Unur had blocked all the wells. They were absolutely stuck with no choice but to retreat.

To the immense embarrassment of all involved, and realising that the game was up, the Crusaders were forced to retreat back into Outremer. On the way, they were constantly menaced by mounted Seljuk archers and lost many men on the march. Eventually they made it back to port and sailed home almost immediately.

Playing the blame game

Despite the prophetic visions of Bernard of Clairvaux and his immense oratory on the subject, the Second Crusade was a complete and total failure. Medieval chronicler William of Tyre very clearly attributed the failure to the local leaders in Outremer rather than to Louis or Conrad:

> *The men returned to their own kingdoms by the same route that they had come, and held in suspicion all the ways of our princes, rightly declining to take any part in their plans. This was the case not only while they remained in the East: even after they returned to their own lands they remained mindful of the wrongs they had suffered.*

William's judgement is a little harsh. The Second Crusade hadn't exactly been going well when it arrived in Antioch, and a third of the army was lost at Dorylaeum only two weeks after leaving Constantinople! Everybody was at fault for one of the most disastrous military campaigns in medieval history. The knock-on result of the entire affair was that European monarchs and nobles were less willing to lend support to the leaders of Outremer in the future.

The big winner in the Second Crusade was Nur ed-Din, despite never facing the Crusader army in battle. In April 1154 he finally captured Damascus. Unlike the Crusaders, he secured a mole inside the city who let down a rope to help his soldiers get inside and open the gates. The threat to Outremer of an unfriendly Damascus was huge. In addition, within 30 years another Crusade was needed to resist an even greater threat – Saladin, the Muslim ruler of Egypt and Syria (see Chapter 15).

Chapter 15

Pitting Richard I Against Saladin: The Third Crusade

As I describe in Chapter 14, the Second Crusade was a total failure. It was meant to strengthen the position of the kingdom of Outremer (the Crusader-controlled states) but in fact did the complete opposite. For a time Crusading went seriously out of fashion. European kings and nobles were far keener on starting fights with each other than making journeys to the Holy Land.

In 1165, Pope Alexander III asked for a further Crusade, but all the relevant parties were otherwise engaged. None of the Western European kings were prepared to go; in particular, Henry II of England and Louis VII of France were far too busy fighting each other to bother turning up. Perhaps the entire notion of Crusading was at an end?

No such luck. Everything changed in the 1180s when a fresh Crusade was launched. Two men dominated the new contest – Richard I and Saladin. This chapter is all about their successes and encounters in the Holy Land.

Turning Up the Heat: The Rise of Saladin

The man who historians refer to as Saladin was born Salah ad-Din Yusuf in around 1137. He was a Kurd whose family came from Armenia, but he was born in the city of Tikrit in modern-day Iraq. The Kurdish people originally came from an area around the borders of modern-day Iran, Iraq, Turkey and Syria now known as Kurdistan and had been incorporated into the Great Seljuk Empire.

As a young man Saladin was in the service of the Seljuk leader Zengi (whom I discuss in Chapter 14) and lived in the city of Damascus. Historians know little about Saladin's early years, but he was extremely well-educated and, despite his Kurdish background, developed a deep knowledge of Islam and Islamic customs, and became a Sunni Muslim (see Chapter 7).

Coming out on top in Egypt

Saladin's military career began under his uncle, Asad al-Din Shirkuh, who was one of the leading generals loyal to Nur ed-Din, the man who controlled the whole of the western Seljuk empire (flip to Chapter 14 for more on Nur ed-Din). In 1164 a civil war took place in Egypt. Shawar, the vizier who oversaw the territory for the Fatamid caliph, was driven out by a local rival. Shawar requested help from Nur ed-Din, who in turn despatched Asad al-Din Shirkuh, along with his nephew Saladin, to help restore Shawar to power.

Working with his uncle, Saladin did well in Egypt – to put it mildly. The force led by his uncle Shirkuh won a great victory against the rebel forces and as a result managed to take control of Alexandria and the other major cities. However, Shirkuh didn't much fancy giving back the power he'd acquired.

Shawar, who had asked for their help, was left in a bit of a no-man's-land. He sought help from Jerusalem and formed an alliance with its leader King Amalric, but the arrangement didn't work. In 1169 Shawar was assassinated, allegedly by Saladin, and Shirkuh became the new vizier. Shirkuh also didn't last long in the position and was dead by the end of the year.

With Shirkuh dead, the caliph made Saladin the new vizier at the age of just 32, and within another two years he had been awarded the title of Sultan. Saladin instantly became one of the most powerful men in the world.

Sweeping all before him

The possession of Egypt meant that Saladin had huge wealth and military strength at his disposal – and he made the most of it. Over the next 20 years, he fought a series of campaigns that extended his influence throughout Syria and Mesopotamia. The death of King Amalric of Jerusalem in 1174 also helped to expand his influence. Amalric's successor was his son Baldwin IV, who was just 13 years old and suffering with an illness that developed into leprosy. Outremer descended into political chaos as various pretenders for the throne jockeyed for position.

Within ten years Saladin had managed to unify all Nur ed-Din's territories and incorporate them into his growing empire. Aleppo, Damascus and the other towns of the regions fell to him. By 1185 Saladin's territory completely encircled the kingdom of Outremer, which looked very small and vulnerable in comparison (see Figure 14-1 in Chapter 14).

Taking Jerusalem

Sensibly the kingdom of Outremer signed a peace treaty with Saladin in 1180, and yet things still didn't go well. Poor Baldwin IV eventually expired of leprosy in 1185 and was replaced by his own nephew, the handily named Baldwin V. He managed only 17 months in power, however, before his own death. His mother, Sibylla, replaced him and her husband Guy became king. This unsteady, complicated situation was about to become even worse.

Reckless Reynald

Having signed a treaty, Outremer was technically at peace with Saladin. The treaty was sensible considering that Saladin commanded territory between the Nile River and Edessa and was able easily to raise an army that would dwarf the military strength of Outremer. Saladin wasn't a man to mess with – unless you were the reckless Reynald of Chatillon (check out the next section 'Breaking the truce').

Reynald arrived in Outremer as part of the Second Crusade (which I cover in detail in Chapter 14) and stayed, becoming one of the princes of Antioch. In 1156 Reynald decided that he wanted to attack Cyprus and needed funds to do so. He asked the Catholic Patriarch of Antioch – the pope's representative in the region – to fund a military expedition. When the Patriarch said no, Reynald had him stripped naked, covered with honey and tied to the top of the citadel. Humiliated and exhausted (and probably quite sticky), the Patriarch had a change of heart and financed the expedition.

Reynald duly went off to invade Cyprus, raping and pillaging his way around the island. In the process, he upset the Byzantine emperor Manuel I, who was responsible for Cyprus. The emperor brought his army to Syria, threatening Reynald's estates there and forcing him to return. Overwhelmed by the size of Manuel's forces, Reynald was forced publicly to grovel in front of him, and when Manuel visited Antioch, Reynald was required to lead Manuel's horse into the city like a defeated enemy, as a public humiliation.

The following year, while he was on a raiding expedition, Muslims captured Reynald and he spent the next 17 years held captive in Aleppo. His long stay in prison was partly because nobody wanted to pay his massive ransom of 150,000 gold *dinars* (500 kilograms or 79 stone of gold – a huge sum at the time) and partly because everybody was sick to the back teeth of him.

Eventually the Byzantine emperor Manuel I coughed up the cash in 1176. Whilst he can't have been keen to do so, Reynald was the second husband of Constance of Antioch, the mother of Manuel's wife – the empress Maria. So effectively he spent the equivalent of millions of pounds to bail out his wife's stepfather! Reynald was released. Free – but as wild as ever – Reynald's biggest blunder was yet to come.

Breaking the truce

In May 1187, Reynald of Chatillon decided he wanted to engage in his passion for raiding (see the preceding sidebar 'Reckless Reynald' for more on Reynald's other exploits). He chose as his target a Muslim trading caravan that was travelling between Cairo and Damascus. The raid was successful, and Reynald took considerable plunder. The caravan, however, was technically under the protection of Saladin; by attacking it Reynald broke the peace treaty between Outremer and the great Muslim leader.

This episode and the events surrounding it form part of the 2005 film *Kingdom of Heaven*, directed by Ridley Scott. The film is well worth seeing, with some fantastic battle scenes giving a visceral idea of what medieval warfare was like. Also, Brendan Gleeson plays Reynald and gives him just the right mixture of arrogance, barbarism and stupidity!

Fighting the Battle of Hattin

Saladin had stuck to his peace treaty with Outremer, but Reynald's attack gave him the excuse that he needed to attack the Crusader states. During late May and early June 1187, Saladin gathered his forces before attacking the town of Tiberias (around 150 kilometres or 93 miles north of Jerusalem). His army was huge, with around 30,000 regular troops being supplemented with many more volunteers.

King Guy of Jerusalem was in a quandary. Taking the field against Saladin meant almost certain defeat, but if he did nothing he was sure to be accused of cowardice. In the end chivalry won out. Guy received a message from Tiberias that the Countess of Tripoli had been captured. Her husband, Raymond of Tripoli, argued that she should be left to get on with it as Guy shouldn't risk the kingdom for the wife of one of his vassals, but Guy decided that he had to intervene militarily.

The Frankish army of around just under 20,000 marched out on 3 July and camped in the valley beneath a set of two hills called the Horns of Hattin. When the Muslim army appeared, the Franks set at them in a desperate charge. Saladin opened his lines and let the Franks advance. He then closed around the Franks, completely surrounding them. The result was a massacre, and virtually the entire Frankish force was destroyed in one day.

Muslim forces took a huge number of prisoners at the battle, including King Guy and Reynald. Both were brought to the tent of Saladin. Remarkably, a scholar and personal friend of Saladin called Isfahnai provides an eye-witness account of what happened.

According to Isfahnai's account, both King Guy and Reynald were brought in gasping with thirst after the battle, and Saladin offered them water. Guy thanked him before drinking but then gave some to Reynald without asking Saladin for permission to do so. Saladin then said to Guy:

'You did not ask permission before giving him water. I am therefore not obliged to grant him mercy.' After pronouncing these words, the sultan smiled, mounted his horse, and rode off, leaving the captives in terror. He supervised the return of the troops, and then came back to his tent. He ordered Reynald brought there, then advanced before him, sword in hand, and struck him between the neck and the shoulder-blade. When Reynald fell, he cut off his head and dragged the body by its feet to the king, who began to tremble. Seeing him thus upset, Saladin said to him in a reassuring tone: 'This man was killed only because of his maleficence and perfidy [disloyalty]'.

Guy spent the next year imprisoned in Damascus but Saladin eventually released him in 1188 and allowed him to return to his family.

After such a victory the fall of Jerusalem was inevitable. Saladin first moved to capture the towns of Acre, Beruit and Sidon. On 2 October 1187 he officially took control of the city of Jerusalem. The takeover was entirely peaceful; no looting or violence. He restored the city's mosques but allowed its Christian churches to remain open for pilgrims.

Outremer was virtually wiped from existence. All that remained were the ports of Tyre and Tripoli – everything else was under Saladin's control. Something remarkable would need to happen for the situation to change, but within two years the rather remarkable Richard I arrived on the scene.

Readying for Round Three: Europe Prepares for Crusade

The fall of Jerusalem sent shockwaves around Europe. The Franks had held the city for just 88 years. The Europeans felt that losing the city to Saladin was like driving the final nail into the coffin of Outremer. When news arrived in Italy in the autumn of 1187, a new call for Crusade was put together.

Pope Gregory VIII responded very quickly to the news and issued something known as the *Audita tremendi*, one of those large papal special offers to encourage European monarchs to sign up for a long, hard battle. Gregory repeated the offer that Pope Eugenius made before the Second Crusade (check out Chapter 14 for more): all Crusaders were guaranteed places in Heaven and their property would be protected while they were away. The offer had worked before, but would it work again?

Dealing with false starts and empty promises

Crusading had gone out of fashion in the years following the Second Crusade, but the fall of Jerusalem was a huge shock. Despite the risks, nobles from around Europe began making their way to the Holy Land arriving in Tyre or Tripoli. Knights and adventurers from Denmark, Flanders, Hungary and elsewhere all made the journey. A small flotilla of ships from London also joined them. The forces were gathering.

Although losing Jerusalem to Saladin was a shock to most Europeans, going on Crusade was a difficult endeavour. For a monarch, Crusading was hugely expensive and very time-consuming. Although individual nobles were able to make a healthy profit from Crusading, a king had to pay for his army. He was unlikely to recoup those costs from an expedition, never mind make a profit.

The following sections look at some stumbles along the way to assembling the Third Crusade.

On again, off again: Henry II and Philip II Augustus

Henry II, king of England, was one of the first European monarchs to write back to Pope Gregory confirming his desire to fight – but an obstacle stood in the way. For the past few years Henry had been at war with the French king Philip II Augustus. The main bone of contention was the lands in what is now France that Henry claimed as his own, partly due to his marriage with Eleanor of Aquitaine (turn to Chapter 14 for more background details). In January 1188 the two kings met at Gisors in northern France and agreed to a truce in their war to allow them both to take the cross and join the Crusade.

Calling a truce was easy compared to raising money for the new Crusade. Having been at war for so long, neither the English nor the French king had the funds. In a council held at Le Mans, both kings agreed to introduce a tax known as the 'Saladin Tithe' to raise funds.

English chronicler Roger of Howden describes the details:

> *Everyone is to give a tenth of his income and property in the present year in the form of alms as a subsidy for the land of Jerusalem . . . Excommunication has already been pronounced against anyone who does not legitimately pay this tithe in the presence of the assessment of whose duty it is to collect it.*

Unsurprisingly the 'Saladin Tithe' was about as popular as Reynald of Chatillon was diplomatic (check out the earlier section 'Breaking the truce' for more on Reynald's exploits). People were forced to pay it but they protested. Philip Augustus was eventually forced to abolish it in 1189. Nevertheless the tax did the job and raised a huge amount of money.

A war of words

Frederick obviously wasn't planning on using any surprise tactics in waging his battles in the Third Crusade. In fact, he wrote a letter to Saladin demanding that he vacate Jerusalem and elsewhere if he wanted to avoid a war, telling Saladin:

> *With God's help you will find out by experience what our conquering eagles can do, our battalions of many races . . . You will discover that my own right hand, which you accuse of being feeble with age, has not forgotten how to wield a sword.*

Saladin responded to Frederick in kind. Unsurprisingly, Saladin seemed equally confident in his own ability, threatening that after he defeated Frederick, he would travel to Europe and take control of his empire. Saladin rather threateningly added:

> *The combined forces of Christendom have twice come against us in Egypt, once at Damietta and once at Alexandria . . . but you know how on both occasions the Christians returned, and the end to which they came.*

A bit of playground bragging, but impressive words nonetheless.

England and France were all set for a new Crusade, when another problem emerged. The peace treaty between Philip Augustus and Henry II was blown apart after Henry's own sons (with the support of Philip) made an attack on Henry! A new war began in 1189, and the Crusade was put on hold.

Ready, Freddie? Frederick I

While Henry and Philip continued to fight among themselves, Frederick I, the Holy Roman Emperor, was the first to make a move, leading a Crusade army from Germany in March 1188.

Frederick was known as *Barbarossa* meaning 'red beard' and had been a successful and relative long-serving emperor. Now 67 years old he must have seen recapturing Jerusalem and defeating Saladin as a final achievement in a glorious career. Unfortunately for him, things didn't quite work out like that.

Frederick managed to recruit a huge army of over 30,000, by far the biggest that had ever gone on Crusade under a single commander. It was so big in fact that he was unable to find enough ships to transport it and was forced to march overland to the east.

Arriving at Constantinople, Frederick found that he and his army weren't really wanted there. The Byzantine emperor, Isaac II Comnenus, refused to give the army shelter or food, and Frederick's forces were continually attacked by bandits and raiders as they made their way through the empire. Isaac clearly felt threatened by Frederick and the size of his army, but his obstructive behaviour almost forced Frederick into laying siege to Constantinople.

Eventually Frederick's army crossed the Bosphorus, but the journey east took a terrible toll. They slowly progressed through Asia Minor, fought several battles against the Turks and struggled on to the Taurus mountains. After making camp by the Goksu River, Frederick stripped off and plunged into the water to cool down. It was the last thing he ever did, because he drowned shortly afterwards, in front of his devastated army. The expedition ended right there. The biggest army ever assembled for a Crusade never even reached as far as Syria. Some of the men made their way to Acre to fight under new commanders, but the rest disbanded and began the long trudge home.

Roaring into battle: Richard the Lionheart

Around the same time that Frederick went for his fatal swim, Henry II of England died too. Age and illness finally caught up with him during the wars with France and against his own sons. He was succeeded by his son Richard, known as *couer de leon* or the 'lion-hearted'.

Richard had revolted against his father at the suggestion of Philip Augustus of France, and consequently the French king wasn't upset to see Richard take the English throne. Along with his new title of King of England, Richard became Duke of Normandy and Count of Anjou as well as Duke of Aquitaine and Count of Poitou – quite a haul! He went on to become one of the most famous figures in medieval history, as well as one of the most controversial.

Selling England by the pound

England was definitely Richard's least favourite territory. Essentially, we would now regard him as French, speaking the language and having grown up in the country, although he wouldn't have considered himself as such. He visited England only when he took control of it. Having taken the throne, he regarded England as one huge cash machine to fund his activities. He allegedly said, 'I would sell London if I could find a buyer' – and he certainly drained every last penny of revenue from his new kingdom.

Richard had already pledged to go on Crusade prior to becoming king, and so after gaining the crown, he set about raising cash for the expedition. Henry's treasury had been filled with the Saladin Tithe (see the earlier section 'On again, off again: Henry II and Philip Augustus'), but those funds were soon spent on the wars he fought against his own sons.

Richard raised taxes in England to swell his coffers and took a fee of 10,000 marks from William of Scotland to release him from his subservience to the English throne. Eventually, Richard was able to raise an army of around 8,000 men and 100 ships. He took a huge amount of supplies with him: 14,000 pig carcasses, immense stores of cheese, beans and wine as well as 50,000 horseshoes! It must have taken a while to pack it all, but by July 1190 he was ready to set sail.

A mass of contradictions and controversy

Richard I is heralded as a great English king, but the facts don't quite add up. To English eyes Richard was essentially a foreigner who, in common with most of the nobility, didn't speak English and made his distaste for England very public. All in all his time in England was a dead loss. Specifically:

- He spent just six months in England organising finances for the Third Crusade before leaving, never to return.

- He derided England as 'cold and always raining' and was upset about the lack of tournaments, which his father Henry II had banned.

- His coronation was spoiled when anti-Semitic riots broke out across London and thousands of Jewish people were massacred throughout the country.

Rumours surrounded Richard throughout his reign, and historians today still debate his character and even his sexuality. Before he even left on Crusade, he was dogged with gossip about his relationship with Philip Augustus. The chronicler Roger of Hoveden wrote that the two kings 'slept in the same bed' and that 'passionate love [existed] between them'. Other stories allege huge cruelty when he raped and pillaged his way through his military campaigns in France.

Although details are sketchy, one thing is certainly true: before going on Crusade he had to swear an oath to a priest renouncing his past wickedness!

As for England, Richard left the job of running it to his advisors. Richard's brother John wasn't given control of the country, and some people claim that Richard barred him from entering the country, perhaps concerned that he would try and seize it. Richard must have changed his mind though because by 1191 John was back in England and ruling it as regent (see Chapter 17).

Sojourning in Sicily: A marriage of inconvenience

Richard and Philip Augustus embarked on Crusade in July 1190, but became distracted. Arriving in Sicily in September, Richard took the opportunity of resolving a dispute with the ruler of the island, Tancred Count of Lecce. Tancred had seized the throne after the death of the previous ruler, William of Sicily, who was Richard's brother-in-law. This meant that Richard's sister Joan was still inside the city being effectively held prisoner by Tancred.

In an abrupt change of mission, Richard laid siege to the town of Messina and eventually captured it. Richard's actions put Philip Augustus on edge; he disliked the way that Richard was turning the Crusade to his own interests.

To make things more difficult, Richard further upset Philip by becoming engaged to, but then refusing to marry, Philip's sister Alice. The refusal was bad enough, but his reason was that Alice had slept with his father, Henry, when she was a guest at his court as a young girl! Philip had had enough; he set sail from Sicily without Richard at the end of March 1191.

Shortly afterwards Richard agreed to marry Berengaria, the daughter of the king of Navarre (in the Pyrenees, in modern-day France). The marriage was a great diplomatic arrangement, strengthening the southern borders of his territory in Aquitaine.

But just before his marriage to Berengaria, Richard departed for Cyprus, taking her with him. At the time, Cyprus was in the hands of a man called Isaac Ducas Comnenus, who had conned his way into power by convincing the former governor that he was his replacement, sent from Constantinople. When Richard turned up, Comnenus must have thought that the king had been sent by the Byzantine emperor to oust him! In the event, that's exactly what Richard did. While Richard rested on the island, Guy, the exiled king of Jerusalem, arrived along with some Templar knights (Chapter 14 contains more on these warrior monks). Richard led them in the 'liberation' of the island, no doubt enjoying himself hugely in the process.

Shortly afterwards, Richard married Berengaria in Limassol and finally sailed for the Holy Land. He arrived in June 1191, a year after setting out – but now with a new wife and a management interest in Sicily and Cyprus!

Duelling for Dominance: Richard versus Saladin

When Richard finally arrived in Outremer in 1191, he found himself in the middle of a difficult situation. Not only was the kingdom reduced to just two cities (Tripoli and Tyre), but also it was further split into two factions. (A noble from Outremer could start an argument in an empty room!)

Vying for Outremer

Ever since the fall of Jerusalem (which I cover in the earlier section 'Taking Jerusalem'), Outremer had been split into two groups. Guy was the king of Outremer, but shortly after Saladin's capture of the Holy City, a man called Conrad of Montferrat arrived in the Holy Land and began asserting himself.

Conrad's father William was captured during the battle of Hattin (see the earlier section 'Fighting the Battle of Hattin') while Conrad travelled to assist him. Conrad made his way to Tyre and slipped in during Saladin's siege of the city. He managed to rally the population sufficiently to resist Saladin and later refused to surrender even when Saladin threatened to kill his father. Eventually Saladin gave up and left, leaving Conrad as the master of Tyre.

All this was well and good, but Conrad's new position put him somewhat at odds with King Guy, who was still claiming to be the master of Outremer, which included Tyre. Over the next few years the pair jockeyed for position.

Besieging Acre – for years

King Guy had to make his mark and assert himself as the rightful ruler and Conrad's superior. In August 1189 he took his army to the town of Acre (around 100 kilometres or 62 miles north of Jerusalem) which was under Muslim control, and laid siege to it. The attack was a good idea in theory because Acre was a port that would make a great launch pad for a further attack on Jerusalem. Unfortunately for Guy, it didn't work out well in practice. Guy's army wasn't large enough to take the city, and Acre was relatively well provisioned by sea. Also, soon after Guy arrived, Saladin did too, with his army, although initially he didn't attack Guy's men.

The siege of Acre turned into the longest in medieval history and reached a point where Guy and Saladin's armies were regularly fraternising with each other as the siege dragged on, despite the fact that they were frequently involved in skirmishes with each other!

As the siege dragged on, food became scarce and the behaviour of the besieging army increasingly savage. A contemporary chronicler paints the following desperate picture:

> *A measure of wheat small enough to tuck under your arm was selling for a hundred gold pieces, a fowl for twelve shillings and an egg for sixpence. Priceless chargers were slaughtered for their meat. They devoured the horseflesh sometimes without even skinning them. Horses' guts were sold for ten shillings.*

Some reports talk of cannibalism as the situation became ever worse.

Philip and Richard arrived in the region in the summer of 1191. The siege had been in place for more than two years and showed no sign of drawing to a close. Unfortunately, poor Philip, who arrived first in the region, immediately came down with a nasty disease known as *arnaldia,* thought to be a type of scurvy. This condition has no modern equivalent, but its symptoms include hair loss, pustules, blotches on the skin and fingernails falling out. To make matter worse, as soon as Richard arrived in Acre, he caught the disease too!

The Crusade seemed about to grind to a halt again, but Richard plunged into the middle of the siege of Acre to help Guy, commanding from his sickbed. The fresh troops he brought were vital to ending the attack. Eventually, by 12 June, with sickness rife in the city and no prospect of relief from Saladin, who didn't want to get into an open battle with the Crusaders, Acre caved in to them. King Guy had the city back – 25 months after he first attacked.

Dealing with diplomatic baggage

During the siege, Richard demanded a meeting with Saladin who, unsurprisingly, politely declined. Instead Saladin suggested that Richard meet with his brother al-Adil. Richard in turn refused, and Saladin left the Crusaders to squabble amongst themselves. They didn't disappoint:

- Richard and Philip disagreed about who should rule Outremer. Richard supported Guy; Philip supported Conrad because they were cousins.

- Philip intensified the squabbling by deciding that he wanted half the territory that Richard had taken in Cyprus during their earlier voyage to the Holy Land (as I discuss in the earlier section, 'Sojourning in Sicily: A marriage of inconvenience') claiming that they'd agreed to split all spoils between them before setting out.

- A man called Duke Leopold of Austria, the last remnant of Frederick Barbarossa's Crusade (see 'Ready, Freddie? Frederick I'), claimed that he should be in command, just to complicate matters. Leopold had been at the siege of Acre for two years and felt that he deserved to fly his banner over the city just as much as Richard and Philip, and was pushing for a three-way split!

- Acre was full of rich Genoese and Pisan merchants wanting guaranteed trading rights in the cities, who tied themselves to Conrad or Guy.

Richard made some tough decisions. After much arguing, agreement was reached that Guy would remain king (in Acre) and that Conrad would be lord of Tyre, which gave both the Italian merchant cities a trading base. Sounds like a neat enough plan, but nobody was particularly happy. Especially not Leopold of Austria after Richard tore down his standard and threw it in the moat around Acre! Leopold went home in a huff.

Philip soon followed Leopold back to Europe. By this point Philip was worn out with the constant bickering among the nobles, fed up with Richard's endless self-promotion and presumably none too pleased that his hair had fallen out. Before he left he was forced to swear an oath to Richard that he wouldn't threaten his territories until he himself returned. Richard was probably relieved too. Philip's presence had also been frustrating to him. According to the English chronicler Richard of Devizes, the king had found Philip's presence to be 'like a hammer tied to the tail of a cat'!

Regaining Jerusalem (sort of)

All the arguments about leadership notwithstanding, in reality Richard was in charge in the Holy Land. His first decision was what to do with the 2,700 Muslim survivors of the garrison at Acre. Not wanting to hang around to negotiate their release with Saladin, he had them killed – every last one – outside the city walls and in full view of Saladin's army.

Venturing on: The Battle of Arsuf

Richard set out on an absurdly optimistic march to Jerusalem, around 60 kilometres or 37 miles away, through enemy territory and in the height of summer. His army was not large, and the march was incredibly heavy going. By early September, they reached the small town of Arsuf, just outside Jaffa, and Saladin attacked, bringing his entire army into the field. Amazingly, despite repeated attacks, Saladin's army failed to break through the Crusaders' lines. Instead Richard surprised them by charging himself.

At the advance of the heavily-armed Europeans, Saladin's army broke. The result was a tremendous victory, and shortly afterwards Richard marched into and captured the city of Jaffa.

Negotiating and a bit of battling

Richard's army was now only a march away from Jerusalem, but the problem he faced was whether he would be able to hold the city after taking it. Also, he was in a strong position on the coast, but as soon as he ventured inland he knew he would lose the support of his ships.

He chose to negotiate with the Muslim forces, and met with Saladin's brother, al-Adil. According to some sources, Richard offered al-Adil his sister Joan with the idea that the two rule Jerusalem as king and queen! Unfortunately for history, Saladin turned this intriguing idea down. Instead, Richard and al-Adil had a big feast and parted as friends. This rather anti-climactic conclusion can't have been what Gregory VII had in mind when he called for Crusade.

Negotiations eventually resulted in a treaty whereby Saladin kept hold of Jerusalem but agreed to allow Christian pilgrims. The Europeans were to retain the territory they had recovered. So Jerusalem was not in any real sense regained. Richard was being pragmatic though. He realised that he had nowhere near enough men to hold the city against Saladin's forces and if he did take the city it would be lost fairly swiftly afterwards. In the circumstances, free passage for pilgrims and keeping the lands that they'd already taken was a fairly good deal.

With negotiations complete, however, events took an unfortunate turn. On the eve of Richard's departure from Acre in July 1192, Saladin's army suddenly appeared at Jaffa. Richard rushed to the scene but found that Jaffa had been completely routed, worse still Richard and a tiny force (only around 50 knights and some infantry) were left isolated outside the ruined city. Their attack had been entirely independent of Saladin. His troops had acted of their own volition, wanting revenge for the massacre of prisoners at Acre.

Days later, a few hundred troops attacked Richard's remaining forces. The majority of Saladin's army had already mutinied after sacking Jaffa, though; they'd had enough of war. So, too, had both commanders: Saladin had fallen ill, and Richard was anxious to get home because he was concerned about the activities of his brother John back in England (see Chapter 17).

In September 1192, Richard and Saladin signed a three-year peace treaty. Jerusalem stayed in Muslim hands, but Outremer continued to exist in the form of its various coastal towns. Essentially, the Third Crusade finished in an unsatisfactory draw.

Ending unhappily

Neither Richard nor Saladin profited from their agreement:

- Richard suffered a shipwreck off the coast of Italy on his way home and was forced to journey over land. He travelled in disguise but near Vienna was captured by Leopold of Austria, who hadn't forgotten Richard's insults at Acre (remember him from the earlier section 'Dealing with diplomatic baggage'?). Leopold imprisoned Richard and set a massive ransom of 150,000 marks. Richard's mother eventually raised the capital, but Richard was to stay in captivity for the next 12 months before it could be paid. Chapter 17 has more on how this situation played out.

- Saladin fared no better. Having fallen ill in the aftermath of the battle at Jaffa, he never really recovered. He died on 3 March 1193 in Damascus at the age of 67. His empire quickly dissolved into in-fighting between his sons, but Outremer was too weak to take advantage.

In the following years, European religious and military leaders tried again to recruit fresh Crusade armies, but none of these efforts were particularly successful. For the time being, both the Muslim and Christian sides remained content with what they had.

Chapter 16

Following the Fourth Crusade and Other Failures

The Third Crusade didn't turn out as the Western European powers expected. Despite some notable victories, the contest between the Christian and Muslim forces ended up in a draw. As Chapter 15 describes, the kings of England and France took massive armies to the Christian states of Outremer in the Middle East and came back without a great deal to show for the effort.

The idea of Crusading may have lost some of its allure, but from the late twelfth century, and throughout the thirteenth century, various groups again ventured eastwards or engaged in Crusades within Europe against people whom the Church decided were enemies.

In this chapter, I discuss the end of the Crusading period and cover the truly bizarre events that took place in Europe and elsewhere.

Playing a Game of Smash 'n' Grab: The Fourth Crusade

After the chaos of assembling and coordinating the Third Crusade (which I cover in detail in Chapter 15), the papacy initially struggled to drum up interest in a new expedition. Between 1195–1198, a group of German troops led by Emperor Henry VI did venture eastwards but met with little success. In fact, Henry never made it to Jerusalem, dying at Messina, Italy.

Nevertheless, in 1198 Pope Innocent III decided the time was right to ask for another Crusade, to aid the failing kingdom of Outremer and gain full and permanent control of the cities of the Holy Land. He orchestrated a vast plan, applying to many groups and hoping for the best.

Upping the ante: Bigger papal bargains

Because Crusades cost a fortune, major figures such as the kings of France and England had to take the cross and underwrite all the expenses. Pope Innocent III quickly realised that the great nobles of Europe weren't interested in a new expedition.

Crusade was still popular with ordinary people though, who had little to lose and everything to gain. Although the risk of death was obvious – and great – the chance to make a new life for themselves elsewhere and perhaps become wealthier with more land to their name was a powerful incentive. But an even bigger inducement was also on offer.

Innocent made the Fourth Crusade an even better spiritual deal than previous ones by promising not only that participants would have all their sins wiped away, but that they would also definitely enter Heaven and get a 'greater share of eternal salvation'. A great deal indeed!

Struggling to find a leader

Persuading the leading nobles of Europe to take part in a new Crusade proved more difficult. In 1200, however, England and France signed a truce in their ongoing war and some leading Frankish nobles signed up for the Fourth Crusade, among them Theobald, Count of Champagne, who was elected leader. At roughly the same time Pope Innocent applied a new tax on Church revenues to pay for the expedition.

Unfortunately, just as the campaign was gaining momentum, Theobald of Champagne fell gravely ill and died in 1201. One of Europe's leading noblemen, Boniface of Montferrat, replaced him. Boniface was a good choice but no friend of Pope Innocent. One of Boniface's closest associates was Philip of Swabia, who had claimed the title of Holy Roman Emperor but was denied by Innocent III.

The Fourth Crusade finally had a leader, but one likely to do his own thing. Which is exactly what Boniface did, as I discuss in the following section.

Securing Venetian transport

A logistical problem that arose early in the Fourth Crusade was transporting the army eastwards. This situation was solved when papal envoys travelled to Venice and arranged for Venetian-provided ships to transport men and 50 armed galleys to protect the fleet and give naval support.

Unfortunately, not quite enough people turned up to board the Venetian ships. The Venetians had been hired to transport around 35,000 troops and 12,000 at the most actually arrived. In fact, the Crusade was so short of the pope's estimates that the organisers owed the Venetians around 34,000 marks for ships and provisions that they didn't need – and they didn't have the cash to pay Venice.

The Venetians were traders (check out Chapter 18 for more details) and knew how to make a deal. Their leader, known as *the doge*, was Henry Dandalo. Although he was 81 years old and completely blind at the time of the Crusade, he was still able to wheel and deal. Specifically, he promised that if the Crusaders assisted Venice in its war with Hungary and helped attack the Adriatic port of Zara (in modern-day Croatia) on their way east, he would cancel the Crusaders's outstanding debt. Boniface and friends didn't have much choice, and so the deal was made.

Innocent III was furious when he heard about the Venetians hijacking the Crusade for their own purposes, but the Crusaders ignored him: Boniface and the Venetian doge were no friends of the pope. The expedition sailed from Venice in the autumn of 1202, and the port of Zara was taken without much resistance.

Unfortunately, the peaceful occupation of Zara was undermined when the Frankish and Venetian armies took a dislike to each other. Geoffrey of Villehardouin was on the Fourth Crusade and gives this account:

> *Shortly after this* [the taking of Zara] *the most unfortunate conflict exploded between French and Venetian soldiers. Scuffles broke out and soon spread, everyone rushed for their arms and battles raged in every street with swords, lances, crossbows and spears. There were many wounded and killed.*

Tensions were on the rise and were about to get worse.

Sacking Constantinople

The Crusaders wintered in Zara and planned their next move. At this point they came to a quite remarkable decision – to make their next target the city of Constantinople.

Changing direction

Taking Constantinople was a million miles from Pope Innocent III's plan to regain Jerusalem, but the Crusade leaders didn't care. The pope threatened excommunication, but what else could he do? In the event, Innocent sent a letter expressing his disapproval and forbidding the Crusaders from going ahead, but they had already left by the time it arrived.

The Venetians and the Crusaders had their own reasons for attacking Constantinople. For the Venetians, the decision was economic: taking Constantinople would give them total trade dominance in the region. The Crusaders, however, were offered an attractive deal by Alexius (the future Alexius IV), a Byzantine prince who had joined the Crusade at Zara. His father, Isaac Angelus, had been blinded and imprisoned by the current Constantine emperor Alexius III, Isaac's own brother. Alexius said that if the Crusaders helped him get rid of the emperor and gain the throne, he would give them anything they wanted – including a cash reward and, crucially, a formal acknowledgement that Rome was the overlord of Constantinople. The Crusaders were never going to say no.

Plotting and counterplotting

In late May 1203, the combined Frankish and Venetian force set sail for Constantinople. The journey was relatively easy and when the armies arrived, they sailed around the walls of the city parading Alexius on deck, hoping that this display would provoke the people of the Constantinople into revolt. This plan failed.

Instead they were forced to attack: the original Frankish, Crusader army from the land and the Venetians from the sea. The battle featured a remarkable episode in which the elderly, blind doge was carried ashore at the head of his army waving the flag of Saint Mark; he was determined to lead them into battle just as the other Crusade leaders were doing. The armies encamped around the city, and the siege began.

Byzantine defeat seemed clear from the start, and so the weakened emperor, Alexius III, did a runner in the night leaving the city without an emperor. The Byzantine response was to release Isaac Angelus from prison and make him emperor again!

The Byzantines hoped the Crusade army would go away after they elevated Isaac Angelus to emperor, but the Crusaders didn't back down and stayed encamped outside the city. Alexius III may have fled, but Alexius IV had promised the Crusaders a cash reward for their help. In August 1203 the young prince was officially crowned Emperor Alexius IV, alongside Isaac, and they agreed to rule as co-emperors. Meanwhile, the Crusaders prepared to collect their reward.

The treasures of Venice?

One of the most famous results of the sack of Constantinople was the manner in which Venice was decorated with the proceeds. A huge number of valuable items were taken and still survive in the Italian city, including holy icons and relics and many Greek and Roman antiquities.

Indeed, the fabulous bronze horses that still stand in St Mark's Square in Venice were looted from the Hippodrome during the sacking of Constantinople. These sculptures, known as 'the Greek Horses' because they date back to classical Greece, were separated from a bronze sculpture of a chariot. The horses there now are copies but you can still see the originals in the Marciano Museum in Venice, along with many other 'acquired' Byzantine artefacts!

Awaiting payment

Alexius IV owed the Crusaders something like 200,000 marks, provisions for their men and a detachment of around 10,000 Byzantine mercenaries to join them on a mission to Egypt. Unfortunately, he had a bit of a problem – no money. His predecessor had been fond of splashing out, and despite being the richest city in the world, Constantinople was absolutely broke.

Alexius asked the Crusaders to hang on for a year or find something else to do while he made some money. The doge and his fellow Crusader leaders were unimpressed with this suggestion, but for several months the two forces hung around Constantinople like an army of occupation. The bored soldiers continually got into fights, vandalised public monuments and at one point even accidentally set fire to a large area of the city.

Alexius and Isaac were soon taken out the equation when they were murdered by a rival called Murzuphlus, who promptly seized the throne and demanded that the Crusaders go home.

Taking the city

The situation had to change, and fairly soon the Venetians managed to persuade the Franks that the only way forward was to sack the city. In April 1204, they launched an attack. The European armies easily gained control of the city, and the soldiers were given three days to pillage. They didn't waste the opportunity; Constantinople was completely ravaged. The violence was terrible and the booty seized extraordinary, as related in the following quote by the knight and historian Geoffrey of Villehardouin:

> *Each of the powerful men took gold objects or whatever he wanted and stole away with it . . . and the booty was never shared amongst the common soldiers and poor knights, all they ever received was some of the plain silver. The rest of the treasure was wickedly hidden.*

At this point, both the Crusaders and the Venetians forgot about their mission to the Holy Land. Byzantium had fallen, and that was enough. They crowned Baldwin of Flanders as the new Latin emperor of Constantinople and divided the territory of the empire up between Boniface and the Venetian doge.

For the Crusaders, taking Constantinople was a victory, of sorts. A Venetian, Thomas Morosini, was elected as Patriarch (the first Latin cleric to take this role in the Byzantine church) and a large part of the East was effectively reclaimed in the name of the Western Roman Catholic Church, without a single Westerner in the campaign having arrived in Outremer.

Leading Byzantine nobles fled the city and founded new fledgling states in Nicaea, Epirus and Trebizond. They would have to wait over 50 years before managing to wrestle back control of the city, in 1261.

Crusading in Europe

The outcome of the Fourth Crusade – specifically the taking of Constantinople – was rather different than Pope Innocent III imagined (see the earlier section 'Sacking Constantinople'). But, despite threatening excommunication to the Crusaders, the Eastern states were returned to the control of the Roman Church. Ignoring the fact that victory over the Byzantines was very much a side effect of the Crusaders's and Venetians's lust for cash, the papacy launched a new series of Crusades, this time throughout Europe.

Crusades had taken place within Europe before (check out Chapter 14 for more details), mainly aimed at non-Christians who lived within the wider boundaries of the continent. Innocent III was quick to act in a similar way in the early part of the thirteenth century.

Converting the Baltic region, again

An official Crusade in the Baltic took place in 1198, but in 1204 Innocent appointed Albert, archbishop of Riga (in modern-day Latvia) to lead a new expedition against the pagan people living in Livonia. Albert was determined to convert these people to Christianity, and his expedition was manned by Augustinian and Cistercian monks to preach the gospels to the Livonians. Just in case they weren't convinced, he also took along a large body of Templar Knights (whom I discuss in Chapter 14) to kill a few people as alternative examples.

In a series of campaigns that lasted more than 20 years, forced conversions took place across Eastern Europe. By the time Albert died in 1234, modern-day Estonia and Latvia were entirely converted to Roman Christianity. In many ways Albert's campaigns formed one of the most successful Crusades because thousands of people were converted to Christianity as a result of them. His campaigns had very different aims to those of the Crusaders who went to the Holy Land, but had a much more successful outcome.

Reclaiming Castile: The Reconquista

After Innocent III developed a habit of proclaiming Crusade, he just kept doing so. His target after Eastern Europe was the far west of Europe, targeting the Muslim caliphs who had retaken territory from the Christian kingdom of Castile, in modern-day Spain. Innocent had received a request for support from Peter II (who lived 1178–1213), the king of Aragon in northeast Spain.

In 1212, Innocent proclaimed Crusade against non-Christian enemies, and the armies of Castile, Aragon and Navarre were joined by knights from Portugal and France under the command of Alfonso VIII of Castile. In July 1212, Crusading forces won a massive victory over Muslim forces at the town of Las Navas de Tolosa.

This process, which historians call the *Reconquista,* dates back to the first Muslim gains in Spain during the eighth century. The Reconquista carried on all the way through until the fifteenth century and included the siege of Lisbon in 1147 that I look at in Chapter 12. Innocent III's proclamation of Crusade undoubtedly gave the Reconquista fresh impetus.

Fighting the enemy within: Heretics a plenty

By far the greatest and most famous of Pope Innocent III's proclamations was against those he thought of as enemies of the Church within the kingdoms of Western Europe. These campaigns were known as the *Albigensian Crusades.* *Albigensians,* perhaps better known as *Cathars,* were heretics that Innocent III wanted to eliminate.

Meeting some heretics

During the second half of the twelfth century, the heretical group the *Cathars* sprung up in southern France and became extremely popular even among the aristocracy. Their most prominent supporter was Raymond VI of Toulouse who tolerated their activities in his lands. Many different groups of Cathars existed, but in general they supported two heretical beliefs:

- ✔ **Dualism:** According to this belief, love and power were incompatible, and therefore the existence of one God, who was both all-powerful and all-loving, was impossible. Dualists thus believed in the existence of two gods, each representing one element.

- ✔ **Gnosticism:** According to this belief, the physical world was evil and created by an imperfect god. By extension, human souls were divine and trapped in this world. Only death could free humans and enable their souls to join with the god of love.

Both views put Cathars completely at odds with the Catholic Church, an institution that Cathars considered to be created by an imperfect god.

Countering Cathars: The Albigensian Crusade

Pope Innocent III spent many years trying to overturn Cathar influence in southern France, without success. But in January 1208 his legate Peter of Castlenau was murdered, reputedly on the orders of Cathar supporter Raymond of Toulouse. In response, Innocent proclaimed a Crusade against the Cathars.

The resulting Albigensian Crusade was an enticing prospect to potential Crusaders because Innocent promised them Raymond's wealthy and fertile lands if they took up arms. By the middle of 1209, a huge army of around 10,000 men gathered at Lyon, intending to march south.

Massacring at Beziers

The campaign progressed successfully. Nobles, such as Raymond, who tolerated the Cathars, tried to negotiate, but their envoys were refused an audience. The Crusade captured a number of small villages before arriving at the town of Beziers. The attackers demanded that true Catholics leave the town and the Cathars surrender, but they received no response.

The next day the army attacked, and the town fell. In the frenzy that followed, the entire population was massacred, Catholic and Cathar alike. Estimates of the numbers killed are as high as 20,000. In a letter to Innocent III, Arnold abbot of Citeaux describes the horrific events:

> *Our forces spared neither rank nor sex nor age. About twenty thousand people lost their lives at the point of the sword. The destruction of the enemy was on an enormous scale. The entire city was plundered and put to the torch. Thus did divine vengeance vent its wondrous rage.*

Suddenly the kind of massacre and brutality in the name of God that had been carried out in the Holy Land was happening in the middle of mainland Europe.

Nobody expects the Albigensian Inquisition

One result of the Albigensian Crusades was particularly sinister: the Crusade's religious fervour eventually turned in on itself.

In 1229, with *Languedoc* — formerly Cathar-controlled regions of southern France — under French control, Pope Gregory IX initiated the *Inquisition*, an institution intended to investigate those suspected of heresy.

Over the next 100 years, thousands of people were tortured and burned as suspected Cathars, with the full backing of the papacy. This institution Latin was the forerunner of the Spanish Inquisition that began in the fifteenth century.

Burning heretics for decades

The Albigensian Crusade didn't finish after the horrors of Beziers. Unsurprisingly, the Cathars were on the retreat after the massacre, but they were remorselessly pursued by the Crusade leaders, in particular one Simon de Montfort. The Crusaders's next target, in 1209, was the mountain town of Carcassone, which quickly fell. Many other towns and villages subsequently surrendered without a fight.

Captured Cathars were offered the choice between returning to Catholicism or death. If they refused to convert, they were burned at the stake, sometimes hundreds at a time. By 1211 many Cathar strongholds had fallen, and their leaders rounded up. Senior knights were hanged and around 700 other Cathars burned in a huge execution.

Campaigns against the Cathars, and revolts by them, took place almost continually over the next 20 years. Eventually the French king, Louis VIII took the cross in 1226. Campaigns continued under his successor, the child-king Louis IX, and in 1229 Raymond of Toulouse was captured, publicly whipped and forced to make the French king his heir.

The big winner in the Albigensian Crusades wasn't the papacy but the French crown, which eventually inherited a huge amount of territory and a real foothold in the south of the country.

Finishing with the Final Crusades

The Crusades didn't go terribly well in the first quarter of the thirteenth century. Although Constantinople did fall under Latin control (see the earlier section 'Sacking Constantinople'), Outremer hadn't received any substantial military support since the short-lived German Crusades over 25 years earlier.

The mystery of the 'Children's Crusade'

One of the strangest and saddest stories associated with the Crusades is that of the so-called 'Children's Crusade'. Historians still debate the true nature of this unofficial Crusade, but are unlikely to ever resolve the issue because so little written evidence of the episode and its consequences exists.

The traditional version of the Children's Crusade claims that a small boy began preaching in Germany in 1212, claiming that Jesus had called him to bring together an army of children to march on Jerusalem. The boy was remarkably successful and gathered together a group of around 30,000 runaways who walked all the way to the southern French coast where they expected the sea to part and allow them to march to Jerusalem. When this didn't happen, they negotiated free passage from a number of merchants and sailed off never to be seen again. Apocryphal contemporary sources claim that the children were sold into slavery in Tunisia or died in a series of shipwrecks.

Modern historians have argued that this traditional story is probably based on the movement of two groups of young people (not children) who came from France and Germany. The French group never left the country, whereas the group from Germany (about 7,000) ventured as far east as Marseille, but broke up when the Mediterranean didn't part in front of them. Many tried to make their way home, but many others were captured and sold into slavery at the French port.

Whatever the truth, a vast number of young people in the early thirteenth century were apparently moved by preachers to leave their homes and walk hundreds of miles in a bizarre attempt to stage a Crusade. Huge numbers probably lost their lives – or certainly their liberties – as a result.

The Fifth Crusade in 1218 was a total disaster. Having targeted Egypt to strike at the heart of the Muslim power base, the invading army was almost entirely destroyed by the army of Al-Kamil, the Ayyubid Sultan, at Damietta on the northern coast of Egypt. The period of Crusading was coming to an end – but two further significant expeditions did take place.

Regaining Jerusalem: Frederick II and the Sixth Crusade

One man who made a massive impact on the Holy Land in the final years of the Crusades was the Holy Roman Emperor Frederick II, who was known as *Stupor Mundi* – the 'Wonder of the World'.

The wonderful world of Frederick II

Frederick II was an extraordinary man, but then again you have to be to get a name like *Stupor Mundi*. He spent most of his young life in Sicily, where his father Emperor Henry VI gave him his first title of king of the island. Eventually, he controlled an empire that included Germany, Italy and Burgundy, as well as Sicily.

He was unusual for a Holy Roman Emperor in that he was extremely literate, being fluent in several languages (including Arabic), and had a huge interest in all branches of science and knowledge. In fact, he was much more like an Arab leader: his court was full of astronomers and he regularly contacted the great scholars of the age to ask questions of them.

He was hugely sceptical about religion and openly denounced large parts of the Bible as fables and stories and took a notably tolerant and even interested attitude towards people of other faiths living within his lands. He was known to read the Koran.

Devoted to science, particularly the natural world, he was a skilled falconer and possessed a huge menagerie of exotic animals. His interest in human beings was rather more sinister, and he is said to have practised experiments on live victims, including disembowelling two prisoners to ascertain who had better digested his meal that evening! Another experiment involved starving a victim to death in a barrel to see whether his soul was visible emerging through the hole in the top of the barrel when he died!

When he died in 1250, the Medieval World was certainly less colourful without him.

Frederick had been keen to go on Crusade ever since taking the crown as emperor in 1215, but Pope Innocent III ignored him. Innocent enjoyed being 'top dog' in organising Crusades and didn't want one led by anybody too powerful – just look at what happened when the Fourth Crusade went its own way under the leadership of the Doge of Venice (flip to 'Securing Venetian transport' earlier in this chapter).

Getting his way

Frederick eventually got his way when Innocent died and was succeeded by Honorius III in 1216. Honorius had no objection to Frederick and wanted a successful Crusade. Frederick needed no convincing: he was keen to add Jerusalem to his massive empire (see the earlier sidebar, 'The wonderful world of Frederick II') and add honour and glory to his successes.

In 1220, Frederick announced he was going on the Sixth Crusade and asked for volunteers. He even persuaded Honorius III to excommunicate anybody who offered to go and then didn't turn up.

Unfortunately, one of the people who didn't turn up was Frederick himself. Delayed by his own business, he didn't get around to engaging with a Crusade until 1227. During this period he married Isabella, the daughter of John of Brienne the king of Jerusalem. Clearly the war he intended for Jerusalem and beyond was about more than God and the Church – he was looking to expand his empire to include Jerusalem as well.

Holy (dis)orders

During the early thirteenth century, Outremer became increasingly divided and unstable. One of the reasons for the disorganisation was increasing competition, and in some cases, open warfare, between the Holy Orders of Knights in the region. I talk about the Templars in Chapter 14, but equally powerful in the Holy Land were the Knights of St John of the Hospital – called 'Hospitallers' because they built hospitals for pilgrims in Jerusalem – and the Teutonic Knights.

The original purpose of these orders when they were established in the twelfth century was to protect pilgrims and Christian visitors to the Holy Land, but the orders became powerful institutions, hugely rich from trade revenues and taxes, and in almost total control of the cities of Acre and Tyre. The influence of these various knights spread throughout Eastern and Central Europe, and their commercial and banking activities were underpinned by successful Crusading against pagan peoples all over the Medieval World. Unfortunately, their increased factionalism and infighting disabled the Crusader states at a vital time, and they must bear some of the responsibility for the eventual collapse of Outremer. Despite possessing the means to defend, their infighting allowed enemies to take advantage.

The orders had evolved a great deal from their original intentions, well-expressed in the sworn oath of the Teutonic Order: 'I promise the chastity of my body, and poverty, and obedience to God, Holy Mary and you the Master of the Teutonic Order, and your successors according to the rules and practice of the order. Obedience until death.' By the thirteenth century, the latter part was very much the most influential aspect of these immensely rich and powerful knights.

Making a false start

By the time Frederick was ready to leave, Honorius had died and been replaced by a new pope, Gregory VIII, who was much less keen to indulge a headstrong emperor such as Frederick. Gregory's concerns were too little too late, however, because in August 1227 Frederick set sail.

Within two months, though, Frederick was back in Italy suffering from a mystery disease. While he was out of action, Gregory excommunicated him, which meant that, technically, he was unable to lead a Crusade.

Crying for help

Just as this Crusade seemed to be off, it was back on! Frederick received an extraordinary letter from Al-Kamil, the Ayyubid Sultan who had defeated the Fifth Crusade at Damietta. Al-Kamil was under threat from a revolt by his brother and made Frederick an astonishing offer: if Frederick provided him with military aid, Al-Kamil would give back Jerusalem in exchange. The deal was so good, Frederick must have almost bitten his hand off!

Frederick set sail immediately for Acre, ignoring Gregory VIII and his excommunication. The Sixth Crusade became a deal between monarchs.

Retaking the Holy Land

Everything seemed set for a glorious triumphal cap on Frederick's reign, but when Frederick arrived in Acre, he found a very different situation to the one Al-Kamil described in his letter. Specifically, Al-Kamil's brother was already dead and the sultan no longer needed Frederick's help!

Al-Kamil recognised, however, that he was in an embarrassing position and was forced to give in. On 18 February 1229, he officially handed Jerusalem over to Frederick's Frankish forces. Not a single sword had been raised in anger.

With typical humility Frederick crowned himself 'King of Jerusalem' and 'The Last Emperor'. The pope responded by excommunicating him once more and banning all religious services in Jerusalem, the holiest of cities. Happy days.

Frederick left his new kingdom soon after taking Jerusalem and returned to find that the pope had organised a military invasion of some of his territories. He spent the rest of his life fighting papal interference and very soon forgot all about Jerusalem. Crusading was old news, and the papacy was more concerned about heretics in Europe (see the earlier section 'Fighting the enemy within: Heretics a plenty').

Experiencing the last hurrah

By the middle of the thirteenth century, the Crusading period was drawing to a close but one last campaign took place. Although this effort was again driven by a cry for help from the East, Europe wasn't able to respond in time.

Beginning the end

In the middle of the twelfth century, the Mongols and Genghis Khan (see the earlier sidebar 'If anyone can, Genghis Khan') emerged as a new and terrifying threat from the East. Part of the reason for the weakness in the Muslim leadership, which provoked so many civil wars during the twelfth century, was pressure from these new invaders, coming westwards from the very Far East.

In particular, the Egyptian sultan was a worried man. His rich cities were clearly the next targets of the unstoppable Mongol army, and he needed friends and allies. In 1240 he struck a deal with the Franks of Outremer to return all former lands west of Jerusalem to Frankish control in return for military support. Unfortunately the Franks were in no position to take advantage of the additional lands. Two prominent Holy Orders within the Frankish population, the Templars and Hospitallers, were virtually at war with one another, with the cities of Tyre and Acre almost functioning as independent states (the earlier sidebar 'Holy (dis)orders' has more details on these squabbling knights).

Instead of Outremer, the sultan looked to the Khwarazmian Turks, a warlike people who the Mongols had displaced and forced westwards, for help. They became his mercenaries, but he was unable to control them and they attacked Jerusalem in 1244: the Franks were too preoccupied with their internal fighting to protect it. Almost the entire Christian population of 6,000 was slaughtered, the holy sites desecrated and the city destroyed.

Taking the cross: Louis IX

The response from Europe to the fall of Outremer was deafening silence. The world had changed since the first Crusade in 1196, and the Muslim forces no longer seemed to pose the threat that they once had. European monarchs and the papacy were more concerned with internal heretics such as the Cathars. Europe's only connection with Jerusalem was the steady supply of pilgrims journeying there.

One man, however, did respond – the French king Louis IX. He had to, really. When news of the sacking of Jerusalem broke, he was ill, probably with malaria. He promised that if he recovered he would take the cross. Sadly for him, he got better. Given the way that his Crusade went, he may have been better off sticking with malaria.

Louis IX took more than four years to get ready for a Seventh Crusade. The quest was specifically a French expedition, although the pope paid for it. Nobody else wanted to go; Frederick II even advised Louis not to bother.

Messing around by the river

This Seventh Crusade was doomed from the start. Louis's plan was to invade Egypt and unseat the sultan, before taking back the cities of the Holy Land. Louis sailed to Cyprus to use it as a base for attacking Egypt and left there in May 1249 with the intention of landing at Damietta, the Egyptian port and taking the city. However, Sultan as-Salih Ayub knew that Louis was coming – Frederick II had written him a letter tipping him off! Not the best of starts.

For a short time, things were more promising. Damietta was eventually captured and by November 1249 the Crusaders were advancing towards the Egyptian town of Mansourah in the Nile delta region. The Nile proved a continuing problem for the Crusaders: in order to cross the many branches of the river, wood was taken from ships to help build causeways, and many men were lost when they tried to swim.

If anyone can, Genghis Khan

Genghis Khan, leader of the Mongols, was an absolute leader, and his people numbered hundreds of thousands. In 1141, the Seljuk Sultan had sent a force against the Mongols near Samarkand (in modern-day Uzbekistan), and the Mongols had utterly destroyed them. Although he never came as far as the Mediterranean himself, the chaos and upheaval that Genghis caused had a huge impact on Outremer and the surrounding states.

By the time he died in 1227, Genghis Khan's huge empire stretched between the Caspian Sea and the Sea of Japan. The situation continued under Genghis's successor, Ogedai Khan. The Mongol army continued to push west and hundreds of thousands of people were displaced and fled into Syria where they sold themselves into the service of the local emirs.

In February 1250 the Crusade army attempted an attack on the Muslim camp outside Mansourah. Despite initial success, the army was quickly surrounded and, more importantly, cut off from any potential escape route. Louis IX and his nobles were eventually found in a small village nearby and captured by the sultan's troops.

Paying the price

Getting captured was hugely embarrassing for Louis IX: it was also expensive, really expensive. The ransom was set at a massive 400,000 livres. To put this amount in perspective, the annual income of the kingdom of France at the time was probably around 250,000 livres.

The French nobles had to take out a massive loan from the Templar Knights to pay for Louis's release. They also had to give up Damietta. The end result was that nothing had been gained from the Seventh Crusade at absolutely vast expense.

Blundering on

But Louis wasn't finished yet! He spent the next four years in the Crusader kingdoms of Acre and Jaffa trying to rebuild their defences and heal the huge issues between the various nobles and the Holy Orders of Knights who were still pretty much openly at war with each other.

Back when Louis was laying siege to Damietta in 1248, he had sent an embassy to the Mongol Khan, providing him with gifts and asking for support. In 1251, three years later, Louis finally got an answer, and the news wasn't good. The Khan stated that he readily accepted the gifts and was pleased to accept Louis as a vassal!

The Khan also insisted that as his new subordinate, the king of France must send him a tribute every year. His tone was rather threatening:

> *We command you to send us a yearly tribute of gold and silver if you wish to retain our goodwill. Otherwise we will destroy you and your people as we destroyed others who rebelled against us.*

Thundering west: Mongols

The Khan's words weren't an idle threat; they were a promise. In 1256, the Mongol army moved westwards led by Ogedai Khan himself. All the traditional heartlands of the East were utterly destroyed and armies routed along the way. The Muslim caliph was killed in Baghdad, and the former Seljuk Empire completely finished off.

To Louis IX, the Mongol advance through Muslim territory must have seemed like deliverance, but it wasn't because the Mongols didn't stop there. They advanced on Aleppo in Syria, and the city fell. Soon after Damascus was under threat and then Antioch. The Prince of Antioch submitted to the Khan as did the Emir of Damascus. By 1259, the influence of Islam was being utterly eradicated from the Holy Land – not by a Crusader army but by a pagan ruler who was also wiping out the last remnants of Western influence.

Fortunately for the Franks, Ogedai Khan died later in 1259, and the majority of his army returned to Mongolia to dispute succession before turning on the Crusader states. Outremer wasn't totally finished, but had experienced a close-run thing.

Ending things: The Mameluks

The death of the Mongol leader, Ogedai Khan, failed to save Egypt. Khwarazmian Turks – who were responsible for the pillaging of Jerusalem (see the earlier section 'Beginning the end') and known as the *Mameluks*, which means 'owned' – were in the service of the Egyptian sultan, as-Salih Ayub, as mercenaries. When he passed away during Louis IX's Crusade, the Mameluks rose up, killing his successor and seizing control of Egypt.

They named their own sultan, a man called Kutuz ibn Abdullah. As warlike as any Mongol Khan, Kutuz ibn Abdullah began systematically destroying all opposition to his sultanate. He left the Crusader states alone for the time being, only proving what minnows they had become, and instead headed for a confrontation with the Mongols. The two sides came together in battle at a place called Ain Jalut, known as 'The Pools of Goliath' in modern-day Palestine, on 3 September 1260. For the first time in history, a Mongol army was completely defeated in open battle.

Within a few years the cities of Aleppo and Damascus had fallen to the Mameluks and a new sultan called Baibars built an empire stronger and more fearsome than that of Nu red-Din or Saladin (turn to Chapters 14 and 15, respectively). The Holy Orders and small groups of European nobles made various small-scale attempts to protect the Crusader states, but these came to very little, mostly because of the petty squabbling and infighting of the Frankish nobles. In 1271, Prince Edward of England (the future King Edward I – check out Chapter 17) arrived in Tyre. Disgusted by the infighting and political intrigue that he found, he left without going on a campaign.

In many ways, the Crusader states lasting as long as they did was a surprise. In 1289, Tripoli fell to the Mameluks and in 1291 the Mameluk army arrived at Acre. The situation was hopeless. The Franks attempted a night-time raid on the Mameluk camp, but it ended with disastrous consequences, as told by the Mameluk chronicler Abu al-Fida:

> *Seeing that our troops had begun to outnumber them, the Franks fled back to the town. The Mameluk troops managed to kill some of them. As dawn broke al-Malik al-Muzaffar, leader of the Mameluks, had a number of Franks' heads fixed to the necks of the horses which the Mameluk troops had captured that night, and sent them to Sultan al-Ashraf Khalil.*

Acre fell shortly afterwards and the city was razed to the ground on 18 May. Within the month, the Franks abandoned Tyre and shortly afterwards Sidon and Beirut. By 1 June 1291, Crusader rule anywhere in the Middle East had come to an end.

Critiquing Crusading

Various sporadic attempts were made in Europe during the fourteenth century to revive interest in campaigns in Outremer, but none came to anything. Hugely expensive foreign missions with no guarantee of success were out of fashion. New issues and causes were ripe throughout Europe (see Part IV for details).

Crusader rule and the kingdom of Outremer lasted for a little under 200 years. A Muslim state run by former slaves, known as the Mamluk Sultanate of Egypt, replaced it; a state that created a system of financial and social control the likes of which the Crusaders were never capable. The sultanate lasted for hundreds of years and was still in place at the beginning of the nineteenth century.

In 1297 Pope Boniface VIII decided to canonise the recently deceased Louis IX because of his Crusading valour. The decision was hugely ironic: the folly of Louis's Crusade created a far harder-line and more destructive enemy of Christianity in the Mameluks than the First Crusade had been called to defeat almost exactly 200 years before.

Part IV
Dealing with Domestic Dramas: Parliament, Priories and Plagues (1200–1300)

The 5th Wave — By Rich Tennant

AT THE BEGINNING OF THE HUNDRED YEARS WAR

"The peasants are pillaging the castles, the plague has killed another 10,000 people, but good news Your Highness—the war shouldn't last much longer."

In this part . . .

In this part, I examine what was going on in Medieval Europe during the thirteenth century. Highlights include international traders making a packet, monasticism spreading throughout the region and Marco Polo travelling to China. Quite a lot of things went wrong too; King John of England was absolutely incompetent, the papacy managed to have bizarre arguments with itself and the Black Death killed millions. Quite a busy old time, really.

Chapter 17

Having Trouble in England: John, Henry III and Edward I

In This Chapter

▶ Getting into trouble with King John and the Magna Carta

▶ Forcing Henry III to create parliament

▶ Rising up against Edward I with William Wallace

During the thirteenth century, Western Europe moved closer to the geographic boundaries and political institutions recognised today. In addition, as the century progressed, the differences between England and France became even more pronounced, and the way England was governed changed enormously.

Most of these changes happened by accident rather than design, particularly during the reign of King John who was as controversial in the thirteenth century as he remains today. After John, Henry III and Edward I both experienced their own problems with their barons and other enemies as England and the British Isles proved very difficult to rule.

Reliving the Ruinous Reign of King John

King John of England is a hugely controversial figure. Was he a rubbish king or just unlucky? Whatever the case, he seems to have been massively unpopular during his reign (1199–1216), and chroniclers at the time were critical about him and his record.

John wasn't helped by the fact that he inherited the throne from his brother, Richard I, who was something of a medieval superstar (check out Chapter 15 for more on Richard) and certainly a big, bold personality. John's reputation has probably suffered in comparison, but he did get off to a tricky start.

Splitting with France

Richard I died on 10 April 1199. He wasn't in England at the time; in fact he never returned after he left to go on the Third Crusade (as I describe in Chapter 15). Richard was killed at a place called Chalus-Chabrol in southwestern France, where he had been campaigning to protect his French territories. Despite being extremely active with medieval ladies, Richard died without leaving an heir. As a result, the throne of England became vacant.

Ascending the throne

Although Richard left no direct heir, two contenders did exist:

- Richard's younger brother John, who had been regent in England from the time Richard left on the Third Crusade.
- Richard's 12-year-old nephew Arthur (the son of Richard's dead brother Geoffrey).

The contest, such as it was, ended swiftly. On 25 April 1199, John was invested as the Duke of Normandy in Rouen and then just over a month later crowned as the new English king at Westminster.

The entertaining death of Richard I

Typically for Richard I, even his death was a good story. As with everything in his life, his death has a hint of the unbelievable about it but most sources cite something along the following lines.

Richard had been besieging a small castle at Chalus-Chabrol in France. One evening, while inspecting the defences without wearing his armour, an enemy crossbowman who had been taking pot shots at Richard's army all day saw the king and let an arrow go. The arrow just missed Richard, who applauded the archer and challenged him to try again. The crossbowman did so, and this time hit the king in his left shoulder.

Richard staggered back to his tent where his surgeon bodged the job of removing the arrow.

The wound soon turned gangrenous, and Richard fell into a fever. The castle had fallen by this time, and so he asked that the crossbowman be brought before him. The archer turned out to be a young boy. Showing characteristic chutzpah, Richard didn't have the boy killed but instead awarded him 100 shillings and gave him his freedom.

Richard died soon after, in the arms of his mother, the aged Eleanor of Aquitaine who was an impressive 77 years old at this point. Unfortunately for the crossbowman, one of Richard's mercenary captains decided to take revenge on him. He was recaptured and flayed alive before being hanged.

Young Arthur's supporters tried a brief rebellion in 1200, but it was easily beaten back by John who then signed a deal with the French king, Philip Augustus, which confirmed him in all his French possessions and territories, and restricted Arthur to some land in Brittany. Figure 17-1 outlines the division of lands.

The agreement with France was just about the last occasion that things in John's life went so smoothly! Although he was newly crowned, the king was 33 years old and very experienced in all the aspects of being a monarch – which makes what happened next all the more difficult to understand. Modern historians still argue today whether John was incompetent or merely unfortunate. Read on for what happened, and then make up your own mind.

Complaining to a higher authority

In 1202 the barons of Poitou, a territory just south of Brittany, put in a complaint to Philip Augustus about John. They were unhappy with a war that John had carried out against their allies in Brittany, and that he'd married a woman called Isobel of Angouleme, who they alleged was already betrothed (or engaged) to another man, Guy of Lusingnan!

The relationship between England and France at this time was extremely complicated. John held territory in France as well as the title 'Count of Poitou', meaning that he was the lord of that area. However, Poitou was technically overseen by the French monarch and whoever was the Count of Poitou had to submit to the king of France as his overlord. Just because John also happened to be the king of England and the Duke of Normandy didn't make any difference to his role in Poitou.

Philip heard the barons's complaints and summoned John to attend a court hearing. John refused to attend, and Philip claimed that as a result all John's French territories were forfeited and everything that had been taken from Arthur should be returned to him. This wasn't really fair as Philip should only have really taken Poitou, the area that the argument was about. Nevertheless, at a stroke John lost the French territories that English kings had spent centuries building up!

Going from bad to worse: Losing Normandy

John was hardly able to take the loss of his French territories lying down, and the result was war. Just like Richard before the Crusades, John faced the problem of mobilising his army. He needed the full support of his English barons so that their men undertook to serve in the king's army, but this support wasn't immediately forthcoming. Nevertheless, at first, John managed a successful campaign in France during 1202–03, and he seemed about to reassert control. Although the French king had officially taken away John's territories, places such as Normandy, where the barons ignored Philip's decision, were still loyal to him.

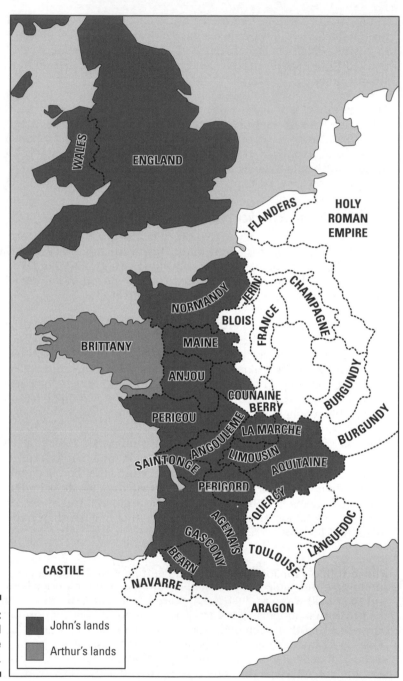

Figure 17-1:
England
and France
around 1200.

John's lands

Arthur's lands

The mysterious fate of Arthur

Nobody is entirely sure what happened to Arthur after his uncle John's forces captured him. The only facts are that Arthur was imprisoned in 1203 and never seen again.

The traditional story is that John kept him prisoner in the castle of Rouen in Normandy, France, before John personally killed him and threw his weighted corpse into the River Seine. Another version has John ordering that Arthur be castrated (to avoid the problems of any descendants) and the boy dying of shock after the presumably horrendous operation. One of John's lieutenants claimed that this was the case but later changed his story and claimed that Arthur was still alive. The likeliest explanation is that Arthur died in captivity, but how and by whose hand is open to question.

The case of Arthur is one of the main reasons why John was famed as a tyrant. (He also imprisoned Arthur's sister, Eleanor: she remained in captivity until her death in 1241.)

During the 1202–03 war with France, John's nephew Arthur revolted. During a remarkable episode, John's forces captured Arthur while he was attempting to kidnap his own grandmother, the 79-year-old Eleanor of Aquitaine!

Eleanor had been making her way to Arthur to try and dissuade him from attacking John. Arthur got wind of this and caught up with Eleanor at a place called Mirabeau (in Provence, southwestern France), laying siege to the castle where she was staying. Fortunately for Eleanor, John arrived and drove Arthur's troops off, capturing him in the process.

The event was clearly the last straw for Eleanor who entered a convent shortly afterwards. She died there three years later at the age of 82 – a grand old age for the time.

Whether or not John then killed Arthur (see the sidebar 'The mysterious fate of Arthur), he certainly suffered for it. His war, which had been going well, took a decisive turn after Arthur's imprisonment. Brittany, however, which had always been loyal to Arthur, revolted against John, as did many of the barons of Normandy. Philip Augustus turned his attention to the duchy, whose support for John was tepid and getting weaker. Instead of just invading, Philip Augustus campaigned like a modern politician, claiming that John wasn't to be trusted and that he'd deserted the duchy.

Philip's machinations worked. In the summer of 1204, Philip Augustus made an official entry into Normandy, the duchy having completely gone over to his side. Of all the territories that had been held in France and Normandy, only the Channel Islands now remained loyal to the English king. For the first time since 1066, the king of England was isolated across the channel.

Collapsing further

The loss of French territories and the revolt of the duchy was more than enough to cast John as an ineffectual king, but worse – indeed, much worse – was to come.

Losing Normandy and the French lands didn't just affect the English crown. The vast majority of English nobles who had lands in the regions were now in grave danger of losing them, and consequently of withdrawing their support from John. John forced people to make a choice: if they paid homage to Philip for their French lands, they had to give up their lands in England. Philip responded in kind. Within a few years, the relatively young countries of England and France effectively became two completely separate entities for the first time.

Reacting to the pope saying 'nope'

Most of the European rulers that I cover in this book seem unable to go a whole reign without somehow upsetting the pope. John was no different, but he did go several years before managing to come into conflict with the papal powers.

The Archbishop of Canterbury, Hubert Walter, died in 1205. Both the chapter of Canterbury cathedral and John had their preferred candidates for a successor, and an argument ensued. Just to complicate matters, Pope Innocent III declared that the papacy should choose because only it had the right to do so (see Chapter 13 for all the details of these investiture debates). The papacy named its chosen candidate, Stephen Langton.

John refused to accept the pope's decision, and the situation soon turned into a mini-investiture crisis. Innocent III placed an *interdict* on England (a forced closure of churches), and John happily closed them down and confiscated their properties and estates, making a tidy sum for the crown in the process! Innocent was enraged and excommunicated John in 1209.

John carried on regardless, but by 1213 Innocent was calling on European leaders to crusade against heretics and proposing tougher measures that foreign leaders could have interpreted as a virtual licence to invade. Another concern for John was that he really didn't want to give the barons another stick with which to beat him – being declared an enemy of the papacy would not have gone down well with them – and so he was finally forced to back down in 1213 (see the sidebar 'A question of interpretation'). He signed a humiliating treaty in which he agreed to pay the papacy an annual tribute of 1,000 marks in return for papal approval. Humiliation at the hands of Innocent III was just another blow to John's prestige.

A question of interpretation

The reign of King John is one of the most controversial in medieval history due to the huge debate about John's decisions and policies that continues to this day. His dealings with Pope Innocent III are a great case in point. At the time, being forced to back down to the pope in 1213 was seen as a humiliating defeat and was a great blow to his prestige with the nobility of England. However, by Tudor times John's actions were interpreted as a bold strategy. The Tudor king Henry VIII had forced a complete break with Rome and to the Tudor political mind John was an amazing figure who had tried to do the same thing 300 years before Henry.

Recent historians have found yet a further interpretation of events. At the time of John's disagreement with Innocent III, King Philip of France was also in trouble with him but managed to get onside more quickly and regain papal support. This presented the very real possibility that Philip might try and invade England, claiming that he was representing the interests of the Pope. Accordingly, modern historians have suggested that coming to terms with the pope, however humiliating, was actually a clever move to try and ward off a potential attack by Philip.

John's reign throws up many such talking points. Was he useless, unlucky or actually quite smart and simply misunderstood? It's all a question of interpretation.

Pushing the barons to breaking point

In 1211, John had to suppress an uprising in Wales led by Llywelyn I, the Prince of Gwynedd (north Wales), who was the effective ruler of the principality. Innocent III had approved of this revolt, regarding it as a Crusade against John, the enemy of the papacy!

Dealing with the revolt in Wales forced John to suspend his plans for renewing the war with France. Unfortunately, he didn't put off his French plans completely. The campaign that began in 1213 was a disaster, culminating in defeat at the Battle of Bovines (near modern-day Lille) in July 1214. The war left 1,000 English dead and 9,000 captured, and the defeat forced John to pay huge financial settlements to the French crown.

The Battle of Bovines was the last straw for the English nobles. Confidence had totally evaporated in John. Many had revolted during the Welsh rebellion and also following John's excommunication. By 1215 the English monarchy was in crisis.

Agreeing to the Magna Carta

John met with his deeply dissatisfied barons on 15 June 1215 at Runnymede. He was forced to agree to the 'Great Charter' (in Latin, 'Magna Carta'), one of the most famous documents in world history.

The main point of the Magna Carta was that it forced the monarch to acknowledge that his power was not absolute, and that in fact it was controlled by law. All freemen were also granted certain privileges and rights, many of which are now foundations of English law. Concepts such as *habeas corpus* – the right of appeal against unlawful imprisonment – find their roots in the Magna Carta.

Probably the most significant part of the Magna Carta was the creation of a council of barons whose job was to ensure that the charter's actions were enforced. The council never actually came into force, but simply through being prepared to create it John suffered loss of face. Clause 61 of the charter describes the council:

> . . .*we give and grant to them the underwritten security, namely, that the barons choose five-and-twenty barons of the kingdom, whomsoever they will, who shall be bound with all their might, to observe and hold, and cause to be observed, the peace and liberties we have granted and confirmed to them by this our present Charter.*

This clause almost completely disempowered John as king. He effectively signed away the power of the monarchy by agreeing to be supervised by a council. Although he rubbished clause 61 as soon as he rode away from Runnymede, he was unable to escape it. The clause caused a fatal blow to his prestige as well as forming the basis for the idea of a parliament, which came to fruition under Simon de Monfort in 1258. See 'Playing a game of Simon (de Monfort) Says' later in this chapter.

Reaching an ignominious end

Unsurprisingly, John never recovered from the blow of signing the Magna Carta. Shortly afterwards, Prince Louis of France invaded England, at the invitation of many of the barons who had met with John at Runnymede.

John was forced into an emergency tour of the country in an attempt to raise an army, and during this time, he suffered his last great humiliation. While travelling through East Anglia, he took a roundabout route to avoid crossing the treacherous channel known as The Wash. However, he was so concerned about being caught by the French that he sent his baggage train across the water to escape any potential raiders; this decision was a tragic mistake. An unexpected high tide swept in and sank his treasury, crown jewels and all. Friendless and deserted by his barons, he was now also completely broke.

The game was up, and John fell gravely ill very shortly afterwards. He died of dysentery a few days later on 19 October 1216, at the age of 49. His reign had been a catalogue of woes from beginning to end. (To see how he compares to some other great medieval failures, flip to Chapter 25.)

Making the Best of a Bad Job: Henry III

In 1216, when King John died, the English monarchy had pretty much reached its lowest ebb (as I describe in the preceding section 'Reaching an ignominious end'). Fortunately, John left only one possible heir, a nine-year-old son! In many ways this boy – who would quickly become Henry III – was on to a winner from the start of his coronation, because it was unlikely that things could get too much worse!

The barons who had undermined John saw the accession of a child as the perfect opportunity to enforce the Magna Carta, and so they proclaimed Henry as their king. A deal was signed with Prince Louis of France at the treaty of Lambeth in 1217, and for the next ten years a regent called William Marshal, the Earl of Pembroke, controlled the country until Henry came of age.

Pitting baron against baron

Henry reached adulthood in 1227, at which point the period known as his Personal Rule began, a period marked by troubles. Unsurprisingly, Henry struggled to enforce his authority over the barons who had been running the country while he was growing up, but a series of other issues also didn't help matters.

Probing the problem with Poitevins

Part of Henry's problem came from his own inner circle of advisors, men who were hugely unpopular in England. They were mostly *Poitevins* from the Poitou district of France, from where Henry's family came. In some cases, these advisers were related to him.

Poitevin influences immediately put Henry at odds with the English nobles who had revolted against his father, King John. Ever since John lost his French territories, the nobility of England had begun to think of themselves as separate from France and resent others who they considered as foreign usurpers.

Playing a game of Simon (de Monfort) Says

One of the principal 'foreign upstarts' in England at this point in Henry's reign was Simon de Monfort. He was the Earl of Leicester but French by birth, and he descended from the nobility of Flanders. At first a keen ally of the king, de Monfort became an enemy when Henry publicly accused him of seducing his (Henry's) sister, forcing Henry to allow their marriage.

De Monfort was appointed to administrate the English territories in Gascony, in the south of France, but Henry then tried to charge him with corruption. Much to Henry's displeasure, a council of barons acquitted de Monfort, but worse was to come and Henry had made a serious enemy.

De Monfort began to gather support among the 'English' barons who were keen to ensure a return to the original Magna Carta and force the king to rule under the principles set out in the charter, including the discarded clause 61 about the council of nobles.

Events came to a head in 1258 when Henry was forced to attend a meeting in Oxford organised by de Monfort and seven leading barons. A new treaty was signed. Building on the Magna Carta, it destroyed the absolute power of the monarchy, replacing it with a council of 15 barons that dealt with the business of the kingdom. Council decisions were to be reviewed three times a year at a meeting known as a *parliament*. Henry would continue to rule but as little more than a puppet king. The English parliament had been created.

Bursting out in civil war

Henry III signed the renewed charter under pressure and spent the next few years trying to get out of it. In 1262, he received the backing of the pope, who issued an official *papal bull* (a legal pronouncement) that refuted the charter and absolved Henry from any duty to follow it.

Civil war was inevitable and followed soon afterwards. De Monfort and the rebellious barons were very successful, winning a string of small victories. Finally they met Henry and his supporters at the Battle of Lewes in May 1264.

De Monfort wrote to Henry asking him to submit to the demands of the barons, but he received the following letter (preserved by a monastic chronicler) in response:

> *Since, from the war and general confusion existing in our kingdom, which has all been caused by you, and by the conflagrations and other lawless mischiefs, it is distinctly visible that you do not preserve the fidelity which you owe to us, and that you have in no respect any regard for the safety of our person, since you have wickedly attacked our nobles and others our faithful subjects, who have constantly preserved their fidelity to us. Witness my hand* [meaning 'signed by me', the writer]*, at Lewes, on the twelfth day of May, in the forty-eighth year of our reign.*

Henry's words were brave but ultimately hollow. He lost the battle and was taken prisoner. For the next year or so, the monarchy was effectively abolished and de Monfort's barons ruled through the new parliament. Such a situation didn't happen again until the English Civil War in the seventeenth century.

Recovering the crown: The battle of Evesham

But the monarchy wasn't out of power for long. Henry's eldest son Edward was also captured after the Battle of Lewes, but he escaped shortly afterwards and set about gaining support for a comeback.

England was in total uproar, and the three years up to 1265 are known as the Second Barons' War. De Monfort and his rebellious barons were supported by the Welsh prince Llywelyn ap Gruffyd, and western England was the main area of conflict. Eventually the barons and Edward met outside Evesham, a small market town in Worcestershire.

The choice of battleground was very much Edward's. Following a tactical victory, he cut off Simon de Monfort from many of his supporters who were on the other side of the river Avon. De Monfort's forces were outnumbered almost two to one. The battle was furious and extremely bloody; Simon de Monfort and his son were both killed and the king's supporters won a vital victory.

The aftermath of the battle was almost as disturbing. Simon de Monfort's corpse was mutilated – his head, hands and private parts were cut off by furious royal supporters. Furthermore, Edward disinherited any noble who had taken part in the rebellion and their lands became the property of the crown.

Passing quickly

Henry was finally released from captivity following the battle of Evesham, but his reign only lasted for another seven years. He died in 1272 at the age of 65 and was buried in Westminster Abbey.

Edward was his obvious successor, but he had been on Crusade since 1268 and was still out of the country. His expedition was a failure, however, and he became frustrated by the political situation in the Crusader states of Outremer (as I describe in Chapter 16). He was on his way home when he heard the news of his father's death. He spent further time in Gascony before eventually he returned to England in 1274 and was crowned Edward I. Another tumultuous reign was about to begin.

Rudolf the 'No Show' Hapsburg

Around the same time that England was in uproar, a new and powerful family was making a name for itself in Germany. Rudolf of Hapsburg was the German king (and took the title 'King of the Romans') between 1273–1291.

On becoming king he showed that he had taken on board the lessons of previous Holy Roman Emperors' battles with the pope, and immediately renounced any imperial rights in Italy and promised to go on Crusade. The vast majority of his reign, however, was spent fighting to protect and expand his territory within Central Europe.

His most significant achievement was taking control of Austria and Styria (modern-day southern Austria and Slovenia) and securing them for his descendants. This act had two far-reaching impacts; first, these territories formed the core of the modern-day country of Austria, and second, they became the bedrock of the Hapsburg dynasty.

The House of Hapsburg became the dominant royal family of Europe for hundreds of years. Between 1470 and 1740 every Holy Roman Emperor that was elected came from this very extended family, which eventually branched out into Spanish and Austro-Hungarian sections.

Rudolf himself is most famous for being the first of the Hapsburg kings, and the rest of his reign wasn't really that distinguished; he never brought peace to a troubled and divided Germany and never went on that promised Crusade! As a result, he appears in Dante's epic poem *The Divine Comedy*, sitting outside the gates of Purgatory and being mocked as 'He who did not do what he ought to have done'.

Haggling over Homage: Edward 1

Edward I was crowned as king of England in 1274, and by then the rebellious England nobility had settled down a bit; and yet he still faced huge challenges throughout his reign. He spent a great many years producing legislation that would restore some powers that the crown had lost under John and Henry III. Edward was, overall, quite successful, but the main problem he faced was a series of wars based around the concept of *homage* – the ceremony where a feudal tenant publicly promised loyalty to his lord.

Paying homage to the French monarch had caused problems for King John, and Edward faced similar issues both at home and abroad. The key problem with homage was that it obliged one man to make a public display of his subservience to another. Most people today would find this action a bit embarrassing, but with medieval kings and nobles who commanded armies and vast estates, paying homage was a massive issue and a huge amount of blood was spilt as a result.

The situation was even more complicated during Edward's reign because Henry III had signed the Treaty of Paris with the French king in 1259. In this treaty, Henry had promised that he and all his descendants would do homage to the French king for all the territories that they possessed. As a young prince, Edward had agreed to this too.

Waging Welsh wars

Edward's first homage controversy was with Wales. The Welsh nobility had joined in with Simon de Monfort's revolt during the second Barons' War (for more, flip to the earlier section 'Recovering the crown: The battle of Evesham'). Their leader, a man called Llywelyn ap Gruffyd, had done pretty well out of the revolt because he became the first to be granted the title of Prince of Wales. Others in Wales were less pleased, in particular the lords of what was known as the 'Welsh Marches', the territory on the border between England and Wales.

Continual revolts within this territory took place throughout Edward's reign, and he fought a series of battles to try and put them down. As ever, the key issue was paying homage to a foreign king.

By 1284 Edward had had enough and put in place the Statute of Rhudlan, which incorporated Wales into England while simultaneously providing it with its own administrative system that exactly mirrored the English one. Wars with the Welsh continued until, in 1301, the king also made his eldest son (also named Edward) the first English Prince of Wales, which is the title that Prince Charles holds today.

Losing himself in France

Edward I had been frustrated in his attempts to go on Crusade in 1268, but it remained an ambition. However, he also realised that no Crusade stood any chance of success unless the leading monarchs of Europe were willing to work together. He spent much of his early reign in fruitless diplomacy as other kings scuppered his plans for unity. He finally gave up when Acre fell in 1291 (turn to Chapter 16 for more details) and the last chance for a successful Crusade had clearly passed.

With that in mind, Edward changed tack completely and started causing some trouble himself! His attention switched to the one French territory that he had left, the Duchy of Gascony, for which he had to pay homage to the French king!

Tall stories?

Edward I is famously known as 'Longshanks', meaning 'long legged' or 'long shinned'. Numerous medieval rulers have been called tall by their contemporaries, with some leaders who were just of average height given the distinction based on their imposing presences. In Edward's case though, references to his height seem to be true.

In 1774, Edward's tomb in Westminster Abbey was opened by the Royal Society of Antiquaries. Despite the fact that he had been dead for more than 450 years, his body was apparently well preserved. Measurements were taken of the corpse and he was found to be about 185 centimetres (6 feet 2 inches) in height. This made him very tall by medieval standards, probably taller than the average medieval man by 20–21 centimetres (8 inches). Longshanks indeed!

Edward was also known as the 'Hammer of the Scots'. See the section 'Taking up the Great Cause: The Scottish Question' and decide for yourself whether this name was accurate!

Edward spent several years in Gascony up until 1294 when something unfortunate happened. Several murderous fights had broken out between French sailors and their English and Gascon counterparts, and ships were torched as a result. The French king Philip IV summoned Edward to Paris to explain this situation and he refused to go. In response Philip declared Gascony forfeited to the French crown – a tactic that Edward was all too fond of using on the Welsh!

A brief and pointless war ensued. Although Edward had support from other French nobles, he eventually had to give up and go home. Gascony was left under the control of the king's officials because Edward had other problems to attend to, specifically a Scottish revolt.

Taking up the Great Cause: The Scottish question

Relations between the kings of England and Scotland had never been as hostile as between England and Wales. Technically, a question of homage was the culprit here: the English king was the overlord of his Scottish equivalent, but for many years nothing like the same level of opposition to this situation had existed in Scotland as had in Wales. In fact, relations had been quite cordial with several intermarriages and no significant revolts.

In 1286, King Alexander III of Scotland died without leaving a male heir. His daughter Margaret was married to Eric II of Norway, and they had a three-year-old daughter, also called Margaret. A treaty was arranged between Eric and Edward I that she would marry Edward's one-year-old son (also called Edward, the Prince of Wales). This arrangement would still keep Scotland one step removed from the control of the English crown.

Unfortunately, like many great plans, this one didn't work out. In 1290, at the age of seven, Margaret died while crossing from Norway. Her death left Scotland without an heir, an issue that came to be referred to at the time in both England and Scotland as 'The Great Cause'.

A total of 14 people put their names forward as official candidates and rather surprisingly the king of England was asked to make the decision as to who would be the Scottish king! Eventually, in 1292, Edward chose John Balliol ahead of his chief rival Robert the Bruce, and put him in place with the use of the English army.

Drumming up that braveheart spirit

John Balliol's coronation was ruthlessly enforced by the English army, but his leadership lasted only until 1296. As soon as the English military presence began to drift away, a rebellion was begun by the charismatic William Wallace.

Wallace was a knight and landowner who turned out to be an inspired general and leader of men. He and his rebels routed a much larger English force at Stirling Bridge in 1297 and forced Edward to respond. Over the next six years, Wallace fought a guerrilla war against the English, avoiding open battle and engaging in almost continual raiding on English forces and territories.

Unfortunately for William, he lost the diplomatic war. During this time Edward I managed to bribe and convince many Scottish nobles to come over to his side. Eventually in 1305 Wallace was captured by his own side and handed over to the English, who had him publicly executed in London before installing English nobles and pro-Edward Scots to run England.

The exploits of William Wallace are memorably shown in the film *Braveheart* (1995). If you can get past Mel Gibson's slightly shaky accent, the depictions of medieval warfare are fantastic. Edward I is portrayed as an almost pantomime villain and the film plays very fast and loose with the facts, but it's still well worth a watch. Be warned though, the film's incredibly – and realistically – violent. Never more so than in showing Wallace's grisly death by evisceration and beheading!

Butting heads with Bruce

Scottish resistance didn't end with the death of William Wallace. In February 1306, Robert the Bruce (the grandson of one of the contenders for the throne ten years earlier) had himself crowned Robert I, King of Scotland.

In the years that followed, he crushingly defeated the English army on several occasions. The brutality of Edward's response served only to rally more people to Robert's cause. Robert I ended up ruling until his death (possibly from leprosy) in 1329. Scotland's independence from England had been won.

Ending things in a draw

Edward I died in July 1307 at the age of 68. He was immediately succeeded by his eldest son Edward II.

Edward I's reign still divides modern historians. Traditionally, he's been seen as a king who tried to create constitutional government out of the mess that the Magna Carta created. Whether or not this view is true, England was certainly more settled at his death than at that of his father Henry III.

Chapter 18

Meeting Medieval Monks and Merchants

*B*y the thirteenth century, two communities had become extraordinarily influential in the Medieval World: Monastic orders and merchant guilds.

✔ *Monastic orders* were religious communities living under one roof where everyone followed a particular version of Christianity with its own exclusive practises and beliefs. The lives of medieval monks and nuns were interesting and different from those led by the vast majority of people, and they played an important role in wider society.

✔ *Merchant guilds* were collectives of merchants and trading companies who came together to combine their efforts in search of greater trade dominance. Guilds cornered the market in the big cities and established new trade routes to far away and hard-to-reach places.

In a sense nothing was new about these groups. The influence of religion and the need to eat and to make money had always provided some of the biggest influences on the medieval mind. The institutions that grew out of these concerns, however, were much more than the sum of their parts.

In this chapter I take a look at the emergence of these two new medieval powers whose interests and influence came to play a part in the big decisions being made in the Medieval World.

Contemplating the Religious Orders

As I discuss in Chapter 9, Christianity experienced a massive upsurge during the ninth and tenth centuries throughout the Medieval World. The intensity of people's beliefs and the way that faith dominated their lives increased hugely. Most historians think that one of the main reasons behind this surge in belief was the influence of the monastic orders. The following sections explore who these people were, what they did during the medieval period and how they became vital to the working of society during the tenth and eleventh centuries.

Examining the origins of monasticism

Throughout history, certain people have tried to separate themselves from the day-to-day stresses of the everyday world and seek a simpler, if more self-disciplined, life of religious prayer and contemplation. *Monasticism*, the practice of renouncing worldly pursuits and fully devoting one's life to spiritual work, appears in all religions and throughout many regions of the world. In the turbulent times of the early Middle Ages, more and more men and women sought refuge in religious communities.

Although monasticism in Greek literally means dwelling alone, total seclusion was rarely possible, even during medieval times. In order for religious groups to be able to function, they had to continue to integrate with the rest of society – they needed supplies of food and other essentials that they couldn't entirely produce by themselves. The monasteries and abbeys that thrived during the medieval period did so because they were able to combine a life of spiritual contemplation with an active role in their local communities.

Meeting the man who thunk of being a monk: St Benedict

St Benedict (AD c. 480– c. 550) is the man most credited with the concept of Christian monasticism. Although informal monasticism had existed before Benedict, becoming popular in the West by the fourth century AD, he was the first person in Western Europe to codify the lifestyle and be specific about the role of monks and nuns in society.

Benedict, the son of a nobleman from Umbria in Italy, founded 12 communities for monks in Italy, as well as a large monastery in Monte Casino. One of the most famous orders of monks is the order of St Benedict (check out 'Calling the role: Notable orders' later in this chapter), but he wasn't really responsible for starting it. Benedictine monks chose to live by his principles rather than join a specific order that he established. Benedict was eventually made a saint by Pope Honorius III in 1220.

Anchorites and coenobites

Over the centuries and up to the present day, many religious people have interpreted the roles of monks and monasteries in vastly different ways. Two groups that illustrate the extremes of the range of interpretations are anchorites and coenobites.

An *anchorite* is somebody who completely withdraws from the world, often to the extent of being a hermit and living apart from any other human being. Anchorites devote themselves entirely to religious contemplation, eating and drinking only the bare minimum to exist. Many anchorites managed to withdraw by bricking themselves up in a small cell within a building. Not a great deal of fun, but then fun isn't the point of monasticism!

One of the most famous *anchoresses* (female anchorites) was St Julian (1342–c. 1416). Her original name is unknown; she was named after her church in Norwich, England. She spent more than 40 years living in a small cell in the church, which you can still visit today. She recorded her experiences and visions in a series of highly influential, mystical writings.

In contrast to anchorites, *coenobites* believe that they're duty bound to live and work in religious communities. They reside in communal, religious accommodation set within the larger and more complex buildings of a monastery. They work along with their fellow monks or nuns instead of bricking themselves up in small cells.

Coenobite life can still be pretty quiet. Established in the sixteenth century, the Trappist order of monks vow only to speak when absolutely necessary and discourage idle or conversational talk. Nobody knows whether their vow is the origin of the expression 'Keep your trap shut!'

Benedict is rather ironically considered to be the father of Western monasticism – ironically because he himself was more like a hermit than a monk and spent a large amount of his adult life living in seclusion in Subiaco (about 40 kilometres, or 25 miles, east of Rome).

Benedict's most significant influence was through a document called 'The Rule', in which he set out the role and purpose of a monastic community. The Rule suggests that these communities face inward and be concerned with their spiritual health, but also look outward to the world and address the spiritual health of all people. In other words, The Rule gave monks a new purpose: to go out and pray for their neighbours and work in their communities. The Rule placed no greater value on either activity, suggesting a moderate middle way between individual spiritual concerns and the spiritual health of the wider world. In doing so, it virtually set a template for monastic life.

Get thee to a nunnery!

Monastic life wasn't a male-dominated activity. An equally important, if different, role was played in medieval society by female orders. A community of nuns was known as a *convent* or a *nunnery*. These communities were established along the lines of all the religious orders mentioned in 'Calling the roll: Notable orders', except the Carthusians.

Nuns took very similar vows to their male counterparts, undertaking a vow of chastity, poverty and obedience. Convents tended to be as self-supporting as possible and were perhaps slightly more withdrawn from the outside world than monasteries. For this reason, many young women were often sent into convents by their families. The process of placing a girl into a convent was similar to betrothing her to a husband in that the family were expected to find a dowry that was in this case payable to the church. However, women would join convents via a variety of different means: many older women would join after the death of their husband or to live out their final years in quiet contemplation.

Women could join a convent as an oblate or a postulant. An *oblate* was a child given to a convent as a small baby to be brought up as a nun.

This would often be done with children found deserted and occasionally with illegitimate children of the nobility. A *postulant* was a mature person seeking admission to the convent, who would be considered a postulant until approved for training – a process that took a matter of weeks. A girl or woman that passed through the postulant stage would be then considered a *novice* and be in full religious training. This stage would last for one year, after which she would take the full vows and be thought of as a *nun*.

A nun was effectively married to God, so on becoming a nun a ceremony was carried out in which she would wear a ring symbolising this. Nuns would then take on roles within their own internal community, usually having some specific duty concerned with running the convent or educating the novices. Other nuns would have a role in the wider world, the most common being that of an *almoner*, dispensing care and supplies to the poor and the sick and praying for the spiritual health of their locality. Convents were a closed world and the nuns inside weren't usually allowed to leave, so few of them became the big business that monasteries developed into.

Calling the roll: Notable orders

A huge variety of Christian religious orders developed in the Medieval World, and many continue to the present day. Here are the major monastic orders with medieval roots:

- ✓ **Benedictine:** These monks follow St Benedict's Rule, although each community interpreted (and continues to interpret) it differently. Benedictine orders were particularly prominent in England and France during the Middle Ages.

- ✓ **Carthusian:** Founded by St Bruno in 1084, near the village of Chatrousse in the French Alps, the Carthusians are one of the most reclusive of all Christian monastic orders. The monks live in their own cells, and speaking is rare except for religious chanting and scriptural readings during communal services. They are renowned for producing the famous Charteuse liqueur.

For a great insight into the original Carthusian monastery, La Grande Chartreuse, take a look at the 2005 film, *Into Great Silence*. Containing hardly any talking and no narration, this fascinating documentary follows a year in the community through the lives of the monks.

- **Cistercian:** This self-sufficient, austere order, also known as the 'White Monks' because of the colour of their robes, is enclosed (known as *eremitic*). They interpret St Benedict's Rule very literally. Members spend their lives in prayer and contemplation and in physical labours that support their communities, sometimes involving agriculture or the brewing of ale! The first Cistercian community was founded by Robert of Molseme in 1098 near Dijon in France.

  Cistercian communities tended to be founded in remote places a fair distance from other communities. Because of this trait, the ruins that still survive are in some very exposed and romantic places like Fourtenay in France and Poblet in Spain.

- **Dominican:** This order, founded by St Dominic in France in 1216, has long focused on teaching and education within the wider community. Many of its members also held and continue to hold important and influential positions of state, including many popes.

- **Franciscan:** This order was founded by followers of St Francis of Assisi, who was inspired by a sermon in 1209. The order originally had a strict attitude towards ideas of poverty and abstinence, which provided the basis for a number of controversies and debates in the thirteenth and fourteenth centuries, such as the great papal arguments that you can read about in Chapter 19.

Going about monastic work

As I outline in the preceding section, the different monastic orders and the lives of the monks and nuns were varied, as were the ways in which the orders engaged with their local communities.

Most orders were based in *abbeys*, which were essentially large monasteries or convents. Abbeys were far more complex institutions than those of the smaller, more contemplative monastic orders. The difference was similar to visiting a modern-day school as against a university campus. Each abbey was run by an abbot or an abbess, who was the spiritual leader of the abbey and the surrounding community.

By far the most influential medieval abbeys were Gorze in Lorraine and Cluny in the Burgundy region of France. See the later sidebar 'Cluny – Toeing the corporate line'.

Cluny – Toeing the corporate line

Founded in 909, Cluny Abbey in Burgundy was founded on land donated by William I, Duke of Aquitaine (875–918). It became an international brand and a symbol of the new Benedictine monastic way of life. By the twelfth century, nearly 2,000 other European abbeys and monasteries were associated with Cluny.

The theological research and teaching that took place at Cluny was hugely influential on religious thought throughout the whole Medieval World. Not coincidentally, Pope Urban II used the influence of Cluny to call for the First Crusade in 1095 (turn to Chapter 11 for the origins of the Crusade). In a world where international communication was far more difficult than today, the spiritual influence of a large abbey was tremendously important.

Indeed, the following curse leaves little doubt of what would befall anybody who didn't respect the institution. Duke William issued this curse upon anybody who failed to show Cluny a suitable level of respect:

First indeed let him incur the wrath of almighty God; and let God remove him from the land of the living and wipe out his name from the book of life, and let his portion be with those who said to the Lord God: Depart from us; and with Dathan and Abiron [who rebelled against Moses in the Old Testament] *whom the earth opening its jaws swallowed up, and hell absorbed while still alive, let him incur everlasting damnation. And being made a companion of Judas, let him be kept thrust down there with eternal tortures, and, let it seem to human eyes that he pass through the present world with impunity, let him experience in his own body, indeed, the torments of future damnation, sharing the double disaster with Heliodorus and Antiochus* [treacherous kings], *of whom one being coerced with a sharp blow scarcely escaped alive; and the other, struck down by the divine will, his members putrefying and swarming with vermin, perished most miserably.*

Building up the abbeys

By the eleventh century, coenobite abbeys were the centres of their local community. Abbeys were mighty constructions. They typically contained the largest local church, which also served as the focus of abbey life. The church was surrounded by areas for the monks and nuns to eat, sleep and work, as well as the *Chapter House* where theological debate took place.

Abbeys also provided education for both *novices* who wanted to join the order and the general population. Infirmaries were available to provide medical care for individuals inside and outside the abbey. Most abbeys also had guest quarters for hosting important secular and religious visitors or to shelter pilgrims on their way to various shrines.

Probably the best preserved and the most studied of these institutions is the Abbey of St Gall in Switzerland. First erected during the ninth century, this abbey features more than 30 separate buildings, each with specific purposes in the working of the community. It was and is an incredible site and you can still visit today.

Considering the cold, hard cash

By the thirteenth century, more than 50,000 abbeys covered the Medieval World. Most were incredibly efficient and almost self-sufficient, which allowed them to produce surpluses that they then traded.

The value of the abbeys's agricultural land was also immense. After the monarchs of Europe, the churches were the biggest landholders. This value often made them a target for acquisitive kings, the most famous example occurring during the Tudor period in England with Henry VIII's dissolution of the monasteries between 1536–1541. (See *The Tudors For Dummies* by David Loades for lots more about this.)

The situation for convents was very different. Being so much more closed off from the world they were unable to trade, and were usually much poorer as a result. Convents depended on the support of local communities who valued the spiritual care they received in return.

The following Domesday Book entry from 1086 (Chapter 10 contains much more on the Domesday Book) gives an indication of the wealth of the Abbey of St Peter in Winchester, England:

> *The same Abbey holds Miceldevre in demesne [Micheldever in its territory]. In King Edward's time it was assessed at a hundred and six hides. It is now assessed at eighty-five hides and half a yardland. Here are seventy-two ploughlands; nine in demesne. Sixty-four villeins and twenty-eight cottagers have twenty-five ploughlands. There are twenty-two serfs; a mill, which yields thirty pence; thirty acres of meadow; and woods for four hogs. [. . .] The value of the whole manor was in King Edward's time sixty pounds; and when it came into possession forty pounds. The abbot's demesne is now worth fifty-seven pounds.*

Unusually, this particular abbey lost value following the Norman invasion of 1066 (which I describe in Chapter 10). But the property's value soon rose again, in tandem with the rising economic power of all the abbeys and monasteries. Eventually, these institutions became big players in the other great medieval revolution – the revolution in trade.

Balancing Profits and Losses: Medieval Trade

Trade had thrived in Europe ever since ancient times. In both the Greek and Roman periods, trade was extensive, with goods such as silks, spices, wine and metals travelling huge distances. Even the fall of the Roman Empire didn't massively impact trade because people still needed goods. But in the thirteenth century, trade in Europe went through a major transformation and expansion – and it never looked back.

Changing the very nature of trade

During the thirteenth century, trade blossomed within nations, internationally and even across continents. The big movers in this change were Italian merchant cities such as Venice, Pisa and Genoa. These cities were relatively peaceful and secure, which provided them with opportunities to expand their trading operations significantly. As the following sections describe, they introduced big changes in how trade was organised, paid for and accounted to drive this trade, as opposed to any single, specific event.

Hiring agents

Traditionally, merchants had been always on the move, travelling with their goods and being present at the point of sale. This arrangement changed in the thirteenth century when mercantile businesses in Italy became prosperous enough for the merchants to stay at home. A three-stage process developed: merchants employed specialist goods carriers who made their livings by transporting things from place to place, delivering items along established trade routes to distant agents, who sold the items at prices determined by the merchants. Figure 18-1 shows the major trade routes of the day.

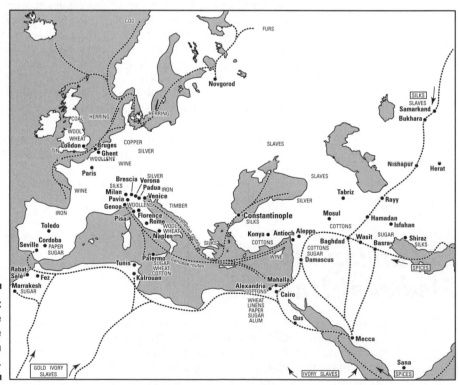

Figure 18-1:
Major trade routes in the thirteenth century.

The following letter is an excellent example of this new three-stage trade practice. The quote comes from an acknowledgement note dating from 1248, written by an agent to a merchant that he represents:

> *June tenth. In the year of the Incarnation of the Lord 1248. I, Bartholomew, son of the late Benedict of Lucca, confess and acknowledge to you Rolland Vendemmia, of Lucca, that I have had and received from you as an order twenty-three pounds and ten solidi* [Genoese currency], *invested in armor and in prepared silk and gold wire from Lucca and in two cross-bows, renouncing, etc. With that order I shall go, God willing, on the next journey I make to Montpellier, by sea or by land, for the purpose of selling the said things, with God's favor and at the risk of the sea and to your profit. I promise by this agreement to repay you all the capital and the profit of the said order, retaining for myself what I expend for the transport and sale of the goods, pledging all my goods, etc.*

I wonder whether he ever came good on the agreement?

Founding trade colonies

After a while, towns with large numbers of agents began to form their own kinds of colonies. Venice, Pisa and Genoa all had colonies throughout the Mediterranean. The purpose of colonies was to establish a distribution centre for goods as well as a place for agents to be permanently based so that they could find new customers and markets. For example, the territory of Galata in Constantinople was a Genoese colony and they built the large Galata tower that still stands in modern-day Istanbul to protect their interests.

Competition for trade colonies was fierce. For example, Venice's involvement in the Fourth Crusade (which I describe in Chapter 16) was primarily based on the city's desire to establish more control of trade in the Adriatic and colonies in Constantinople. These colonies also provided handy bases for long voyages. Venetian ships travelling to Constantinople were able to stop at a number of (usually island) bases on their way to the Byzantine capital.

Establishing trading companies

The concept of the trading company emerged during the thirteenth century. Merchants had worked together before but usually just agreed to invest jointly in a single voyage or series of trading operations. These arrangements gradually became more permanent to the point where companies were formed.

The main reason for the creation of these trading companies was the evolution of financial practices. Amazingly, all the following practices developed hugely in the thirteenth century:

- **Accountancy** took on the tasks of recording everything that was happening financially. Merchants had previously dealt personally with customers, but now a whole new network of transactions needed to be recorded. These new skills first developed in various Italian cities, particularly Genoa, which developed schools for these 'notaries'.

- **Banking** had been going on for hundreds of years, but during the thirteenth century it got serious and went international. The biggest development was the creation of *bills of exchange*, which freed merchants from having to carry bucketloads of cash around all the time. Instead, bankers as far apart as Paris and Antioch were able to pass credit notes, which encouraged larger deals to take place. Most major European cities became part of an ever-growing network of banks. *Usury* (money lending) also became a far more complex business.

- **Communication** became increasingly important. During the thirteenth century, several Italian cities and business guilds began their own courier services. These companies were in addition to the services started by large religious organisations such as the Templars and the Teutonic Knights (check out Chapters 14 and 16 respectively for more on these groups). A lot of business letters survive from the period and show how up-to-date the authors were with events taking place some distance away.

- **Insurance** was increasingly necessary as trade deals became riskier and more complex. An early system developed in which the ship owner transporting goods advanced a loan to the merchant covering any losses that may occur. Gradually this system changed into separate companies providing this service, enabling merchants to buy insurance cover.

- **Share options** first came into being around the middle of the thirteenth century. Several investors grouped together in a contract, or *commenda*, and agreed to undertake mutually the risks in a series of trading ventures and share whatever profits came out of it as a dividend. Essentially, the stock market was born!

Things didn't always work out in merchants' daily lives. In Shakespeare's play *The Merchant of Venice*, the merchant Antonio gets in trouble with Shylock the moneylender (or usurer) because his ships are lost at sea and he's uninsured. A film version starring Al Pacino (2004) is a good production of this classic play with connections to medieval history and commerce.

Armour for hire!

The range of original documents regarding trade that survive is quite staggering. Modern historians can review original price lists, ship manifests, insurance documents, tax agreements and all manner of other things that I don't have space to include.

One of my favourites is the following, written by a knight wanting to hire some armour so that he could go on Crusade in 1248:

July twenty-seventh. In the year of the Incarnation of the Lord 1248. I, Bonfils Manganelli, of Gaeta, acknowledge and confess to you, Atenoux Pecora, of Gaeta, that I have taken and received from you a certain suit of armor at a rent of seventeen solidi in mixed money now current in Marseilles, which seventeen solidi I have already paid you, renouncing all claims, etc. This armor I should take on the next voyage I am to make across the sea, for the price mentioned, at your risk and for your profit, going across the sea and returning to Marseilles. But if, on the completion of the said voyage, I should make another voyage with the said armor, I promise to pay you by this agreement, as hire for the said armor, one augustal of gold, and on the return from the said voyage to pay you that augustal and to return the armor or its value, namely seventy solidi in mixed money now current in Marseilles, if by chance the armor should be lost through my fault. Or I promise to bring the said armor to your profit under pledge of all my goods, present and future, renouncing the protection of all laws, etc. Witnesses, etc.

This document hints at one of those wonderful lost stories from history. Did the knight make it on Crusade and ever bring the armour back? We'll never know. Incidentally, he was probably paying about 25 per cent of the price of the suit to hire it.

Trudging through Italian trade wars and tribulations

On the one hand, these commercial advances were great boons to people throughout the Medieval World, and yet wherever money was to be made there were also fights to be had. The Italian cities were almost continually in conflict with each other, endeavouring to dominate trade routes and set up new colonies. Several notable conflicts of the era were based in trade issues.

The Sicilian Vespers

Despite its name, the Sicilian Vespers – one of the more interesting episodes in medieval history – has nothing to do with Italians riding scooters. In fact, the Sicilian Vespers took the form of a revolt on the island of Sicily in 1282 against the rule of Charles of Anjou (also known as Charles I), the king of

Sicily. A series of wars followed, lasting all the way through to the beginning of the fourteenth century. The rebellion takes its name from the fact that it began during evening prayers (vespers) on Easter Monday, 1282.

The series of events following the 1282 uprising are extremely complicated, but the relevance to trade is clear: nearly all the great and good of Europe got involved at one stage or another, including the Holy Roman Emperor, because Sicily was so vitally important in the trade of sugar, wheat and cotton. (Figure 18-1 highlights Sicily's prominence in multiple routes.)

The Grand Company

For every legitimate trading company (turn to the earlier section 'Establishing trading companies'), there was a group of what historians politely call 'adventurers' and who we might refer to as robbers or pirates. Piracy was still big business in the Mediterranean (see Chapter 7 for more on early medieval piracy), but groups such as The Grand Company (also known as The Catalan Company) were even more organised.

When the Sicilian Vespers came to an end in 1302, Roger de Flor recruited the soldiers and mercenaries who had become unemployed to form The Grand Company. Roger then offered their services to the Byzantine emperor in his war with the Ottoman Turks in Asia Minor and he was quite successful. However, Roger had political ambitions and was eventually betrayed by the emperor. He took his revenge by ravaging the cities of Thrace and Macedonia and getting very rich from the proceeds.

Continuing to offer their services to the highest bidder, the Grand Company prospered under a number of leaders and eventually set themselves up as the legitimate rulers of large chunks of Greece, ruling in Thessaly and Athens all the way through until 1390. Not bad for a bunch of heavies!

Expanding in the North

Many of the advances in trade happened in Southern Europe, mostly based around the Mediterranean, but the thirteenth century also saw advances in trade in the North:

- Fishing, particularly herring, was one of the biggest industries, which the Scandinavians dominated.

- Wool and the cloth produced from it was the major import/export in England, Flanders and northern France.

- The mines in Germany produced large amounts of copper and silver, which were highly valued in other countries.

ELSEWHERE IN THE WORLD

Marco Polo – to the ends of the earth

The vast expansion in trade also saw Europeans travel farther than ever before. The most significant traveller was Marco Polo (1254–1324). A nobleman and merchant from Venice, Marco Polo is credited with being the first man to introduce Europeans to the people and culture of the Far East. He travelled to Asia Minor, Persia (modern-day Iraq and Iran), China and Indonesia, meeting the Mongol leader Kublai Khan, who asked Polo's entourage to visit because he wanted to meet Europeans. Polo recorded his experiences in a book called *Il Milione*, in which he gives a detailed account of meeting Kublai Khan at his capital located in modern-day Beijing.

At 9,000 kilometres (5,500 miles), the journey from Venice to Khan's kingdom must have seemed almost unimaginably long. In total, Polo journeyed for 24 years (between 1271–1295), during which time he's estimated to have travelled around 24,000 kilometres (15,000 miles).

Ironically when Polo returned home, he didn't move much at all. Venice was at war with Genoa (over trade issues, unsurprisingly), and Marco Polo was captured and thrown in prison. He didn't waste his time though, putting together *Il Milione* during his captivity (although it may have actually been written by somebody else). After being released he returned to Venice and continued to work successfully as a merchant, never leaving the city again. I suppose any more trips would have been a bit of a let-down.

Getting together: The Hanseatic League

Given the relatively separate industries throughout Northern Europe, one development of the thirteenth century was a real surprise. *The Hanseatic League* may sound like a football tournament, but it was an alliance of trading guilds and cities that dominated the coast of Northern Europe all the way through until the seventeenth century. Originally founded in a small way in the eleventh century, the League saw a massive expansion during the thirteenth century as more and more cities joined it.

In essence, the league was an idea similar to the agents and colonies that were used in Southern Europe (see the earlier section 'Changing the very nature of trade'). Merchants within a northern town would form their own guild, or *hansa*. Under its mutual protection they agreed partnerships with guilds in foreign towns and cities, particularly far to the east where the towns were less developed but rich in important commodities such as amber, fur and timber.

The league began in the town of Lübeck in northern Germany, gradually forming alliances with other German cities such as Hamburg and eventually farther east to ports in the Baltic sea. By the mid-thirteenth century, league representatives had travelled as far as the Russian port of Novgorod, over 2,250 kilometres (1,400 miles) away across very treacherous waters.

Gradually the league expanded into Norway, England and Flanders until the vast majority of ports were associated with it, because not being so made life financially difficult. The Hanseatic League worked as pretty much a monopoly on all trade in the region. Member cities often had a *hansa* community where merchants and businessmen lived with their families, much like the colonies founded in the Mediterranean.

In the following 1231 agreement, the town of Riga (in modern-day Latvia) grants a house for *hanse* traders from Lübeck to live in:

> *To all the faithful of Christ seeing these presents, the citizens and consuls of Riga wish the enjoyment of perpetual peace. Since those things which are done lapse with the passage of time, and unless they are corroborated by written testimony, will easily slip the memories of men, and be changed, we wish it to be known to all people both now and in the future that we, on the advice of the citizens of Lübeck, for the preservation of that true love and the constant faith we have in the citizens of Lübeck, have granted a court lying near to the citadel, within the walls of our city, to be held freely with every right and the income therefrom, to be possessed by them and their heirs free and forever. Therefore, in order that no calumny may arise in the future, and in order that all doubt may be removed, we have strengthened this gift of ours, corroborating it in writing and with our seal.*

Finding safety in numbers

The benefits of being a member of the Hanseatic League extended beyond the financial. In the thirteenth century, although the peak of Viking activity was over, raiders from Scandinavia were still a problem (Chapter 8 has much more on the Viking raiders), and league money paid for military protection for its members. The league fought several successful campaigns against piracy in the Baltic, and spent vast revenues to build lighthouses and schools that provided training in navigation and seamanship.

By the fourteenth century, the league's power was so great that it was able to take on entire nations! Between 1361–1370 the league was at war with the king of Denmark, Valdemar. They were successful in this conflict too, forcing the king to hand over 15 per cent of all trade revenues to the league. Formed for the protection of its owners, at the height of its power, the league was more like a Mafia protection racket!

Expanding trade during the thirteenth century had very different outcomes in the north of Europe as compared to the south. Although trade wars were common in both areas, the Hanseatic League was formed, initially at least, for mutual protection, whereas competition was the order of the day in the south. But that's what the free market is all about, I suppose!

Chapter 19

Piling On the Popes: Avignon and the Antipopes

. . . .

In This Chapter

▶ Counting popes at Avignon

▶ Whipping up things with the Western Schism

▶ Calming divisions at the Council of Constance

. . . .

*T*he medieval papacy loved a good argument. As I explore in Chapter 9, arguments between Christian leaders in Eastern and Western Europe produced the first schism during the ninth century. Then, some 200 years later, the *East-West Schism* of 1054 split medieval Christianity into Eastern (Greek) and Western (Latin) branches, which in time became the Eastern Orthodox Church and the Roman Catholic Church.

Well, fast-forward around 300 years, and something even more remarkable happened. The papacy managed to split again, but this time with itself! During the fourteenth century, the papacy divided into two groups – one in Rome and the other in Avignon, France – both of which claimed to have the true pope. Read on to find out more about this truly remarkable series of events!

Reaching Crisis Point: Church versus State

Between 1309–1378, seven separate popes based at Avignon in southeastern France questioned the legitimacy of the pope in Rome. The major reason for this bizarre situation was conflict between Church and State rather than some grand theological debate. But the conflict's roots went much further back in history.

Historians refer to the fourteenth-century period of papal disagreement as *the Avignon Papacy*. Some commentators at the time of the crisis referred to it as *the Babylonian Captivity of the Papacy*, meaning that the good nature of the papacy was held captive by the Beast of Babylon or, in other words, those who supported the alternative papacy in Avignon.

Continuing an eternal argument

The massive problems between papal and secular rulers during earlier centuries were largely centred on the question of *investiture*: that is, whether Church or State had the right to appoint bishops (turn to Chapters 9 and 13 for more details). In the centuries that followed, the divisions of power between Church and State had become even murkier.

The papacy had taken on a big secular role during the Crusades (check out the chapters in Part III) by calling for and recruiting armies. Previously, the monarchs's and nobles's ability to command armies had given them power over the pope. But the papacy's initial success in forming armies added massively to its prestige and influence. The many leading kings and nobles who went on Crusade were essentially 'working for' the papacy.

The papacy's *temporal power* – its mixed role as both secular and religious leader – became only more confusing and also more out of control during the thirteenth and fourteenth centuries. Although the pope was a spiritual leader, he was also a landowner and political administrator. With regard to the Vatican and other papal estates, he had the same powers and responsibilities as a duke or lord.

Making mounds of money

As a landowner, the papacy was rich – very rich. Like any other land or property owner, it had taxes to collect. Following is a quick list of some of the most significant charges that the papacy levelled:

- **Tithes:** The papacy taxed all Church property at 10 per cent of its value, and all communities were expected to contribute 10 per cent of their profits or crop to the papal coffers. The man tasked with collecting tithes was called, somewhat amusingly, a *decimator*. Tithes were by far the biggest source of revenues for the papacy, simply because of the vast amount of territory from which it could raise tithes.

- **Benefices:** A *benefice* was a piece of land given to a priest, bishop or other ecclesiastic and the revenues that derived from it. The intention was that by receiving the land, the priest would be better able to carry out certain spiritual duties as a result and thus receive payment or donations for his services. So, granting a benefice was effectively a form of patronage, like that enjoyed by kings and nobles through the feudal system (see Chapter 3). Competition for the best benefices (and therefore bribery and corruption) was extremely fierce.

- **Annates:** An annate was payable at the end of the first year of any benefice and amounted to the entire profits from the post, paid to the papacy. The size of some bishoprics meant that their annates to the papacy were seriously large amounts of cash.

- **Other taxes:** The papacy also initiated many other taxes for things such as Crusades (both national and international), as well as extra charges, rents, taxes and increases in the amounts payable from benefices and annates.

As well as being hugely profitable these taxes were completely unregulated by anybody except the papacy. They decided what to charge and possessed the administrational system required to enforce that decision across the whole of Medieval Europe. The taxes were all likely to be paid too. Failure to pay taxes could mean the withdrawal of a benefice or, worse, some kind of spiritual penalty. People in the Medieval World were terrified of failing to pass into Heaven (see Chapter 2) and believed that the papacy had the ability to influence their likelihood of doing so.

All these charges and taxes meant that by the late thirteenth century the papacy was very wealthy, which led to the position of pope being zealously fought over – and ripe for corruption. Some of the popes of the later end of this period lived richer and more indulgent lives than kings. They partly financed this lush lifestyle by accepting huge bribes to grant valuable benefices to rich candidates.

During this period, the candidates for the role of pope also changed. Big Italian families such as the Colonna in Rome fought like cats and dogs to get their family members into positions of influence and it became the norm for one of their members to get the job. These types of fights had been going on for centuries, but the scale of arguing and bribery had become breathtaking. Although the period did have its good popes, this situation meant that being spiritually driven to do a good job became increasingly difficult in the bloated political administration that surrounded them.

The first bothersome Boniface

Indulgent popes were nothing new to the thirteenth and fourteenth centuries, and neither was the idea of different people claiming to be pope at the same time. The two issues came together rather nicely in Pope Boniface VII (nothing to do with Boniface VIII, whom I discuss in the later section 'Fighting for the top: Boniface VIII and Philip IV').

Boniface VII was born Franco Ferrucci and seized the papacy in 974 after allegedly having his predecessor, Benedict VI, strangled. Boniface didn't prove very popular in his new job and was forced to do a runner to Constantinople the same year – but not before squirreling away a vast fortune from the papal treasury. While in Constantinople he still claimed to be pope despite the fact that a successor had been appointed, and so he was very definitely an *antipope* – a rival pretender to the true papacy.

In 984 he staged a comeback, returning to Italy and unseating the current incumbent, John XIV, who he had imprisoned and then starved to death! Fortunately, like all the best villains, Boniface got his comeuppance. His second stint as pope proved even less popular than his first; when in July 985 he died, he was *flayed* (had the skin stripped from his body) and his corpse was dragged through the streets of Rome.

Boniface VII's story shows that people had been abusing the position of pope for centuries, but by the fourteenth century, corruption (albeit on a slightly less Hollywood scale) had become endemic and much more systemised.

Fighting for the top: Boniface VIII and Philip IV

By the beginning of the fourteenth century, the papacy was dying in Rome. The infighting between rival families combined with the corruption and indulgence of many high officials was bad enough, but the demands for secular power made matters even worse. The situation finally broke wide open with Pope Boniface VIII in 1301.

Boniface's extreme bull

To be honest, the situation wasn't Boniface's fault. As I mention in the earlier section 'Continuing an eternal argument', the problems with the papacy holding temporal power had been growing, and in 1301 these issues really kicked off. For the previous 20 years, the kings of England and France had been charging the Church and clergy their own secular taxes to help finance wars against each other. The papacy had been protesting against this practice, but the straw that broke the camel's back was the arrest of the Bishop of Pamiers by King Philip IV of France in 1301.

Boniface's response was to issue a famous papal bull (edict) known as the *Unam Sanctam*, which renounced any privileges that had previously been granted to French kings. Boniface followed up the bull a few weeks later with the statement that 'God has placed us over kings and kingdoms'. According to Boniface, every human being on Earth was subject to the pope's authority.

These events opened up again the old argument about primacy between pope and monarch.

War of words – more

Boniface can't have expected Philip to take his bull and subsequent statement lying down, but even the pope must have been surprised at the king's response. After replying in the same tone to the pope, Philip called a council of his nobles at which he accused Boniface of a vast number of crimes including simony (the selling of religious offices – probably true), sodomy (unlikely), sorcery (interesting but unproven) and heresy.

A furious war of correspondence ensued that came to a close only in 1303 when Philip sent his troops to Rome. The pope fled to his home town of Agni, but the king's army caught up with him.

Philip's troops surrounded the town and then captured the pope, as described by the historian and writer William of Hundlehy:

> Not even the pope was in a position to hold out longer. Sciarra [Philip's commander in Italy] and his forces broke through the doors and windows of the papal palace at a number of points, and set fire to them at others, till at last the angered soldiery forced their way to the pope. Many of them heaped insults upon his head and threatened him violently, but to them all the pope answered not so much as a word. And when they pressed him as to whether he would resign the papacy, firmly did he refuse – indeed he preferred to lose his head – as he said in his vernacular: 'E le col, e le cape!' which means: 'Here is my neck and here my head.' Therewith he proclaimed in the presence of them all that as long as life was in him, he would not give up the papacy.

Boniface was deeply affected by the attack, and some sources say that they saw him being beaten. Whatever the case, he died a few weeks later, ushering in an era of great confusion.

Establishing the New Papacy in Avignon

Boniface VIII may have bitten off more than he could chew (check out the earlier section 'Fighting for the top: Boniface VIII and Philip IV'), but at least he was an able politician. Without him, the papacy descended into political chaos. Remarkably, two years after Philip's attack and Boniface's death in 1303, the papacy moved its seat from Rome to France. I sort through all the details in the following sections.

Fleeing to France

In 1309, Pope Clement V made the remarkable decision to relocate the papal seat from Rome to the city of Avignon in southern France. Initially meant to be a temporary decision, it lasted until 1378.

This move became known as the 'Babylonian Captivity', because despite the fact that Avignon wasn't legally the property of the French king, he effectively controlled it. Also, during this period, every pope between the move to Avignon and the return to Rome was French.

Despite the recent problems with the French king, moving the papacy to Avignon actually made sense, because the town was far removed from the murderous infighting happening in Rome:

- ✔ Avignon was located in the southern Languedoc region of France, well away from the French king's court and his major sphere of influence.

- ✔ Avignon had adjacent territories, such as the city of Arles, which were loyal to the Holy Roman Emperor rather than the French monarch.

- ✔ Avignon represented a neutral space between two powers, much like a kind of medieval Switzerland!

- ✔ Avignon was centrally located in Western Europe, making constant contact with the rest of the Medieval World that much easier.

Living like kings

In Avignon, the papacy became much more like the court of a monarch than the seat of the highest representative of the Church. Senior posts within the administration were given to family members, and the popes spent lavishly. John XXII, Benedict XII and Clement VI were all famed as popes who spent recklessly and lived indulgent lives.

Avignon certainly fit the bill for this kind of indulgence. The town was dominated by the monumental *Palais des Papes* (or Papal Palace), which was constructed during the period. Overlooking the river Rhone, this Gothic palace – the largest still standing in Europe – covers more than 15,000 square metres (or 161,400 square feet). You can still visit it today.

Unsurprisingly this new palatial lifestyle received a fair amount of disapproval, including criticism from two of the most famous figures in European literature. The Italian intellectual and philosopher Petrarch (1304–1374) wrote the following letter to a friend in 1340 that makes plain his distaste for what he found in Avignon:

The long-lasting effects of the *Defensor Pacis*

Sometimes criticism of the Avignon papacy took on a very political edge. One of the most famous cases was that of Marsilius of Padua (1275–1342). Marsillus was a noted Italian scholar and politician who got involved in a much bigger fight than he was used to.

In 1324, Pope John XXII was involved in a war of words with the reigning king of Germany, Louis IV (who was looking to be crowned Holy Roman Emperor and finally was in 1328) over the usual issue – who was superior in the eyes of God. In response to this very public argument, Marsilius produced a text called the *Defensor Pacis*, one of the most famous medieval texts. In it, he set out what he thought were the main arguments for the supremacy of the emperor and how the papacy had constantly claimed more rights and powers than it was due. Marsilius argued that the state was entirely separate from religious authority and had power over it.

Unsurprisingly the *Defensor Pacis* didn't go down terribly well with Pope John, and Marsilius was forced to flee France. Equally unsurprisingly, he was welcomed with open arms by Louis IV, who later made him Bishop of Milan despite the fact that Marsilius was a layman. The *Defensor Pacis* turned out to be a hugely important document, much quoted and referenced by later thinkers and leaders to define the idea of sovereignty.

> *Now I am living in France, in the Babylon of the West. . . Instead of holy solitude we find a criminal host and crowds of the most infamous satellites; instead of soberness, licentious banquets; instead of pious pilgrimages, preternatural and foul sloth; instead of the bare feet of the apostles, the snowy coursers* [swift, expensive horses] *of brigands* [robbers] *fly past us, the horses decked in gold and fed on gold, soon to be shod with gold, if the Lord does not check this slavish luxury. In short, we seem to be among the kings of the Persians or Parthians, before whom we must fall down and worship, and who cannot be approached except presents be offered.*

Italian poet Dante Alighieri (1265–1321) was also hugely critical of the contemporary Church in his most famous work *The Divine Comedy*. In this following brief excerpt from the first part called the *Inferno*, Dante's disdain is very clear:

> *Ye who the things of God, which ought to be*
> *The brides of holiness, rapaciously,*
> *For silver and for gold do prostitute.*

Breaking Up: Another Schism and the Antipopes

As I describe in Chapter 9, a massive schism occurred between the Western and Eastern Churches in 1054, which some historians refer to as the 'Great Schism'. In 1378 another schism happened – which is, helpfully, sometimes also known as the 'Great Schism'! The 1378 schism – also known as the Papal Schism and the Western Schism – featured the Western Church splitting within itself. Shortly afterwards two men claimed to be pope at the same time. Prepare to be confused!

Returning to Rome: Gregory XI

Problems first began under Pope Gregory XI. In 1376 Gregory ended the Avignon Papacy (which I describe in the earlier section 'Establishing the New Papacy in Avignon') when he decided that the seat of the pope should again be in Rome. Gregory had spent most of his tenure as pope trying to eliminate heresies in Europe, such as condemning the writings of John Wycliffe (see Chapter 22), but a conflict with the city of Florence played the biggest part in his thinking.

The War of the Eight Saints

In 1372, at the start of this conflict known as the War of the Eight Saints, Gregory made clear that he intended to return to Rome and expand the papal estates throughout Italy. This plan annoyed the city of Florence, which feared it would lose territory. Along with the city of Milan, eight Florentine magistrates (the 'eight saints') instigated a revolt in the papal states in 1375.

A brief period of unrest followed and Gregory was forced to return to Italy earlier than anticipated. He made the Florentines pay for the revolt by excommunicating all members of their government and putting the city under an *interdict*, which meant that no religious services were permitted to take place there. The interdict lasted for the next two years.

So, the most significant reason for returning the papacy to Italy was a threat to the revenues of the papal estates, rather than being motivated by a desire to restore Rome as the seat of papal authority. Several Popes had in fact wanted to return to Rome before this point, but the unsettled political situation in Italy made doing so impossible. Now, returning to Rome had become vital.

Election fever: Urban ascends

Gregory XI didn't do particularly well following the War of the Eight Saints because he died shortly afterwards in 1378 at the age of only 42. His death meant that an election was necessary. Unsurprisingly, a huge public clamour called for an Italian, specifically a Roman, to be elected in his place. Campaigns for the papacy threatened to turn violent in Rome, and the cardinals feared a mob uprising. Eventually they decided on a Neapolitan who took the name Urban VI.

Initially, the selection of Urban seemed to settle the issue, but the cardinals soon regretted their decision. Urban was very different from previous popes. Extremely devout, he lived a simple lifestyle and was suspicious of the rich, pampered cardinals who had arrived from Avignon. (For most of them, Avignon was the only papal home they had known in their lifetime, and Rome was a strange and new experience.) The mob weren't too pleased either: Urban may have been Italian, but he wasn't Roman.

Of pope and antipope

What happened next was remarkable. Many of the cardinals fled Rome for the small town of Anagni, where they decided to have another go and elect another pope! This time they settled on a man who took the name Clement VII. He travelled to France with the cardinals and established a new court in Avignon.

Therefore, two different but official popes existed. Rivalry for the papacy had raged before, but for the first time the same set of cardinals had elected two different popes, both of whom had a claim to being legitimate! Clement VII is usually referred to as the *antipope* because he was the second to be elected, but in many ways his claim was more legitimate because Urban VI hadn't been a cardinal when he was chosen, and therefore Clement was technically his superior.

Kings and rulers now had to pick sides. The popes themselves didn't really matter; the real decision was whether a person recognised Avignon or Rome as the seat of papal power. Lots of other interests were also at stake. For example, the king of France fairly obviously supported Avignon, and consequently the king of England supported Rome, and so therefore the king of Scotland supported Avignon; the Holy Roman Emperor of course supported Rome! These choices had nothing to do with Urban or Clement; older rivalries were simply at play.

The antipope was able to exist and function comparatively easily. After all, Avignon already had a beautiful palace and papal court. Also, despite missive after missive from Rome denouncing the antipope, he had the backing of, among others, the French king. Why quit?

The impasse continued as follows:

- ✔ **In Avignon,** when Clement VII died in 1394, he was replaced by a successor, Benedict XIII, who maintained the court in Avignon just as it had been since the beginning of the century.

- ✔ **In Rome,** when Urban VI died, he was replaced by Boniface IX in 1389. He in turn died in 1404 and in an attempt to solve the situation Roman cardinals offered not to elect a new pope in the hope that Benedict would resign too. The Roman cardinals were turned down flat and so proceeded to elect Innocent VII.

The situation seemed likely to go on for some time.

Healing the split: The Council of Constance

Part of the difficulty in solving the pope/antipope situation was purely down to a legal tangle that the conflict had caused. *Cannon law* – laws devised by the Church to run its own affairs – governed the papacy. Any dispute over the election of a pope needed to be resolved at a full meeting, or *ecumenical council*, and only a pope was able to call these meetings. Neither pope nor antipope was likely to call a council at which he was likely to be asked to resign – even if one of them had called a council, the rival was unlikely to attend: a tricky situation.

But the situation didn't stay tricky for much longer. For several years theologians argued over whether changes could be made to cannon law. Leading theologian Jean Gerson argued that the Church had the right to change the law if it was defending itself and that the current situation demanded such action. Surprisingly, Gerson managed to get leading lawyers to agree to this idea.

In 1409, a meeting was organised between Pope Gregory XII (who succeeded Innocent VII in 1406) and antipope Benedict XIII. They were supposed to meet at the town of Pisa in Tuscany, Italy, but at the last moment, both sides pulled out.

To make matters worse, the general frustration with the situation had caused both sets of cardinals to look elsewhere for leadership, so they abandoned their popes and instead elected another one – Alexander V. That's right, three popes were now in place simultaneously! Alexander only managed a year in office before he died in 1410 and was replaced by yet another pope – John XXII. The situation was getting ridiculous.

Calling the council

The situation required another four years before it was completely resolved. The German King Sigismund called a full ecumenical council in the town of Constance in southern Germany. Sigismund, who would later become Holy Roman Emperor, had his own issues to discuss involving the borders of his kingdom with Poland, but the main business of the council was to resolve the mess that the papacy had become.

At the time that the council was called, three men claimed to be the pope:

- **Gregory XII:** The Roman antipope was abandoned by the cardinals in 1409, but still in place in Rome.

- **Benedict XIII:** The Avignon antipope was abandoned by the cardinals in 1409, but still in place in Avignon.

- **John XXII:** The 'official' pope and successor to Alexander V was elected in preference to the first two claimants in 1409.

Technically, the man with the greatest claim was John XXII, who was at least the most recently 'officially' elected. Benedict XIII was the only antipope, although he still had backing in France.

Eventually the council decided that the only way forward was to wipe the slate completely clean, and that none of the claimants who came to Constance were acceptable as pope. Gregory XII had already suggested that he would allow the succession of anybody elected by the council and John XXII was persuaded to resign. Benedict XIII was treated rather differently as the antipope: he refused to step down, and so the council excommunicated him!

Meeting the new guy: Martin V

The council then elected a new pope, Martin V. Ironically, Martin came from the Colonna family in Rome – one of the powerful and dominant Roman families, which had motivated Clement V's decision to move the papacy from Rome back in 1305 (check out the earlier section 'Making mounds of money'). The papacy was back in Rome and back in the hands of the Colonna 109 years and about 20 popes later.

But Martin V was not universally accepted. Over the next 20 years, a couple of pretenders appeared as antipopes in the kingdom of Aragon (in modern-day France), but they didn't attract support from anywhere else and every other powerful figure in Europe acknowledged Martin as pope and Rome as the home of the papacy.

Continuing the argument

The Council of Constance wasn't the end of the story. Although the issue of papal leadership was settled, arguments continued all the way through to the nineteenth century. Admittedly these later debates were theological arguments and didn't result in wars or antipopes, but as recently as 1880, theologians were still arguing about whether the line of Roman popes was truly legitimate.

As with some other historical events that I cover in this book, the Schism of 1378 had only a minor impact on the daily life of ordinary people. Debates over papal power had a real effect on everyday life only when the churches were closed due to an interdict (such as in Florence in 1372 – flip to the earlier section 'The War of the Eight Saints'). Military conflict had serious effects of course, but the papal conflicts rarely went that far.

For ordinary Europeans, these arguments were a world away compared to something else that happened during the fourteenth century – a form of bubonic plague known as The Black Death that devastated the continent. Many people thought that the plague was a judgement from God on the sinful times that they lived in, and many cited the papal mess as a cause. Read all about the plague in Chapter 20.

Chapter 20

Facing God's Judgement: Dealing with the Black Death

In This Chapter

▶ Tracing the origins of the plague

▶ Assessing the plague's impact on Europe

▶ Tackling the plague and its consequences

The dreadful pestilence penetrated the sea coast by Southampton and came to Bristol, and there almost the whole population of the town perished, as if it had been seized by sudden death; for few kept their beds more than two or three days, or even half a day. . . .

–Henry Knighton, historian, 1354

*B*etween 1346–1353, Europe was utterly devastated by an appalling disease – the plague. Historians estimate that during this period the disease killed between 30 and 60 per cent of Europe's population: that's at least 75 million people and possibly as many as 200 million. At the lower end, that's more people than live in the United Kingdom, and in the upper range, about two-thirds of the population of the United States. These numbers can be difficult to take in so perhaps the way to think of it is as follows: imagine if between a third and a half of the population where you live died within a short space of time. That's how it would have been.

In this chapter I provide a sense of the massive impact that the plague had on Europe. I examine where the plague originated, how it spread and how people attempted to explain and deal with it. I also look at how Europe slowly tried to recover. Be warned, although fascinating, this chapter covers some gruesome stuff. If you haven't got a strong stomach, look away now.

Journeying Far and Wide: Death Comes West

The great plague probably began in 1346. People today refer to this outbreak of disease as the 'Black Death', but the term is from the nineteenth century and wasn't used at the time. People then would have referred to it as a 'pestilence'. Throughout this chapter I refer to it as a 'plague'.

One of the big ironies of history is that the plague's effectiveness was due in part to the huge expansion in trade that took place during the thirteenth century (check out Chapter 18 for more details). The relatively new, speedier and more efficient trade routes that were established during this period allowed the deadly cargo to travel faster and farther than ever before.

Tracking down the plague's origins

Most historians agree that the plague started among the Mongols, the descendants of Genghis Khan. Their capital in the thirteenth century was at Sarai, on the northwest shore of the Caspian Sea in modern-day Russia. Despite being thousands of miles from Western Europe, the plague managed to spread from Sarai incredibly quickly.

The most well-supported theory is that the disease began within the squirrel population around the Volga River, whose fur the Mongols traded with the merchants of Genoa, Italy. As Figure 20-1 shows, the Italian city of Genoa had a trading station at Tana, from which the disease was easily exported throughout the region.

Spreading across Europe

As soon as the plague hit the Mediterranean, it became unstoppable because the disease transferred extremely efficiently among rats. Actually, the disease was a bacteria carried in the lice and fleas that attached themselves to rodents. When a host rodent died, the fleas and bacteria simply moved on to another rodent – or several other rodents. These fleas eventually made their way on to human beings who then spread the disease to one another.

Travelling by sea

All Mediterranean ports were full of rats, many of which quickly travelled by ship to other ports hundreds of miles away.

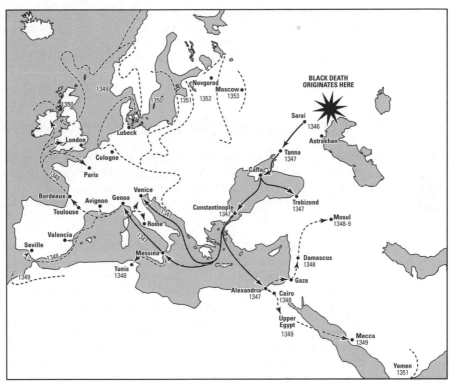

Figure 20-1:
The spread
of the
plague from
1346–1353

Port cities such as Alexandria, Venice and Genoa were some of the first places in Europe that the plague struck. Sicily was another, and Gabrielle de Mussi, a notary from the island, gave this account of its first contact:

> Alas! our ships enter the port, but of a thousand sailors hardly ten are spared. We reach our homes; our kindred . . . come from all parts to visit us. Woe to us for we cast at them the darts of death! . . . Going back to their homes, they in turn soon infected their whole families, who in three days succumbed, and were buried in one common grave. Priests and doctors visiting . . . from their duties ill, and soon were . . . dead. O death! cruel, bitter, impious death! . . . Lamenting our misery, we feared to fly, yet we dared not remain.

Crossing land

After the disease arrived in mainland Europe, it moved incredibly fast. The spread was helped by the numbers of people who fled infected areas but were already infected themselves, thus taking the disease to new areas. Also many plague-infested cargoes were unloaded and moved overland, spreading the disease like wildfire.

From its beginnings deep in Russia in 1346, the plague was everywhere within two years. By 1348 it was virulent throughout Italy, France and Spain and had crossed the channel to Britain and Ireland. To the south, it was in Egypt, along the coast of Syria and Palestine (including the former Crusader Kingdom of Outremer) and had travelled as far as the Yemen.

Creating the perfect breeding ground

The Medieval World was a dangerous place. Illness aside, you were quite likely to get bludgeoned by an axe or a cudgel, cleaved by a sword or pierced by an arrow. As nearly every chapter in this book attests, war was a constant in the Medieval World; you were as likely to get killed fighting as from contracting an illness.

In addition to the potential for violent deaths, the Middle Ages were incredibly unhealthy in general. Cleanliness – or the lack of it – was a major issue. General ideas of cleanliness and hygiene were very basic indeed. Bathing was a luxury available only to a few and was often regarded with suspicion. Rich people were clean, in appearance at least, because turning up at the Royal Court dirty just wouldn't do. But medieval people didn't know that germs and infections caused disease, and so consequently they didn't guard against them. Ironically, bathing actually declined in popularity after the plague because people suspected that it may have been a way that the disease spread. So the greatest disease in medieval history actually encouraged people to wash less!

In addition to personal cleanliness, sanitation and food were major problems:

- Poor people spent a lot of their time in close proximity to their own and other people's faeces. Proper drainage systems were incredibly scarce, and the most common method of dealing with human refuse was to dump it in the street in piles. Human waste was also often disposed of close to, or even in, the local water supply, meaning that most people would be drinking from water already infected with all sorts of bacteria.

- Rotting meat was a major issue. The most common way of storing meat was to use salt, but people often ate meat that was decayed. The scarcity and price of meat meant that many people grabbed whatever they could.

Given these conditions and the fact that people lived in very close proximity, diseases and infections spread like wildfire. Even communities such as monasteries with relatively good sanitation were prone to disease outbreaks, and due to the number of people living in a concentrated spot, abbeys were often riskier places to live or seek assistance.

Nothing humour-ous about this

Medieval medical thought was fairly straightforward. Based on the work of Ancient Greek and Roman physicians, people believed that the entire world was made up of four basic elements: fire, water, earth and air. These elements were represented in the human body by four corresponding humours: blood, phlegm, black bile and choler (also known as yellow bile, like regular vomit).

Medieval physicians believed that as long as these four humours were in order and balanced, a person was perfectly well. If somebody was ill, their humours were simply not balanced. A person's temperament was also able to create an imbalance. For example, people with melancholic personalities were believed to have too much black bile in their systems. This philosophy meant that doctors not only treated illnesses but also individuals's characters.

Doctors used the scent of a patient's blood, faeces, vomit or urine to establish a diagnosis, often without even seeing the patient. Most treatments involved trying to reduce the humour that existed in a patient in too great a quantity. Forced vomiting and bloodletting were popular techniques. Famously, leeches were used to drain the blood and eat away diseased or infected flesh around a wound. Purgatives were used to enforce expulsion. (These medicines weren't always taken orally either; rudimentary medieval enemas involved using a pig's bladder to squirt a foul mixture up the anus. Hard to believe that this didn't have the desired effect!)

In effect, physicians and rudimentary surgeons tried everything and anything. In the vast majority of cases, patients ended up dying. People accepted this outcome and saw visiting a physician as very much a last chance saloon. Most people stuck to praying instead.

Experiencing the symptoms

Several different types of plague seem to have developed during the mid-fourteenth century because the disease mutated, but the most common form was the bubonic plague.

Historians have a lot of accounts of the plague hitting towns and cities, and they are fairly consistent in their descriptions of what happened to people who caught the disease:

- The first stage of the disease was a high fever that forced up patients's temperatures and caused them to spit blood. These symptoms frequently caused death within three days. Many people went to bed with a fever and never woke up again. They were probably the lucky ones.

- The second stage, if the disease developed that far, involved large black growths known as *buboes* which developed in the armpits, neck and groin – the locations of the lymph nodes, which typically fight disease. The growths were incredibly painful, and patients often lingered on for up to five days.

Treating the plague

So what did you do if you had the plague? Well, the simple answer is that you died swiftly and painfully. Medieval medicine wasn't particularly advanced.

People tended to regard catching a disease as a judgement from God (flip to the later section 'Posing theories and propagating persecutions') and medical practices were fairly basic. Treatment from a doctor was expensive and not available for the majority of people. Physicians followed the teachings of Galen and Hippocrates, models from the Ancient World (see the sidebar 'Nothing humour-ous about this' for details).

Responding to the Plague

The plague was swift and terrible: from 1358 to 1360, between a quarter and a third of the population of Europe died. Physicians and medieval medicine were unable to stop it. Antibiotics and the World Health Organisation didn't exist, and methods of communication across long distances were only rudimentary. Most people took the decision to travel a long way away and not come back for a while, but even this strategy rarely worked because the disease moved more quickly than people could travel.

Posing theories and propagating persecutions

Across Europe, people returned to attending church during the plague years to ask God for protection and to figure out whether this devastating illness was a judgement from God. One of the most popular ideas was that the plague was a *miasma* caused by something unpleasant in the air. Many people linked this idea with the plague having been a judgement from God on people's corrupt and immoral lives, much like the story of Noah and the great flood.

Around Europe, all sorts of theories were hit upon as to why this epidemic had begun. Not unusually for the period, some of these theories inspired truly tragic and appalling deeds.

The following horrific and extreme reactions have to be understood in the context of the confusion and panic of the times. People had no understanding of bacterial infection and therefore were unable to work out why the disease had struck or what they needed to do to stop it.

Pointing fingers at the Jews

Jewish communities in Europe were among the first targets for persecution. Anti-Semitic acts were fairly common during the Middle Ages (see Chapters 14 and 15), but the plague persecutions were a new thing entirely.

A key element in people's thinking arose from the fact that the Jewish religion required its adherents to wash on a daily basis, an unusual practice for non-Jews. Additionally, Jewish communities tended not to use water from public wells for their washing. As a result, rumours spread that the Jews had poisoned the public wells and started the disease.

Many accounts exist of such persecutions. Some of the most famous come from Strasbourg where Jews were tortured and forced to confess to the poisoning. Records of these confessions were sent around towns in Germany and as a result thousands of Jews were arrested and burnt alive.

The following chronicler is very insightful about the real reasons behind a 1350 purge:

> On Saturday – that was St Valentine's Day – they burnt the Jews on a wooden platform in their cemetery. There were about two thousand people of them. Those who wanted to baptize themselves were spared. [Some historians say that about 1,000 accepted baptism.] *Many small children were taken out of the fire and baptized against the will of their fathers and mothers. And everything that was owed to the Jews was cancelled, and the Jews had to surrender all pledges and notes that they had taken for debts. The council, however, took the cash that the Jews possessed and divided it among the working-men proportionately. The money was indeed the thing that killed the Jews. If they had been poor and if the feudal lords had not been in debt to them, they would not have been burnt. After this wealth was divided among the artisans, some gave their share to the Cathedral or to the Church on the advice of their confessors.*

Modern historians say that around 350 purges took place across Europe during 1351, wiping out more than 50 large communities. The only place that didn't launch a Jewish persecution was England, but this fact wasn't due to tolerance or understanding: Edward I had already expelled the entire Jewish population from the country in 1290.

Fearing differences

Jewish communities weren't the only ones that suffered. Other groups who were different in some way became the victims of people's anger and need for answers and vengeance:

✔ Leper communities across Europe were rooted out because people feared anybody with visible signs of disease. Even just sporting acne or any other common skin condition became dangerous.

✔ Anyone who travelled was under suspicion. Merchants and other foreigners were chased out of towns and killed. Particularly at risk were the Romany (traveller) communities of Europe who were constantly on the move and therefore suspected of being bringers of the disease.

✔ Travelling monks and friars became victims, although these individuals were most likely attempting to bring alms to the poor and sick.

Becoming whipping boys (and girls)

The plague encouraged a huge loss of faith in the clergy on mainland Europe as people asked what they'd done to stop the spread of the disease and began to look to themselves for answers.

In place of their regular religious practices, many people took to more extreme versions of their faith. For example, the Flagellants appeared as a particularly popular, extreme Catholic sect during this time. Flagellants believed in the mortification of the flesh by continually striking themselves with whips and other items. Their popularity grew hugely during the fourteenth century, particularly in Germany where the 'Brothers of the Cross' were the most famous order, and thousands joined the movement. Unfortunately, Flagellants soon became suspected (by those who didn't share their beliefs) of actually spreading the disease. The Flagellants encouraged vast numbers of people to move from place to place to try and spread the word of their faith and recruit other members and by 1352 towns were closing their gates to them. These measures didn't kill the sect off though, and they experienced periodic revivals throughout the fourteenth and fifteenth centuries despite being banned by some rulers.

Regrouping after the plague: England

Medieval England offers a really good example of how the plague affected society, with England suffering as badly as anywhere else. The plague hit in 1348 and within four years more than a third of the population was dead. During this time King Edward III took some rather bizarre actions in response. Even his family wasn't safe from the plague – his daughter Joan died of the disease in 1348.

Dealing with labour shortages

The vast majority of plague victims in England were from the peasant class who worked the land, and by 1349 too few people were available to work the fields. The labour problem was made worse by the numbers of people leaving their homes to escape the plague and being tempted to work for other land-owners in towns free of the disease, with the promise of higher wages.

Edward III attempted to regain control of the labour market with the Ordinance of Labourers in 1349, which parliament reinforced in 1351 with a bill called the Statute of Labourers. This bill set a maximum wage for labourers that was fixed at wage levels before the plague. The bill also forced any able-bodied man or woman to work (unless they were from the nobility, of course).

These measures didn't go down very well with the peasantry and caused a huge economic depression. Part of the problem was that England was already going through economic problems due to the Hundred Years' War (which I discuss in Chapters 21 and 23), and wages were being put back down to those levels. Additionally, harsh enforcement of these measures was one of the factors behind the unrest that eventually culminated in the Peasants' Revolt of 1381 (turn to Chapter 22 for more details).

Calling for priests

Another area of English employment that suffered during the plague was the Church. The huge numbers of people killed resulted in a scarcity of priests throughout the country. This shortage was ironic, because at this time of great suffering vast numbers of people in England – particularly the nobility – returned to regular worship.

The plague also had a potentially devastating impact in that thousands and thousands of people died without being able to give their confession to a priest. This situation led to some extraordinary measures, as Ralph of Shrewsbury (who was the Bishop of Bath and Wells) ordained that:

> *The continuous pestilence of the present day...has left many parish churches without parson or priest...if they are on the point of death and cannot secure the services of a priest, then they should make confession to each other. . . if no man is present, even to a woman.*

This highlights how serious the situation had become as missing out on the afterlife was probably the greatest fear to the medieval mind. It also gives us a fair idea of some clerics' attitudes towards women.

The shortage of priests meant that the English Church had to put its own house in order and the effect of the plague on Europe meant that they did this without help from Rome. Many historians suggest that these developments weakened the hold of the papacy on the English Church. Rome appointed fewer priests and although more members of the English aristocracy began taking an active interest in Church affairs, some people suggest that this was the first step on the way towards the Protestant Reformation.

Assessing the Plague's Impact

Most of Western Europe had suffered the worst of the plague by 1350, but the disease continued to spread elsewhere. Central and Eastern Europe were next to suffer, with the plague hitting Poland in 1351 and western Russia in the following year. Moscow was the last major city to be contaminated before, ironically, the plague dwindled to a stop in some small towns on the Volga River, only a few miles from where it had first begun seven years before.

Europe must have breathed a sigh of relief by 1353, but the plague wasn't over. A new outbreak occurred in Germany during 1357 and spread across much of Central Europe. Further outbreaks occurred sporadically over the next 100 years into the fifteenth century, including the Plague of Paris that killed 40,000 people in 1466. One of the most famous outbreaks took place in England in 1664, known as the 'Great Plague of London', it ravaged the city for over two years. The greatest pandemic since the Black Death took place in the nineteenth century in China and India, killing around 10 million people, and individual cases have been reported as recently as 1995.

Despite the devastations of the plague, many of the policies of rulers remained relatively similar to before, especially with regard to foreign policy. The best example is the fact that by 1355 the Hundred Years' War (see Chapter 21) had resumed, and England and France were happily battering away at each other again.

Calculating the death toll

The most obvious impact of the plague was the depopulation that followed it. As I mention at the beginning of the chapter, between a third and a half of the population of Europe died from the disease. The vast majority of those who died were from the lower classes. Very few members of the nobility were killed. Not a single monarch or ruler died from the plague except for Alfonso XI of Castile, who is famous only for that reason. Several sons and daughters of monarchs were killed, but the political map of Europe in 1353 looked remarkably similar to that of 1346. One reason for this was that the wealthy were more able to lock themselves away in isolation from the disease and restrict whom they came into contact with.

The areas most affected were the towns and cities of Europe – places that packed thousands of people in close proximity and had unsanitary conditions. Some of the figures are quite startling. For example, the population of Florence, Italy, was reduced from 110,000 to around 50,000. More than 50 per cent of people who lived in Florence died or fled in the course of just three years.

The Malthusian interpretation

The plague that we call the Black Death has produced some interesting and controversial theories over the years. Economic historian Thomas Mathus put forward one of the more interesting at the beginning of the nineteenth century.

Mathus claimed that the plague was an inevitable consequence of the tendency of human beings to over-reproduce. He suggested that on a generational basis, humans would reproduce beyond the available food supply and accordingly some catastrophe – such as an act of God or great reckoning – would take place to reduce the numbers to an acceptable level. He argued that by the middle of the fourteenth century, Europe was overpopulated and that the Black Death was just the latest in a series of reckonings.

Mathus's idea is thought-provoking, but modern historians argue that Medieval Europe was overpopulated a long time before the Black Death arrived. His ideas were very unpopular during his lifetime, and he was subject to huge personal criticism and abuse.

Many impacts of this depopulation were economic. Goods were scarce, the transport of them dangerous and people had less money to spend. High prices and low spending power tipped Europe into its first big recession. However, social mobility was greatly increased. Figures aren't available, but huge demographic changes must have taken place as groups of people moved from one area to another. Also, the scarcity of labour meant that some people were possibly better off financially and may even have managed to raise their social status. Some people could have moved from being the lowliest kind of serf to enjoying a position of greater privilege in a different place.

Affecting culture

One of the more interesting aspects of the plague is the impact it had on cultural life. The disease and its effects became a very rich topic for writers and artists and profoundly affected the way people felt and lived their lives.

Many historians and commentators have written about the increase in *morbidity* following the plague, with writers and artists finding inspiration in subjects like death, dying and purgatory. Certainly, medieval art and literature from the middle of the fourteenth century show a much greater interest in death and other morbid subjects.

Doctors in disguise

One of the most obvious and unusual impacts of the Black Death was the bizarre outfit that doctors began to wear as a result. Even when the worst of the pandemic was over, physicians were still very much at risk of coming into contact with the disease. As a result, they adopted a strange new form of dress.

They wore long leather coats, coated with wax for further protection and tucked into leather breaches so that the skin wasn't exposed. On their head they wore wide-brimmed leather hats to shield them from infection and to identify them as doctors. They were probably very easy to recognise because they also wore primitive gas masks that stuck out in front of the face. Long and shaped like a bird's beak, the masks were filled with herbs and spices to protect against *miasma*, the bad air that many believed transported the plague (flip to the earlier section 'Posing theories and propagating persecutions'). Accordingly, they were known as 'Beak Doctors'. Their stunning outfit was topped off with a long cane with which they could examine, touch or ward off people without any bodily contact. If you bumped into a doctor in this garb in the street you were probably as likely to die of shock as the plague!

One of the most popular subjects to arise after the plague was *La Danse Macabre* ('The Dance of Death'). This theme was popular in art, music and literature. The works allegorically focus on the common fate of every individual, whatever their status in life, and typically involve the figure of Death as a skeleton, leading a group of various individuals on the journey to the great beyond. Dramatic representations of this subject were also popular and commonly performed.

The plague and its impact was also irresistible to the great writers of the time (as well as modern-day authors). The Italian writers Petrarch and Boccaccio discussed the subject in some of their greatest works, and it also features in *The Canterbury Tales* by Geoffrey Chaucer. Plague eventually became an actual character, taking on a personification like a pagan god. Medieval folklore features lots of depictions of plague, mostly shown as a bent old woman wielding a broom who brought death to anyone caught in her sweeping: an effective and chilling analogy.

Part V
Ending the Middle and Beginning the Age of Discovery
(1300–1492)

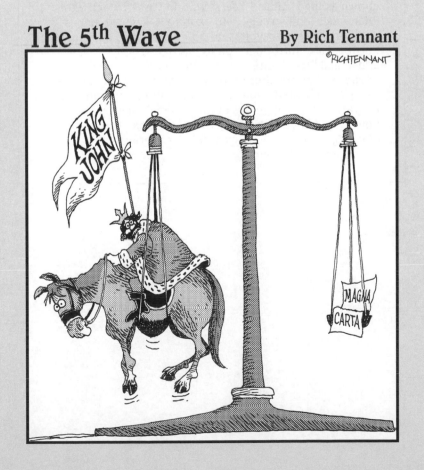

The 5th Wave   By Rich Tennant

In this part . . .

The Middle Ages come to an end in this part, but not before England and France engage in the epic conflict known as the Hundred Years' War. In Part V, I tackle this infamously long struggle and explore its consequences, including peasant revolts and political change all around Europe. I also introduce you to murderous English kings and a mad French one, while saying farewell to the Byzantine Empire after more than 1,000 years of unnecessarily complicated administration. Culture fans can look forward to the beginnings of the Italian Renaissance before the Middle Ages truly draw to a close with the amazing journeys and accidental discoveries of Christopher Columbus.

Chapter 21

Beginning One Hundred Years of War

*T*he Hundred Years' War is one of the most famous conflicts in history. In many ways it was the culmination of years of fighting over territory between the rulers of England and France. At the time, the conflict may well have seemed like the war to end all wars: of course, it wasn't (and it wasn't 100 years of uninterrupted fighting either).

The war was an incredible confrontation that raged for generations. The Hundred Years' War is so important partly because it was the first time that England and France engaged in a clear and sustained war. The conflict also caused a rise in nationalist feelings in the two countries, which hadn't previously existed.

In this chapter I look at why the war started and how the fortunes of both sides swung back and forth throughout the fourteenth century. The conflict was sustained over such a long period that one chapter just isn't to cover it! I look at the second half of it in Chapter 23.

Laying the Groundwork for a Long Struggle

The Hundred Years' War didn't last for exactly 100 years. Technically, the war took place over 116 years, from 1337 to 1453, but I suppose the Hundred and Sixteen Years' War just didn't have much of a ring to it. Then again, this period also included long periods of peace (around 35 years in total), and so the events are probably more accurately described as the Eighty Five Years' War. Again, not a great name!

In addition, the Hundred Years' War wasn't one war. Technically, it was a series of separate wars and invasions, but because the fighting generally took place in the same areas and involved the same people and issues, historians consider these wars and battles as a single unified conflict, broken into four periods:

- ✔ The Edwardian War (1337–1360); see 'Beginning the Battle: The Edwardian War', later in this chapter.

- ✔ The Caroline War (1369–1389); see 'Recovering with the French: The Caroline War', later in this chapter.

- ✔ The Lancastrian War (1415–1429); see Chapter 23.

- ✔ The period of French recovery, following the impact of Joan of Arc (1429 onwards); see Chapter 23.

Life went on despite or even because of the conflict. An awful lot else happened during the fourteenth century, such as the plague we now call the Black Death (flip to Chapter 20 for all the gory details of the plague), while the war was ever present in the background. For people not directly in the war zones, the main impact was financial due to the extra taxes and price hikes. Unlike modern conflicts such as the Second World War, the lives of many people, particularly in England, were relatively untouched.

Delving into dynastic ding-dong

So why did the Hundred Years' War begin? Well, unsurprisingly, like so many conflicts during the Middle Ages, the big dispute was over the control of territory. In this case, the dispute was a big one – specifically, who was the true king of France.

People had been attempting to combine the rule of territories in what is now modern-day France and England since the Norman invasion of England in

1066 (which I describe in Chapter 10). In the fourteenth century the situation exploded into a massive confrontation.

Reaching the end of the Capetian line

For centuries France had been ruled by a series of first-born sons in the Capetian line, the descendants of Hugh Capet, the first king of France who died in 996. Over the next four centuries the Capetian kings had never had full control over the land that comprises modern-day France. In fact, many English kings and nobles had held territory there.

The Capetian king, Philip IV, died in 1314 and left four children: three sons, Louis, Philip and Charles, and a daughter, Isabella. Isabella was married to King Edward II of England and had produced a son with him, also called Edward. This situation made the young English prince the nephew of the new French king. Edward's lineage became very important. He was a *Plantagenet*, the royal household descended from Henry II (1133–1189) who came from the duchy of Anjou and therefore always had an interest in France.

The new French king was Louis IX, but he died within two years and was succeeded by his brother, Philip V, in 1316. Philip didn't last long either, dying in 1322, and his younger brother Charles IV soon replaced him.

Putting Edward III in a tricky spot

One of Charles's first challenges was to beat off a small English invasion in 1324; English forces were trying to reclaim some lands in Bordeaux that had once been in English hands. Known as the Gascon War, the conflict was a complete failure for the English – and very much a foretaste of what was to come.

In fact, the war was such a failure that it led to the English king, Edward II, being deposed from the throne, and his young son Edward III replacing him in 1327. This shift meant that the king of England was now the closest living male relative of the king of France. Trouble was brewing! (The later sidebar 'Salic law versus feudal law' highlights the details behind the impending controversy.)

Looking at the reasons for war

Although Edward III's claim for the French throne was a big motivator for the beginning of the Hundred Years' War, two other big issues had a part to play:

- **Trade and revenues:** Despite being the king of England, a large amount of Edward III's revenues came from his territories in France, particularly Gascony (see Figure 21-1). French kings had made continual attempts over the past 100 years to take Gascony back; Edward, however, was keen to preserve his territory there, particularly because a large amount of wine came from Gascony!

> ✔ **Homage:** Homage had been an issue for a series of English kings (see Chapter 17). Because they possessed lands in France they were obliged to pay homage for them to the king of France, as their feudal lord. This situation had been confirmed between Henry III and Louis IX at the Treaty of Paris in 1229. Any opportunity to end the obligation would have been welcome to Edward III.

The war began in this context. Edward III certainly had a valid claim to the French throne but it was more than just a desire to be king that encouraged him to invade. Economic concerns and the desire to free himself of the issue of homage were equally important motivations. In many ways, his claim to the throne was a means to an end.

Stepping in discreetly: Philip of Valois

The situation brewed for about 15 years before it finally came to a crunch in 1328 when Charles IV died. He had no sons, only a daughter. His wife was pregnant, and so people in France held out hope for a male heir.

The only surviving Capetian was a man called Philip of Valois who was the nephew of King Philip IV who had died in 1314 and the grandson of the previous king. Philip of Valois had a claim, but it was a loose one. However, he did have the huge advantage of being in France; upon Charles's death, he was immediately regent.

When Charles's unborn child proved to be a girl, Philip of Valois was crowned as King Philip VI. He became the first of the Valois kings, a new French dynasty.

Gathering the storm

Unsurprisingly, the news of King Philip VI's coronation didn't go down very well in England. Although French law said that Philip was the rightful king (see the sidebar 'Salic law versus feudal law') as far as feudal law was concerned, Edward III was the only candidate.

Nowadays a complicated and expensive legal case would be the answer. In the fourteenth century, the solution was much simpler – sort it out with a nice big war.

In the short-term, however, Edward III was forced to accept the situation. He was still very young (aged just 16 in 1328) and very much under the influence of his mother, Isabella, and Roger Mortimer, his regent. He had problems enforcing his rule at home and dealing with invasions by King David II of Scotland. Edward managed to defeat David in 1333, but David, who had become an ally of Philip VI, fled to the French king's court.

Salic law versus feudal law

The French nobility knew that a problem was building up between France and England, and they argued for the importance of Salic Law. This law referred back to the Salian Franks who had settled in Germany after the end of the Roman Empire (flip to Chapter 4 for more details) and whose laws had provided the basis for the Holy Roman Empire and the Kingdom of France.

Salic law held that a throne or *fief* (lands awarded to a person) couldn't be inherited through a female member of the family line. For example, although previous French kings had died childless, proponents of Salic law argued that their throne couldn't pass to the sons of their sisters (their nephews) because doing so was against Salic law.

So at the beginning of the fourteenth century, French nobles argued that despite the fact that Edward III was the nephew of Charles IV, he was never a candidate to inherit the throne of France because the crown would have to pass through a female line (in this case, his mother, Charles's sister, Isabella) to reach him. Thus, upholding Salic law was a convenient argument from a French point of view as well as one steeped in centuries of tradition. Very handy, especially as this form of Salic law probably wasn't even *codified* (made official law) at this point. (Some historians argue that Salic law wasn't codified until 1350, well after the war had started.) Salic law continued to be applied in France, Germany and elsewhere throughout the Middle Ages, and in some areas of Europe, all the way through until the nineteenth century.

In England the situation was different; the English crown was inherited through feudal law, which prioritised bloodline over gender and made Edward III the *only* legitimate heir to the kingdom of France.

Beginning the Battle: The Edwardian War

Having successfully dealt with Scotland (turn to the preceding section 'Gathering the storm'), Edward III was free to consider what to do about the newly crowned king of France, Philip VI. The problem was more than Philip becoming king; lands in Gascony in southern France that technically Edward held (see Figure 21-1) were sure to come under threat from the new French monarch as he looked to eliminate any support that Edward might have in France. Within a year, war between England and France began. This period of the conflict, the Edwardian War, lasted between 1337–1360.

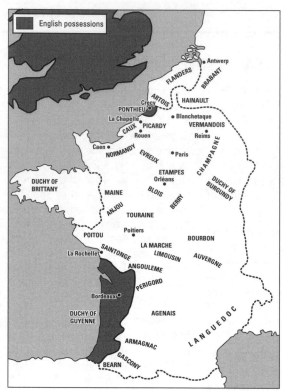

Figure 21-1:
English and French possessions around 1337.

Spinning the 'wool war'

Despite the fact that the war was about the conflict between the English and French kings, the Low Countries – modern-day Belgium and southern The Netherlands – were the first places affected by the manoeuvring from England (see Figure 21-1). These areas were technically independent of the French king, but they were attractive to Edward III because they would provide a much needed foothold in northern France.

The Low Countries were also worth gaining control of because of the huge revenues that Edward could derive from them. Economic concerns were at the heart of this conflict. Indeed, Edward's strategy for getting hold of the territory was an economic one – manipulating the cloth trade.

Cloth making was the area's main industry, and it relied upon English wool. Knowing this, Edward banned the trade of Low Countries' cloth unless the region elected a new government that supported him. Edward's effort was rather like modern-day trade sanctions, and it worked. By 1338 a new court was in place, and Edward crossed the channel to make Antwerp his base of operations.

Feeling a credit crunch

At this time, French ships were menacing England across the channel, and the poorly equipped and funded English navy was unable to respond effectively. These attacks were another reason why Edward had to establish a base in mainland Europe, because otherwise he was unable to guarantee his supply lines across the channel.

Money was a problem in general, and Edward was forced to borrow huge amounts from Italian bankers as well as English moneylenders. Interest payments were huge, and Edward even had to mortgage his crown!

So, the war took on another aspect. Aside from Edward's claim to the French throne and his own desire for more territory, his efforts now had to be successful in order to stop him from going bankrupt. He needed big, positive results – quickly. As events turned out, he wasn't ready to invade France until September 1339.

Fighting – and taunting – the French

Edward III's army invaded France in 1339, and the soldiers followed what was essentially a scorched-earth policy. Instead of rushing straight into an open battle, they set about laying waste to the land that they passed through. The idea was to reduce these areas to dust, taking booty of value and destroying fortifications. In so doing they hoped to make a profit from their attacks and prevent the French king from reoccupying the territory.

Philip VI pretty much let Edward get on with his attacks. The area that Edward was raiding was a fair distance from Philip's location and the destruction didn't really impact upon Philip or his army.

Edward moved his army to La Chapelle (see Figure 21-1) and gave Philip the opportunity to come and attack him, but Philip declined. Edward shrugged his shoulders and left French territory because he didn't want to pursue Philip further south and risk getting cut off from his supply lines.

Things continued in a similar vein over the next few years. England won a victory at sea in the Battle of Sluys in June 1340, when a freshly constructed English fleet virtually destroyed their French opposition in maybe the biggest sea battle of the Middle Ages. England captured 190 French ships, and accounts claim that up to 18,000 French soldiers and sailors lost their lives.

This victory was landed a vital blow in Edward's campaign. He was now able to attack across the channel knowing that he could land easily and that the French king was unable to attack England across the sea.

Unfortunately, the sea victory didn't help with Edward's main objective because later in 1340 Edward was again unable to force Philip into battle. Edward returned home hugely in debt and with no real profits from his efforts. He was able only to pay off a few of his creditors and was forced into signing a nine-month truce with Philip.

Edward also made another move late in 1340 when he began to formally refer to himself as the King of France and sign treaties and make agreements under that name. This move meant that anybody who now supported him in France could claim that they weren't committing treason, and were merely supporting the rightful king. It also meant that his supporters in Flanders were supporting their true feudal lord.

Surveying fights elsewhere in France

While Edward was fighting in the north of France, war was also going on in other parts of France. Since the beginning of the conflict, Philip had been waging a vicious war and trying to regain control of the few remaining territories that were loyal to Edward in Gascony, but he wasn't making a great deal of headway.

The situation became more complicated in 1341, when John III the Duke of Brittany died without an heir. Two men, John of Monfort and Charles of Blois, fought a short war of succession. Neither France nor England was really able to intervene; both had their own problems, and Edward was too busy raising taxes to try and pay off his debts. This situation meant that yet another war, this time independent of Philip and Edward, began on mainland France.

Taking the Advantage: England

The first years of the Edwardian War proved to be a bit of a failure for England and events are probably best described as a draw. However, things changed when the English army returned to France in 1345. Edward III took with him a freshly recruited army of nearly 10,000 men along with his 16-year-old son, Edward the Prince of Wales, who was to have a massive impact on events and make a name for himself as 'the Black Prince'.

Fighting all the way

The English army was advancing with only one intention – an open battle with the French – and this time the French were unable to avoid the impending fight. Philip VI realised the high stakes and began advancing through Normandy, gathering a large army made up of all his feudal lords, supporters and their troops to take on the English.

Edward III's second campaign in France was very different from his previous effort as he finally faced the French king in battle. This time the English army looted its way through Normandy, seizing property and burning French towns. They met two French armies at Caen and Blanchetaque (see Figure 21-1) in July and August and won victories over both. These French armies were just Philip's advance party; his full army arrived in the middle of August. At this point, the two large armies began circling each other in an attempt to find decent ground.

Overstating the huge importance of the impending battle is impossible. For the defeated side, any comeback would be expensive and laborious. Recruiting a fresh army would take years, and many nobles were likely to be killed or captured and held for ransom (a popular way of making money out of warfare). The situation was victory or nothing, because for the loser the results may well have meant permanent defeat.

Meeting at last: The battle of Crecy

Nearly a decade after the beginning of the war, the English and French armies finally faced each other on 26 August 1346, in one of the most famous battles of the Middle Ages. Like many other medieval battles, it took place somewhere fairly insignificant. Crecy was a very small town south of Calais of no great importance, but it was surrounded by flat agricultural land ideal for fighting.

A new kind of battle

Crecy is a famous battle not only because of its outcome, but also because many historians regard it as being the point at which the old Medieval World of chivalry came to an end. Normal war practice was to take prisoners, particularly nobles, and then hold them for ransom, but in the vicious, bloody carnage of Crecy all that changed. Whatever their status, men were finished off and murdered before they could surrender.

The chronicler Jean Froissart gives a chilling account of English knife-wielding killers known as *misericordias* or 'mercy killers':

> *Then ye should have seen the men at arms dash in among them and kill a great number of them: and ever still the Englishmen shot whereas they saw thickest press; the sharp arrows ran into the men of arms and into their horses, and many fell, horse and men, among the Genoways* [Genovese; French allies], *and when they were down, they could not relieve again, the press was so thick that one overthrew another. And also among the Englishmen there were certain rascals that went afoot with great knives, and they went in among the men of arms, and slew and murdered many as they lay on the ground, both earls, barons, knights, and squires, whereof the king of England was after displeased, for he had rather they had been taken prisoners.*

Edward wasn't thinking in humanitarian terms. No doubt the heavily in-debt king was displeased with all the potential ransoms that were lost.

Crecy was also notable as possibly the first time that a cannon was used in a major European battle. Known as 'Ribaldis' and developed in Italy, this simple cannon was first employed in Europe in around 1345. Accounts from Crecy suggest that one was fired on two or three occasions during the battle: the cannon probably terrified more people than it killed.

Philip's army vastly outnumbered Edward's. Accounts vary, but the majority of historians suggest that an English army of around 15,000 faced a French force at least 35,000 strong. Despite the numerical disadvantage, the English forces won a crushing victory at Crecy. This success was partly due to overconfidence from the French, as well as several other important factors:

> ✔ The French army consisted mostly of knights – mounted warriors on horseback – whereas the English had a large body of infantry in their force. This made the French technically more mobile but less able to fight effectively at close quarters.

✔ The English used the traditional longbow, whereas the French used the more modern and complicated crossbow, something that would be very important at the battle of Agincourt nearly 60 years later, towards the end of the war (check out Chapter 23 for much more on this most famous of medieval battles), but at Crecy the longbow won the day.

The French first attacked with crossbows, but they made no impact on the English infantry. The crossbowmen were able to fire only one or two arrows a minute, and their arrows didn't pierce armour. In contrast, the English archers replied by firing three times as fast and the French knights's armour was unable to withstand their arrows. The crossbow attack failed, and the French knights were forced to charge straight into English arrow fire.

Again and again the French knights charged at the English lines, incurring heavy losses every time. To make things worse for the French, Edward had positioned his forces at the top of a small hill. As the day wore on, the damp conditions and the hooves and feet of horses and men turned the sloping ground into a soggy bog. The French knights and their horses became exhausted by having to plough through it.

In all, the French made 16 charges but were unable to break the English lines and Philip VI was injured in one attack. By the early evening he'd had enough and called for the army to retreat, with appallingly heavy losses.

More than 1,500 French knights were killed along with 11 noblemen. Total French casualties numbered around 15,000 as opposed to around 300 English. The battle of Crecy was an astonishing victory for England.

Rising up with the Black Prince

The battle at Crecy was an amazing victory, but Edward III was never able to press home his advantage. Although he followed up Crecy by capturing Calais, in 1348 the plague known as the Black Death hit Europe (turn to Chapter 20 for all about the plague) and the devastating impact meant that the war was suspended for some eight years with neither king in any position to launch an offensive and returning to their own domestic affairs.

Philip VI died in 1350 and was replaced by his son John II, known as 'John the Good', and the war moved into a new phase. See the later sidebar 'John is a good boy' for more details on John.

A very potent promenade

The Black Prince is most famous for adopting the military strategy known as the *chevauchee* (from the French word meaning 'promenade'). The tactic, which he used on campaign during 1356, was a particularly brutal form of destroying the land that an army travelled through. Towns were raided and looted, and crops burnt to prevent land being used again for some time. The effect was intended to be psychological as much as practical. The idea was to suggest to an invaded people that their king was unable to protect them. In many ways the idea was nothing new. Edward III had followed a similar policy when invading in 1339, but with the Black Prince it was applied on a much bigger and more destructive scale.

The Black Prince's methods worked, and many historians suggest that the *chevauchee* contributed to the peasant uprising called the *Jacquerie*, which took place in 1358 (the later section 'Collapsing in France' has more on this uprising). In practical terms, the revolt forced the French king to come to battle.

The man leading this new phase of the war was Edward's son, also named Edward, but known as the Black Prince. When the war resumed in 1356, he was 26 years old and had become a fearsome warrior. From a very young age, he'd shown a keen interest in military affairs and became a feared opponent at tournaments (see Chapter 11 for more on these events).

Historians can't agree on the origin of Edward's nickname, and no surviving sources from the fourteenth century refer to him as such. Some people suggest that the name stems from wearing black armour and others that it was because of the colour of his coat of arms. I prefer the argument that it refers to his apparently explosive temper and generally violent attitude.

Edward the Black Prince was at the head of an invasion that sailed around the Atlantic coast to land in Gascony in 1356. At this time, English forces were secure in the north of France, and the Black Prince was attempting to catch John II in the middle. The plan worked. The sides met in battle at Poitiers in west, central France on 19 September 1356.

Poitiers was another crushing victory for the English army. Amazingly, employing the same tactics as at Crecy allowed the English to win again. French armour was still vulnerable to the English archers and by making a feint to the left, the infantry lured the French knights into charging and exposed them to attack.

Around 3,000 French were killed or wounded and more than 2,500 captured – among them King John II.

Collapsing in France

Unsurprisingly, the kingdom of France went into meltdown after John II's capture. The country hadn't yet recovered from the ravages of the Black Death, and two massive and humiliating military defeats – at Crecy and Poitiers – within a decade caused further problems.

In addition, for four years after Poitiers, France was a kingdom without a king. The French people had had enough and remarkably, during the next stage of the Hundred Years' War, the greatest threat to the kingdom of France came from its own subjects.

Experiencing social unrest and the Jacquerie

After the capture of King John II, the States General – the French equivalent of Parliament – tried to take control but failed. Various nobles took the opportunity to settle old scores and seize back territory from the king and the kingdom of France had no effective government.

Another problem was the growing economic crisis. In order to try and recover their losses from Poitiers, the French nobility were forced to raise taxes to pay for new armies. A law was also passed that allowed landowners to take money and property without compensation and, even worse, forced all peasants to fight if their masters' property came under attack.

After the ravages of the Black Death and the famines that followed, mandatory military service was the last straw. In 1358, things came to a head with a peasant uprising in France. The revolt, known as the *Jacquerie* because of the padded jackets all peasants wore, pitted class against class. Years of subjugation and mistreatment boiled over into an astonishingly bloody and violent response. Although the revolt had no particular structure, a general mood of unrest turned into peasants rising up against their masters.

Nobles were the main targets, with their agents and tax collectors even joining in the revolt. The chronicler Jean Froissart gives a shocking account of the violence that took place, although he may well have been slightly exaggerating. Froissart was from the Low Countries and his patron was an English queen who would have presumably been pleased by these stories of French struggle:

> *These mischievous people thus assembled without captain or armour robbed, beat and slew all gentlemen that they could lay hands on, and forced and ravished ladies and damosels, and did such shameful deeds that no human creature ought to think on any such, and he that did most mischief was most praised with them and greatest master. I dare not write the horrible deeds that they did to ladies and damosels; among other they slew a knight and after did put him on a broach [spit] and roasted him at the fire in the sight of the lady his wife and his children; and after the lady had been enforced and ravished with a ten or twelve, they made her perforce to eat of her husband and after made her to die an evil death and all her children.*

Restoring order, brutally

Eventually, the *Jacquerie* came to an end, perhaps because no overall plan was in place other than to try and kill off all the nobles in France. More than 150 noble houses were affected and thousands of people were tortured and killed. But soon some kind of co-ordinated response was arranged.

This response came from the splendidly titled Charles the Bad of Navarre. Charles was very much the enemy of the Prince Regent and nominal French leader (the soon to be Charles V), and wanted to use the crisis to mount a challenge for the throne. Charles the Bad tricked one of the most prominent rebels, Guillaume Cale, into meeting him for talks and had him tortured and decapitated. The massed group of 20,000 peasants that had followed Guillaume were then mercilessly chased down and slaughtered by Charles's knights.

Across France, various nobles followed suit and thousands of peasants were lynched during the summer of 1358. The *Jacquerie* was over.

Pressing pause: A time for peace

The chaos in France was too much for the Black Prince to resist, and in 1360 he invaded again. With the French king, John II, still in captivity, France was under the nominal control of the Dauphin (Prince Regent) Charles V.

Despite France's unsteady circumstances, the English attack wasn't a success. The English army attacked Reims and Paris, but managed to take neither city. Their only reward was some ravaging of the already ravaged French countryside.

John is a good boy

John II gained his nickname 'the Good' from events that followed his capture by the English during the battle of Poitiers. After four years of captivity, the treaty of Bretigny that was signed in 1360 set John's ransom at a massive 3,000,000 gold crowns, around double the annual income of France. John was released from captivity to return to France and raise his ransom. In his stead, his son Louis was held in Anjou and several French nobles in England.

Soon afterwards, however, the hostages held in England escaped and fled back across the channel; Prince Louis escaped from Anjou in 1363. John was appalled by these acts and felt that his word had been broken by others. In one of the most remarkable events of the Middle Ages he travelled to England and gave himself up as a hostage!

Sadly, soon after his arrival back in England, John caught an unknown illness and died in April 1364. During his time in England he was treated like a hero and very much as a symbol of chivalry. For John, honour was above everything – including the liberty of his son and even his kingdom.

The treaty of Bretigny was signed in 1360, which confirmed that the Black Prince now held Calais and also considerably more territory in the southern duchy of Aquitaine. The treaty also stipulated that there would be peace for the next nine years. For the time being the Hundred Years' War was on hold.

Recovering with the French: The Caroline War

Historians generally consider the next stage of the Hundred Years' War (1369–1389, and named the Caroline War after the new French king, Charles V, who had been crowned in 1364) to be one of French recovery. In truth this period was more like a series of English disasters than a great French comeback, but the events meant that by the end of the fourteenth century, the conflict between the nations was balanced on a knife-edge.

Stoking the flames of war

During the 1360s France recovered. Charles V established his rule, and several nobles who stood against the French monarch (see the earlier section 'Collapsing in France') changed their minds and returned to serving him. Charles cleverly picked small targets, including Poitiers, and took these cities back from the English, gradually reducing their possessions in France.

The English response was again to take up the policy of *chevauchee* in an attempt to undermine Charles V's authority and also cause difficulties for the large French army if it tried to live off the land.

Jean Froissart described the raiding, which proved to be as brutal as ever:

> Then the [Black] prince all the others with their companies entered into the city, ready apparelled to do evil, and to pill and rob the city, and to slay men, women and children, for so it was commanded them to do. It was great pity to see the men, women and children that kneeled down on their knees before the prince for mercy; but he was so inflamed with ire, that he took no heed to them, so that none was heared, but all put to death. There was no pity taken of the poor people, who wrought never no manner of treason, yet they bought it dearer than the great personages, such as had done the evil and trespass. There was not so hard a heart within the city of Limoges, and if he had any remembrance of God, but that wept piteously for the great mischief that they saw before their eyes: for more than three thousand men, women and children were slain and beheaded that day, God have mercy on their souls, for I believe they were martyrs.

Yet again innocent people were being butchered in this most bloody of medieval wars.

Busting the English at Biscay

The first big action of this new stage of the war was a massive naval encounter off the coast of La Rochelle in the Bay of Biscay (see Figure 21-1). In June 1372 the English fleet under the command of John of Hastings met the French in the biggest naval encounter since the Battle of Sluys in 1340. Accounts differ as to what happened in the battle, but the end result was a massive defeat for the English.

This defeat was a huge blow to the English, because since Sluys the English fleet had dominated the channel and protected the island from invasion. Continuing to do so was now far more difficult and opened up an opportunity for the French king. The defeat also made defending English territories in southern France far more difficult, because the naval route through the Bay of Biscay was the only way to keep communications and supply lines open.

Regrouping: The Plantagenets need a new plan

Worse was to come for the English throne as the Plantagenet dynasty experienced some very unexpected setbacks. Within five years, they had a new king – and not the one that they were expecting. In June 1376, the Black Prince died at the age of 46. He had been ill following his return from France in 1371 with what chroniclers referred to as a 'wasting illness'. Few people had more impact on the Hundred Years' War.

The following year, his father was dead too. Edward III died almost exactly a year after his son in June 1377 at the age of 65, most probably of a stroke. The deaths left the English crown in something of a crisis. The only available male heir was his 10-year-old grandson Richard, the son of the Black Prince.

The new king, Richard II, was supported by a council of advisors, but was still unable to continue the war properly. Within two years England was dealing with its own *Jacquerie* in the form of the Peasants' Revolt (which I describe in detail in Chapter 22). For the time being the French were able to make relatively easy progress at recapturing lost territory from the English, which they did until a truce was signed in 1389. Huge changes were necessary in England before the war fully resumed (I take up this aspect of the story in Chapter 23).

Chapter 22

Pausing the War: Dealing with Unrest at Home

*T*he fourteenth century saw Medieval Europe buffeted by numerous wars, invasions, population movements and the devastating effects of the plague, later known as the 'Black Death', with the peasants bearing the brunt of these events. With little property of their own, they depended on the charity – and all too often the work bordering on exploitation – given to them by others to live. Life was harsh, brutal and for many short.

Peasants had always suffered more than other groups in society, but the fourteenth century saw attempts to change this situation. Across Europe, and particularly in England as I describe in this chapter, groups of peasants protested and took up arms to try and improve their lives. Yes, the peasants were revolting – and so watch out as you read on!

Getting Riled Up in England

In some ways England was slow to respond to the mood of unrest in Europe. Several other revolts took place before things came to a head in England (see the later sidebar 'Of lettuce and liberty: Rebellion throughout Europe'). Still, the English Peasants' Revolt of 1381 is probably the most famous of the revolts, due to its organisation and the threat that it posed to the monarchy.

All peasants aren't equal

The trouble with a word such as 'peasants' is that it suggests one large mass of poor people. In fact, the situation was more complicated. *Peasant* basically means 'one who works', indicating people who weren't rich enough in land to subsist only from the profits from their estates, but those who actually had to work for a living.

A huge variety of grades within the lower classes existed. For example, a *yeoman,* who worked what was called a *yardland* (around 30 acres), still had to work it for a living but was a world away from an unfree serf who would

have had far less – possibly just a very few acres. Similarly, the lower classes also included *freemen* or *husbandmen,* collectively known as *artisans,* who although free from bondage to a lord still had to work to survive. Often they had trades, such as blacksmith or cooper (a maker of barrels) and owned the premises where they worked.

None of these people would have described themselves as peasants though because the word wasn't used at the time. True serfs were referred to as *rustici* (country dwellers) or *villeins.*

Rooting out the causes of revolt

The revolt was a long time coming, and many of the reasons had been smouldering away for generations, even centuries. Although specific triggers for the revolt did exist (as I describe in the later section 'Taxing everyone'), the general cause was the terrible conditions that were imposed on the lower classes through serfdom. The revolt was also prompted by the sudden change to working conditions caused by the Black Death.

Serfing through life

Most lower-class people lived in a state of *serfdom*, which was the basis of the feudal system. *Serfs*, or *villeins*, were unfree peasants tied to working on the land on which they lived. They were forced to labour on the land of their master, taking on whatever tasks they were told to do and with no freedom to move elsewhere or right to seek other opportunities or higher wages. Landowners owned their serfs in almost the same way that they owned the land on which the serfs worked, in that they were valuable property. Serfs weren't exactly slaves as they were able to run away, but doing so would leave them with very little option for what they could then do with their lives. Serfdom wasn't quite slavery, but it wasn't too far from it either.

The Black Death in the middle of the fourteenth century significantly shook up the system of serfdom. Millions of serfs died, resulting in labour shortages throughout England. Many serfs tried to seize this opportunity to move on and seek better wages elsewhere. Their mobility was a huge threat to the nobility, and in 1351 King Edward III passed the 'Statute of Labourers', which made switching positions illegal and set wages at a maximum level, based on amounts from before the Black Death in the 1340s. The statute was probably difficult to enforce, but it likely stopped many people from grabbing a new-found freedom.

Serfs were able, however, to free themselves from their bondage in a couple of ways: if their lords volunteered to free them or the serfs ran away. If after running away, they managed to live somewhere else for a year and a day, they were declared legally free. Sounds easy, right? Well, not quite. Serfs who fled their homes were legally barred from taking other work, and so they had an almost impossible time surviving anywhere else. Many serfs on the run ended up living in forests and becoming outlaws.

Taxing everyone

Whether people were villeins, serfs, artisans or yeomen, they were all affected by the Hundred Years' War. Whilst the battles may have mostly taken place across the Channel, the taxes raised to fund the military campaigns were very much a problem for the English population. The conflict dragged on for a good part of the fourteenth century (check out Chapters 21 and 23) and was ruinously expensive for England.

Much of the war was financed on credit, with Edward III borrowing heavily from foreign bankers in Italy and the Low Countries. However, the money needed to be paid back and further cash raised. The only way to do that was through taxes. Eventually, in 1377, Edward raised money through a *poll tax*. The poll tax was set at a fixed amount regardless of an individual's wealth and possessions, as opposed to an *income tax* based on what you earn or own.

In 1377 Edward III died and was replaced by his ten-year-old grandson Richard II. Richard's advisors, in particular John of Gaunt (see Chapter 21 for more on him), wanted to raise funds to continue the war with France, and they almost tripled the first poll tax that was set in Richard's name in 1381. The tax was raised from 1 groat (4 pennies) to 3 groats (12 pennies) and applied across the board with no exceptions. As far as many peasants were concerned, this rise was the last straw.

Telling the tax collector to fob off in Fobbing

Not paying the poll tax presented an easy way for people to protest. In many cases, they couldn't pay it, and so refusing to do so was easy. According to accounts from the period, the first recorded incident of refusal to pay was in a village called Fobbing in Essex.

In May 1381 a man called John Bampton was sent to collect the taxes from Fobbing. The villagers refused to pay and were led in their protests by a man called Thomas Baker. Interestingly, Thomas Baker was a landowner and was considered a yeoman rather than a serf. When the local justice of the peace arrived to demand the cash, the villagers attacked him and sent him packing – the revolt was on!

IN THEIR OWN WORDS

Lollardy – The people's Church

At the same time as the peasantry in the south of England were refusing to pay tax, a whole new religious movement based on the equality of all human beings was growing in influence. Known as *Lollardy*, the movement was based upon the teachings of John Wycliffe (c. 1325–1384), who had been expelled from Oxford University in 1381.

Specifically, Wycliffe was expelled for his belief that the Roman Church had become corrupt and that the true Church was represented in the 'Community of Believers' who abstained from pomp and ceremony and based their lives purely on the Bible. One aspect of this belief was that the Bible needed to be translated into English and made available to all peasants to read and study. Lollards challenged whether the Church was any more capable of making a man into a good priest than through simple study of the Bible. They despised the rituals and mysticism of Roman church services and the mass, believing in simple community ceremonies.

Their views proved very timely. Along with Wat Tyler's economic challenge, Lollardy represented another way for peasants to challenge authority and call for the Church to be taxed and pay the dues being forced on to the poor.

The Lollards were proposing a kind of medieval socialism where all things were held in common. The chronicler Jean Froissart quotes the Lollard priest John Ball as follows:

My good friends, things cannot go on well in England, nor ever will until every thing shall be in common; when there shall be neither vassal nor lord, and all distinctions levelled; when the lords shall be no more masters than ourselves. How ill have they used us! and for what reason do they hold us in bondage? Are we not all descended from the same parents, Adam and Eve? and what can they show, or what reasons give, why they should be more the masters than ourselves? except, perhaps, in making us labour and work, for them to spend.

Interestingly, Froissart describes John Ball as the 'crazy priest' and those involved in the revolt as 'the evil-desposed', probably because his patron had been the English queen and the crown still perceived Lollards to be a threat. He was probably exaggerating a bit too. Lollardy survived long after the Peasants' Revolt, and many of its beliefs formed the basis for Protestant thought during the English Reformation.

Revolting with the peasants

The protest at Fobbing was the first act of peasant defiance. Within a few weeks, dozens of similar incidents occurred across the counties of Essex and Kent. Villagers didn't stop at refusing to pay tax: they formed themselves into armed gangs, daring officials to press them for payment and in some cases marching to London to make their protests to the king and to parliament.

Ganging up with Wat Tyler

In June 1381, a large band of men formed in Kent under the charismatic leadership of Wat Tyler. Tyler and his Kentish men marched towards London and met up with the contingent from Essex before arriving in Blackheath, in south London, on 12 June.

Many others joined the protestors and great speeches were made, including one by John Ball, a campaigning Lollard priest (see the later sidebar 'Lollardy – The people's Church'). Despite the number of people massing on London, the situation didn't degenerate into extreme violence. Sporadic attacks were made on specific properties, however, most of which belonged to or were associated with John of Gaunt, the 14-year-old King Richard II's uncle and chief advisor.

Sources at the time claim that the king himself rode out to meet the peasants on 14 June, at which point he was presented with their demands. These included the sacking of his advisors and the end to serfdom. Both sides agreed to meet again the next day.

Storming the Tower of London

Up to this point, the revolt in London was a peaceful affair, but all that changed in the blink of an eye. At roughly the same time that Wat Tyler and his party were meeting with Richard II, another group of protestors were making their presence felt in a far more dramatic fashion. In an incredibly violent episode, they attacked and burnt down several properties, including the Savoy Palace owned by John of Gaunt.

More astonishingly still the violent protesters stormed the Tower of London, the most significant of London landmarks associated with the monarchy. Unfortunately, various notable men heavily associated with the poll tax were inside the tower. Among the nobles rounded up and murdered were Simon of Sudbury, the Lord Chancellor and also the Archbishop of Canterbury, as well as Robert de Hales, the Lord Treasurer. The revolt had taken on a much more dramatic and sinister turn.

Doling out disaster at Smithfield and St John's Field

The following day the rebels again travelled to a public meeting with King Richard, on the site of the meat market at Smithfield. From the start, this meeting had a more fractious and unpleasant feel to it than the encounter with Richard II just a day earlier. Wat Tyler apparently arrived slightly drunk and the proceedings had a clear edge to them.

As he rose to speak to the king, Tyler was alleged to have drawn a dagger. At this point two men stepped forward and ran him through with their swords, mortally wounding him. When Tyler disappeared from view, the crowd went into uproar shouting out to ask where he was. At this point Richard II stood and made the memorable claim that 'You shall have no captain but me.' He then asked them to disperse and meet up again at St John's Fields, which was then an area of agricultural land owned by the Church in south London.

Of lettuce and liberty: Rebellion in Europe

The Peasants' Revolt of 1381 in England certainly wasn't the only uprising during the fourteenth century. In Chapter 21, I discuss the *Jacquerie* in France, and several other significant uprisings occurred around this time as well:

✔ **The Ivalyo Rebellion:** In 1227, one of the most remarkable revolts – known as the Ivalyo rebellion – took place in Bulgaria. This uprising was arguably the most successful of all time. Ivaylo was the nickname of a swine-herder who proved to be an extremely charismatic leader. Given how badly he probably smelled, his charisma was fortunate! He was at the head of a peasant uprising that was so successful that it forced the nobility of Bulgaria to make him emperor! He proved good at that too, winning a series of military victories against the neighbouring Byzantine Empire. His luck ran out when some of his supporters turned on him, and he fled into the Mongol Empire where he was assassinated soon afterwards. For someone who had led such an adventurous life his nickname is curious; it means 'lettuce' in Bulgarian!

✔ **The Flanders Uprising:** Between 1323–1328, a peasant uprising occurred in Flanders. Like the 1381 revolt in England, the Flanders episode was caused by excessive taxation, this time imposed on the orders of Louis I, the Count of Flanders. Riots and violent protests followed for a number of years led by a farmer called Nicolaas Zannekin. Several towns were captured along with Louis I, who was imprisoned. Order was eventually restored by the French king, Charles IV, but not until the rebels were defeated by his successor Philip VI in 1328.

✔ **The Estonian Revolt:** Between 1343–45, a huge uprising took place in Estonia on the far eastern borders of the Holy Roman Empire. The Teutonic Knights had conquered the territory as part of their Crusading in Europe (see Chapter 16) and had imposed a German-speaking ruling class. In 1343 the indigenous people rose up in an anti-German and anti-Christian revolt. In one night, nearly 2,000 people were slaughtered and hundreds of churches burned. The Teutonic order retaliated in similar style and a guerrilla war resulted over the next two years before the revolt leaders were eventually hunted down and killed.

✔ **The Revolt of the Ciompi:** In 1378, Italy saw its own peasant uprising, the Revolt of the Ciompi. The *ciompi* were textile workers in Florence who weren't part of any trading guild and had no representation. Their uprising made demands for legal changes to give them greater representation. They forced themselves into power, with their leader Michele Di Lando assuming a major government post. Although initially successful, the revolt soon fell apart with infighting among the ciompi and other minor guilds, culminating in a deadly street fight. For a while at least, they did force a change in the government of Florence. A statue of Di Lando still stands today in the Loggia del Mercato Nuovo, in Florence.

All these revolts have one thing in common – they eventually failed. None of the rebel leaders were able to cope with a coordinated armed response from a government or monarch. They also show that by the fourteenth century the lower classes of Europe were pushing at the boundaries of their class systems in previously unseen ways. Revolutionary politics were born during this period and the leaders of these revolts became heroes for those who later pushed for political change.

Whilst the peasants were settling there a militia of around 7,000 was put together and fell on the rebels at St John's Field. All the rebel leaders were arrested, including the Lollard priest John Ball (check out the earlier sidebar 'Lollardy – The people's Church'). Immediately any concessions made by the king were revoked.

The militia didn't stop there either. Richard then took his troops to Kent to search out any further dissenters. Many were arrested, but in time the king relented as this contemporary chronicle describes:

> *Afterwards the King sent out his messengers into diverse parts, to capture the malefactors and put them to death. And many were taken and hanged at London, and they set up many gallows around the City of London, and in other cities and boroughs of the south country. At last, as it pleased God, the King seeing that too many of his liege subjects would be undone, and too much blood spilt, took pity in his heart, and granted them all pardon, on condition that they should never rise again, under pain of losing life or members [genitals], and that each of them should get his charter of pardon, and pay the King as fee for his seal twenty shillings, to make him rich. And so finished this wicked war.*

In the end, around 1,500 rebels were arrested and condemned to death. The revolt was brutally ended and nothing tangible was achieved. What it did do, however, was show how dangerous a peasant uprising could be and many people cite it as the first event of radical British politics.

Regarding Henry IV: Bolingbroke Seizes Power

Richard II was able to claim that he successfully put down the 1381 Peasants' Revolt, but that affair was only the beginning of his problems. Ever since his father had died, because of Richard's young age a committee had in effect been ruling England. Powerful men who had served under Edward III advised Richard and ran the show. Sooner or later he was going to have to deal with their threat to his authority, but in fact that threat came from somebody else, his first cousin and childhood playmate, Henry Bolingbroke.

Perusing Henry's path to power

Henry was the son of John of Gaunt, who was the third son of Edward III and had been advising and pretty much controlling his nephew Richard II since he'd become king. Furthermore, John was most unpopular with the rebels of the Peasants' Revolt because he'd been the main mover behind the hated Poll Tax.

Henry was born in 1366 at Bolingbroke Castle in Lincolnshire from which he took his name. He grew up at court alongside his cousin Richard. When Richard became king in 1377, Henry continued to be a part of the court because his father was effectively in charge.

Participating in an uprising and Crusading

In 1387 Richard II suffered the first internal uprising against him. The 21-year-old king was presented with a demand from parliament that he sack his chancellor Edward de la Pole. Richard refused and a coalition of knights formed against him. Henry was involved in this revolt, but when Richard successfully suppressed it, Henry wasn't punished – instead he was elevated from an earl to a duke!

Although Henry escaped punishment, he may not have been totally confident that he wouldn't eventually suffer reprisals because he spent most of the 1390s involved in Crusading activity in Europe. Between 1390–92, he fought with the Teutonic Knights against revolts in Lithuania, laying siege to the capital of Vilnius. The siege was unsuccessful and so Henry followed up with a journey to Jerusalem, which was no longer in Christian hands. These campaigns seem to have been a kind of training exercise in both war and political diplomacy, developing skills that Henry later put to great use during his own reign.

Going into exile

By the end of the fourteenth century, the relationship between Richard and Henry seems to have completely broken down. Richard was childless and also heavily in debt. Henry's family group, the House of Lancaster, was a clear threat to the king; it was wealthy and had blood connections to the throne. In addition, Henry had returned from Europe as a famous warrior and politician. His potential was clear – as was his threat to Richard.

In December 1397 Henry became involved in a big argument with the Duke of Norfolk, Thomas de Mowbray, which was to be settled by a duel of honour. To prevent bloodshed, Richard exiled both of them – Henry for ten years. He went to live in Paris – not a bad place to be exiled!

Making a comeback

Richard must have felt safe from the threat of Henry, but the feeling didn't last long. In 1399 John of Gaunt died, and as his heir Henry expected to return home and take up his position. Instead, Richard disinherited Henry, exiled him for life and claimed the estates for the crown! Richard's actions gave Henry the excuse he needed to stage a major comeback, and Richard pretty much brought it on himself.

Henry landed on the Yorkshire coast in June 1399 with only a small group of followers. Within a few weeks he had gathered together huge support across the country. Richard II was an unpopular king because of his cruel tax policies, and few now rose to defend him.

Desperately seeking Richard

Nobody is sure of the exact fate of Richard II. Historians know that he was imprisoned in the Tower of London and that shortly afterwards he was moved to Pontefract Castle in West Yorkshire. Henry had promised to spare his life and would probably have done so, but in the months after Henry assumed power, news of a counterplot emerged.

Several leading nobles including the Earls of Kent and Somerset were arrested and revealed, under torture, that they'd been plotting to assassinate Henry and reinstate Richard. Richard was unlikely to have been involved in the plot, but it must have suggested to Henry that he was too dangerous to be kept alive. Most historians agree that Richard died some time during February 1400, but how is unknown: poison or being left to starve to death are the most popular theories.

But the story doesn't end there. For years after his death rumours persisted that Richard was still alive – despite the fact that his body was publicly displayed in St Paul's Cathedral! A few years later a man emerged in Scotland claiming to be Richard and was used as the figurehead for several revolts. This man's identity isn't known, but many considered him mentally ill; he died in poverty in 1419. His is a curious tale that tells a great deal about the medieval mindset: clearly conspiracy theories were as popular then as they are today!

Richard had recently gone to Ireland on campaign and had to rush back to deal with the crisis. Eventually he met with Henry at Flint Castle in Wales. He agreed to abdicate on condition that his life was spared. He was immediately imprisoned in the Tower of London.

Although delayed by political problems, Henry's coronation eventually took place in October 1399. England had a new king, Henry IV.

Muddling through an unhappy reign

After all the action and skulduggery that preceded it, Henry IV's reign was a bit of a let down. He ruled for just 14 years and most of it was spent dealing with problems at home and potential revolts. His reign is important, however, because it paved the way for the succession of his son, Henry V and his famous campaigns in the resumption of the Hundred Years' War (I discuss Henry V in more detail in Chapter 23).

Rebelling against the rebels

Henry IV came to the throne on the back of plot and rebellion, and he in turn suffered from similar events throughout his reign. (Check out the sidebar 'Desperately seeking Richard' for details of various plots against Henry.) Even more serious were his problems in Wales. In 1400 Owain Glyndwr proclaimed himself the Prince of Wales and its true ruler. The revolt that took place lasted for the whole of Henry's reign and wasn't concluded until 1415, when it was eventually put down by Prince Henry (also known as Henry of Monmouth and the future Henry V). Glyndwr was never captured and disappeared into hiding in 1412, never to return.

Equally serious was the revolt of Henry Percy, the Duke of Northumberland, and his son, also named Henry but better known as 'Hotspur' in 1403. This revolt joined with Owain Glyndwr and the Welsh and put up Edmund Mortimer, a distant relative of Edward III, as an alternative king. This rebellion was extremely serious and drew a great deal of support from barons who were disenchanted with the king. The revolt was ended only by the Battle of Shrewsbury in July 1403, when Hotspur was killed. Again, the king's son, Henry of Monmouth, led the defence.

Suffering war at home, enjoying peace abroad

Given the horrendous problems that Henry was having at home, he was probably relieved that the Hundred Years' War was still suspended. In 1389, Richard II had signed a peace treaty with France that still held. Both France and England were experiencing huge domestic problems and weren't ready for war. Although Henry had planned French campaigns, problems at home meant that they were never able to take place. Equally, France was hamstrung by the French king, Charles V, gradually losing his mind and challengers for the throne emerging. Unsurprisingly the peace treaty was regularly renewed and carried on until 1415.

Dying a rather messy death

Henry IV suffered bad health from early on in his reign. As time went on, he became progressively worse with more responsibility being handed over to his son. Initially, Henry IV suffered from a terrible skin disease that may have been a form of leprosy or some kind of psoriasis, but from 1405 onwards he began to suffer attacks that sound like epileptic fits. Eventually in March 1413 he died at the relatively young age of 47. His son, Henry of Monmouth, was already running the kingdom for all practical purposes, and so the transition was relatively smooth. On 9 April he was crowned Henry V. The Hundred Years' War was about to start again!

A strange and unusual visitor

One remarkable foreign policy event did take place during the reign of Henry IV – a visit from the Byzantine emperor, Manuel II Paleologus. Manuel was the first Byzantine emperor to visit Western Europe, and in 1400 he travelled to both France and then England. He was trying to drum up military support for a war against the Ottoman Turks, who were carving their way through the old Byzantine Empire (as I describe in Chapter 24). While in England, Manuel stayed at Eltham Palace in Greenwich, and his wealthy exotic appearance amazed everybody at court. He left with funds from King Henry but no troops.

Chapter 23

Turning the Tide of War (Twice!): Henry V and Joan of Arc

*W*hen the Hundred Years' War resumed in the fifteenth century, two fascinating individuals came to the fore: King Henry V and Joan of Arc. Their actions dominated the final period of the war, and its fortunes swung with them. From the devastating campaigns fought by Henry to the amazing turnaround inspired by the woman known as the Maid of Orleans, the second half of the war – approximately 38 years – is a gripping story.

In this chapter I visit some of the war's sprawling battles and piece together how this seemingly endless conflict eventually drew to a close.

Envisioning English Triumph: Henry V and the Lancastrian War

As I describe in Chapter 22, King Henry IV planned campaigns in France but was never able to put them into action. Therefore, the peace of 1389 between England and France continued steadily throughout his reign.

When Henry V became king in 1413, he had one big agenda in mind: invading France. His overall objective was to become king of both countries, but a more pressing issue was to regain control of the Plantagenet lands that previous kings had held in southeastern France – and of the revenues that they produced. Surprisingly, Henry very nearly pulled this ambition off during the phase of the war known as the 'Lancastrian War'.

Travelling the road to Agincourt

When he became king at the age of 27, Henry V was already an experienced commander. He had fought against his father's enemies in both Wales and England and was very keen to cut his teeth in France. From the English perspective, the moment was ideal to resume the Hundred Years' War: Charles VI of France was widely known to be suffering from a serious mental illness and was plagued by revolts from the French nobility, including his own brother, Louis of Orleans.

France was weakened, and Henry wanted to take full advantage. The only likely problem was money, but parliament granted Henry the authority to charge a 'double tax' for the war, and he was able to put together an army that was around 12,000 strong. Henry was in a fortunate position with this. His predecessors had raised revenues through a 'poll tax' payable by all, which had led to the Peasants' Revolt of 1381 (see Chapter 22), whereas Henry's tax was payable only by the nobility who would potentially gain booty if he was successful. Nevertheless, if he hadn't been he might have ended up with trouble on his hands!

Invading Harfleur

In August 1415 Henry sailed for France. Very few among the party knew where they were headed, because Henry was hoping to surprise the French with his choice of landing spot. The target was the French fortress at Harfleur on the Seine estuary (see Figure 23-1), and having landed in Normandy the English army made its way there. Henry was keen to use Harfleur as a base to strike farther inland, just as Edward III had used Calais years earlier (check out Chapter 21).

Taking Harfleur was a large task, because it was a huge fortress with 26 towers, various fortifications and a broad, deep moat. Henry laid siege to it, launching several unsuccessful attacks until the outer fortifications fell on 17 September. The siege was arduous with many English troops dying from dysentery after apparently drinking rotten wine and unclean water. The rest of the fortress surrendered soon afterwards and by 22 September, Harfleur was in the hands of the English.

Marching into the mud

Having secured Harfleur, in October Henry moved on with the intention of marching to Calais. The port was in English hands, and Henry and his men would be able to winter and resupply there. Unfortunately for Henry the long siege at Harfleur gave the French opportunity to organise their response and the French army was now in the field, led by Charles d'Albret, the Constable of France.

The French intention was to intercept the English before they made it to Calais: and they managed to do so. The French army had greater numbers than the English and was growing all the time as more and more French noblemen joined it with their companies. Also, torrential rain slowed down the English, and they soon realised that they wouldn't make Calais before meeting the French. On 25 October, the two sides encountered each other in a muddy set of fields in northeastern France near woods locally known as Agincourt.

Pinpointing the Battle of Agincourt

The battle that followed is one of the most famous in medieval history. The battlefield was a relatively narrow strip of land between two large woods: Agincourt and Tramecourt.

The two armies were very different in composition and approaches to fighting:

- ✔ **The English army** was made up of around 1,500 men-at-arms (fully armoured soldiers) and nearly 7,000 longbowmen, the archers who caused chaos at Crecy and Poitiers over 50 years earlier (flip to Chapter 21 for the story of these battles). They were very keen to get on with the fighting as quickly as possible.

- ✔ **The French army**, although slightly larger in numbers (around 10,000 troops), was mostly made up of men-at-arms along with around 1,500 knights. The French were hesitant to begin fighting at first because they were still waiting for around 2,000 further troops to arrive.

Eventually the French cavalry were hampered by the mud and the tremendous, unrelenting volleys of arrows fired by the English archers who were positioned on both sides in the woods. Driven back towards their own lines, the cavalry ran straight into its own infantry who had begun their advance!

Chaos followed. The heavily armed French found moving in the mud incredibly difficult. In the brutal three-hour melee that followed, the English infantry attacked and were joined by their archers who, having run out of arrows, picked up axes, hatchets and daggers. Everybody piled into the bloody, muddy carnage including Henry and the French commander Charles d'Albret. After some time, the French tired and were overcome; thousands were lost in the mud and unable to retreat to their own lines.

Few reliable sources for the battle exist, but the result was obviously a huge victory for the English. Most modern historians agree that at least 4,000 Frenchmen were killed with the English losing only around 500. Many French nobles were killed too, including Charles d'Albret. Several thousand French prisoners were taken, but Henry became concerned that the remaining French were regrouping for another attack and had them all executed, so that his army would be able to move quickly.

Conquering France (almost)

Agincourt was an almost complete victory. The French government was already tearing itself apart, split between the rival Dukes of Burgundy and

Orleans, King Charles VI was suffering from bouts of insanity (according to some sources, he often convinced himself that he was made of glass) and the army had now been utterly defeated in the field. France was in no position to respond. The way seemed clear for Henry V to press home his advantage and possibly end the war by uniting the two kingdoms. Over the next four years he nearly managed it.

Enjoying favourable international relations

Agincourt certainly got Henry noticed in Europe. The following year, 1416, Henry received an embassy from King Sigismund of Hungary (1368–1437), one of the most powerful rulers in Europe, who would go on to become Holy Roman Emperor. Sigismund was visiting Western Europe to try and heal the divisions in the papacy that had followed the Great Western Schism (turn to Chapter 19 for more), but he dropped in on Henry in 1416 while he was in the area.

Sigismund's original intention seems to have been to try and make peace between France and England, but he was so impressed with Henry as a statesman that he eventually signed a mutual cooperation deal with him! This event in turn had another positive effect for Henry, because Duke John of Burgundy, who had held himself independent from the French crown, met with Henry and declared him to be the true king of France.

Henry's good fortunes didn't stop there. Again in 1416 Henry won another important victory. France was still allied with the Italian city of Genoa, and a Genoese fleet had besieged Harfleur. After an immense seven-hour naval battle, the English were victorious and the channel was back under English control. Henry was on a roll.

Taking Rouen, slowly and brutally

With fresh allies and quite a lot of momentum, Henry resumed campaigning in 1417 and very quickly took control of the whole of south Normandy. His next target was the important city of Rouen (see Figure 23-1), which was tremendously wealthy from the weaving industry and the export of its products down the Seine to Paris, from where they were exported across the whole of Europe.

Henry quickly surrounded Rouen and laid siege. The city was now completely cut off from the north coast, as well as from Paris to the south. The siege was hard and brutal. The citizens of Rouen forced out the women and children that they were no longer able to feed, hoping that the besieging army would feed them. But the English ignored them and without food or shelter, they died dreadful deaths of starvation in the fields around Rouen. Another set of innocent victims of the war.

The siege dragged on for more than 18 months, and the city didn't fall until January 1419. The French nobles who had continued to resist were executed, and Henry moved south towards Paris.

SEEN ON SCREEN

Agincourt: Too few sources to shake a sword at

Although Agincourt is one of the most famous events in medieval history, no reliable sources or accounts of the battle exist. Although historians have a good idea of how the battle progressed, the numbers involved vary hugely depending on which source you read. Famously the events of the reigns of Richard II, Henry IV and Henry V are all captured in the plays of William Shakespeare (1554–1616). Shakespeare's history plays have generated a huge amount of academic debate concerning how close they are to the 'facts' and from where Shakespeare got his information.

The text of *Henry V* certainly gives an idea of the size and scale of the conflict that took place in France. The two most famous cinematic versions of the play – starring Laurence Olivier in 1944 and Kenneth Branagh in 1989 – offer thrills and insights. The more recent version is probably the best and gives a great impression of the mud, grime and unrelenting violence of the campaign. Famously, however, the 1944 version has a terrific scene showing a huge volley of English arrows at the crucial point in the battle. Both are well worth checking out if you have the time.

Henry now travelled wearing the appropriate ducal robes of Normandy, clearly making the political point that he was laying claim to the old Plantagenet lands and titles (see Chapter 21). A nice piece of medieval political spin!

Zeroing in on Paris: the Treaty of Troyes

The English army was outside Paris by August, although their advance didn't go without incident. Shortly after they arrived Henry's new French ally, John of Burgundy, was assassinated by supporters of the Dauphin, the French heir to the throne. John's death didn't derail Henry though, because the French king had no choice but to negotiate with an English army parked outside his capital.

In the early months of 1420, the Treaty of Troyes was signed. It made Henry heir to the French throne (still occupied by the failing Charles VI who wasn't expected to live much longer). All Henry had to do was wait and he would combine the thrones of England and France. The deal was sealed in June 1420 by Henry's marriage to Catherine of Valois, the daughter of the French king. For once this doesn't just seem to have been a political match and considerable attraction existed between Henry and Catherine. The scene between them at the end of Shakespeare's *Henry V* shows them very much in love and there is reason to believe that this wasn't too far from the truth.

The Treaty of Troyes was an amazing result for Henry and a terrible one for France, but the French government was still in crisis and the king barely in touch with reality.

Amazingly, copies of the text of the Treaty of Troyes still exist. Following are some of the more important clauses in the treaty. Basically the agreement gave Henry complete power in the event of Charles's death and also absolutely outlawed the Dauphin, Prince Charles – and this document was drafted before the Dauphin had the Duke of Burgundy assassinated!

> *6. After our [Charles VI's] death, and from that time forward, the crown and kingdom of France, with all their rights and appurtenances, shall be vested permanently in our son [son-in-law], King Henry [of England], and his heirs.*

> *7. . . . The power and authority to govern and to control the public affairs of the said kingdom shall, during our lifetime, be vested in our son, King Henry, with the advice of the nobles and wise men who are obedient to us, and who have consideration for the advancement and honour of the said kingdom*

> *24. . . . [It is agreed] that the two kingdoms shall be governed from the time that our said son, or any of his heirs shall assume the crown, not divided between different kings at the same time, but under one person who shall be king and sovereign lord of both kingdoms; observing all pledges and all other things to each kingdom its rights, liberties or customs, usages and laws, not submitting in any manner one kingdom to the other.*

> *29. In consideration of the frightful and astounding crimes and misdeeds committed against the kingdom of France by Charles, the said Dauphin, it is agreed that we, our son Henry, and also our very dear son Philip, duke of Burgundy, will never treat for peace or amity with the said Charles.*

Upsetting the best-laid plans of mice and men

Everything seemed set for Henry to succeed, but as you know from reading this book (or even scanning some of the headings in Chapter 24), history rarely turns out as planned.

Henry returned to England with his new wife at the end of 1420 and was planning a campaign to mop up the last elements of resistance in France for 1421. In June 1421 he crossed the channel again – for the last time.

During 1422 the English army was laying siege to the town of Meaux (see Figure 23-1) when Henry suddenly fell gravely ill with dysentery. He lasted only until August when he died at the age of 35. Suddenly everything that he and England had fought and planned for was reduced to nothing.

Henry V's only heir was his young son, Henry, born just the year before. He was technically heir to the French throne, a fact that proved horrendously difficult to enforce. Actual power transferred to John, Duke of Bedford, who became the regent for the new infant king in France. Henry's youth meant that he was unable to lead troops into battle until he came of age in 1436. The delay was fatal to his chances of successfully claiming the French throne.

Recovering with the French: Riding to the Rescue with Saint Joan

Ironically, the desperately ill and half-mad Charles VI outlived his great rival Henry V by two months, maintaining the crown in French hands until his death in October 1422. With the English regent John, Duke of Bedford, unable to enforce the succession of Henry VI, the French crown passed to the previously outlawed Dauphin who became Charles VII.

But as the following contemporary chronicle shows, Charles VII inherited a kingdom in a desperate state:

> *Charles VI being dead, Charles VII succeeded to his father in the kingdom, in the year of our Lord 1422, when he was about twenty-two years of age. In his time, owing to the long wars, wars which had raged within and without, the lethargy and cowardliness of the officers and commanders who were under him, the destruction of all military discipline and order, the rapacity of the troopers, and the general dissolution into which all things had fallen, such destruction had been wrought from the Loire to the Seine – even to the Somme – the farmers were dead or had fled, and almost all the fields had for many years lain without cultivation or any one to cultivate them.*

Charles wasn't really able to do much to turn the situation around over the next seven years, and the English continued to capture towns and pillage territory.

In 1428, however, the war took an entirely new direction, under the influence of an illiterate, 17-year-old shepherdess.

The story of Joan of Arc is one of the most famous in all history, never mind medieval history. Her remarkable achievements and the events in which she was involved are almost legendary. However, Joan didn't win the Hundred Years' War on her own! Her great achievement was to stop the advance of the English army that had been carrying on since 1415. After that, Charles VII was then able to turn the tables and carry the war to the English. Having said that, Joan's life is still one of the most incredible stories.

Rising from the bottom

Medieval history features several people from the peasant classes who made major impacts, including individuals such as Peter the Hermit and Wat Tyler (discussed in Chapters 12 and 22 respectively), but Joan was something else altogether.

She was born in a small village in the east of France in 1412. Her parents were rural folk, and her father owned 50 acres of land. Nothing about her upbringing hinted at what she went on to do. The area in which she lived was still loyal to the French king despite the fact that it bordered the lands of the Duke of Burgundy, who was allied with England.

Taking the initiative

From a young age Joan had visions and claimed that she heard voices in her head. Furthermore, she claimed that these voices were those of Saints Michael, Catherine and Margaret. The saints repeatedly told her that her destiny was to drive the English out of France and that she would accompany the Dauphin (Charles VII) at his coronation.

Many people have visions and hear voices, but Joan was determined and acted on them. In 1428, at the age of just 16, she talked a friend of the family into taking her to Vaucouleurs, in Normandy, where some of the French army were garrisoned. She begged the garrison commander to take her to the French court, but he sarcastically dismissed her. She didn't give up though; the following January in 1429 she was back, demanding to be taken to the king and predicting in detail that the French army would be defeated in a battle near Orleans (see Figure 23-1).

When the prediction came true a few weeks later, Joan was taken to the French court at Chinon and granted an interview with King Charles VII. Managing to get this far seems remarkable, but France was in a desperate state in the war. Anything that offered hope was lapped up. Indeed, desperation seems the only explanation for what followed.

The 17-year-old Joan, standing in borrowed armour, asked the French king if she could be placed at the head of the relief force being sent to break the English siege at Orleans. Amazingly, the king said yes!

Mounting a holy war

Historians have put forward one overriding reason for Joan's amazing ascent to power and her ensuing success: she turned a tired and exhausting conflict into a religious war, rather like the Crusades (see the chapters in Part III). She had been ordered by the saints to take up the fight, and this religious aspect was used as very effective propaganda. To ensure that no risk of bad PR existed, the Dauphin even checked out Joan's background – to make sure that she wasn't hiding any sinful skeletons in her closet!

That Joan managed to achieve what she did is a testament to her skill as a leader and an orator. She must have had some force of personality to make her arguments convincing to both kings and nobles and the common soldiers.

To be able to move in both worlds is the mark of a true leader and is something said of commanders like Alexander the Great, Julius Caesar and Napoleon Bonaparte.

Joan arrived at Orleans in late March 1429 and quickly engaged with the French military leaders. She also began sending letters to the English leaders. Joan was illiterate and must have dictated the letters, but they clearly show how she perceived herself and her role. The following is a good example:

> *King of England, and you, Duke of Bedford, who call yourself regent of the kingdom of France . . . settle your debt to the king of Heaven; return to the Maiden* [Joan herself], *who is envoy of the king of Heaven, the keys to all the good towns you took and violated in France.*

Recovering miraculously

Joan certainly brought a fresh impetus to the conflict. For the best part of the preceding decade, the French forces had taken a cautious approach. But under Joan's influence, they took the fight to the English.

By early May, the forces under Joan had won three consecutive victories, capturing three fortresses in the process, despite Joan being effectively excluded from several war councils by nobles who still didn't completely trust her. Regardless, she insisted on a full assault against the English stronghold called Les Tourelles. On 7 May, despite receiving an arrow wound in the neck, she led the charge against the fortress.

The attack was successful and drove the English army away from Orleans. This incredible series of events persuaded Charles VII to make Joan the co-commander-in-chief of the French army, and she didn't waste any time. Within a period of just a few months, Joan turned the war in a new direction:

- ✔ She won an astonishing victory over an English relief force at Patay, a battle that turned into a complete rout – despite receiving a direct blow to the helmet from a cannonball during the battle!

- ✔ In late June the French army made the considerable journey to Reims and by 16 July the city was back in French hands. Inside the city, Charles VII was finally able to be truly crowned as king of France – Reims was the city where French kings were traditionally crowned. It was a hugely symbolic moment in the war.

Joan spent the rest of 1429 engaged in an attempt to retake the outskirts of Paris from the English, although her efforts ultimately failed. During the winter break from campaigning, she was rewarded with noble status and had her position as co-commander-in-chief renewed. Her intention was again to take the war to the English in 1430, but unfortunately for her events didn't quite work out that way.

SEEN ON SCREEN

The legacy of Saint Joan

The story of Joan of Arc doesn't end with her execution in May 1431. Even at the time, most people regarded her trial as a farce and the verdict even more so. More than 20 years later in 1452, Pope Calilxtus III ordered an investigation, which led to a retrial in 1456 that found Joan innocent and stated that she was a martyr and condemned those who had convicted her. In 1909 she was beatified by the Catholic Church and 30 May is still celebrated in France and elsewhere as her feast day. The French also have a public holiday in her honour on the second Sunday in May.

In the 500 years that have passed since her death, Joan has been an inspiration for some of Europe's greatest writers. She features in the works of Shakespeare, Mark Twain, George Bernard Shaw and Jean Anouilh, as well as in an opera by Giuseppe Verdi. More recently she has been used as a symbol by extreme right wing French politicians. Several films of her life have been made, too. She was famously played by Ingrid Bergman in 1948; a visually impressive recent version was made in 1999, starring Milla Jovovich as an excellent Joan.

May 1430 found Joan at the city of Compiègne, which was under siege by the English-allied Duke of Burgundy. During a skirmish she was captured by the Burgundian troops and taken prisoner. As I mention in Chapter 21, high-ranking prisoners were often ransomed back to their families, but Joan was a commoner and despite her recently acquired noble status her family had no money. Amazingly, Charles VII didn't intervene.

In the end the only people who met Joan's price were the English and despite Philip being their ally he charged them the full price. She was sold to the English as a prisoner of war.

Going on trial and meeting her end

Instead of holding on to Joan and waiting for a ransom to be paid, the English put her on trial in Rouen – for heresy. Despite the fact that Joan had been their greatest enemy, the English would normally have had to treat her with honour like any other prisoner of war of status. However, the opportunity to rid themselves of a difficult opponent and win a big propaganda victory was far too great to turn down.

English lawyers claimed that Joan was a 'false soothsayer' who had invented her visions and undermined the authority of the Church by doing so. She was also accused of cross-dressing! Clearly in battle she had to wear armour but this was used as a charge against her and she was portrayed as a deviant who wanted to change her gender.

The ensuing trial was a complete joke. The English refused Joan a legal representative and were basically unable to substantiate their claims against her. A record of the trial still exists in which Joan shows that she was as capable in an intellectual battle as in a physical one.

Sadly for her nothing made a jot of difference and she was convicted of heresy. Despite the fact that heresy was only a capital offence for repeat offenders, she was sentenced to death. On 30 May 1431 she was burned at the stake in Rouen. After her execution her body was burned twice more – to convince the watching public that she hadn't escaped. Her ashes were then thrown in the Seine to avoid them being used as relics. Joan was just 19 years old.

Wrapping Up the Hundred Years' War

The Hundred Years' War didn't finish with the death of Joan of Arc, but her passing certainly moved the conflict into its final phase. English influence was on the wane. The victories that Joan won put the French on the offensive and the English in retreat. Figure 23-1 shows how more of France was returning to the control of the French king, Charles VII, by 1430 (see Figure 21-1 in Chapter 21 for a comparison with how the map of France looked nearly 100 years earlier).

Realigning at the Congress of Arras

In 1435 representatives of England, France and Burgundy met at the town of Arras near to Calais (see Figure 23-1). This period was a difficult time for the English, because the Duke of Bedford (Henry VI's regent in France) had died just the week before the meeting was concluded, which meant that he was unable to influence the Treaty of Arras that was signed on 21 September.

The treaty finally made peace between Charles VII and Philip, Duke of Burgundy, and cut out the English completely. The peace allowed Philip to keep all the territories that he had already occupied during the war and enabled him to shift his campaigning towards extending his territory into the Low Countries.

The Duke of Burgundy's shift of allegiance from England to France changed the war forever. Henry VI was apparently reduced to tears by the betrayal, and mobs attacked Burgundian merchants in London. The new alliance made an English win incredibly difficult, and yet simply pulling out would seem like a defeat. To add to the English problems, Henry VI came of age in 1437. The English needed to fight a defensive retreat and were now led by an untried 16-year-old leader.

Figure 23-1:
France in
1430.

Retreating, little by little

For the next 15 years the English army continued campaigning in the form of a gradual withdrawal and Charles VII was able to spend several years reorganising the French government of his war-torn country. In addition, he changed the nature of the French army. Previously it had been made up of levies from his nobles, but now he was able to create a professional standing army that was completely loyal to the crown.

Whereas Joan of Arc had taken the war to the English and actively sought battle, Charles went back to the plan of his predecessors and avoided open battle wherever possible. Instead, he focused on retaking towns and cities across the north of France. In 1449 the French army finally recaptured the city of Rouen, which had been an English stronghold for nearly 50 years.

The English presence in France was tiny and dwindling every day and by 1451 only Calais remained in English hands.

Ending the matter

The last English efforts to strike back at Charles VII came in 1453. Under the leadership of Lord Talbot, a small force of English and Gascon troops attacked a French camp at the battle of Castillon. The conflict was important for two reasons:

- ✔ The rout of the English troops was effectively the last battle of the Hundred Years' War.

- ✔ The battle was the first in Europe in which the use of cannons was decisive.

Following the battle, the forces of Charles VII moved into Bordeaux and the final end came. All English territories that remained fell back into French hands and English interests in France ceased.

The defeat had a devastating effect on Henry VI, who slipped into a bout of insanity. His government began to collapse around him, bringing into existence the Wars of the Roses during which Richard Duke of York (the father of Richard III) was persuaded to assume control of the country.

As the Hundred Years' War struggled to a conclusion, another epic contest was also coming to an end. On 5 April 1453, the armies of the Ottoman Sultan Mehmet II finally gained control of Constantinople and brought the Byzantine Empire to an end. You can read all about these events in Chapter 24.

Assessing the legacy

Like many conflicts the Hundred Years' War ended on a bit of a downer. Most of its epic struggles – Crecy, Poitiers, Agincourt and the French recovery under Joan of Arc – took place years before the war's official conclusion.

The biggest impact of the war was that it left the English bankrupt and the Lancastrian dynasty (Henry IV, V and VI) fatally undermined, bringing about the Wars of the Roses between the houses of Lancaster and York.

At the time, the events of 1453 must have just seemed to the English and French like a temporary end to hostilities. After all, their war had been going on in one form or another since 1337; surely the fighting would resume soon.

But it never did. The huge cost of the conflict and the internal problems that both countries faced prevented the war from being resumed.

Ironically the biggest consequence of the Hundred Years' War was the one thing that Edward III had been trying to prevent when he invaded France in 1337 – England and France permanently became two separate countries under individual rulers.

Although they desired control of French lands and were related to the French aristocracy, successive English kings became truly English. What was a war over inheritance turned into one between two different countries:

- ✔ The kings of England had become ever more distinctly English and even began using the English language at court. The war also left England geographically isolated from the rest of Europe, an island apart from the mainland.

- ✔ France had suffered the physical impact of the war but become stronger and more unified under their king. By 1453 the King of France was in a far more powerful position than he had been in 1337 and his vassals were more loyal to him as a result.

The French landscape and many of its buildings still show real physical evidence of the war. Many historians argue that the continuing uneasy relationship between the two countries can be traced back to the events between 1337 and 1453.

Chapter 24

Moving On from the Medieval Era

....

....

So when did the Middle Ages come to an end? As I say in Chapter 1, historians have been arguing over this point for years and show no sign of stopping. In general, they agree that the period ended in the fifteenth century, although the official moment at which it ceased is very much open to debate. Some historians even argue that the medieval period carried on into the sixteenth century. For the purposes of this book, I have chosen the end of the fifteenth century as the cut-off point.

In this chapter I look at some of the major events of the fifteenth century and consider how the old medieval way of life came to an end. From my point of view, the Middle Ages – and this chapter – definitely finish with the discovery of North America by Christopher Columbus in 1492. But before bidding 'That's all, folks!', this chapter covers a few final flourishes and fascinating beginnings.

Heading Back to the Future: The Renaissance

Most historians agree that the Renaissance is the period that grew from the Middle Ages. Between the fourteenth and seventeenth centuries, a massive cultural change spread across Europe, beginning in the Italian city of Florence.

The Renaissance takes its name from the French word meaning 'rebirth' that derives from the Italian word *Rinascimento*. The Renaissance is fascinating because instead of being a historical period, it describes a big cultural change. But this cultural change was so widespread across Europe that the term has come to be identified as a historical period such as 'Middle Ages', signifying a period of time between the Medieval World and the early modern era.

In this section I look at how the Renaissance happened within the final years of the medieval period and what was so significant about this new phase.

Digging for the Renaissance's roots: Cold hard cash

The Renaissance – which began in the Tuscany region of Italy, in particular its biggest city Florence (around 240 kilometres, or 149 miles, north of Rome) – was all about culture: it comprised a revolution in art, architecture, music and philosophy inspired by the great works of Ancient Greece and Rome. This revival had begun in the fourteenth century with scholars like Petrarch (1304–74) who were fascinated by the study and translation of classical texts. That said, however, the Renaissance took place only because of a new preponderance of money: lots and lots of Italian cash!

As I discuss in Chapter 18, during the thirteenth and fourteenth centuries Italy led a revolution in trade throughout the Mediterranean. However, Italy itself wasn't a unified entity in the fifteenth century and wouldn't actually become one for around another 500 years.

The development of trading and financial services made the big cities of Italy – such as Florence, Pisa, Venice, Milan and Genoa – incredibly wealthy and influential. Added to these cities was the wealthy and influential Rome, which was also home to the pope (apart from that Avignon business – check out Chapter 19 for more on Avignon and the antipopes).

Money was incredibly important in Italy because it bought power. Nobody had overall control of the state, and instead the peninsula was made up of competing, and frequently feuding, city states. The lack of a monarchy or even a nobility like the rest of Europe meant that social mobility was available for people with money, including the Medici family in Florence (see the later sidebar 'Five fantastic guys' for more on family founder, Lorenzo).

Feeding on the stream of culture

Just as trade brought money into Italy, it also brought new ideas and foreign influences. The gradual decline and eventual fall of the Byzantine Empire (flip to the 'Bidding Bye-Bye to Byzantium' section later in this chapter) encouraged huge numbers of intellectuals and artisans from the East to travel westwards in the hope of finding new patrons. Cash-rich Italy was just the place to come to because its new moneyed political leaders were looking for big juicy cultural status symbols on which to spend their money.

The travellers also brought with them ancient texts that had been lost in Christian Western Europe for centuries. These poems, plays and texts on art and architecture, which the early Catholic Church had considered pagan, were all rediscovered during this period.

Italy's wealthy leaders also had more leisure time to spend reading and indulging in the arts than other European nobles. While Henry VI of England, Charles VII of France and all their attendant nobles spent their money on the seemingly endless pursuit of the Hundred Years' War (which I relate in Chapters 21 and 23), leading Italians were able to spend money on painting, sculpture, architecture and immense and impressive libraries to house their burgeoning collections of classical texts and artefacts.

Italy's renewed interest in art and culture didn't just express itself in rich men reading ancient poetry and building fine palaces: it also involved a reignited passion for learning. In the following quote from Niccolo Machiavelli's *History of Florence*, he explains how Lorenzo de'Medici encouraged this passion for learning throughout Tuscany (the later sidebar 'Five fantastic guys' has more on Machiavelli and Medici):

> *Lorenzo took the greatest delight in architecture, music and poetry; and many of his own poetic compositions, enriched with commentaries, appeared in print. And for the purpose of enabling the Florentine youths to devote themselves to the study of letters, he established a university in the city of Pisa, where he employed the most eminent men of all Italy as professors. He built a monastery for Fra Mariano da Chianozzona, of the order of St Augustine, who was a most admirable pulpit orator. And thus, beloved of God and fortune, all his enterprises were crowned with success, whilst those of his enemies had the opposite fate.*

Extending the Renaissance throughout Europe

Although the Renaissance started in Italy and was based in the ancient cultures of the Mediterranean, the movement soon spread throughout Europe. The late fifteenth century saw what historians consider to be the *Northern Renaissance* in Hungary, Poland, The Netherlands and Germany. This cultural flourishing was mostly expressed through art and literature that showed a pronounced and greater interest in the ancient world and classical and mythological themes. It was also expressed in huge building programmes. The Holy Roman Emperor Maximilian I (1459–1519) was the first big patron of the arts during the northern Renaissance and filled his court with artists and scientists.

Five fantastic guys

The Renaissance was absolutely bursting with talented and influential people. These days the term *Renaissance man* is used to describe somebody who has a wide array of cultural interests and that's exactly what a noble and influential man was expected to have in the fifteenth century.

Following is a quick guide to five of the greatest Renaissance men:

- **Lorenzo de'Medici (1449–1492):** Very much the father of the Renaissance, Medici was an Italian statesman who effectively ran the city of Florence during the second half of the fifteenth century. His family operated the Medici bank, which had become fabulously wealthy during the big trade expansion of the previous century (which I describe in Chapter 18). A massive patron of the arts, he sponsored the careers of many of the great artists of the period and was also responsible for huge building programmes throughout Florence. As a skilled politician he managed to survive numerous assassination attempts – something else that was very popular during the Renaissance. After his eventual death (from natural causes), the hub of the Renaissance moved from Florence to Rome.

- **Leonardo da Vinci (1452–1519):** Arguably the greatest figure of the Renaissance, Leonardo was interested in everything and worked as a hugely talented artist, writer and inventor. As well as producing famous paintings such as the 'Mona Lisa' and 'The Last Supper', he also produced incredible journals filled with his studies of anatomy, science and engineering. His 1505 book *The Codex on the Flight of Birds* contains plans for several flying machines, including two versions of something like a helicopter. A true individual, nobody like da Vinci had come along since Aristotle, and probably no-one like him has come along since.

- **Michelangelo Buonorroti (1475–1564):** Probably the most famous artist of the Renaissance, Michelangelo began his career sponsored by the Medici family in Florence. He is as famous for his sculpture as for his painting, in particular 'David' which you can still see in Florence today. Probably his greatest work was the painting of the ceiling of the Sistine Chapel in the Vatican. He had incredibly high standards and was known for his exacting temperament, which resulted in his famously broken nose after he criticised a student and was punched in the face!

- **Niccolo Machiavelli (1469–1527):** Machiavelli was probably the greatest philosophical figure of the Renaissance, writing texts such as *The Art of War* and most famously *The Prince*, a treatise on how to succeed in politics. The low and cunning tactics that he sometimes advised have led to the term 'Machiavellian' to describe an untrustworthy and coldly ambitious person. During his political career he was responsible for the Florentine militia and also worked as a diplomat. He was eventually deposed from office and tortured before his release and retirement.

- **Baldessare Castiglione (1478–1529):** Not as famous as some of the other people I mention, Castiglione was a courtier, soldier and author. He wrote a book called *The Book of the Courtier* that perfectly describes life, manners, education and conduct in a Renaissance court. The book was hugely influential during the Renaissance and shows how the idea of chivalry developed further from medieval ideals and became more political. Castiglione's work also illustrates how social mobility became possible during the Renaissance, because individuals were able to develop courtly and aristocratic manners through practice and schooling, instead of these useful assets being restricted to birth and status.

The Renaissance took slightly longer to reach France and England who were locked into the Hundred Years' War all the way through until 1453 (turn to Chapter 23 for the conclusion to that conflict). In England the first real effects of the Renaissance came during the Tudor period, where Henry VIII filled his court with humanist scholars like Erasmus. Later on, the reign of Elizabeth I during the sixteenth century, saw the production of the plays of William Shakespeare and Christopher Marlowe as well as the philosophical enquiries of Francis Bacon. Across the Channel in France, the greatest impact of the Renaissance was felt in the duchy of Burgundy which had connections with the Low Countries and the developments there and was visited by many Flemish and also Italian artists.

Bidding Bye-Bye to Byzantium

Ironically, just as Western Europe was rediscovering the culture of the Ancient World through the Renaissance, the last remaining civilisation that had survived the fall of Rome was brought crashing to an end. In 1453, the Byzantine Empire that had existed for more than 1,000 years, dating back to the time of Constantine in the fourth century, was savagely ended.

In May 1453, the Ottoman Turk Sultan Mehmet II successfully captured the city of Constantinople, and the new Ottoman Empire was founded in Asia Minor.

Making way for the new Turks

Byzantium had been in trouble for a while. In Chapter 22, I mention the visit of the Byzantine Emperor, Manuel II Paleologus, to France and England in 1400. He had been looking to build up support for a Crusade-like war against the Ottoman Turks who were threatening the city of Constantinople. By that point he was getting desperate because the Byzantine Empire was hanging by a thread.

The Ottomans first came into contact with people from Western Europe in 1227 when they migrated into the Great Seljuk Empire in Anatolia (the eastern part of modern-day Turkey). The already established Seljuk Turks were struggling themselves at the time and the Ottomans continued farther west across modern-day Turkey under their leader Ertugrul. In 1299 the Ottomans established a town near the Marmara, the sea between the Black Sea and the Aegean. This new settlement was right in the middle of the lands that had formerly been part of the Byzantine Empire but over which the emperor now had no control.

When Ertugrul died, his son Osman replaced him as leader. Using his name, Europeans began referring to the people as 'Ottomans'. They were a war-like people and over the next 100 years were amazingly successful in gaining control of territory across the Balkans and the eastern Mediterranean.

Crusading for the sake of trade

The expansion of the Ottomans brought them into conflict with Europe's great trading cities who had established colonies throughout the eastern Mediterranean (check out Chapter 18 for more details). In 1387 the Ottomans took the important port of Thessalonica from the Venetians and in 1389 the battle of Kosovo destroyed the kingdom of Serbia and added the region to the growing Ottoman Empire.

Europe responded by launching the last real attempt at a Crusade in 1396. This time the quest wasn't about reclaiming the Holy Land from Arab control but preventing a new enemy from threatening trade interests. The Holy Roman Emperor Sigismund I led contingents from around Europe including Hungary, France, Venice and Poland. The campaign culminated in the Battle of Nicopolis (in modern-day Bulgaria) on 25 September 1396. Accounts of the battle vary, but the result was a massive defeat for the Crusaders, with thousands killed in battle and thousands more prisoners executed.

The failure at Nicopolis was very much the last stand against the Ottomans, and after that the leaders of Western Europe left those of the eastern countries to it. As for the Ottomans, their eyes turned to the one remaining prize in the region – the ancient and magical city of Constantinople.

Taking Constantinople, in all its faded glory

By the beginning of the fifteenth century, the Byzantine Empire was in tatters. Indeed, it was barely an empire, just the outlying districts around the once-great city of Constantinople. Even the city itself was fading, and throughout the first half of the fifteenth century its population gradually drifted away to make their lives elsewhere. Many of its intellectual and artistic inhabitants found their way to Italy and helped to create the Renaissance.

The Ottoman Sultan Mehmet II still desired to control the city. Despite its failing fortunes, Constantinople remained the jewel in the crown for the Ottomans, a potent symbol of how far they had come. From Mehmet's perspective, he hoped the conquest would make him the most successful sultan ever. As he became forever known as 'Mehmet the Conqueror', he was probably right! In addition, the city had important strategic significance; it was the gateway to the Black Sea and a potential springboard for further campaigns westwards into Europe.

The end came for Byzantium fairly swiftly. Mehmet moved on the city at the beginning of April 1453 with a massive force of more than 100,000 men. Barely more than 5,000 remained within the walls of the city to defend it. The emperor, Constantine XI, was desperately awaiting the arrival of a relief force from Venice.

Initially the defenders managed to repel the Ottoman advances even when their walls were battered by cannon fire. But in late May news came through that no Venetian fleet was coming and all hope left the defenders. The final assault came on 29 May. The emperor was cut down in the fighting and Constantinople fell.

Launching a new empire

The Byzantine Empire had existed for more than 1,100 years. The people who fled the city headed for Trebizond on the Black Sea, where an independent empire continued for a while until Mehmet mopped up this settlement in 1461.

Constantinople itself became the centrepiece of the Ottoman Empire. With its name changed to Istanbul the city flourished again as part of a new empire that lasted all the way through until 1923.

Given that the Hundred Years' War also finished in the same year as the fall of Constantinople (as I describe in Chapter 23), 1453 may appear to be a pretty good year to identify as the end of the Middle Ages. But one more set of events really brought the medieval era to a close – the beginning of the age of exploration.

Exploring a Whole New World

As the then-known world collapsed or reinvented itself, a whole new one was being discovered. The fifteenth century was the age of exploration, heralded in particular by the activities of two men: Vasco da Gama and Christopher Columbus.

Sailing to the East: Vasco da Gama

Vasco da Gama (1460–1524) was one of the first explorers of the Age of Discovery. Born in Portugal he was the son of a knight and probably studied mathematics. During his youth, Portugal was becoming an increasingly important trading power, particularly when the influence of Venice and other Italian cities began to fade after the fall of Constantinople and the loss of their trading colonies in the eastern Mediterranean.

The Age of Discovery

Columbus and da Gama were only two of the many Europeans who engaged in exploration during what historians refer to as the Age of Discovery. For about 150 years from the end of the fifteenth century, a whole group of people set out to explore the limits of the known world and chart and map its boundaries.

The Crusades (see the chapters in Part III) had seen Europeans gain knowledge of Asia Minor and the Near East, but only as a by-product of a series of wars. The Age of Discovery saw people make even longer and more hazardous journeys just to find out more about the world they lived in.

In a way, the boom in exploration that began in the late fifteenth century was quite natural. The Renaissance revived ideas about discovery and enquiry in terms of both science and philosophy, and as an extension, acquiring greater knowledge of the Earth's surface became a passion for many people.

Traders at this time were particularly interested in developing a single non-stop route between the Atlantic Coast of Portugal and India, and Vasco da Gama was the man who succeeded. During his life he made three voyages around the Cape of Africa to the East. Europeans knew about India – Alexander the Great had been there 1,700 years earlier – but da Gama's triumph was to develop a route to the popular trading region of the Indian Ocean, a route that nobody had previously sailed. Opening up this route brought in huge amounts of money from the extra trade in exotic goods, such as spices, that could be found there.

Vasco da Gama's voyages established a route that thousands of trading ships followed in the years to come. Connecting with the Indian Ocean also moved the focus of trade from the Mediterranean. As the Middle Ages came to an end, the world must have seemed like it was getting bigger all the time.

Another important factor motivating the increased knowledge of the globe was the opportunity that exploration offered nations to expand and colonise overseas. Previously this kind of expansion had involved sending an army over the borders into a neighbouring country and engaging in bloody battles. Now opportunities existed to set up new states hundreds or even thousands of miles away. Portugal was at the forefront of the trend, and by the early sixteenth century it had colonies on the eastern and western coasts of Africa: its empire was also building up elsewhere on the other side of the Atlantic.

Going off the map: Christopher Columbus

Whereas Vasco da Gama went east, Christopher Columbus (1451–1506) very famously went west. Like Vasco da Gama, historians know little about Columbus's early life. He was born in the thriving Italian trading city of Genoa but moved to the Portuguese capital Lisbon when he was a young man. Here he worked in a cartographer's shop, something that obviously fired his interest in navigation. Alongside his brother he spent many hours calculating routes and journeys.

Columbus's great voyages came about because he was trying to solve the same problem as Vasco da Gama – find a quicker sea journey to India and the East. Whereas da Gama sailed round Africa, Columbus believed that if you sailed west across the Atlantic you would reach Asia from the other side. Simply put, he was aware that the Earth was a globe but he didn't realise that the American continent was between where he wanted to go!

Financing the voyage

One of the largest problems that Columbus had was money. He was turned down twice by the King of Portugal (John II) but eventually received funding from Spain. The two ruling monarchs, Ferdinand II of Aragon and Isabella of Castile, agreed in 1489 to fund him. Their own experts had told them that the expedition was doomed to fail as they believed that Columbus had got his calculations wrong, but the two monarchs ignored the experts. They wanted to prevent Columbus from taking his ideas elsewhere.

Here's a portion from their actual letter to Columbus, giving him permission:

> *For as much of you, Christopher Columbus, are going by our command, with some of our vessels and men, to discover and subdue some Islands and Continent in the ocean, and it is hoped that by God's assistance, some of the said Islands and Continent in the ocean will be discovered and conquered by your means and conduct, therefore it is but just and reasonable, that since you expose yourself to such danger to serve us, you should be rewarded for it. And we being willing to honour and favour You for the reasons aforesaid.*

'Discovering' the New World

Columbus departed on 3 August 1492 from the Spanish port of Palos de la Frontera. By 12 October land had been sighted, which turned out to be an island in the Bahamas (possibly the one now known as San Salvador). He spent time exploring the islands and establishing harmonious relationships with the local people, before setting off to explore the northeast coast of Cuba and then heading back to Europe.

Columbus made three more visits to this part of the world, although he still thought that he'd reached the east Asian peninsula! That's why he referred to the natives as 'Indios' and why Native Americans were called Indians for many years.

Of course, Columbus wasn't the first European to reach this part of the world. Leif Eriksson and a bunch of Vikings had, somewhat incredibly, made the trip to North America more than 500 years earlier (as I describe in Chapter 8), but Columbus was the first person to establish full contact with the indigenous people. His first contacts allowed other Spanish and Portuguese adventurers to expand their countries's empires into Central and South America during the century that followed.

To celebrate the 500-year anniversary of Columbus, in 1992 several films were made about his voyages. *1492: Conquest of Paradise* is probably the best of them and features Gerard Depardieu as Columbus. Although a little bit of a trudge, the film does show the incredible scale of the journey and gives a good idea of the tricky political situation that Columbus found himself in when he returned. If you just can't satisfy your Columbus fix, you can always watch the comedy *Carry on Columbus* (1992) instead!

Columbus's voyages truly brought the Middle Ages to an end. Although his discoveries didn't directly affect ordinary people, they did tie two parts of the world together that had previously not even known about each other. More than 1,000 years had passed since illiterate Germanic tribes smashed down the remnants of the old Roman Empire. Now kings of England and France were in place, and a sultan ruled Constantinople. New towns and cities were created with universities that were rediscovering the achievements of the Ancient World and using this knowledge to build a whole new world.

Part VI
The Part of Tens

In this part . . .

This part is all about picking out the best of the Medieval World and flagging up some things that you may want to look at again or in more detail. Get ready to meet some nasty and perhaps unlucky rulers, as well as some exceptional medieval people who changed the world. I describe some of the more unusual pastimes that medieval people enjoyed – quite a lot of which were, unsurprisingly, violent. I also compile a thank-you list for all the things that the Medieval World provided, including modern languages, beer and football to name just three. Enjoy!

Chapter 25

Ten Rubbish Rulers

In This Chapter

▶ Cringe-worthy kings

▶ Bad, bad Byzantine emperors

▶ Reckless warlords

*B*eing a ruler isn't easy; you're responsible for absolutely everything and any decision you make can have ramifications and consequences for years and years, even after you die. The Middle Ages saw hundreds of people taking the role of king, queen, emperor, duke and all sorts of other positions of power. Some of them were exceptional and most just muddled through – but a few made a really spectacular hash of things. Others never got the chance or were killed before they were able to do anything good.

In this chapter I take a look at ten people who I think were particularly bad in leadership roles. The following list is just my personal opinion, of course, and you may beg to differ. That's what studying history is all about!

King Stephen of England (c. 1096–1154)

Although I find this hard to write, the one English king who shares my name is considered by most historians not to have been terribly good. Stephen was the grandson of William the Conqueror (Chapter 10 has all about William's exploits) and the last Norman king of England, reigning between 1135–1154. Stephen was unfortunate in that he came to the throne at a time when opinion was split on who should be the new monarch. His predecessor, Henry I, had wanted his only surviving child – daughter Matilda – to assume power, but she was unable to gather enough support from the nobility.

Stephen thought that he could do better and seized the throne, but within four years he'd lost most of his support and England was plunged into a period called 'The Anarchy', which lasted for the rest of his reign.

He remained on the throne until his death but had already signed an agreement that his children would be passed over in the line of succession, in favour of Matilda's son Henry (the future Henry II). Stephen isn't known to have achieved anything significant in his reign and when he died his only impact was to have caused a decade-long civil war!

The contemporary chronicler Walter Map described Stephen as follows:

> *A man of a certain age, remarkably hard-working but otherwise a nonentity* [a nobody] *or perhaps rather inclined to evil.*

Essentially, he wasn't even good at being bad!

King John of England (1166–1216)

Countless Robin Hood stories and movies have portrayed King John as one of the villains of English history, but he's more accurately described as one of England's most ineffective kings. Whether due to a lack of talent, bad luck or cruel fate, he seemed to fall out with everybody and everything that he touched went wrong. In fact, identifying anything in his reign (1199–1216) that went well is pretty much impossible. Quite whether it was his fault is a subject that I tackle in Chapter 17 but I couldn't exclude him from this chapter.

Most famously John was forced to agree to the Magna Carta in 1215, a treaty that made the king responsible to a group of barons (effectively a forerunner to the English parliament) and put legal limits on regal power (check out Chapter 17 for more details). Whilst most of it never came to pass it was nonetheless a humiliating event for John. His final humiliation was losing most of his treasury in an estuary on England's east coast known as The Wash, the Crown Jewels being swept away by an incoming tide.

John also managed to fall out with Pope Innocent III, who forced the closure of all the churches in England and then excommunicated him in 1213! Oh yes, and many people accuse him of murdering his nephew Arthur. Eventually, in 1216 John died of dysentery, which some people alleged was caused by eating poisoned plums or drinking too much cider. Given his record of bad results, such an ending definitely fits!

Vortigern (c. 450)

Vortigern was a fifth-century warlord in Britain who seized control of an area in the southeast of England when the Roman Army withdrew. Historians know little about him or even if Vortigern was his real name. The one thing that's recorded about him is that he made one of the worst decisions in history.

Looking to secure his kingdom, Vortigern came up with the bright idea of employing a group of mercenary soldiers from overseas. These soldiers were Saxons from the Low Countries (modern-day Belgium and The Netherlands) who had spent the last century continually raiding the English coast.

According to sources that are possibly apocryphal, a group of Saxons readily agreed to Vortigern's proposition and settled in the east of England. They rather liked the area and invited over some more of their relatives. In no time at all, enough had arrived to overthrow Vortigern and kick-start the Anglo-Saxon domination of England (as I describe in Chapter 3). Another version of the story suggests that they revolted when they weren't paid. Whether the precise details of the event are accurate or not, the story lingers and certainly qualifies Vortigern for inclusion in the 'rubbish ruler' category!

Charles 'The Bad' of Navarre (1332–1387)

With a name like Charles 'The Bad', I was quite unable to omit ol' Charlie from this chapter. He was officially called Charles II of Navarre, where he was king from 1349–1387. He was quite successful in that he gained lands in Normandy and elsewhere in France, but the manner in which he became so successful is the source of his nickname.

Charles was probably the most untrustworthy person in medieval history, and if you've read the rest of the book, you know that the competition for that title is pretty fierce! Charles was married to the daughter of King John II of France and was jealous of the Royal Constable, Charles de la Cerda, and so the king had de la Cerda murdered! This killing was just the start of a lifetime of treachery that saw him switch sides during the Hundred Years' War on two occasions, be imprisoned by the French king and join forces with a notable Catalan freebooter who was later excommunicated by the pope!

Charles received his comeuppance though. In 1387 he became so unwell that his physician ordered him to be wrapped in a linen sack at night, presumably so that he didn't harm himself whilst he slept. Unfortunately the treatment didn't turn out too well:

> *One of the female attendants of the palace, charged to sew up the cloth that contained the patient, having come to the neck, the fixed point where she was to finish her seam, made a knot according to custom; but as there was still remaining an end of thread, instead of cutting it as usual with scissors, she had recourse to the candle, which immediately set fire to the whole cloth. Being terrified, she ran away, and abandoned the king, who was thus burnt alive in his own palace.*

Louis V of France (c. 967–987)

King Louis V is a curious case. Although he's known variously as Louis 'The Lazy', 'The Indolent', 'The Do Nothing' and 'The Sluggard', none of these nicknames are his fault. He was the son of the former king, Lothair, the last Carolingian monarch in France (I discuss the Carolingian family in Chapter 4). Even though Louis was crowned in 979, he didn't actually take power until Lothair's death in 987. Sons were often crowned as co-emperor as a way of avoiding challenges from other pretenders by making sure the son was firmly established in the role by the time the father eventually died. In Louis's case this meant that he ruled for only one year (the probable reason for his nickname).

Nothing went terribly well for him though. When he was 13, he married a woman 20 years older than him (Adelaide of Anjou), but she ran off after two years. Eventually Louis died in May 987, possibly poisoned by his own mother! Perhaps Louis 'The Hard Done By' would have been more appropriate!

John 1 of France (1316–1316)

This story is a sad one. Known as John 'The Posthumous', he had the shortest reign in medieval history. He was the successor of King Louis X. When Louis died in June 1316, his wife Clementia of Hungary was pregnant. She gave birth to a boy on 15 November and named him John. The tiny infant was the next king of France, but within five days he too had died.

Infant mortality was common in the Middle Ages, but many people believe that John's uncle, Philip of Champagne, was responsible for his death, because he replaced John on the throne, becoming Philip V. One story suggests that Philip kidnapped John and put a dead infant in his place. In the 1350s an Italian man turned up in Provence claiming to be the now adult John. He was immediately thrown in prison and died there in 1360. Nobody will ever know for sure what happened to the shortest-lived ruler in French history.

Louis X of France (1289–1316)

The father of John I of France (check out the preceding section) also gets into this chapter. Louis X was king of Navarre and king of France for only two years between 1314–1316. Despite dying relatively young, he managed to earn the nickname Louis 'The Quarreller' (or 'The Turbulent' or 'The Stubborn') and does seem to be the sort of person who was able to start an argument in an empty room. Throughout his time as king of Navarre, he was in almost continual dispute with his nobles and things weren't much better domestically.

His first wife was Margaret of Burgundy, until in 1313 Louis's father, Philip IV, accused her of adultery and Louis had her imprisoned. Within 18 months she was dead, in what contemporary sources considered to be very suspicious circumstances – particularly considering that he married Clementia of Hungary only five days later! Modern historians aren't so sure about all of this, suggesting that Margaret possibly died from a cold, but at the time many people suspected Louis. Mud sticks, it would seem. Whilst there doesn't now seem to be too much evidence of bad behaviour, his contemporaries were clearly able to believe he was capable of anything.

Louis X died entertainingly though, from infection possibly worsened by having drunk too much wine after a particularly strenuous game of 'real tennis'. The account of his death is the first mention of tennis in history and Louis's sole contribution to the game!

Justinian II of Byzantium (669–711)

The Byzantine emperors were a fascinating bunch. Assassinations, imprisonments, uprising and usurpations were the order of the day, and many rulers suffered cruel and unusual fates. One of the more interesting examples is Justinian II, known as the 'Split-Nosed'. Justinian ruled the empire twice: first between 685–695 and then from 705 to his death in 711.

First time around he became hugely unpopular with everybody for raising taxes massively to finance his luxurious lifestyle. One of his generals called Leontius led an uprising, captured Justinian and cut his nose off in the belief that doing so would prevent him from becoming emperor again (emperors were supposed to be unblemished). Instead Justinian went off to a Black Sea port, plotted a comeback and regained the throne in bloody style in 705.

He wasn't much more successful the second time though; a second rebellion rose up and this time they executed him. He gets into this chapter for being rubbish twice!

Justin II of Byzantium (c. 520–578)

Plenty of medieval rulers had the word 'mad' added to their name and although nothing is funny about mental illness, the truth is that many of them could have made it into this chapter. One such ruler from the early medieval period is the Byzantine emperor Justin II, known somewhat inevitably as Justin 'The Mad'. His reign was pretty much a complete disaster, during which time the Byzantines were almost permanently at war with the Persian Empire and lost control of all their lands in Italy.

Justin can rightly be blamed for most of his empire's problems, but his increasingly frequent bouts of insanity caused him to abdicate the throne in 578. By this point his behaviour had become even more bizarre. According to the chronicler John of Ephesus, he was continually pulled round the palace on a wheeled cart, biting any attendants that came close to him. Only the constant playing of organ music calmed his rages, and so had to accompany his every waking hour. Even worse were the rumours that night-time saw him engage in bouts of cannibalism! Justin died a few years after abdicating, having spent his time in isolation in a quiet royal palace. A sad story.

Aethelred 'The Unready' (968–1016)

The list of rubbish rulers wouldn't be complete without one of the most famously poor kings: Aethelred II, known as 'The Unready' Whilst he wasn't a raging success, his nickname is a little unfair. 'Unready' didn't have quite the same meaning at the time as it does now, and a better translation is probably 'The Ill-Advised'. Nevertheless, he must have had some pretty bad advisors.

Aethelred was the Anglo-Saxon king of England between 978–1016. He reigned for quite a while and was moderately successful – except for one key event. Throughout his reign England was buffeted by continuous attacks from the Vikings. In 1013, the Viking king, Sweyn, was intending to invade with the goal of conquering the country. Aethelred was unable to gain enough support to organise the defences of England and so he abandoned the country and fled to Normandy! When he eventually returned, the situation had changed and most of England was under the control of the Danish king, Cnut (turn to Chapter 3 for more on Cnut). Aethelred fell off his horse soon afterwards and died. No great loss.

Chapter 26

Ten Medieval Pastimes

Medieval life was difficult, dangerous and unhealthy. In Christian Western Europe, most people lived with one eye focused on the afterlife and did everything possible to ensure that they would get to Heaven. Despite these conditions, however, medieval people still knew how to enjoy themselves. In this chapter I look at some of the more bizarre ways in which they let the good times roll. Warning – don't try these things at home!

Playing Football

Yes, that's right. The world's most popular sport originated in the Middle Ages – although medieval football was a world away from the modern game that millions know and love today. In fact, football in the Middle Ages was popular in England but considered to be a sinful and perverse pastime by anybody not involved in it because people let themselves indulge in reckless behaviour when playing. Then again, when you see how they played it, you can understand why.

The traditional day for football was Shrove Tuesday when matches were held throughout the country. These events were more like a battle than a game though, with whole villages pitched against each other, hundreds of players involved and the goals placed several miles apart. Games lasted most of the day and people literally fought for the ball (which was usually an inflated bladder), resulting in serious injuries and even deaths. Edward III went so far as to ban the game in 1336, but nobody took any notice and it carries on today – although in a *slightly* more organised form!

Savouring Subtleties

Gastronomic curiosities known as *subtleties* were popular among the nobility during the Middle Ages. They took the form of small, intricately made dishes that were served between courses at a banquet. Known as *entremets* in Old French, they began as simple oat dishes in amusing shapes, but by the fourteenth century European rulers were demanding ever more complex and impressive subtleties from their cooks. Before long, the creations were only partly edible, with more and more non-edible elements being added – including people!

Popular subjects included models of castles with tiny figures, replicas of animals and even life-size models of human genitalia made out of pastry! Sources describe some incredible creations, such as a huge wooden model of Jerusalem for Emperor Charles IV in 1378, which was accompanied by several soldiers performing an attack on it from a model wooden boat on wheels! Another famous example was a banquet given by Philip the Good of Burgundy in 1454 in honour of the fall of Constantinople, which involved a giant pie that held four musicians. Not so subtle really!

Trying Out Charms and Remedies

Despite the fact that most of Western Europe became Christian during the Middle Ages, some pagan traditions continued. In Anglo-Saxon England, even after conversion, *charms* – protective spells that were repeated to ward off evil or bad luck – continued to be very popular. People spoke hundreds and hundreds of different brief verses to ward off trouble, such as a charm to ward off a swarm of bees and one to stop people from stealing your cattle.

Similar to charms were *remedies* that gave instructions on what to do to ward off problems. This idea is slightly different to how we now understand 'remedies' – as a way of helping to deal with something that has already happened. Many medieval remedies are contained in *Bald's Leechbook*, which was composed during the tenth century. Among the many suggestions is the following remedy to ward off the effects of a chattering woman:

> *Against a woman's chatter: eat a radish at night, while fasting; that day the chatter cannot harm you.*

Make sure that you write that down for use next time you sit beside a major talker on the bus or train!

Enjoying Music and Dancing

Wherever a celebration was taking place in the Middle Ages, you'd find people enjoying music and dancing. In particular, people danced themselves and watched performing troupes. The performances were more like acrobatic displays and often involved tumbling, juggling and dangerous activities involving weapons. Edward II was a big fan of dance. In 1313, he was entertained by 'Bernard the Fool and his 54 nude dancers', which must have been quite a spectacle!

Minstrels were by far the most popular medieval entertainers. These musicians travelled far and wide, playing a variety of fantastically named instruments such as nakers (small drums), sackbuts (early trombones), crumhorns (curved wind instruments) and tabors (drum-like tambourines). (You can see examples of these instruments at the Mary Rose museum in Portsmouth, England.) If they were good, minstrels were able to earn a tremendous amount, far beyond the income of most people. The aforementioned Edward II was particularly generous in paying minstrels – up to £1 a time – which was the equivalent of several months wages for a skilled worker.

Hocking Your Friends

Historians know little about the medieval sense of humour. Surviving examples take the form of sarcasm in correspondence or the laboured 'jokes' made by fools and jesters. *Hocking*, one of the more famous games played in England, does give a sense of medieval people's idea of fun. Essentially a kidnapping for amusement, hocking involved taking people prisoner and then ransoming them back to their families in a kind of parody of how noble hostages were taken after battles (as I describe in Chapter 21).

Hocking was meant to be carried out on high days and feast days, and sometimes women captured men and vice versa. Unfortunately, the games often spilled over into violence and sexual assault. A popular way of catching people was to lay a noose on the ground so that the unwary stepped on it and were catapulted upside down into the branches of a tree. Hilarious!

Cucking

Cucking was a familiar but bizarre public punishment (and therefore also public entertainment!) during the Middle Ages. Several Anglo-Saxon sources describe similar reprimands for women (mostly) who were considered gossips or scolds, and the Domesday Book also refers to the practice.

The woman in question was trussed to a stool at the end of a pole by her accuser. The pole was levered up and down. In the case of *cucking*, the woman was levered into the air and left suspended so that the crowd were able to mock and possibly throw things at her. Sometimes this involved the stool being continually lowered into a river so that the victim came close to drowning. A similar punishment was a *Skimmington ride* that involved the victim being paraded through the streets to general abuse. That these activities were considered acceptable and public displays tells you a lot about the medieval mindset.

Hunting for Sport

Hunting was the most popular pastime for the European nobility during the Middle Ages. Indeed, many rulers were absolutely obsessed with it. One reason for hunting's popularity was because it was considered to be training for battle. The skills developed on the hunt would prove invaluable to a young man who later wanted to go to war as a knight or man-at-arms.

Hunts were very organised, with ten or so carefully established stages, and were carried out from horseback, with hounds or with the aid of trained hawks and falcons. The most popular animals to hunt were the *hart* (an adult male red deer), wild boar and wolves, although other animals such as bears, foxes and badgers were also common quarry.

Hunting was exceptionally dangerous (not least for the animals!), and many European rulers were killed while hunting. Most famous was William II (known as William Rufus) the king of England and son of William the Conqueror. He was killed by a stray arrow in the New Forest (in Hampshire, England). The hunt was also a great opportunity for assassination: many people were killed in 'hunting accidents' that appeared to be very carefully arranged!

Laughing Aloud at Mummery

Mummery literally means 'disguising', and the word was used in England to describe a certain kind of dramatic performance that was very popular across Medieval Europe. The plays used masks and few words to recreate famous scenes from history and folklore. The performances would be put on anywhere, sometimes for the delight of an invited audience of nobles or sometimes just in the street as a kind of public protest.

Disguising games were a much simpler version of mummery that people at court used to entertain other nobles. Masked players – often the nobles themselves – acted out scenes and played tricks on people, often with quite cruel and unusual results such as lampooning them, tripping them or covering them with unpleasant substances. Essentially, these events involved nobles arriving in fancy dress as pirates or priests or something similar. Eventually they whisked off their masks to reveal who they truly were. Apparently people found the whole show hilarious: it takes all sorts I suppose.

Going Ga-Ga for Goliards

Another form of medieval humour was practised by *goliards*, wandering students and scholars who composed satirical verses and gave live performances that mocked and lampooned the Church. Goliards and their work were popular throughout Medieval Europe, and in particular in the universities that were founded in France, Germany, Spain and Italy: rather like a medieval version of an undergraduate review show.

Some goliard activities still seem quite amusing today. Often they would dress as women, lead donkeys into the church or play dice on the altar. Their pranks had a serious point to them; the accompanying poems railed against the increasing power of the Church and perceived abuses. These activities were frequently outlawed by Church authorities but that didn't stop goliards from playing their pranks.

Jousting the Day Away

Probably the most famous medieval pastime was *jousting:* combat between two knights on horseback that took place at tournaments. You can read more about this activity in Chapter 11, but I mention it here as well because it was second only to hunting in popularity with the medieval nobility.

The first recorded joust was in 1066 in France, but by the twelfth century it was amazingly popular throughout Europe. Basically jousting was yet another medieval pastime that involved people trying to kill each other and practising methods of doing so. Huge sums were gambled on the outcome, with people frequently making or losing fortunes. The knights themselves became the closest thing that the Middle Ages had to celebrities.

Jousting was incredibly dangerous. The jouster who was hit felt the power of a blunt tipped lance travelling at over 60 kilometres (or 37 miles) per hour. One historian has suggested that, travelling at that speed, the blow was equivalent to being struck with a hammer that weighs half a tonne. Few survived the impact from an incoming lance.

Chapter 27

Ten Great Castles

*M*uch evidence of medieval life still exists today: documents, tombs, churches, statues and battlefields all remain. The most iconic and visible image of the Middle Ages, however, is the castle (check out Chapter 10 for more on medieval castle-building).

Hundreds of medieval castles still stand in one form or another all around Europe and beyond. In this chapter, I look at some of the greatest: all these buildings are open to visitors and are well-documented in books and online. That said, all castles are great for different reasons and definitely worth visiting.

Krak des Chevaliers, Syria

Very much the daddy of surviving medieval castles, Krak des Chevaliers is in a different league to almost anything else. From its dominant position on top of a 650-metre-high (2,100 feet) hill in a place called the Horns Gap, it guards the only route between Antioch and the ports on the Mediterranean Sea – a position of immense strategic importance.

Construction began on the site in 1031, when the Emir of Aleppo built a small fortress. Captured in the early twelfth century by the Crusaders, this building was given to the Knights of St John of the Hospital (known as the Hospitallers, who feature in more detail in Chapter 16) in 1142, and they spent 100 years expanding the castle into the immense form that it still displays today.

The castle is almost a small town, capable of holding a garrison of 2,000 and defended by a huge curtain wall, 30-metres (or 90 feet) thick, and with seven massive 9-metre (or 29 feet) wide guard towers. The structure also originally had a moat – as if it needed any more protection!

The Tower of London, London, England

The original tower, known as the White Tower, is the key architectural treasure here. William the Conqueror built the large keep in 1078. It features two floors, a basement and a gallery and contained everything for the king's living quarters, including a chapel, a hall and a chamber for receiving guests and conferring with advisors. Quite a complicated building, the design was more akin to a comparatively modern construction like the White House in Washington than just a basic stone keep. After William, a great deal more building was done on the site and the White Tower is now just the central part of a much larger complex of buildings.

The White Tower, however, is also important because of what it represented as opposed to just what it contained. It was built as a clear statement to the people of England that they were now under the control of a new power, and the tower would have dominated the skyline for miles around. The White Tower was also used as a jail for important political prisoners and became greatly feared: the idea of being sent to 'The Tower' was absolutely terrifying throughout English history. Having said that, the first official prisoner escaped! In 1100, Henry I imprisoned the Bishop of Durham in the tower and he escaped using a rope that someone smuggled to him inside a pot of wine.

Tintagel Castle, Cornwall, England

Little remains of the actual building, but Tintagel in southwest England is still an incredibly evocative place for anybody interested in medieval history. Located on a small peninsula that sticks out into the sea, Tintagel really does feel as if it's on the edge of the world. Originally a Roman settlement, the ruins that remain date back to a thirteenth-century building on the site.

Most people visit Tintagel, however, for completely different reasons: the castle has been associated for centuries with the legend of King Arthur. In the twelfth century the writer Geoffrey of Monmouth claimed that it had been the site of the castle of Uther Pendragon, who he identified as Arthur. As a result, when Richard of Cornwall built his castle on the site in 1233, he made sure that it was constructed in an older and more ancient style so that it fitted with the legend. Although the associations with Arthur are unlikely to be true, the legend just makes an already evocative place even more so!

Caernarfon Castle, Wales

Constructed by Edward I in the late thirteenth century, Caernarfon Castle is a whopping great statement of intent by an English king in northeast Wales. Edward finally put down the Welsh revolt in around 1283 and set about building a series of castles across the country so that he was able to maintain royal authority in the region. Caernarfon is by far the biggest and most impressive of these structures. It was also expensive, costing around £23,000 to build, which was the equivalent of the entire royal revenues for a year!

Construction began on the site in 1283 and carried on for more than 30 years. Edward died in 1307, long before the castle was even close to being completed. Even now it remains unfinished: you can still see gaps in large sections of wall that were left for joints from further walls to be put in. The design of the castle is interesting too. Edward I had been on Crusade (as I describe in Chapter 16) and liked the look of Constantinople and its city walls, and so he used them as a basis for the design of Caernarfon.

Kenilworth Castle, Warwickshire, England

The Hundred Years' War involved a lot of castle building throughout England, and not only because people feared a French invasion. Many of the commanders in the war had in fact made loads of cash from their campaigns and wanted to spend it on building imposing castles. Kenilworth Castle is a great example of this impulse.

Like many other structures from the period, a fortress already existed on the site in Warwickshire (in the centre of England). In the thirteenth century, it belonged to the rebellious Simon de Monfort (see Chapter 17). In 1364, however, John of Gaunt (who crops up in Chapter 22 about the Peasants' Revolt) began to turn it into a true castle fit for a king, building a great hall to receive guests and expanding the lake that covered three sides of the building. The castle became a lavish and indulgent palace that changed hands many times over the following centuries. In 1575, Queen Elizabeth I visited the castle, at the time owned by Robert Dudley, the Earl of Leicester. He entertained the queen incredibly lavishly, spending the modern-day equivalent of £180,000 on feasts and entertainments!

Bodiam Castle, East Sussex, England

The current building is another product of the Hundred Years' War. It was begun in 1385 by Sir Edward Dalyngrigge, a knight of Edward III who had fought in France. Bodiam is worth mentioning because it's a near perfect example of a castle built to a quadrangular, square plan. The structure is entirely symmetrical with outer walls built exactly around the inner courts.

Having made his fortune in the war, Dalyngrigge was given permission by the young King Richard II (flip to Chapter 22 for more on Richard's reign) to turn his old fortified manor house in East Sussex, in the south of England, into a true castle, but Dalyngrigge didn't mess around with renovations and instead built a completely new castle! The building is completely surrounded by a moat and no army was able to approach without being seen because of its excellent defensive location. Despite all this protection, or perhaps because of it, the castle has never been attacked.

Wartburg Castle, Eisenach, Germany

Possibly the most dramatic castle in Europe, Wartburg is a ruined medieval structure built over 300 metres (or 984 feet) above the nearby town of Eisenbach in Thuringia, central Germany. The original building was established in the middle of the eleventh century by the Count of Schauenburg, one of the rulers of Thuringia, and became the seat of power in the area for the next 400 years.

Even without its powerful associations, Wartburg is an amazingly dramatic place, hovering above the valley and accessible only by a drawbridge from the one road in. Anyone seeking access another way faces a bit of a climb!

Bizarrely for such an imposing building, it became a cultural centre and the venue for the *Sangerkreig*, a contest for minstrels dating back to 1207. Musicians flocked from all around Europe to sing at the castle. Records don't indicate whether performers who displeased the judges were pushed off the walls!

Malbork Castle, Malbork, Poland

Like the Hospitallers and the Templars, the order of the Teutonic Knights (check out Chapter 16 for more) also built a huge number of castles. One of the most famous is Malbork Castle in the north of Poland, which was first constructed in around 1274 when the Teutonic Knights were in charge of the region then known as Prussia. The castle was a huge project and expanded several times as new knights arrived after the fall of the Crusader states. It eventually became the largest fortified Gothic building in Europe. The nearly 52-acre site was entirely surrounded by walls and comfortably housed nearly 3,000 knights. Malbork became the dominant building in the region and hosted meetings of the Hanseatic League trade guild when it was founded in the fourteenth century.

Rather more sinister is the impression that Malbork made upon leading Nazis more than 500 years later. They decided that the castle was their ideal Teutonic fortress, and it hosted many Hitler Youth Camps.

Caerphilly Castle, Caerphilly, Wales

Caerphilly is a massive Norman castle in the south of Wales that remains in remarkably good condition. The castle – constructed between 1268–1271 by nobleman Guilbert 'The Red' de Clare, the Earl of Gloucester – is the second biggest castle in Britain (after Windsor Castle) and was built on an island in the middle of a dammed lake.

Caerphilly is a good example of a *concentric castle*. This type of castle is effectively a 'castle within a castle' – several rings of walls surrounding each other, sometimes without a keep. Not many of this type of castle survive in their original form, although Krak des Chevaliers (turn to the earlier section 'Krak des Chevaliers, Syria') is another good example. Visitors are always impressed by its famous leaning tower. Nobody is entirely sure whether subsidence or cannon-fire damage in the civil war caused this angle!

Guedelon Castle, Treigny, France

Guedelon is something else entirely – a brand new medieval castle! That may sound like a bit of a contradiction in terms, but it's true. Guedelon is an archaeological project involving the building of a brand new castle in the style of the thirteenth century, using only tools and techniques that were available at the time as well as building materials available in the local area.

Construction began in 1999 in Treigny, Burgundy, and is scheduled to finish at some point in the 2020s. The team responsible hope that by carrying out the project, they can discover more about how medieval technology functioned as well as what life was like working on a project of this size and scale.

I can't wait to see how this amazing project turns out. If you want to know more, check out the project's website at `www.guedelon.fr` and see how they're getting on!

Chapter 28

Ten Medieval People Who Changed the World

In This Chapter

▶ Examining the empire builders

▶ Questioning the big thinkers

▶ Meeting the people behind big changes

*T*his book features an awful lot of important people; many of them did great things and were responsible for huge changes in history, including the creation of new kingdoms and whole new countries. Within this large group, however, are people who went a step further, people without whom the world wouldn't be as it is today. In this chapter I discuss some key characters from medieval history who really did change the world.

You'll quickly notice that all the people featured here are men. This isn't because medieval women made no important contributions – far from it. Women like Hildegard of Bingen and Eleanor of Aquitaine were very important in medieval history, but because of the way that society worked at the time and the tendency of medieval historians not to write about them, few women were able to make an impact like the people I do include in this chapter.

The individuals in this chapter are all subjects of (or at least major players in) recently published biographies, histories and historical fiction. If you enjoy the Middle Ages and want to find out more about the period, look for books about any of these people.

Charlemagne (742–814)

The first superstar of the Medieval World – Charles the Great, known as Charlemagne – was the man who united the old Roman provinces of Gaul and Germania and created the Holy Roman Empire. He spent his life in near-constant military campaigning and was responsible for creating the Frankish Empire that continued in one form or another for the next 1,000 years.

In addition to his military might, Charlemagne brought a sense of unification and homogeneity to a very disparate group of peoples who happened to be living near each other. He was also responsible for the 'Carolingian Renaissance', ushering in a new era of learning and vastly increasing the number of literate people in that part of Europe. He became the model for European rulers before the millennium – involving himself in every aspect of the running of his empire and personally making war in order to both defend and expand it. Many later rulers, including most Holy Roman Emperors, tried to copy him but nobody really succeeded. Read all about him in Chapter 5.

Anselm of Canterbury (1033–1109)

You can't move for the bounty of ecclesiastics in the Medieval World. But some stand out more than others, and Anselm is one of them. He was an Italian who became a Benedictine monk and then a philosopher. While holding the post of Archbishop of Canterbury between 1093–1109, he found himself involved in some of the biggest theological issues of the day, such as the controversy over investiture (see Chapter 13).

Anselm is most famous for establishing the idea of *scholasticism*, a method of blending Ancient Greek philosophy with Christian theology to achieve greater understanding of both subjects. Anselm encouraged others to analyse and debate the key arguments within important texts. This made Anselm pretty unique at the time, especially for such a high-ranking cleric, and his views and activities weren't universally popular within the church. Other people did follow him though, and more than 300 years before the Renaissance, they and Anselm began the process of rediscovering the Ancient Greek World.

William of Normandy (c. 1027–1087)

Where to start with William the Conqueror? He was the first man to combine the rule of England and territories in France (the Duchy of Normandy); he also ended Anglo-Saxon rule in Britain after more than 400 years. He built the Tower of London, initiated the Domesday Book (which surveyed who owned what pieces of land throughout England) and established a new system for governing the country by building castles and creating a dynasty that lasted for nearly 100 years through to 1154 (check out Chapter 10 for more on William's achievements).

William wasn't the first person to do many of these things, but he was the first ruler who did them all together. In many ways he became the model for a medieval king due to the swiftness with which he was able to enforce his will on the territories under his control. Tough, uncompromising and brutal – with an eye for the main chance and a keen head for figures – he wasn't a man to mess with!

Pope Urban II (c. 1035–1099)

Medieval history includes a preponderance of popes, but a few stand out, principally Urban II. He was responsible for founding the *Roman Curia*, a kind of civil service for the Vatican, which helped to run the Catholic Church throughout the Western World. He was also a powerful opponent of the traditional Church problems of lay investiture, simony and clerical marriage (pop to Chapter 13 for more details on these issues).

All his positions and proclamations, however, pale in comparison to his one undeniable contribution to history. Urban was the first pope to preach Crusade, calling on the monarchs and rulers of Western Europe to take up arms against the Muslim World and reclaim Jerusalem for Christianity. He was responsible for kick-starting a brutal and yet incredible period of history, which lasted for more than 200 years and is still felt in the uneasy relationship between the Western World and the Islamic World today. Venture to Part III to begin your own journey through the Crusades.

Kublai Khan (1215–1294)

The fifth of the Mongol emperors and the grandson of Genghis Khan, Kublai Khan was always destined for greatness. His reign was an amazing globe-trotting adventure involving invasions of Japan and Vietnam, campaigns in southeast Asia and the creation of an empire that spanned a fifth of the surface of the globe. Yes, that's right, 20 per cent of the Earth!

Kublai Khan became a legendary figure in Europe, where his campaigns and achievements must have made even the greatest European monarchs feel pretty small in comparison. In 1275 he received a visit from the European explorer Marco Polo, who recorded his experiences in his *Il Milione,* or *Description of the World* (travel to Chapter 18 to find out more).

Thomas Aquinas (c. 1225–1274)

A great theologian and thinker, Thomas Aquinas is held by many historians to be the greatest of all medieval ecclesiastics. He was an Italian-Dominican priest and a leading academic of his time, holding the chair of the University of Paris twice and travelling to many of the great cities of Europe, teaching and debating.

Aquinas is most famous for championing the idea of *natural theology* – religious belief based on reason and ordinary experience rather than on faith and supernatural experiences. His views were controversial at the time, particularly because he believed that no absolutes existed and that religious ideas and beliefs could be debated and discussed in the way that philosophy allowed.

Aquinas was unpopular in his own lifetime and condemned by many people. After his death, however, he was canonised by the Church; he was someone who spent his whole life searching for truth.

John Wycliffe (1320–1384)

An English academic and theologian, John Wycliffe was the reformer who kick-started the Lollard movement in England and was expelled from Oxford University for his beliefs. Wycliffe believed that religion was for all and shouldn't be controlled by one central Church. In particular, he was against the hierarchy and politicisation of the Catholic Church and how it had become an institution. He personally translated sections of the Bible into English and distributed copies to the lower classes in England.

He argued strongly that the Church should be poor and not concerned with property and material wealth. These beliefs brought him into conflict with the Church authorities and the monasteries, but his arguments struck a chord with the people. The English Peasants' Revolt of 1381 (which I describe in Chapter 22) was partly inspired by his words, and although it failed, the rebellion set a template for radical politics that lasts until today. In standing up to the Catholic Church and arguing for secular power over it, he foreshadowed the Reformation that was to come.

Johannes Gutenberg (1398–1468)

Johannes Gutenberg may have had the greatest impact of all the people in this chapter. A German goldsmith and printer, he is credited as being the first person to develop moveable type printing from which he developed the Gutenberg printing press.

One of the most significant inventions in history, the Gutenberg press helped develop a system that allowed books to be created, produced and distributed to many more people. Previously scripts had to be laboriously copied out by hand, an expensive and time- consuming process. The Gutenberg press was an amazing change; even in the advent of blogs and digital publishing, written communication still follows the basics of Gutenberg's publication model.

Gutenberg's first printed book was the Bible, produced in 1455, and 48 copies still exist. Overestimating the importance of Gutenberg is impossible: without him, you wouldn't be reading these words now!

Lorenzo d'Medici (1449–1492)

Lorenzo d'Medici was an Italian banker and politician, and effectively the ruler of the Italian city state of Florence for a large part of the fifteenth century. He was responsible for a great deal of social change and for turning Florence into an economic power. But his greatest achievement was being the man who arguably began the Italian Renaissance, a new stage of world history (turn to Chapter 24 for all about this cultural revolution).

Through his patronage of the arts (and that of his descendants) and immense building programmes, d'Medici brought a whole generation of artists, artisans, architects and academics to Florence. He started the careers of men such as Leonardo da Vinci and Sandro Botticelli as well as countless more. His efforts inspired other Italian cities to compete with one another for talent and cultural works, which resulted in a surge of creativity and the beginning of a whole new era. Quite an achievement.

Christopher Columbus (c. 1451–1506)

The man who first made contact with the American continent clearly changed the world. Originally from Genoa in Italy, Christopher Columbus's greatest achievement was actually something of an accident. He sailed westwards hoping to reach India and found America in the way! Having said that, he established contact between two parts of the world that didn't know each other existed. In these days of the Internet and instant communication with anywhere on the planet, isolation of the Americas from the other continents is almost impossible to imagine.

Columbus had to fight to get his great voyages going, touting himself around the royal courts of Portugal and Spain (flip to Chapter 24 for more details). When he returned he became enmeshed in political struggles, but by then he'd moved history on to the next stage.

Chapter 29

Ten Great Medieval Innovations

In This Chapter

▶ Creating new countries and languages

▶ Banking, buying and selling

*T*he medieval period is certainly full of more violent wars, horrid plagues, nasty murders and arguing clerics than you can shake a mitre at. But some amazing developments also took place during the 1,000 years of the Middle Ages, and I describe several of them in this chapter.

Creating Europe

Europe as a landmass had been around for millennia and in a sense just the names changed during the medieval period. But, on the other hand, many of the countries that you now know, and the idea of national character, came into being during the Middle Ages. For example, the Treaty of Verdun in 843 (see Chapter 6) was intended to divide the Carolingian Empire into three parts; in doing so it created the land areas known today as France and Germany, from which these two countries developed their very different identities and cultures. The medieval period also saw the creation of Portugal and Spain, and by the end of the Hundred Years' War, the vibrant identities of England and France were well-established – as was their mutual rivalry.

Developing New Languages

One thing that helped to develop distinct national identities was the birth of modern European languages. Throughout the medieval period, the major language of official life was Latin but the actual everyday languages that people spoke varied hugely. French and German were born in the Middle Ages, as was the predecessor of the language that we now know as English.

The arrival of the Anglo-Saxons in Britain in the fifth century (check out Chapter 3) led to the development of a new language that blended with the French spoken by the Norman conquerors after 1066. This combined language eventually became Old English – the language of Chaucer and the immediate predecessor of modern English. By the fifteenth century, new languages were being widely spoken and appearing in mass-produced books.

Inventing Books

The invention of the Gutenberg Press in the middle of the fifteenth century led to the creation of printing, publishing and the book. What you're holding in your hands now was possible only because of the invention of Johannes Gutenberg, a goldsmith and printer from Germany. Books had existed before Gutenberg but had to be laboriously copied by hand and were expensive and unavailable to all bar the elite. The books produced by Gutenberg changed this. Although not accessible to everyone during the period, because of their cost, books began to be reproduced with much greater frequency and variety.

Bringing About Banking

Banking as you know it came into being during the Middle Ages. During the fourteenth century, the Italian merchant cities developed vastly more complicated banking, accountancy and insurance systems (turn to Chapter 18 for more details). These systems in turn led to the expansion of trade (see the following section, 'Establishing World Trade') and more international money exchange between countries. Medieval investors were the first to be able to buy shares in a company, and as a result companies began going international. The next time you fill in a tax return or get charged for unarranged borrowing, remember that you have the Middle Ages to thank!

Establishing World Trade

The Middle Ages saw trade become truly international. During the fourteenth century, Italian cities such as Genoa, Pisa and Venice began to develop colonies and outposts abroad as permanent bases for their merchants to use. These usually took the form of small settlements of dwellings close to a big city or port. Huge companies and corporations developed, enabling merchants to stay at home and send their goods to agents to sell for them. The same thing happened in northern Europe with the Hanseatic League. This period saw incredible expansion but also new threats, such as the rapid spread of diseases (the Black Death rampaged throughout Europe from 1348).

Improving Navigation and Cartography

To satisfy the demands for expanded trade (see 'Establishing World Trade'), navigators and cartographers had to refine their skills. The travels of men such as Marco Polo (c. 1254–1324), Vasco da Gama (c. 1460–1529) and Christopher Columbus (c. 1451–1506) broadened people's horizons, answering questions about the shape of the Earth and about its inhabitants. The introduction of the compass in around 1300, probably from China, also helped matters immensely.

Map-making improved during the Middle Ages too. One of the greatest surviving documents of the time is the Hereford *Mappa Mundi* ('Map of the World'), which was produced around 1300. The document is drawn on a single sheet of vellum and measures around 150×130 centimetres (59 inches $\times$ 51 inches) – by far the largest surviving medieval map. Marked with a mixture of geographical, historical and religious sites, the map is a great example of how the medieval mind was trying to synthesise new discoveries with the traditional teachings of Christianity.

Setting Up Universities

The universities of the Middle Ages collected and developed much of the new learning of the time. In the late eleventh and early twelfth centuries, universities were created in France, England and Italy. The first of these was the University of Bologna, established in 1088.

Initially these new institutions taught mostly theological subjects and some practical skills such as financial controls and logical debate. By the fourteenth century, universities had become home to a different type of intellectual who was interested in all aspects of academic inquiry. With the renewed interest in humanism (the rediscovery of the literature and learning of the ancient world), which developed during the early years of the Renaissance, Europe's universities flourished even more (flip to Chapter 24), becoming centres for artistic and cultural study, often using the new languages of Medieval Europe.

Combating with the Cannon

Of all the military developments during the Middle Ages, such as crossbows and plate armour, cannons are probably the most significant. They weren't invented by Europeans and probably came into being through the work of Arabs or Mongols, but they were first introduced to Europe in the fourteenth century, figuring at the siege of Metz during the Hundred Years' War. Within a few decades, they were vital to military tactics and crucial in ending the Hundred Years' War – the final battle of the war (at Castillon, in 1453) was won by French cannons. Cannons also helped the Ottoman Turks to seize Constantinople in the same year (check out Chapters 23 and 24, respectively). The cannon was the first step towards the era of gunpowder warfare.

Taking On Sports

Medieval people spent much time trying to kill animals (through hunting) or each other (through jousting and tournaments), but also had time to develop two of the most popular sports in the world today. The form of football that I mention in Chapter 26 was more of a violent, lawless mob scrap than a match for the World Cup, but was still the game on which modern football is based.

A form of tennis – now known as *real tennis* – also came into being in the Middle Ages. You can still see a real tennis court in Henry VIII's palace at Hampton Court, but the game started much earlier, developing from a hand-ball game that was played in France. The first English monarch that we know to have taken an interest was Henry V, and the game became massively popular across Europe in the two centuries that followed. Although a tough and energetic game, it was still considerably less dangerous than jousting!

Innovating and Inventing

The Middle Ages introduced many small but important innovations to the world. I don't have enough space to describe them all, but here's a list of some of the most interesting medieval inventions:

- Horseshoes (ninth century)
- Arabic numerals (introduced to Europe in the tenth century)
- Oil paint (thirteenth century and then developed by Jan Van Eyck in The Netherlands around 1410)
- Mirrors (twelfth century)
- Magnets (twelfth century)
- Wheelbarrows (twelfth century)
- Hops in beer (eleventh century)

Having finished writing this book, I intend to take advantage of this last invention!

Index

• *I* •

• N •

• O •

• P •

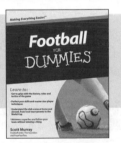

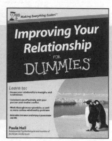

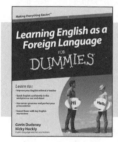

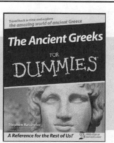